Aral Sea

Caspian Sea

...MENIA

ATROPATENE

...UCID

...ESOPR.

Tigris

MEDIA

·

SELEUCEIA

BABYLON

BABYLONIA

·SUSA

KINGDOM

HYRACANIA

PARTHIA

BACTRIA

·PERSEPOLIS

Persian Gulf

PERSIA

THE HELLENISTIC AGE

THE WORLD HISTORY
OF THE JEWISH PEOPLE

FIRST SERIES: ANCIENT TIMES
VOLUME SIX: THE HELLENISTIC AGE

GENERAL EDITOR
(SECOND TEMPLE PERIOD)
ABRAHAM SCHALIT

ASSISTANT EDITOR
ELIYAHU FELDMAN

MANAGING EDITOR
ALEXANDER PELI

JEWISH HISTORY PUBLICATIONS LTD.

THE HELLENISTIC AGE

POLITICAL HISTORY OF JEWISH PALESTINE
FROM 332 B.C.E. to 67 B.C.E.

EDITOR

ABRAHAM SCHALIT

RUTGERS UNIVERSITY PRESS, NEW BRUNSWICK

LIBRARY OF CONGRESS CATALOGUE NUMBER 64-15907

ISBN 0-8135-0710-3

PRINTED IN ISRAEL BY PELI PRINTING WORKS LTD., GIVATAYIM

CONTENTS

PART ONE: THE HELLENISTIC ENVIRONMENT

CHAPTER I: THE POLITICAL BACKGROUND

V. Tcherikover

CHAPTER II: THE CULTURAL BACKGROUND

V. Tcherikover

V

CONTENTS

PART TWO: HELLENISTIC PALESTINE

CHAPTER III: THE POLITICAL SITUATION FROM 332 TO 175 B.C.E.

V. Tcherikover

CHAPTER IV: SOCIAL CONDITIONS

V. Tcherikover

CHAPTER V: THE HELLENISTIC MOVEMENT IN JERUSALEM AND ANTIOCHUS' PERSECUTIONS

V. Tcherikover

CONTENTS

PART THREE: THE WAR OF LIBERATION

CHAPTER VI: THE HASMONEAN REVOLT AND JUDAH MACCABEE'S WAR AGAINST THE SYRIANS

M. Avi-Yonah

CHAPTER VII: THE FIRST HASMONEAN RULERS: JONATHAN AND SIMEON

J. Klausner

CONTENTS

CONTENTS

CHAPTER XI: DOMESTIC POLITICS AND POLITICAL INSTITUTIONS

A. Schalit

AUTHORS

ILLUSTRATIONS

Between pages 42 and 43

MAPS

PREFATORY NOTE

This volume covers a period of about three hundred years — from the fourth to the first centuries B.C.E. Topically it embraces the Hellenistic Period — the political history of the Jewish people in Palestine from Alexander the Great's conquest of the East almost until the consolidation of Roman power in Syria and Palestine. This was a period in the history of the East replete with great changes and important consequences. Alexander the Great's conquests opened wide the countries of the East and paved the way for the penetration of Greek civilization in its new form — Hellenism. The Jewish people did not remain unaffected and was swept along by the mighty current which overflowed neighboring regions both near and far. The process of these events and the counter-movement which arose among the Jews for survival both as a nation and as a culture are described in this volume.

Professor Tcherikover portrays the penetration of Hellenistic culture and the changes which this brought about among the peoples of the East; the reaction of the Jewish people following the collision with the Western world is described in the chapters written by Professor M. Avi-Yonah and Professor Joseph Klausner. The crowning point of this reaction and its significance as a phenomenon of world-wide historical importance was the establishment of the Hasmonean dynasty. The discussion embraces events as far as Queen Salome, i.e., it covers the history of the independent Hasmonean kingdom. The chapter dealing with the domestic politics of the Hasmonean state describes the internal developments inherent in the political attitudes of the Hasmonean dynasty and their implications for Jewish history during and after the Second Temple Period. This chapter was written by the editor.

Preparing the material for publication was no easy task. Two of the contributors, Professors Tcherikover and Klausner, did not live to see the book's appearance. Editing the work, which had been Professor Tcherikover's task, was assigned to the writer, who had to deal with the manuscripts without being able to consult the authors when doubts arose concerning their intentions. As a rule, the editor held that no changes were to be made in the original manuscripts of the two authors unless there was an obvious error. Furthermore, no attempt whatsoever was made to introduce the slightest change in their views even in instances where the editor's differ from them. The guideline adhered to by the editor was that the responsibility for the opinions expressed in the chapters in question lies solely with the authors. This also applies to the maps appended to the various chapters. The reader will find that they contain details which are in some cases at variance with the conventional views. However, these details agree with the contents of the relevant chapters. Accordingly, the editor saw no possibility of altering them even if he disagreed with them.

The notes dealing with all the references to sources and the literature are given in full, just as they had been written by the authors, unless their citation was superfluous since they had been mentioned elsewhere. In a number of instances, new bibliographical details unknown to the authors were mentioned. Notes added by the editor are in square brackets and bear the attribution "Ed."

Quotations from the works of Josephus were taken from the English translation by H. St. Thackeray and R. Marcus published in the Loeb Classical Library; the quotations from the Books of the Maccabees were taken from the English translation published in E. R. Charles' *Apocrypha and Pseudoepigrapha*, I, Oxford, 1913. For quotations from the Babylonian Talmud use was made of the English translation edited by I. Epstein and published by the Soncino Press, London. However, passages which the authors or the editor felt required a different translation, were rendered in accordance with their views.

The names of persons and places appearing in the Bible are given in their biblical form as they occur in the English translation of the Old Testament published by the Jewish Publication Society of America, Philadelphia, 1955, or in the conventional orthography familiar to the English reader. Hellenistic place-names in Palestine are generally given in parentheses following the biblical form. This practice was adhered to both in the text and in the notes, as well as in the maps — with the exception of the map of Palestine under the Ptolemies and the Seleucids, in which Hellenistic place-names are given together with the biblical designations in parentheses.

Names appearing only in Greek sources are usually given in the form in which they appear in the English translations mentioned above of Josephus and the Books of the Maccabees or in the conventional English form.

These rules also apply to quotations taken from the above-mentioned English translations.

Complete consistency may nevertheless not have been adhered to in every case and now and then there are exceptions to the above-mentioned rules.

The volume's illustrative material was selected by Professor M. Avi-Yonah and the editor would like to thank him for accepting this task.

The editor also wishes to express his gratitude to all the members of the editorial staff who labored to prepare this volume for publication.

ABRAHAM SCHALIT

Jerusalem, July 1971

ABBREVIATIONS FOR BIBLICAL BOOKS

Ex.	Exodus	Jer.	Jeremiah
Lev.	Leviticus	Ps.	Psalms
Num.	Numbers	Prov.	Proverbs
Deut.	Deuteronomy	Neh.	Nehemiah
Josh.	Joshua	I Chron.	I Chronicles
I Sam.	I Samuel	II Chron.	II Chronicles
II Sam.	II Samuel		

ABBREVIATIONS FOR TALMUD
AND RABBINICAL LITERATURE

'Arak.	'Arakin	Meg. Ta'an.	Megillat Ta'anit (ed.
'Av. Zara	'Avoda Zara		Z. Lichtenstein,
B. Batra	Bava Batra		*HUCA*, VIII–IX
Bek.	Bekorot		[1931–2], 257-351)
Ber.	Berakot	Mid.	Middot
Cant. R.	Canticles Rabba	Naz.	Nazir
Deut. R.	Deuteronomy Rabba	Pes.	Pesahim
Eccl. R.	Ecclesiastes Rabba	Qid.	Qiddushin
'Eduy.	'Eduyyot	Sanh.	Sanhedrin
'Eruv.	'Eruvin	Shab.	Shabbat
Gen. R.	Genesis Rabba (ed.	Shev.	Shevuot
	J. Theodor and Ch.	Suk.	Sukka
	Albeck, Jerusalem,	Ta'an	Ta'anit
	1965)	Tosaf.	Tosafot
Git.	Gittin	Tosef.	Tosefta (ed. M. S.
Hag.	Hagiga		Zuckermandel,
Ket.	Ketubbot		Jerusalem, 1963)
Lam. R.	Lamentations Rabba	Yer.	Yerushalmi (Jerusa-
Lev. R.	Leviticus Rabba		lem Talmud)
M.	Mishnah	Yev.	Yevamot
Ma'as. Sh.	Ma'aser Sheni	Zev.	Zevahim
Mak.	Makkot		

ABBREVIATIONS FOR GREEK SOURCES

Ant.   —   Josephus Flavius, Jewish Antiquities

C. P. Jud.   —   V. Tcherikover and A. Fuks (eds.), Corpus Papyrorum Judaicarum, I–II, Cambridge Mass., 1957–60

P. Iand.   —   K. Kalbfleisch (ed.), Papyri Iandanae, Leipzig, 1912

P.Lille   —   P. Jouguet (ed.), Papyri grecs (Institut Papyrologique de l'Université de Lille), 1907–1908

P. Lond.   —   F. G. Kenyon and H. I. Bell, Greek Papyri in the British Museum, London, 1893–1917.

Macc.   —   Maccabees

PCZ   —   C. C. Edgar (ed.), Zenon Papyri, (Cairo, Musée des antiquités egyptiennes)

PSI   —   Publicazioni della Società Italiana per la Ricerca dei Papiri Greci e Latini in Egitto: Papiri Greci e Latini, Firenze

P. Tebtunis —   The Tebtunis Papyri, London, 1902–1938

War   —   Josephus Flavius, The Jewish War

ABBREVIATIONS FOR JOURNALS
AND SCIENTIFIC LITERATURE

AASOR	—	Annual of the American Schools of Oriental Research
ASTI	—	Annual of the Swedish Theological Institute
BAr	—	Biblical Archaeologist
BASOR	—	Bulletin of the American Schools of Oriental Research
BIES	—	Bulletin of the Israel Exploration Society (Hebrew)
CAH	—	Cambridge Ancient History
Graetz, Geschichte	—	Geschichte der Juden von den ältesten Zeiten bis auf die Gegenwart
HUCA	—	Hebrew Union College Annual
IEJ	—	Israel Exploration Journal
JEA	—	Journal of Egyptian Archaeology
JjGL	—	Jahrbuch für jüdische Geschichte und Literatur
JPOS	—	Journal of the Palestine Oriental Society
JQR	—	Jewish Quarterly Review
MGWJ	—	Monatschrift für Geschichte und Wissenschaft des Judentums
PAAJR	—	Proceedings of American Academy of Jewish Research
PL	—	Patrologia Latina
RB	—	Revue Biblique
RE	—	Paulys Realencyclopädie der classischen Altertumwissenschaft (Neue Bearbeitung begonen von Georg Wissowa, fortgeführt von Wilhelm Kroll und Karl Mittelhaus)
REG	—	Revue des Études Grecques
REJ	—	Revue des Études Juives
Schürer, Geschichte	—	Geschichte des jüdischen Volkes im Zeitalter Jesu Christi
ZAW	—	Zeitschrift für die alttestamentliche Wissenschaft
ZDPV	—	Zeitschrift des Deutschen Palästina-Vereins
ZNW	—	Zeitschrift für die neutestamentliche Wissenschaft

HEBREW-ENGLISH TRANSLITERATION

1. All Hebrew names found in the Bible are given as they appear in the English translation of the Holy Scriptures by the Jewish Publication Society of America, Philadelphia, 1955.

2. Those names that are familiar to the English reader are rendered in their customary, accepted spelling (e. g. Caesarea).

3. All other Hebrew names and words are transliterated as follows:

א   Not noted at beginning or end of word; otherwise by ', e. g. pᵉʾēr or pĕʾēr (פְּאָר), mēʾīr (מְאִיר).

ב	b
ב	v
ג	g
ג	g
ד	d
ד	d
ה	h (unless consonantal, ה at the end of the word is not transliterated)
ו	w
ז	z
ח	ḥ
ט	ṭ
י	y
כ	k
כ	ḵ
ל	l
מ	m
נ	n
ס	s
ע	'
פ	p
פ	f
צ	z
ק	q
ר	r
ש	sh, š
ש	s
ת	t
ת	t (Except in the word בית – beth)

a) The *dagesh lene* is not indicated, save in the letters ב and פ. *Dagesh forte* is indicated by doubling the letter.

b) The Hebrew definite article is indicated by *ha* or *he* followed by a hyphen, but without the next letter doubled, e. g. *ha-shānā,* not *ha-shshānā.*

־	a	ֶ	e
־ֲ	ă	ֱ	ĕ
ָ	ā	וּ	ū
ָ	o	וֹ	ō
ֳָ	ŏ	ֻ	u
ֵ	ē	ִ	i
ֵ	ē, ēi	ִ	ī

Sheva mobile (שוא נע) is indicated thus: ᵉ or ĕ. Neither long vowels nor *sheva mobile* are indicated in proper names.

ARABIC-ENGLISH TRANSLITERATION

ٴ — ' (not indicated at the beginning of a word)	ض — ḍ
	ط — ṭ
ب — b	ظ — ẓ
ت — t	ع — '
ث — th	غ — gh
ج — j	ف — f
ح — ḥ	ق — q
خ — kh	ك — k
د — d	ل — l
ذ — dh	م — m
ر — r	ن — n
ز — z	ه — h
س — s	و — w
ش — sh	ى — y
ص — ṣ	

The Lām of the definite article ال is assimilated before a solar letter. Proper names familiar to the English reader are rendered in their customary spelling.

XXII

THE HELLENISTIC AGE

PART ONE: THE HELLENISTIC ENVIRONMENT

CHAPTER I

THE POLITICAL BACKGROUND

by V. Tcherikover

A. The Jews and the Western World

IN THE SUMMER of 322 B.C.E. in the course of the victorious campaign that was to take him as far as the Indus Valley in western India, Alexander of Macedonia incorporated Palestine to his vast realm. This conquest constituted a turning point in Israel's history. Prior to it the life of the nation had developed as part of the world of the Orient, the direction of Israel's history being determined by the mighty kingdoms of the East — Egypt, Babylon, Assyria and Persia — whose intervention in the internal life of Palestine had so often been decisive. The culture of the Orient, especially its religion and literature, had a determining influence in the formation of Israel's civilization both when it attempted to emulate other cultures and to adopt their values, or in instances when it resisted foreign values and developed its own individual cultural patterns. In every aspect — political, social, and cultural — Israel was an integral part of the Ancient East. The Bible remains the eternal monument of this distant age when Israel was linked to the great civilization of the Orient. In one sense it is true that the Bible is the ultimate and most exalted embodiment of the culture of the Ancient East.

Then came the great change. The conquests of Alexander the Great brought not only Palestine into the framework of the Western world and its culture, but all the lands of the Middle East which had previousl been centers of Oriental civilizations as well. Alexander's conquests created a new world, whose emergence, however, did not mean a complete break with earlier civilizations. Rather, diverse elements of the ancient civilizations were fused into the foundations of a new cultural structure of uniform aspect which came to be known as the "Hellenistic world." This world was the framework for Palestine's future political and economic life, and within it the people of Israel were to develop their national culture.

It is easy to understand how the sudden transition to another, totally different, cultural pattern was bound to bring about a severe crisis in the people's life. Hellenism made its influence felt in various ways. Politically it was highly important for the Jews to become acquainted with the typical political institutions of the Greeks, viz., the *polis* — city state, in which the principles of free citizenship were established for the first time in the history of mankind. The Jews came to know the Greek *polis* within the boundaries of their own country, where the Greek cities played a very important political and economic role. They also encountered them abroad, in the numerous lands of the dispersion, even in countries apparently still incapable of absorbing this Greek autonomous institution. The fact that the ancient states of the Orient had now become part of the Hellenistic world was also of great importance for Israel's political development. For as long as the Hellenistic states remained powerful and stable, Israel represented merely a small and insignificant area within the great Hellenistic world, but the moment they crumbled and were supplanted by a number of independent states, Israel was afforded the opportunity of inaugurating an independent political existence of its own. Significantly enough, the Jewish state which was established within the Hellenistic world and through a hard struggle against it, was organized according to the familiar Hellenistic pattern.

Israel's cultural life was influenced by many aspects of Greek civilization. New forms of life, introduced from Greece, forced their way into the traditions of the Orient and became predominant in the Jewish communities both in Palestine and in the Diaspora. Even the Greek preoccupation with physical fitness and athletic games, so characteristic of the Western spirit and so entirely alien to that of the Orient, found loyal supporters within Jewish society. The influence of Greek thinkers on Israel was less pervasive, but only insofar as the Jewish population in Palestine was concerned. In the Diaspora, and especially in such major centers of Hellenism as Alexandria, the Jews were among the most faithful readers and admirers of Greek literature. The ideas of the Greek thinkers penetrated deeply the Jewish communities of the Diaspora. Among Alexandrian Jews a strong literary trend came into being which strove for a synthesis, or at least a compromise, between Judaism and Hellenism. Hellenistic influences were also felt in the economic, social and legal life of the Jewish community.

The conquests of Alexander the Great marked the beginning of a crisis in the life of the Jews and Judaism. It is the historian's task to discover the various points of contact between the two nations, and to reveal the manifold forms resulting from the encounter between the ancient Jewish tradition and Hellenistic civilization.

B. ALEXANDER THE GREAT AND THE CONQUEST OF THE ORIENT

The conquest of the East by Alexander is usually considered a great political achievement of the Greek nation, since the civilization which became established throughout Alexander's vast kingdom was Greek. In effect, however, this conquest was neither carried out by the Greek nation nor with its approval. The real conquerors were the Macedonians, a nation of mixed racial origin, who cannot be considered the bearers of Greek culture.

Macedonia and its kings are known from a very early period of Greek history, but it had never previously played any considerable political role in Greek affairs. It is doubtful whether the Macedonians belonged to the same race as the Greeks. They were probably the product of a mixture of Greeks with Illyrian, Thracian and other north-Balkan tribes. The Macedonian tongue resembled Greek but the spoken language differed so much from the Greek vernacular that the Greeks had difficulty in understanding it.[1] Macedonia's political and social structure was also foreign to the Greek spirit. Kingship, which had been abolished in Greece at the dawn of her history, was preserved in Macedonia down to the 4th century. In Macedonia however, as in the ancient Greek cities, the king was not deified after the Oriental manner and though possessing absolute power, he had to reckon with the opinion of the aristocracy and the military commanders.

Because of her geographical position in the north of the Balkan Peninsula Macedonia was bound to become a military power. Otherwise she would have been destroyed by the barbarians in the north. This accounts for the excellent military training given to Macedonian soldiers and also for the active participation of the Macedonian aristocracy in the command and internal organization of the army. And since the Greeks were considered excellent soldiers, skilled in military tactics by land and sea, it was natural for the Macedonians to learn from them and adopt their principles in tactics and strategy. Not content with mere imitation, they also introduced many improvements. For instance, it was the Macedonians who transformed the skirmish line of Greek infantry into the "phalanx"[2] with its enormous impact. Another improvement they introduced was in the function of the cavalry, which had not been much used in mountainous Greece (except in Thessaly), but played a leading role in the Macedonian army. The cavalry was recruited almost entirely from the aristocracy, while the infantry was enlisted from the free peasantry. The close associates of the king were the nobles, called *hetairoi* (ἑταῖροι) or the King's Companions. In fact the "Companions" ruled the army and often the whole state, especially in cases where the king was a weakling or a minor.

The Greeks considered the Macedonians a nation with barbaric habits and cruel governing methods. Only the royal family was excepted from this view and its Greek origin recognized. According to common Greek legend, the Macedonian kings were the descendants of the mythological hero Heracles from Argos in the Peloponnesus. This notion nevertheless had a certain justification, since the Macedonian kings regarded themselves as the bearers of Greek civilization in their country. They introduced Greek as the official language at Court and in the administration and spread Greek culture among the Macedonian aristocracy, even inviting Greek writers, poets, and thinkers to visit them. Macedonia can be termed the first "Hellenistic state" many years before the beginning of the "Hellenistic period." The Court of the Macedonian kings spoke Greek, enjoyed performances of Greek tragedies, and perhaps even discussed philosophical topics. But the mass of the Macedonian people remained in a state of barbarism and oppressed, as before, by despotic kings. The Greek principles of autonomy, democracy, and freedom of speech and opinion remained unknown in Macedonia and the Greek *polis* itself, the institution in which all these principles had been created and developed, never became familiar to the mass of the Macedonian people.[3]

In the year 359, King Philip ascended the throne of Macedonia and in the course of a few years transformed the country into a powerful kingdom. Philip cherished aspirations of imperialistic expansion which brought him into conflict with the Greek cities, at first with those situated in Thrace, on the northern coast of the Aegean Sea, and later also with the cities of central Greece. On the battlefield of Chaeronea (338 B.C.E.) the independence of classical Greece came to an end, and Philip became the absolute ruler of the whole of Greece.[4]

Macedonian mastery of Greece supplied the pretext for a conflict between Macedonia and Persia. The terms of the agreement known as the "King's Peace," concluded in 386 B.C.E. between Sparta (at that time the most powerful city in Greece) and the Persian king Artaxerxes II, conferred on Persia the right to interfere in Greek internal affairs;[5] but Macedonia's conquest of Greece put an end to Persia's influence there. Actually, however, there was another, more concrete basis to the conflict between Macedonia and Persia. In his drive to expand the borders of his kingdom, Philip conquered Thrace, which brought him to the Sea of Marmara, the Straits of the Hellespont (the modern Dardanelles) and the Bosphorus, thereby gaining control of the important maritime route from the Aegean Sea to the Black Sea, on which Persia also had her eye. Thus enlarged, the kingdom of Macedonia bordered on the western satrapies (i.e. provinces) of

Persia, constituting a constant threat to the power of the Persian king in Asia Minor. War was, to all appearances, inevitable. Philip began making preparations for the struggle and even sent one of his most capable military commanders, Parmenion, to Asia Minor to launch military operations.

As part of his strategy to enlist the support of the Greek cities, he revealed his plans to their representatives assembled at Corinth in 338 B.C.E., when the so-called "Corinthian League" was formed under his leadership. An adroit diplomat, Philip assumed the guise of a Greek patriot and declared that the Macedonian war against Persia would be a "war of vengeance" for all the destruction Greece had suffered when the Persians under Xerxes had overrun the country. The Greeks, however, remained hostile to Macedonia, and although they acquiesced in Philip's plans and acknowledged him as supreme commander, they did so only because they dared not oppose the king's will openly.[6] And, indeed, only about 7,000 men were contributed by the Greek cities to the army which eventually conquered the East, and this force cannot be regarded as having played a decisive role in the campaign. There were 7,000 more Greek soldiers in the army, but these were mercenaries, and the military strength of this force was more or less balanced by that of the Greek mercenaries in the service of the Persian king.[7] The amazing achievement of overthrowing the Persian kingdom and establishing mastery over the Orient was entirely the accomplishment of the Macedonian army and its king.

In the midst of his war preparations, Philip was assassinated by one of his officers in the wake of a court intrigue (336 B.C.E.). The task of carrying out his plans fell to his son Alexander, who succeeded to the throne at the age of twenty.

Alexander made no changes in the plans for the campaign. He renewed Philip's alliance with Greece and received from the Greeks the supreme command, and the same honors which had been conferred on his father. Even the slogan of a "war of vengeance" against Persia was retained, although the Greeks showed even less enthusiasm for it than they had before. But the fact that it was not Philip, a man of 50, but his young son, Alexander, who took it upon himself to carry through the plan of the Persian war was to acquire great historical significance. With all his political and military acumen, Philip was a man of his own generation and his political horizon was accordingly limited to a comparatively small area. The mastery of Greece was the goal of his life; the Persian War was principally intended to secure his power in Greece and to reinforce his control over the Aegean Sea and the commercial route to the Black Sea. It may safely be assumed that the plan of the Athenian writer Isocrates — the conquest of Asia Minor from Sinope to Cilicia — was also adopted by Philip.[8]

Alexander's approach to the problem of the war was something entirely different. The reasons lay not only in Alexander's dynamic temperament but also in the political situation which Philip's conquests had created. The domination of Greece, which had been Philip's supreme goal, was for Alexander an accomplished fact. And if the Persian War was Philip's final political action, for Alexander it was only the beginning. This accounts for the different aims of the campaign. Philip would probably have been content to conquer all the countries adjacent to Greece, without dreaming of the complete destruction of the Persian Empire, whereas it was precisely the crushing of the Oriental kingdom which appealed to Alexander as a sublime aim, worthy of a great war.

Alexander had the support of all his young contemporaries, either because they were devoted to him personally, or because they sought glory and riches. Although the supreme command of troops remained in the hands of Philip's old and experienced general Parmenion, the younger generation gradually took over the most important positions in the army. Differences of opinion between the young and the old often stirred up dangerous political tensions, and in the course of the campaign many of Philip's old veterans were gradually dismissed. Even Parmenion himself was put to death in accordance with a secret order issued by Alexander.[9]

All the energy stored in the young Macedonian aristocracy was concentrated around the king, adding to the enormous driving force so characteristic of Alexander himself. In view of two additional factors — the excellent organization of the Macedonian cavalry and infantry (phalanx) on the one hand, and the political and military weakness of the Persian kingdom on the other, there is no reason to wonder at the powerful impact of his forces and the lightning speed with which Alexander carried out the conquest of the Orient from the shores of the Aegean Sea to India, thereby transforming the face of the world in a few years.

This is not the place for a detailed survey of all the stages of Alexander's victorious campaign.[10] Only the general outline of the campaign will be noted, stressing events directly connected with the subject of this volume.

At the first encounter between Alexander and the Persians near the River Granicus (in the north-western corner of Asia Minor) the Persians suffered an overwhelming defeat, as a result of which the whole of Asia Minor fell into Alexander's hands. In the year 333, the Macedonian army stood at the gates of northern Syria. Here, near Issus (a small town not far from modern Alexandretta), in the narrow passage between the sea and the mountain ridge, a decisive battle between Alexander and the Persian king Darius III was fought. This time Darius led his enormous host in person, but although his forces by far out-numbered Alexander's tiny army, this battle too ended in the total defeat of the Persians. Darius himself abandoned the battlefield and fled, setting his soldiers a disastrous example.

The victory near Issus at once changed the political situation in all the countries along the Mediterranean coast which had until then been under Persian rule. Conquest of the Phoenician coast deprived the mighty Phoenician fleet of its natural bases and one by one all the Phoenician kings hastened to do homage to Alexander. Only Tyre, relying on its strong fortifications, dared resist, but after a long siege it was also taken. After the fall of Tyre, Alexander passed through Palestine, halted only by Gaza, which shut its gates to him. When after a two month siege, Gaza, too, fell, Alexander razed it to the ground. Then he continued on his way to Egypt. In Egypt he met no resistance. The Persian satrap in charge of this rich country, seeing himself entirely isolated and without any hope of help from Darius, preferred to surrender the fortress at Memphis with its Persian garrison. The Egyptians had never regarded themselves as part of the Persian Empire. They hailed Alexander as a liberator from hated masters and submitted to him willingly. The Egyptian priests conferred on Alexander the title of the ancient pharaohs, calling him "Son of Amon-Ra." For his part, Alexander respected the Egyptian gods and treated the local leaders with consideration. However, he felt obliged to further the interests of the Greek population which was quite numerous in the north, especially in the Delta. Accordingly, he founded a Greek city in the western part of the Delta, calling it Alexandria after himself. Before long, Alexandria developed into the largest commercial and cultural center of the Eastern Mediterranean. Alexander retained the Egyptian officials in the towns and villages of the country and appointed two Egyptians to high administrative offices. In this way he publicly demonstrated his goodwill and his intention of allowing the Egyptians to continue living by their own ancestral traditions. However, he left an army commanded by Macedonian officers in occupation of the country, and he put a Greek official in charge of the state's finances, thereby dividing the administration of the country among different authorities in an effort to find the best possible form of government in a joint establishment consisting of Macedonian conquerors and representatives of the native population.[11]

On his way from Egypt to Babylonia, Alexander passed through Palestine again, possibly spending a short time there in order to suppress a revolt in Samaria.[12] But he lost no time on the long march from the Syrian

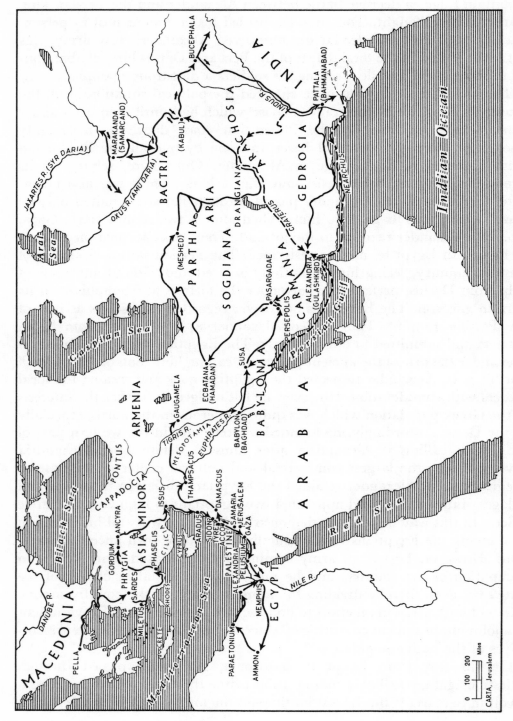

Alexander's Campaign

CARTA, Jerusalem

coast to Mesopotamia. Crossing the Euphrates and Tigris, he met the Persian army for the third time near Gaugamela. Once more, Darius personally commanded his large army. But again he was guilty of the same weakness as at Issus, abandoning the battlefield in the face of Alexander's charge. This time the Persians went on fighting, and there was even a dangerous moment when Alexander's camp might have been encircled. However, the grim battle ended with yet another decisive victory for the Macedonians. Now, all the important centers of the Persian Empire — Babylon, Susa, Persepolis, and Ecbatana — large and wealthy cities with treasures of gold and silver, fell into Alexander's hands one by one.

Having completed this conquest Alexander began his pursuit of Darius who had escaped northwards and managed to reach the Caspian Sea. There, Alexander caught up with him but was unable to take him alive. The Persian satraps had by then rebelled against their weak king who was slain at the moment when Alexander's small force was drawing near. Since Darius left no heir to his throne, Alexander took over the rule of Persia with all its provinces, by the right of conquest, thus becoming the Great King of the Orient, successor to the ancient Persian dynasty of Achaemenidae.

New problems faced him now. The "war of vengeance" of Greece against Persia was over, and Alexander released those Greek soldiers who had taken part in the campaign under the terms of the Corinthian League. From now on the war became his personal concern. There are no really adequate grounds for the assertion that Alexander aspired to found a "world empire."[13] In all his campaigns after the death of Darius, Alexander never crossed the frontiers of Persia. On the other hand, though, the difference between the Persian kingdom and a 'world empire' was not very great, for the boundaries of Persia were almost identical with those of the world as it was known to the Western peoples. After visiting the northern satrapies of Persia Alexander incorporated the valley of the Indus (the modern Punjab) to his kingdom. He then turned back westwards and spent the last year of his life in Mesopotamia. There is reason to think that he looked upon the ancient city of Babylon as the center of his vast kingdom. There is no evidence either of his intention to return to Macedonia or his aspiration to make himself master of the countries to the west (Carthage and others). Both alternatives are possible, but neither assumption can be proved.[14]

Alexander died in Babylon in 323, at the age of 33. In spite of the immense territories he had overrun he may have died with his life's work unfinished, for the conquest of the Orient was only the beginning. The reorganization of the huge kingdom should have followed, and this was not accomplished by Alexander. During his last year, the main task to which he directed all his energy was giving a new shape to the Persian kingdom, now his own. He founded new cities along the borders and settled Macedonian veterans, Greek mercenaries and local people in them. He encouraged the economic development of the Euphrates valley and built a great harbor at the mouth of the Euphrates and Tigris rivers. His final project was an examination of the possibilities of establishing a trade route between Mesopotamia and Egypt by employing the maritime route around the Arabian Peninsula. He did not live to implement this project, but all these actions (and many others not mentioned here) were but a small part of the political and administrative effort needed to put the Persian Kingdom on firm and broad foundations. For Alexander's task had been not only to heal the wounds suffered by Persia in the war, but to bring about a fundamental change in the obsolete methods of government, so characteristic of that country during the last century of its existence.

Alexander believed that the best way of reviving the strength of Persia lay in the fusion of the West and the East into a single political unit. He considered the Western peoples — Macedonians and Greeks — excellent specimens of humanity which could infuse the oriental kingdom with a new spirit. However, he had no intention of following the course which seemed quite logical to his contemporaries, i.e., for the Western peoples to become masters authorized to rule the Eastern peoples by right of conquest. On principle Alexander did not draw any distinction between conquerors and conquered. He was the first among the Macedonians to adopt Persian garb and introduce Persian customs at his court. Alexander strove to rule his kingdom not as a stranger who had conquered the East by military force, but as one on whom the gods had bestowed the right to rule and before whom all peoples in his kingdom were equal. He presented gifts to soldiers who married Persian women (the sources speak of about 10,000 men), and at his command many of his courtiers and nearest friends married Persian women, the daughters of the noblest families. Alexander even enrolled easterners into the Macedonian army. He appointed military commanders from among the Persians and raised an army of 30,000 Persian youths trained in Macedonian techniques. Shortly before his death he was busy organizing mixed military units of Macedonians and natives.

Taking the long view, Alexander was probably right. Historical developments in the course of several centuries confirmed his approach to the problem of the fusion of East and West. Hellenistic culture was a result of this amalgamation, and the entire spiritual development of the ancient world from Alexander onwards, including Christianity, may be resting on the foundations laid by the great Macedonian. But a historical process on a large scale cannot be realized at once, and certainly not by orders given from above. Alexander's great dreams seemed strange and incomprehensible to his contemporaries. The Macedonians felt deeply offended at the very idea that easterners might occupy high offices in the country and be close to the king. On the other hand, eastern peoples were unable to change their nature in the course of a few years, and become genuine adherents of Alexander's policy. Bribery, inefficiency and lack of political discipline remained the basic characteristics of Persian officials under Alexander, just as they had been before him. The fusion of nations which was Alexander's goal could not possibly be realized during his lifetime, and was indeed abandoned immediately after his death. But even if it was not feasible then, the very fact that the fusion of East and West appeared as a powerful political factor at the beginning of the Hellenistic Age is sufficient proof that it was precisely this element which became the distinctive characteristic of the new era.

C. THE PERIOD OF THE DIADOCHI

Alexander's short reign passed like a sudden storm over the Orient. He had destroyed the Persian kingdom and, although he had not had the time to erect a new administrative edifice upon the ruins, his new empire took the place of the defunct state. That empire extended from the River Indus in the east to Macedonia and Greece in the west; and from the River Jaxartes (Syr Darya) in the north to the border between Egypt and Nubia in the south. It is doubtful whether the great conqueror himself would have been able to impose order and discipline throughout such a vast domain. Perhaps countless disappointments lay in store for him. Without him the fate of the empire became less certain. After Alexander's sudden demise the dynasty of Philip and Alexander came to an end and power passed to Alexander's companions-in-arms.[15] There were a number of these generals, each one of them full of energy and initiative, and naturally these men had no interest in maintaining the unity of the empire. Instead, the Diadochi — as the Macedonian generals who succeeded Alexander were called — split up the huge kingdom. A period of long and bloody wars set in; then, gradually, political confusion gave way to the new states which were destined to rule over the world during the whole Hellenistic period.

Some of the basic events of this stormy period (323–301 B.C.E.) determined the political fate of Palestine for many generations, and several of the Diadochi will be mentioned more than once in subsequent chapters.

A brief account of the period which should acquaint us with facts and persons directly connected with our subject is therefore called for.[16]

Although immediately upon Alexander's death the danger of dismemberment of the kingdom became apparent, the Macedonian generals were at first inclined to preserve its unity. Two "kings" from Alexander's family[17] were chosen as the official rulers of the kingdom, an action which demonstrated the Macedonian generals' intention to preserve the dynasty of Philip and Alexander at least *de jure*. One of Alexander's close friends, Perdiccas, a Macedonian of noble birth, was appointed regent for all affairs of state. Perdiccas sincerely attempted to preserve the unity of the huge empire, but he met with the gradually increasing opposition of the Macedonian generals nominated to rule as satraps over the different parts of the empire.

The appointment of these satraps was an innovation contradicting Alexander's policy, which retained the Persian officials of Darius' time at the heads of several satrapies. According to a new order, confirmed by the assembly of Macedonian commanders in Babylon in 323, Persian officials were dismissed and almost all the satrapies distributed among the Macedonian generals.[18] This action effectively ended Alexander's policy of seeking to obliterate the difference between conquerors and conquered and give the Persians (or at least the Persian aristocracy) a share in the government of the state.

Most of the Macedonian generals appointed as satraps had previously served in the army as the faithful lieutenants of their king. Now, for the first time, they achieved political power, but they had a very strange conception of the significance of this transition from military service to administrative office. They considered themselves not officials who had to give an account of their activities to the regent of the state, but independent rulers with unlimited authority whose lands had been bestowed on them as a reward for their assistance in the conquest of the Orient. As a result of this outlook serious conflicts arose with some of the more aggressive satraps, when Perdiccas, in an attempt to bring order into the state, required an account of their activities. In 321, after ruling for about two years, Perdiccas was assassinated by a group of commanders conspiring against him. This was the first step towards the dissolution of the empire.

One of the most capable commanders among the rebel satraps was a certain Ptolemy, who from the very beginning of his career had been striving for complete independence. In 323, when the different lands of the empire were distributed among the Macedonian commanders for the first time, Ptolemy was designated governor of Egypt. But very soon he adopted this rich country as his legal heritage and prepared to go to war against anybody challenging his right to rule it with absolute authority. In addition, he gradually extended his power over the neighboring countries annexing Cyrene in the west (including her five ancient Greek cities) and the countries along the Nile as far south as the borders of Nubia and north to Palestine, which had a special importance in his eyes for strategic and economic reasons. Within a few years Ptolemy succeeded in building up a kind of independent empire, firmly based on the large revenues he drew from the rich Egyptian soil.

Ptolemy was a prudent man of moderate aspirations. Although Perdiccas' death gave him the opportunity to place himself at the head of the whole of Alexander's empire, Ptolemy renounced this high and dangerous office, well aware of the unsteady foundations on which the huge kingdom rested. He was satisfied with a smaller portion which he held with great tenacity. By 323 Ptolemy had already laid the foundations of the first Hellenistic state, although until 305 it was not officially proclaimed an independent kingdom but was considered as a mere satrapy. Only in that year was Ptolemy crowned king. He was the cleverest statesman among the Diadochi, and the state he founded was destined to last longer than any other Hellenistic state.

Another rebel satrap was Seleucus, who obtained Babylon as a satrapy in 321, when a second distribution of the lands of Alexander's empire was made. Seleucus was of the same breed as Ptolemy; he also belonged to Alexander's close friends and top flight commanders, but his political career was much stormier than that of his friend Ptolemy, for the land which fell to his lot was not protected by natural borders like Egypt. Like Ptolemy, Seleucus regarded his satrapy as his share in Alexander's heritage, or rather as his share of the loot, conferred on him as a reward for his assistance in the conquest of the East.[19] In 315 he was forced to flee the country by Antigonus — formerly satrap of Phrygia — who threatened to add Babylon to the Asiatic domains already under his control. Seleucus sought refuge with Ptolemy and lived at his court for about three years. In 312 he returned to his own country, after he and Ptolemy had inflicted a decisive defeat upon Demetrius, the son of Antigonus, at the battle of Gaza. In that year the foundations of the realm known to history as the Kingdom of the Seleucids were finally laid. For some years Seleucus continued to fight Antigonus for his right to rule Babylon, but at last Antigonus was convinced that he would never be able to defeat him. Like Ptolemy in Egypt, so Seleucus in Babylon was not content to rule one land only. He took advantage of the political confusion in the eastern satrapies to extend his power over all the eastern lands as far as the borders of India. After the decisive defeat inflicted on Antigonus in 301, Seleucus' kingdom also extended westwards to include northern Syria and a part of Asia Minor, Thus, Seleucus' kingdom became incomparably larger than Ptolemy's. including most of the lands of the former Persian empire which Alexander had conquered. However it was precisely these huge dimensions that constituted a serious handicap for Seleucus.

This brings us to another of the Diadochi, Antigonus, whom Alexander had appointed satrap of Phrygia in Asia Minor. He never succeeded in establishing an independent state although, after Alexander's death, he played a leading part in the disintegration of the empire. Later on he aimed at the opposite goal, striving to reunite all the conquered lands and establish an empire of his own to supplant Alexander's. Antigonus was already old at the beginning of the Diadochi period, and when he launched a daring war against his numerous enemies he found help and support in his young son Demetrius who was imbued with the same aspiration to extend his power over all the eastern lands. Antigonus and Demetrius waged long, bitter wars against Ptolemy, Seleucus, and other commanders.

Antigonus was the first to call himself "king." He put on the crown in 306, when Demetrius destroyed Ptolemy's fleet near Cyprus and annexed the island to his father's domain. But when, following this victory, Antigonus made an effort to conquer Ptolemy's kingdom and sent out a great expedition against Egypt, he was defeated, the victory giving Ptolemy the excuse to call himself king. Seleucus and two other Macedonian commanders — Lysimachus in Thrace and Cassander in Macedonia — followed Ptolemy's example. Thus the year 305 may be considered as the date when Alexander's great empire was definitely abolished, especially since in the meantime all Alexander's relatives had been eliminated and the ancient Macedonian dynasty which had given Philip and Alexander to Macedonia had become extinct.[20] Again Antigonus made a desperate attempt to subdue all the Diadochi, but once more he failed. After his death on the battlefield of Ipsus in Asia Minor his kingdom was divided among the commanders who had formed a coalition to fight him (301).

In the course of the following twenty years the four Hellenistic kingdoms under Ptolemy, Seleucus, Lysimachus and Cassander, developed and gained in strength. But the historical path of each of them was different. Cassander died in 293, his death being quickly followed by disturbances in Macedonia. His sons were not able to hold on to the throne, and it passed from hand to hand, finally (in the seventies of the third century) falling to Demetrius' son, Antigonus II. The latter was a clever, well-educated man of moderate aspirations who reorganized Macedonia, leaving a state which survived under his sons until the middle of the second century B.C.E. It happened to be the first Hellenistic state to be abolished by Rome.

Ptolemy lived to a ripe old age (283) and left a well-organized kingdom to his son Ptolemy II Philadelphus. Lysimachus' kingdom crumbled immediately after his death. Lysimachus was killed in battle against Seleucus and all the lands which had been his (in the north of Asia Minor, in Thrace and in Macedonia), came into Seleucus' possession. The defeat and death of Lysimachus extended still further the border of the huge Seleucid kingdom, which now stretched as far as Greece. But Seleucus' victory did him no good. The moment he entered Macedonia he was murdered by one of his courtiers. Thus one after the other, the last three Diadochi left the historical arena in the late eighties of the third century. Their death ended the stormy period when lands passed from hand to hand. At last the foundations were laid for more stable political structures: the three Hellenistic states which appeared in the eastern lands and retained power until Rome made its appearance in the international political arena.

D. THE HELLENISTIC STATES.

The successive changes which took place during the period of the Diadochi had a significant influence on the fate of Palestine, a topic discussed in further detail elsewhere in this volume.[21] From 300 until 198 Palestine was under the rule of the Ptolemies. From then until the rise of the Hasmoneans it formed part of the Seleucid kingdom of Syria. During this period a large Jewish community came into being in Egypt, especially in the capital, Alexandria, while at the same time many other Jewish communities were founded in various cities of the Seleucid kingdom. Accordingly these Hellenistic states which played an important role in the historical development of the Land of Israel and the people of Israel, should be briefly discussed.

Although founded by Macedonian conquerors, and with Greeks from Greece proper and from Asia Minor filling the kings' courts and the high offices in the army and administration, it may safely be said that these Hellenistic states were a direct continuation of the Ancient Eastern kingdoms. If, for instance, the administrative methods of Ptolemaic rule in Egypt are examined, the customs and practices, institutions and offices of ancient Egypt are easily recognizable through the thin veneer of Hellenism. The habits of millennia cannot be changed in the course of a few years. Indeed,

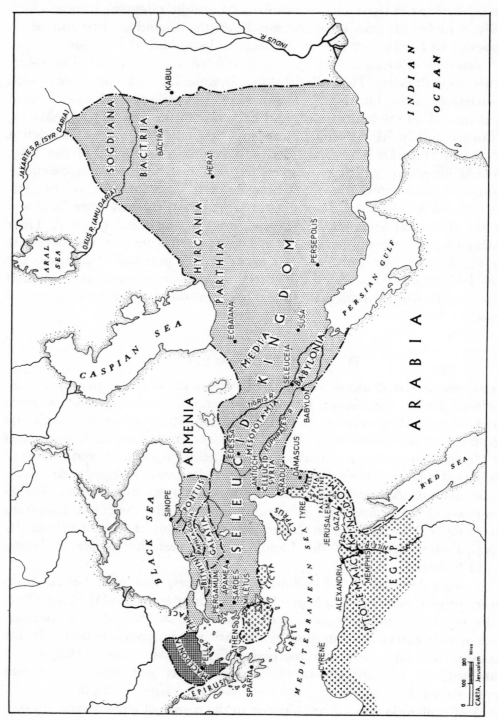

Hellenistic States 275 B.C.E.

the Ptolemies were not interested in introducing fundamental changes in the existing order, since local customs were deeply rooted in the life of the country and had proved their usefulness in the course of thousands of years. In spite of Macedonian domination, the land remained the same ancient Egypt, its soil covered with the Nile waters every year at the flood season, its fields giving abundant crops sufficient not only to feed the local population but also for export, and its inhabitants the same peasants who for thousands of years had cultivated the fields under the strict supervision of the king's officials. Now, a Macedonian king took the place of the pharaoh. Greek officials were appointed to high offices and part of the land passed into the hands of Greek and Macedonian military settlers. But all these changes did not affect the system of government which was the legacy of ancient Egypt.

The priests conferred upon the Macedonian king all the titles which in bygone days had been applied to the pharaohs. The king was considered a deity or the son of a deity. The whole Ptolemaic dynasty was honored as divine, and statues of the kings were placed in temples throughout the whole country. Absolutism, i.e., the untrammelled, despotic power of the king, had ever since the third millennium been the characteristic feature of the Egyptian monarchy, and the same principle continued unchanged in the Hellenistic state of the Ptolemies. The king concentrated in his own person all the features of an absolute ruler. As a god, or the son of a god, he was the link between two worlds, the world of the gods and that of mortals. He was the supreme and sole legislator in the kingdom; no law or local custom could be considered valid without the king's approval. Accordingly, the king was the supreme judge and everybody could appeal to him directly to demand justice. He was regarded as the supreme administrator and all the enormous machinery of Egyptian bureaucracy was at his service. In the economic field the king had unlimited power. He was considered the sole owner of the whole land of Egypt, and numerous sections of economic life — such as the production of many kinds of goods and their sale — were royal monopolies.

The king exercised his power through a very large number of officials. Their main center was at Alexandria, but they were also quite numerous throughout the whole country, even in the remotest villages. These officials were mainly in charge of fiscal and economic matters, such as the collection of taxes, the strict supervision of the king's monopolies, the registration of all property, the measurement of estates, population census, etc. Under the Ptolemies the bureaucratic machine became highly efficient. Its work reached such a level that it could serve as a model for every bureaucratic state. The custom of registering every official paper in the royal offices, the keeping of records in the archives, the composing of standard forms of documents for various kinds of business, the checking of all expenditures and revenues, etc., all these practices attained perfection in the Ptolemaic kingdom. In modern historical literature it is often called "the totalitarian state" and it must be admitted that the name suits it very well.[22]

Principles, however, do not always coincide with real life. According to totalitarian principles, the king had to concentrate every aspect of the political, economic, and administrative life of the state in his own hands. But, by the laws of the kingdom, the throne passed from father to son, and there could arise a case of the king being unable to rule or — in the case of a minor — a regent would have to replace the monarch. Even if a clever and highly capable man were at the head of the government, could it conceivably be possible to concentrate such manifold and complicated tasks in the hands of a single man? Obviously the actual situation rested on other foundations than those demanded by the principles. In consequence, a certain compromise between life itself and the principles of perfect absolutism was reached. Actual government, with all its various administrative branches, was concentrated not in the hands of the king, whose role was sometimes confined merely to the signing of documents, but in the hands of high officials in Alexandria.

Because of the special importance of financial questions, the greatest power was given to the minister of finance, whose title was *dioiketes*. His authority in fact far surpassed the narrow limits of checking expenditure and revenue and embraced the whole economic life of the state. Moreover, the *dioiketes* sometimes interfered in political relations with foreign states and in the appointment of local administrators. In the districts, local power was exercised by governors called the *strategoi*. Each *strategos* represented the king in his own district and was responsible for various branches of government, such as administration, justice, police, army, etc. And, although in theory the peasants could send petitions directly to the king, actually, these petitions got only as far as the office of the *strategos*.

The economic situation likewise revealed a great discrepancy between theory and practice. Theoretically, all the soil of Egypt was regarded as the king's private property; in effect, however, the land was divided into two major categories. One was the "royal land" in the narrow sense of the term, the peasants settled on it being called the "royal peasants," who paid taxes directly to officials appointed by the government. The second group included all the rest of the land and was divided into different categories: 1) "sacred land," i.e. the land allotted to the numerous temples of the kingdom, 2) "cleruchic land," i.e. the land leased to military settlers, and 3) "gift land," i.e. land which the king gave on a temporary basis to his friends or high officials.[23]

In the third century B.C.E., when the Ptolemaic kings were at the height of their power, they even encroached upon lands not under their direct control. For instance, every plot of land leased to a military settler automatically reverted to the royal treasury immediately upon the death of the soldier, regardless of whether he had sons or not. There were even large estates of "gift land" bringing in considerable revenues which were under the control of royal officials, despite the fact that they had been granted to private persons as gifts of the king.

Yet time worked many changes in the nature of the Ptolemaic kingdom. The lands leased to the soldiers began to pass from father to son by right of inheritance, and the principle of private property gradually prevailed over the principle of the king's absolute power. The perennial latent struggle between these two principles blurred the boundary between state and private property (especially if the owner was a high official). Quite often the sources do not make it clear whether the financial and economic actions of a certain official were for his personal gain or were merely a part of the king's general policy. Thus, in the course of time the totalitarian principles of the Ptolemaic state provoked strong opposition forces, able to amend the nature of many branches of the political and economic life in the state.[24]

The organization of the army in the Ptolemaic kingdom also deserves mention, for Jews took an active part in it. The Ptolemaic dynasty was foreign to the local population, and the kings were disinclined to entrust the principal administrative offices to Egyptians. In fact, all the chief charges in Alexandria and the districts were distributed among Macedonians and Greeks, while only the petty offices, such as "head of the village" (*komarch*), or "village-scribe" (*komogrammateus*) were left to Egyptians. The Ptolemies were even more cautious in the question of the defense of the country. The Ptolemaic army was usually recruited from among foreigners. Thus it consisted mainly of Macedonians, Greeks, Thracians, Galatians, etc. However, it was not always possible to bring soldiers from lands across the sea, since these countries were not under Ptolemaic rule. For this reason military colonization had developed on a large scale as early as the reign of Ptolemy II Philadelphus, each settler being assigned a plot of land. As a result of this policy thousands of foreign soldiers were settled on the soil of Egypt. They married native women and a new generation of mixed ethnic origin grew up in Egypt. Following the

Greek-Macedonian pattern, these young people received special military training from childhood, and provided soldiers for the regular Ptolemaic army. In Ptolemaic Egypt, as everywhere else, the army became a vast melting pot, with people of different nations merging into a homogeneous population. For some time different military units were still named after the country where they had originally been recruited, viz. Macedonians, Thessalians, Thracians, Persians, Mysians, etc. By the third century these units had become pseudoethnic groups no longer having any ties with a particular nation or country and open to every soldier, regardless of origin. The plots of land assigned to the foreign settlers were in some cases very large (especially for the cavalry) and this fact quite naturally provoked hatred and envy among the local population.[25]

Throughout the third century the Ptolemaic kings kept the native population under strict control but at the end of the century Ptolemy IV Philopator was forced to enroll several thousand Egyptians as auxiliary soldiers. The moment the natives got weapons into their hands and took an active part in the great victory over the Syrian king (the battle of Raphia in 217), a strong national movement arose among the Egyptians and throughout the second century revolt after revolt flared up. At last the Ptolemies were forced to make concessions to the natives and open government offices (even the highest) to them. From the middle of the second century, the king paid more attention to the needs of the local population and from one point of view he can be regarded as the representative of all groups of the Egyptian population, native and foreign elements.

The Ptolemaic state has been discussed in detail not only because of its special importance in relation to Jewish history (a great number of Jews settled in Egypt in this period) but also because papyri at our disposal have thrown a new light on the political and economic structure of the Ptolemaic kingdom.[26] Investigation of the history and internal organization of the Seleucid kingdom, however, is a much more difficult task. Historians have at their disposal inscriptions from the Greek cities of the Seleucid kingdom, coins, archeological finds, documents or cuneiform tablets, and a few fragments by Greek writers. This material, though very important, is however neither complete nor coherent. Thus only scanty evidence exists about the internal structure of the Seleucid kingdom. This is to be much regretted, for the kingdom also absorbed a great number of Jews. Moreover, from the year 198 B.C.E. onwards, Palestine was an integral part of the Seleucid kingdom, and a proper understanding of the liberation movement of Judah Maccabee and his brothers is impossible without a thorough knowledge of the political and social basis of the Seleucid government.

Like that of the Ptolemies, the Seleucid kingdom was an absolute monarchy. The king was worshiped as a god and was considered the primary source of law and justice. However, the gap between the principles of absolute rule and historical reality was much greater here than it was in the Ptolemaic kingdom. The Seleucids ruled over enormous areas extending from the Mediterranean to the borders of India. Their kingdom was actually a direct continuation of the Persian empire, and this was apparent not only in the immense distances covered. All the defects of the Persian empire — the central government's weakness, the aspiration to independence of different parts of the kingdom, the army's poor organization, and the lack of responsibility on the part of the high officials, all persisted unchanged in the Seleucid kingdom. More than human strength was needed to transform the mixture of peoples under Seleucid rule into an organic whole. Two ways to this end were possible — force and cultural influence. The first way would have meant establishing royal power over all parts of the enormous area by force, including pitiless suppression of national movements, punishing those who transgressed the law with the utmost severity, and so on. It would have been a feasible policy if a powerful and well-organized army had been at the king's disposal. But the same factor giving rise to the weakness of the Ptolemies worked even more strongly in the Seleucid kingdom. It was impossible to entrust the highly responsible role of the defense of the state to the native population since they were anxiously awaiting the proper moment to throw off the yoke of the central government. From this standpoint, the Seleucid kingdom was in a much more dangerous situation than that of the Ptolemies. The Egyptians were generally unarmed and were not considered a warlike people, nor were they well trained militarily; on the other hand, many of the numerous peoples and tribes of Asia Minor, the Iranian plateau, and the far-off satrapies had strong military organizations based on time-honored traditions, and were famous throughout the world as excellent soldiers. Not only was it impossible to convert them into a regular army under Seleucid officers but, on the contrary, strong forces were needed to quell them in times of rebellion.

As in Egypt, the government had a regular army at its disposal consisting of Macedonian and Greek mercenaries. However, large scale recruiting was possible only at the beginning of the Hellenistic period. Later on this source was gradually exhausted and in the 2nd century it dried up completely. Thus, the Seleucids were forced to recruit most of their soldiers from among young Macedonians and Greeks born and raised in the military colonies founded at the time of Alexander the Great and by the first two Seleucid kings — Seleucus I and Antiochus I. In the Seleucid kingdom, just as in Egypt, the descendants of the original soldier-settlers were neither Macedonian nor Greek, for by marrying local women the settlers had intermingled with the population of Asia Minor, Syria, etc. Before very long the terms "Macedonian" or "Greek" ceased to designate the racial origin of a soldier but indicated only the form of his military training.

Without question these professional soldiers constituted a very strong military force, but like all professional or mercenary forces, they were ready to support anybody who would offer them higher wages or promise a bigger share of the loot. Moreover, there were not sufficient "Macedonian" soldiers to protect the vast areas of the Seleucid Empire. Thus, in spite of the dangers involved, the Seleucids were forced to muster auxiliary contingents from among the different peoples of their kingdom. Even this step would have been impossible without making important concessions to these people. The history of the Seleucid kingdom inevitably became the account of the gradual (or sometimes very rapid) dismemberment of a great empire. It represented a kind of duel between the Hellenistic state, anxious to hold on to unlimited power, and the efforts of the Orient to throw off the foreign yoke. The very founder of the dynasty, Seleucus I, had to give up the far-eastern territories bordering on India. Later, in the middle of the 3rd century, the lands of Bactria, Parthia, Armenia, etc., fell away as well.

In all these places chieftains arose to incite the local population against the central government. The most dangerous of them was Arsaces, King of Parthia. He succeeded in founding an independent dynasty which survived not only through the Hellenistic Age, but also through the Roman period up to the 3rd century C.E. Antiochus III, one of the most despotic of the Seleucid kings (223–187 B.C.E.) decided to re-establish his dynasty's rule over the eastern lands cost what it may. He embarked upon a wearisome campaign which lasted for six long years (209–204) and brought him to the most remote borders of the kingdom. Everywhere he waged wars against the rebellious kings, but although at first glance he seemed to be victorious, he did not succeed in abolishing the power of the local rulers. At last he was forced to come to terms with them and to buy their fidelity with important concessions.

Not only did Antiochus' campaign do nothing to lessen the opposition of the Oriental kings, it even led to its increase. Immediately after his death the process of dismemberment of the kingdom was renewed with greater vigor. In the meantime, the Seleucid power in Asia Minor was being whittled away; at first as a result of an unsuccessful struggle against the local tribes and their chieftains, and later because of the intervention of Rome. At the time when the fate of the Seleucids was closely interwoven with that of Israel, that is, the middle of the 2nd century B.C.E., only a small group of lands, corresponding more or less to Syria and Mesopotamia, remained in Seleucid hands.[27]

The alternate method of uniting the Seleucid empire, that of cultural influence, was not easy either. Most modern historians attribute the idea of the Hellenization of the Orient to the Seleucid kings, that is, they hold that the Seleucids strove to spread Greek civilization among the backward peoples of the Orient in order to make it prevail all over the known world. However, this idea is a product of the imagination of modern historians. There is no evidence that the Seleucids even dreamed of implementing such a large and far-reaching project. Indeed, even if such an idea had occurred to them, they would have found it impossible to transform a variety of ancient civilizations, deeply rooted in the life of their peoples, into a uniform Hellenic culture. Not to mention that the founder of the Seleucid dynasty, Seleucus I, married a Persian woman, so that mixed blood flowed in the veins of the Seleucids from the very beginning of their power.

In support of their opinion, scholars point to the great number of Greek cities which the Seleucids founded in the lands they ruled. However, the founding of Greek cities should not be considered identical with the spreading of Greek culture. Admittedly, these cities did serve as centers of Hellenic culture in the Orient, but the purpose of their founding was not cultural but political. The Seleucids were fully aware of the weakness of their position among the numerous Oriental peoples, and by attracting a large number of people from Greece proper, Asia Minor, and Macedonia to their kingdom hoped to secure a solid backing for themselves. These people were granted the right to organize their political life in their new home on the pattern to which they had been accustomed in their own country. In this way scores of cities grew up throughout the whole Orient, especially in Syria and Mesopotamia.[28]

Scholars lay much stress on the fact that the Ptolemies did not build Greek cities in Egypt, and conclude from this omission that the Ptolemies submitted to local Oriental civilization, whereas the Seleucids combatted it valiantly. In fact, however, the Ptolemies erected a great many Greek cities in the lands beyond the borders of Egypt, such as Palestine, Cyrene etc. If they did not do the same in Egypt itself, it was because the Greek *polis* with ancient traditions of freedom and autonomy could easily have destroyed the rigid administration upon which the whole edifice of Egypt's totalitarian state was based.

In any case, the Seleucid kingdom lacked the uniformity so typical of the Ptolemaic state. Not only did the foundation of Greek cities not endanger the integrity of the kingdom, it might actually have strengthened it. Moreover, once the Greek cities had been built, and the local population realized that they enjoyed special political and economic privileges and were regarded as the king's allies, many existing Oriental towns became convinced of the advantages of the *polis*, and transformed their traditional political order to conform to its structure. For, of course, the Seleucid kings saw that it was to their advantage for the rich oriental bourgeoisie to come to terms with the central government, and they lent a helping hand to facilitate this process. The foundation of Greek cities, or the transformation of an Oriental town into a *polis*, may be termed the "Hellenization of the Orient," but it must be borne in mind that this "Hellenization" was not a matter of substituting Western civilization for Oriental culture but only a modification of political forms.[29]

Evidence about the internal organization of the Seleucid state is meager. Supreme power was in the hands of the king, who made decisions after talks with his "friends," i.e. courtiers and high officials. The capital was the center of the state, and from it the king ruled 25 (approximately) satrapies, now called *strategies*, which were divided into 72 smaller administrative divisions. Like the ancient Persian satraps, the *strategoi* were responsible for such varied functions as the army, administration, tax-collection, etc. At first glance, it seems an example of a bureaucratic state par excellence, but in fact in methods of administration it was quite different. The number of officials was not great, and the central government entrusted various economic and administrative branches to representatives of the local population.

While the centralization of power was a basic principle of the Ptolemaic kingdom, the Seleucids (having perhaps no alternative) adopted the opposite criterion of decentralization. The numerous peoples of the kingdom enjoyed a certain degree of autonomy which was officially acknowledged by the Seleucids. There were three kinds of autonomous institutions in the kingdom: the cities, the dynasts, and the peoples. The cities, that is, the Greek *polis*, or the Hellenized Oriental towns, were sure of the special consideration of the government. As pointed out above, they enjoyed a wide measure of municipal autonomy — a distant echo of the "freedom and autonomy" of the classical period — and although they paid taxes to the central government they were regarded as the king's allies. The dynasts, who ruled their peoples and acted as their official representatives before the central government, were regarded as princes or petty kings.

They were a kind of "vassals" of the Seleucid kings, responsible for re-cruiting auxiliary forces for the army and for the collection of taxes in their countries. As for the "peoples" (ἔθνη), they were organized ethnic groups with an aristocratic or theocratic form of government, and they also enjoyed a certain degree of autonomy which varied according to the decision of the king. Having renounced a system of rigid centralization, the kings found wide support in governing the great empire. Of course it goes without saying that *de jure* the king remained the head of the state, and no local, municipal, or ethnic unit was regarded as independent until its autonomy had been precisely determined by the king.[30]

The political situation in the Hellenistic world in the course of the 3rd and 2nd centuries B.C.E. will now be considered briefly. Throughout the 3rd century the Ptolemaic empire was very strong, ruling not only Egypt but also many neighboring lands, such as Cyrene in the west, the lands along the Red Sea to the Bab-el-Mandeb in the east, and southern Syria (including Palestine) in the north. In addition, the island of Cyprus, several cities on the south-west coast of Asia Minor, a number of islands in the Aegean Sea, and even distant Thrace were subject to the Ptolemies.[31] A great fleet patrolling the routes connecting Egypt with her far-off provinces secured Ptolemaic control of Cyprus and a number of places on the coast of Asia Minor and in the Aegean Sea, and protected the trade routes between Egypt and Greece.

Although the conquests of Alexander the Great extended the geo-graphical horizon of the Greeks as far as the borders of distant India, the Mediterranean remained the center of political and economic life in the eyes of the Greeks and Macedonians. Domination of the eastern parts of the Mediterranean had accordingly elevated Egypt in the estimation of its contemporaries to the status of the most important Hellenistic state. Easy communications between Egypt and Greece made Alexandria the greatest city in the Hellenistic world in population, wealth, and culture. The Ptolemies tried more than once to extend their power within Greece proper, but they were always strongly opposed by the Macedonian dynasty founded by Antigonus, son of Demetrius. Even as it was, the Ptolemaic kingdom remained a mighty state, both internally and on the international arena, and throughout the 3rd century it retained the position it had occupied from the very beginning, as the foremost power of the Hellenistic world.

The Seleucid kingdom found itself in a much more difficult political situation. In 312 B.C.E. Seleucus I chose Babylon as the center of his activities and built Seleuceia on the Tigris to serve as the capital of the great eastern empire. The battle of Ipsus (301) brought the lands of northern Syria and part of Asia Minor into his grasp, and this gave Seleucus the idea of transferring the main center of his kingdom from the east to the west, so as to be closer to the Mediterranean world. A new town, Antioch, which was to replace Seleuceia on the Tigris as the capital of the Seleucids, was founded on the river Orontes in northern Syria. But before very long it became apparent that Antioch was not the right place to deal with political affairs of the Iranian plateau and the coast of the Indian Ocean. Accordingly in 293, Seleucus divided the rule of his enormous empire with his son Antiochus, the successor to the throne. Seleucus took the western part, while Antiochus was sent to rule the eastern lands as an independent monarch with unlimited power. This division did not last long, and it is not mentioned further after the death of Seleucus I in 280. From that time on the Seleucid kings unequivocally transferred the center of their kingdom from east to west, without making any provision for the efficient administration of the east.

They had to pay for this move. As pointed out above, national opposition to the Seleucid government started precisely in the east, and it was only with great difficulty that Antiochus III succeeded in securing what was still left and in halting the process of dismemberment. Giving up the east could have been justified only if the Seleucids had succeeded in building a strong kingdom in the west, thereby creating an important political stronghold equivalent to that of Ptolemaic Egypt. But this was not easy. Every attempt the Seleucids made to strengthen their power in the west, and to exercise their influence beyond the borders of the kingdom, met with strong opposition on the part of the Ptolemies who defended their political and economic positions in Syria, Cyprus, Asia Minor, and in every other place where danger threatened their kingdom.

Rivalry between the two states is the main theme of the political history of the 3rd century in the eastern part of the Mediterranean. In the course of the century, five long wars were waged by the Seleucids against the Ptolemies. They are called the "Syrian Wars," although not all of them took place within the borders of Syria, and the early ones quite possibly did not touch Syria at all. The first three wars had no effect at all on the balance of power in the Mediterranean lands. The Ptolemies successfully defended their positions and in the Third Syrian War (246) Ptolemy III Euergetes was even able to inflict a decisive defeat upon Seleucus II and to penetrate quite a distance into his kingdom.

However, with the Fourth Syrian War (219–217), the first signs of a change appeared on the political horizon. King Antiochus III invaded Palestine and conquered it quite easily, to be dislodged by Ptolemy IV only after enormous efforts (including the enrolling of local auxiliary forces) when his troops routed Antiochus at the battle of Raphia.

The battle proved to be the Ptolemies' final success. Fifteen years later a new campaign against the lands of southern Syria initiated by Antiochus III (201–198) found Ptolemy's forces too weak to resist and the empire's most important provinces (Phoenicia, Palestine and Transjordan) were finally incorporated by the Seleucids.[32]

The defeat of the Ptolemaic kingdom had immediate repercussions in several other Mediterranean lands. Macedonia was ready to divide the distant provinces of the Ptolemaic kingdom with the Seleucids, and a number of lands and cities in Thrace and Asia Minor passed to Philip V King of Macedonia, as well as to Antiochus III. It appeared as though the Seleucid kingdom were poised on the edge of a period of expansion, which would enable it to take over the position the Ptolemies had hitherto occupied in the Mediterranean. But at the beginning of the 2nd century, a new factor entered the scene.

Rome began to develop an interest in the affairs of the Eastern lands. The Roman Senate did not look favorably on the rise of mighty Hellenistic states which could threaten the peace of Italy, and decided accordingly on a policy of defending weaker states (which were not dangerous for her) and of reducing the power of the stronger ones. After a series of successful wars, the power of Macedonia and of Seleucid Syria was broken, and the political significance and independence of the Hellenistic states came to an end.[33]

The 2nd century saw a rapid decline of both the Seleucids and the Ptolemies. The native peoples of the Ptolemaic kingdom launched a series of revolts and forced important concessions from the Ptolemies. The central government was paralyzed by a series of intrigues and quarrels at the king's court as a result of which the whole edifice of the totalitarian state began to crumble. In 169–168 B.C.E. Egypt faced new danger. The Seleucid king, Antiochus Epiphanes, invaded the country with the aim of annexing the whole of Egypt to the Syrian kingdom. There is little doubt that he would have succeeded but for the intervention of Rome, which saved Egypt from her dangerous enemy. Antiochus Epiphanes was a great admirer of Rome and knew her strength. Not daring to oppose the Roman Senate, he had no choice but to obey its humiliating order to leave the borders of Egypt immediately and return to his own country. This reverse put an end to all the Seleucids' dreams and plans of setting up a mighty kingdom in the eastern Mediterranean. At the same time the uncompromising opposition of the Oriental peoples to Hellenism succeeded in destroying Seleucid power in the far east.[34]

This was the political framework in which the Jews lived from the time of Alexander the Great onwards. Like every other Oriental people, the Jews — those of the Diaspora even more than the ones in Palestine — came into contact with Hellenistic political institutions at every turn, i.e. with the Hellenistic state and with the Greek *polis*. The Jews' contacts with the Hellenistic state were mainly of a political nature; it rested with the heads of those states to decide whether to confirm or refuse Jewish autonomy, whether to permit or forbid the Jews to live according to their ancestral traditions, whether or not to impose certain Hellenistic political patterns upon them and so on.

With the Greek *polis*, the Jews' contacts were more of a cultural and religious character. The present chapter has outlined the political situation of the Hellenistic states. Another chapter completes the picture with a review of the cultural and religious aspects of Hellenism, for only against this broad background can the impact of Hellenism on the Jewish world be seen in proper perspective.

CHAPTER II

THE CULTURAL BACKGROUND

by V. Tcherikover

A. HELLENISTIC CIVILIZATION

WHEN WE SPEAK of Greek civilization we mean the civilization of the classical period. And rightly so, since it was in the classical period that Greek culture achieved its supreme triumph in epic and lyric poetry, in tragedy and comedy, in historiography and philosophy, in architecture and sculpture. Poets, artists, and philosophers such as Aeschylus, Sophocles and Euripides, Sappho and Pindar, Plato and Aristotle, Phidias and Praxiteles, erected a glorious, eternal monument to the creative power of the Greek people, unique among all the nations of the ancient world. Yet, in discussing the collision between Greek and Jewish culture (a question which will arise more than once in the present volume) it must be borne in mind that this encounter took place not in the classical period, when Greek civilization was at its height, but in the Hellenistic period. What was the specific quality of Greek culture in this age?

Nineteenth century historiography was not much interested in the Hellenistic period, either in its politics or its culture. As regards cultural achievement, it was commonly held that the Hellenistic period was a period of decline and decay. There are no illustrious names in literature or the arts to compare with the great masters of the classical period. Tragedy lost its significance, while comedy, which had played such an important political role in 5th century Athens, dwindled to the narrow confines of middle-class family life. It seems as if the abundant source of Greek creative power which had been gushing for so many centuries had been exhausted, leaving nothing but constant repetition of the same forms of creation which had been so fresh and beautiful when they had first appeared, but which were now gradually declining to the point of extinction.

Such was the common approach of 19th century scholars. However, this century employs other criteria in judging the Hellenistic period. It is indeed beyond question that the creations of the Hellenistic Age were wholly inferior to those of the classical period. Nevertheless, the new age accomplished two tasks foreign to the spirit of classical culture: it spread Greek civilization over immense areas and it fused the elements of Hellenism with those of Eastern civilizations. This fusion laid the foundations for a quite different but no less fertile spiritual development, which was to leave its mark upon subsequent ages and was to contribute to the emergence of the Christian doctrine.

The political background for the emergence of this mixed culture was ushered in by the campaigns of Alexander the Great. As a result Greeks penetrated into the remotest corners of the Orient and everywhere brought with them the basic elements of their national life — their language and literature, their games, their religion and the political structure of a Greek *polis*. Naturally, Greek civilization lost in depth what it gained in breadth. It is impossible to imagine that every small Greek settlement deep in Persia or southern Egypt could preserve its national culture untouched for long, in the face of an alien environment. But, on the other hand, where Greeks settled in great numbers new cultural centers arose, Greek culture struck roots and flourished for many generations.[1]

The life which emerged in the new lands of immigration bore no resemblance at all to that in Greece. A Greek citizen who left his mother-country and went to Egypt or Syria or another Eastern land needed all his energy and talents to hold his own and prosper. The struggle for existence left its mark first of all on the spiritual aspect of Hellenistic man. Living among people who lacked Greek culture (as far as the Greeks were concerned, they lacked any culture at all) developed an urge for conquest and domination among the Greeks. Neither a Greek official beating an Egyptian peasant nor a Macedonian soldier ravaging conquered lands felt any need of restraint, and a man with energy and initiative could without any compunction amass a fortune at the expense of the local population. The Hellenistic Age, and especially the period of the Diadochi, created a particular type of man to whom civil and moral laws did not apply, as it were. Alexander's great generals and their successors set the first example. Men like Antigonus and Demetrius at that time, or Pyrrhus, King of Epirus, a generation later, knew no bounds to their lust for power. They regarded themselves as kings not because they felt any bond with the land they were about to rule, but simply because they wanted power. A determined force of mercenaries was all that was needed to make its general the ruler of immense areas, and could, just as easily, depose him, putting an end to his political career or even his life. Within this unstable world everything depended on luck. To keep going in this life of perpetual change a man had to be strong, resolute, clever and cunning.[2]

This was the situation particularly in the period of the Diadochi, but the tradition of crude force and violence persisted in the Hellenistic states, with the center of gravity shifting from the political to the economic sphere. Papyri from the time of Ptolemy II Philadelphus give an account of two important men: Apollonius, that king's Minister of Finance, and Zenon, Apollonius' personal agent.[3] The forceful dynamic nature of this energetic minister is clearly conveyed by his short notes to Zenon, in which he issues orders to his agent running his estate in Faiyum, to be carried out "without delay" or "as soon as possible." "Turn night into day" writes Apollonius to Zenon, vividly conjuring up the pace demanded for the work on his estate in Faiyum, as well as in the new city of Philadelphia which was about to be built on the site of Rabbath-Ammon under the general supervision of Zenon. We know from other letters to Zenon that not every workman could bear such strain, and many collapsed under the pressure of this intensive work or ran away from the estate.[4] There was no other reason for such a pace than the eager desire of the landlord and his assistants to increase the produce at any price, and to secure the highest profit for themselves. This was the new type of Hellenistic man, molded in an alien environment, far from his mother-country, amidst Egyptians, Syrians, Persians etc. He was a greedy man, eager for riches, who saw nothing but this single aim, the attainment of which justified any means. This type served as a model first for other Greeks of various classes, then for the native peoples, including the Jews. What could these people have in common with refined Greek culture? It is not difficult to understand the astonishment of scholars that among the great number of documents (approximately 1,300) found in Zenon's archives, there is not a single one to tell anything of cultural life or preserve some kind of literary work, except for a short lament in verse written by an unknown poet in memory of Zenon's departed dog.[5] Another papyrus contains a long list of the clothes in Zenon's wardrobe,[6] but there is no catalogue of his personal library; indeed it may be asked whether Zenon possessed any library at all. Businessmen of this kind were destined to turn deserts into cultivated lands, to build towns in the remotest provinces, to plan financial reforms and carry them out, to open new trade routes, to establish workshops and industrial centers, etc.; but one looks in vain for the creators and admirers of culture.[7]

The Hellenistic world, however, had manifold aspects and was rich in human resources. Not everyone was a cruel tyrant, greedy for riches. From Greece came also intellectuals — philosophers, writers and scholars; they too endeavored to establish a new life for themselves in the new lands, their way to success lying in the development of the diverse facets of Greek civilization. They sought protectors of high rank and found them primarily in the kings. In this respect the activities of the first two Ptolemies, who transformed their capital, Alexandria, into the most important center of Hellenistic civilization, were particularly fruitful. It was already during the reign of Ptolemy I that a "Museum" — literally a temple of the Muses — was founded in Alexandria. This was in fact a meeting-place for scholars (something like an "academy" in our days), and beside it the first public library in the world was erected. Within a short time hundreds of thousands of scrolls containing all the works of classical Greek literature as well as the new literary works of Alexandrian scholars and poets were collected in this library.[8]

This great cultural center gave a powerful impetus to the development of Greek science. It may be said that systematic knowledge as understood in our time did not exist before Aristotle, and only in the Hellenistic Age were all the tools necessary for the development and advancement of science created. Astronomy, geography, geometry, anatomy as well as philology, were given a precise definition in the works of Alexandrian scholars. Unfortunately, there is no evidence of other cultural centers in the Hellenistic world (except for an important medical center on the island of Cos); yet the fact that the kings of the Attalid dynasty founded a public library in their capital of Pergamum in Asia Minor, with a view to compete with the Alexandrian library, suggests that Alexandria was not the only center of Hellenistic civilization. And again it needs to be emphasized that although the thorough research conducted by Hellenistic scholars in various scientific spheres cannot be compared with the sublime speculations of the Greek philosophers of the classical period, nevertheless this systematic and cautious study prepared the ground for the development of the exact sciences in the future and left its impress down to our time.

Hellenistic civilization was a many sided whole which embraced numerous different branches of social life. What legacy did the Hellenistic age receive from the classical period? How did it manage to preserve this legacy? How did Hellenistic culture spread its influence throughout the Eastern world?

B. Physical Culture

The first activity of the Hellenized Jews when the Hellenistic movement reached Jerusalem was the erection of a *gymnasium* where Jewish youths were trained in athletics. The first act of an international character performed by the Jewish *polis* Antioch-at-Jerusalem was to send its representatives to participate in the contests which took place that year in Tyre. By these two acts the Jews of Jerusalem secured, as it were, admission into the Hellenistic world. Athletics evidently played a very important role in the life of the Greek nation.

In ancient Greece it did not constitute an isolated cultural phenomenon but penetrated deeply into religious rites, literature and art, and even politics.[9] The religious nature of athletic events is perhaps the most characteristic feature differentiating sports in Greece from games of physical skill in our time. Each of the great games of classical Greece was celebrated in honor of a deeply revered deity: the Olympic and Nemean games — in honor of Zeus; the Pythian — in honor of Apollo, and the Isthmian — in honor of the sea-god Poseidon.[10] The festive openings of the games included sacrificial offerings to the gods, and the games on the whole were usually accompanied by religious ceremonies from beginning to end. Local games celebrated by individual cities (such games were held in many places) were also consecrated to a definite god, usually the chief deity of the *polis*.

The particular holiness conferred from the earliest period upon the Olympic games endowed them with great political significance. People coming to the games from diverse parts of Greece were regarded as being under the special protection of the gods and any harm done to them was condemned as sacrilege. A truce would be proclaimed during the games and all wars and strife between cities or tribes would be suspended (at least formally) for these short periods of time. The victor was honored in a special ceremony on his return home. Sometimes the city-wall would be breached and the victor carried through it, and one of the valuable prizes bestowed upon him was the right to free meals from the City Council for the rest of his life.

Athletic games were not the only manifestation of the cult of the body. Since it was a great honor for a *polis* to have its athletes participate in the contests, it had to attend to the regular physical education of its boys in order to train first-class athletes. Educational institutions in which boys received physical education were called *gymnasia*. There are no details to provide information precisely how, where, and when this institution arose and developed, but it is known that at the end of the classical period the *gymnasium* served as a center of physical culture in Greece's leading cities. At that time two years were added to the normal education in *gymnasia* for special military training. Young men of 18–20 years who received this special training were called ephebes (ἔφηβοι) and were regarded as belonging to the select ranks of the young generation. In the aristocratic cities mostly the sons of rich families were given a *gymnasium* education, whereas in a democratic city, like Athens, *gymnasia* were established for the lower classes too, thus bringing physical training to large masses of the population.[11]

The advent of the Hellenistic Age signaled a turning point in the development of Greek sports. In spite of all the importance attributed to athletics in the classical period, the Greeks were not inclined to accord them precedence above everything else, and sometimes voices of protest were raised in intellectual circles against the exaggerated value placed on athletes.[12] Political life in the classical period was so intense and attracted the interest of the citizens so strongly, that it was able to overshadow all other manifestations of cultural life. In the Hellenistic Age, however, this was not the case. The *polis* had lost its political freedom; wars were no longer waged between cities; democracy had actually ceased to exist and political activity could no longer fill the whole of a man's life. What other bond should now unite the Greeks, dispersed over the immense areas from Persia to Sicily, if not the various manifestations of their culture? And since athletics, especially the appearance of a naked man before a multitude of spectators, were alien to the spirit of Oriental populations, they acquired a particular significance in the Greek cities and became the distinctive mark separating the Greeks from all other peoples.

Thus the great value attached in Greece to athletics from the very beginning of their appearance was enhanced in the Hellenistic period. The *gymnasium* became the center of education and of cultural life in the city. Not only did it fulfil the role of an educational institution in the narrow sense of the word, it also played a political function. For only sons of full citizens had the right to an education in the *gymnasium* and a young Greek was not admitted into the citizens' community until he had completed his gymnasium education and the special training of an *ephebe*.[13] The great games in the Hellenistic Age continued to be celebrated in Greece in accordance with the ancient tradition. Since it was not easy for the overseas Greeks to visit their mother-country often, it became necessary to establish new games in different centers of Greek civilization such as Alexandria, Antioch, the cities of Asia Minor, etc. The Greeks attributed extreme importance to the new games. When a city decided to introduce such events, it had to receive special sanction from the great religious center at Delphi and to secure the consent of every king, tribe, and city, even the most remote. Thus the games attained the level of great Pan-Hellenic undertakings, through which the Greeks demonstrated their national unity to the rest of the world. Accordingly it may be said that a new and most important value was added to the importance of Greek athletics in the classical period — a national one.[14]

Moreover, it was impossible for a stranger to join the ranks of a city's citizens or become familiar with the Greek way of life without acknowledging the importance of athletics. The very notion of full citizenship was from now on connected with *gymnasium* education. No approach to the Hellenistic world was possible without participation in the great Pan-Hellenic festivals in which athletic contests occupied the foremost place. Any Eastern town wishing to acquire the status of *polis* had first of all to overcome the negative attitude of its citizens towards the appearance of naked men in public, an attitude which was the heritage of the ancient Eastern civilizations; and if an Eastern man entered the ranks of citizens, he had to give his sons a *gymnasium* education, so that they might obtain civic rights and be equal to the young Greeks of the city.

C. Religion

We have seen that the attitude towards physical fitness, demonstrated in athletics and games, marked the great difference between the people of the East and West. A great gulf also stretched between the Occident and the Orient in all that concerned religion.

In the lands of the Orient there was a powerful class of priests who scrupulously guarded their monopoly in all religious affairs, both in observing the rituals of the cult with all its various ceremonies as well as in establishing religious principles and preserving them for future generations. The great Eastern religions, such as the Egyptian, Babylonian, Syrian etc., that had developed in the course of hundreds or thousands of years, were the product of the systematic endeavors of the priests. Hence the great mystery veiling the rites and ceremonies whose profound meaning was known only to the priests; hence the tendency to establish permanent religious principles in order to impose them as a divine law upon the large masses of the population. Hence again, the penetration of religion into all the branches of cultural life (law, ethics, literature, politics), since in Eastern lands the priests were not only the keepers of religious tradition but constituted the class of intellectuals as well. In the same way as the king was regarded in the East as the sole ruler governing the material world, so the gods, meaning their representatives the priests and prophets, ruled the spiritual world.

Quite a different situation obtained in the small Greek communities around the Mediterranean. Religion in a *polis* was not a monopoly of the priestly class. Moreover, since priesthood was merely an office like any other municipal post, and therefore open to every citizen, there was no difference between a priest and an ordinary citizen. The priests, like all other officials of the *polis*, were elected by the citizens or appointed by lot, usually for a tenure of one year, and they too were asked, if necessary, to give an account of their activities to the citizens' body. Naturally the priest had to know how to perform a number of duties, such as offering sacrifices, conducting various religious ceremonies, supervising the cult of the local deities, etc., but all those functions any citizen could learn quite easily just as he acquired a knowledge of the city administration when nominated to municipal office. In such circumstances there was no possibility of establishing religious dogmas in Greece, nor was there any way to impose such dogmas upon the citizens of the community.[15]

The fact that every citizen could be elected priest and the position was merely a regular municipal office may seem to us a degradation of religion, yet in the eyes of the Greeks this regulation served, on the contrary, to strengthen religion and its various cults. For it ensured religion's becoming an integral part of the *polis*; indeed the *polis* itself took on the characteristics of a kind of religious institution.

The local deity represented the celestial protector and defender of the *polis*. Any offence committed against this deity endangered the well-being of the *polis* and its citizens. Errors in carrying out religious rites and ceremonies called for immediate amends by complicated purification ceremonies. This is why it was forbidden to offend the official religion publicly, a regulation which at that time referred to orations or discussions held in public, since not much importance was yet attached to the written word, and the circulation of books was extremely limited. Persons who violated this regulation were severely punished by the city authorities. Accounts have survived of a number of trials of the "impious," Socrates' trial being only the most famous among them.[16] These trials, however, had more of a political than a religious nature, since it was not the abstract theories of the philosopher which served as a pretext for accusing him, but the fact that he had dared to offend the gods, thus endangering the well-being of the city. The principle of "separation of state and church" did not exist in Greece since both religion and the state had fused into a single superior unity — the *polis*.

Religion struck deep roots into every aspect of the life of the *polis*. Every citizen participated in the official cult of the local deity as a matter of course. Every official (not only the priest) had to perform in certain circumstances various duties connected with the cult, such as attendance at the festive religious processions, presiding at the games in honor of the god, offering sacrifices for the welfare of the city, and so on. The great festivals in honor of the local deity were celebrated with great pomp. The festival of Panathenaia in Athens, in honor of the city goddess Athena, was famous all over the country, and competed in splendor with the great Pan-Hellenic games.[17] Festivals of this kind were occasions for much sacrificing, mass processions in the city and its environs, visits to the temples, and various ceremonies there under the supervision of priests. The long list of festivals in Athens makes it clear that not a single month would pass without a public celebration, many of which lasted for several days.[18] No wonder the simple citizen felt a strong attachment to the gods.

Athletics, the main interest of city youth, as we have seen, were also closely connected with the cult of the gods. Several cities, moreover, had been sanctified by the role they played in stories of the gods and heroes of Greek mythology, so often enriched by the sublime creations of Greek poets. Even the smallest city in Greece preserved within its walls the tomb of some demi-god or mythological hero who was regarded, according to ancestral tradition, as its founder. Not only would the city as a whole associate its first appearance in history with gods and heroes; each noble and wealthy family would also draw up for itself a genealogical tree reaching back into the mythological period. And since in the eyes of the Greeks that mythological period represented not a product of poetical imagination but the earliest period of Greek history, we may safely assume that the bond between the material world and that of the gods was accepted by the Greeks as a historical reality.

In the Hellenistic period, the *polis* remained both a religious and political institution. As before, the cities celebrated the festivals consecrated to the gods with great pomp, and every citizen, sometimes even every inhabitant of the city, was required to participate.[19] Just as in previous times, every official's activities included the performance of various religious ceremonies in honor of the local deity or other gods. It may even be said that in the Hellenistic period the role of religion in the life of Greek citizens became even more important, since religion, like athletics, was one of the cultural values which united the Greeks regardless of the great distances which now separated the cities. When the Greeks wanted to parade their devotion to their original national culture, the easiest means at hand was a display of the religious element.

During the Hellenistic Age king-worship developed among the Greek population. Kings were deified and offered divine honors, such as altars, the appointment of special priests, sacrifices, etc. It is true that this king-worship lacked any religious feeling and was mainly a matter of politics. Nevertheless its external manifestation was religious in every detail and its observances followed the pattern of the cult of heroes and demi-gods in the Greece of the classical period.[20] Special honors were conferred upon the ruler whose name was connected with the founding of the city; and sometimes the cult of the founder (κτίστης) replaced that of the local god.[21] There is no need to emphasize that the attendance of every municipal official at king-worship was a duty no less and perhaps even more important than being present at the usual religious rites.

The status and rights of the Jewish community in a Greek city will be discussed below on a number of occasions. Were the Jews allowed and moreover were they willing to become citizens in a Greek *polis*? Were they willing to hold office, and if so, how could they reconcile their religious principles with the duty of participating in the pagan cults? How, in general, could a Jewish community whose religion rejected as a matter of principle the existence of the numerous gods of the Greek Pantheon survive within the framework of a Greek *polis*, in which political and religious elements were linked by an indissoluble bond? This is not the place to answer all these questions but it may be useful to note their importance in this chapter in order to emphasize right at the beginning the enormous difficulties the Jews had to face in wishing to become part of the great Greek world.

D. Philosophy and science

No less deep was the abyss which separated the West and the East in other cultural spheres.

In the East, the power of religion over men made impossible the free development of thought, stimulating the growth of philosophy and science. But a different situation prevailed in the West; there religion did not hinder the progress of independent thinking, and the ground was prepared for the elaboration of philosophical systems and the emergence of scientific method.

The appearance of the first shoots of Greek science in Ionian cities in the 6th century B.C.E. gave rise to the style of rational thinking which knows no limits to its inquisitiveness and strives to find the solution of problems by reason only, regardless of popular beliefs and commonly-held opinions. Diverse questions in numerous fields were asked about the universe and its nature, composition and its general aspects, and varied answers were given; philosophical systems attempting to provide a scientific

1.
Alexander the Great
(Louvre)

2.
Ptolemy I
(Ny Carlsberg Glyptothek)

3.
Seleucus I
(Naples, National Museum)

4.
Demetrius I
(Rome,
National
Museum)

5.
Euthydemos of Bactria
(Villa Albani, Rome)

6.
Antiochus IV
(Iran-Bastan Museum, Teheran)

7.
Battle of Issus, mosaic from Pompei
(Naples, National Museum)

8.
"Alexander Sarcophagus" from
Sidon
(Archeological Museum, Istanbul)

9.
Alexander I Balas
(British Museum)

10.
**Antiochus VIII
and Cleopatra**
(British Museum)

11.
Demetrius II
(British Museum)

12.
Antiochus IX
(British Museum)

13.
Tryphon
(British Museum)

14.
Ptolemy IV
(British Museum)

15.
**Antiochus VII
Sidetes**
(British Museum)

16.
Arsaces
(British Museum)

9–16. Late Hellenistic rulers

17.
Head of Olympic Zeus,
Cyrene
(Paribeni)

18.
Zeus on coin of
Antiochus IV
(British Museum)

19.
Inscription giving names of priests
of Zeus at Beth-shean temple

20.
The Nabataean fertility goddess
Atargatis (Khirbet et-Tannur)
(Israel Dept. of Antiquities and Museums)

21.
The Nabataean god Dushara
(Suweida Museum)

22.
Tyche of Antioch
(Vatican Museum)

23.
Sacrifice before race
(Zschietzmann)

24.
Paneas sacred cave and nymphea

25.
The Gymnasia of Pergamum
(reconstruction)

26.
The Tem[ple]
in Perga[mon]
Gymnasi[um]

27.
Athletic games
(National Museum, Copenhagen)

28.
Greeks voting
(Kunsthistorisches Museum, Vienna)

29.
Sidon merchant ship
(Louvre)

30.
Egyptian princess of
the Ptolemaic period
(Metropolitan Museum
of Art, N.Y.)

31.
Agoranomos weight
(Israel Dept. of
Antiquities and Museums)

32—33.
Rhodian jar handles
(Israel Dept. of
Antiquities and Museums)

34.
Hellenistic pottery from Jason's tomb
(Israel Dept. of Antiquities and Museums)

36. Glass bow[l]
(Israel Dep[t.]
Antiquities
and Museu[ms])

37. Hellenistic b[lack]
pot[tery]
(Israel De[pt.]
Antiquities and Muse[ums])

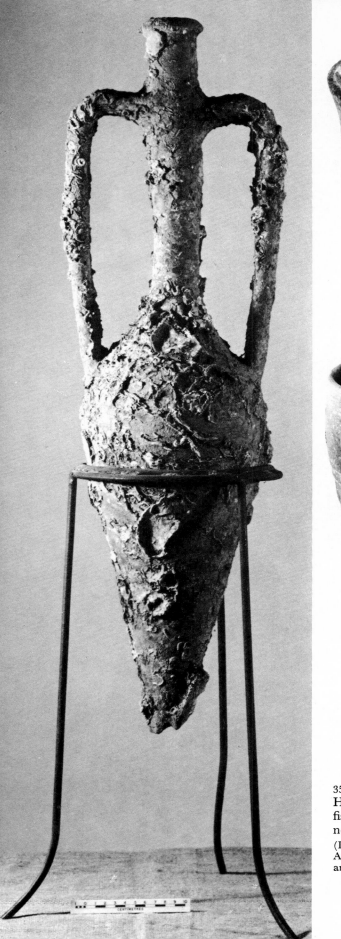

35.
Hellenistic jar
fished out of sea
near Caesarea
(Israel Dept. of
Antiquities
and Museums)

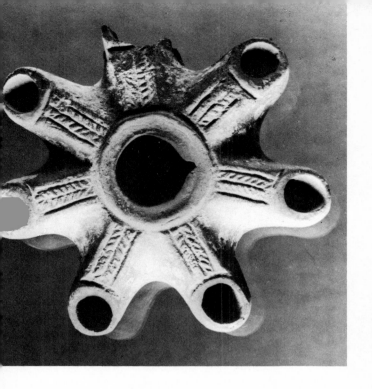

38—40.
Hellenistic lamps
(Israel Dept. of
Antiquities
and Museums)

41.
War elephant on vase
(Villa Giulia, Rome)

42.
Panoply of arms from Rhodes
(Archeological Instit. of
Dodecanese, Rhodes)

43.
Hellenistic mercenary on stele
(Archeological Museum, Istanbul)

44.
Hefzibah
inscription
Antiochus
(Israel
Dept. of
Antiquities
and Museum

explanation of the phenomena of the material world were formulated and the study of culture and the human mind was pursued. Foundations were also laid for the different branches of science, and basic discoveries made in geometry, physics, medicine, etc.[22]

From the Ionian thinkers of the 6th century B.C.E. and the Sophists of the 5th, Greek thought was successively developed by Socrates, Plato and Aristotle, each school and philosopher evolving a particular philosophical doctrine.

This progress of abstract thought in Greece was in sharp contrast to the spirit of the East in general and the Jews in particular. The profound difference between the rational methods of Greek thought and the religious mentality of the Jews as expressed in biblical prophecy is well-known. The world of the prophets steadfastly relied on a single major principle — the bond between God and His people. The mission of the people as a whole and of each individual was to keep the laws and precepts which Moses had been given on Mount Sinai. How remote was this inner confidence of the biblical prophets from the unstable and erratic world of the Greek philosophers, governed by the abstract laws of physics and mathematics, a world in which there was no place for God unless this divinity were completely removed both from the material world and man. How could these two opposite conceptions of the universe and God be reconciled? Was any reconciliation possible at all?

True, the gap separating Greek and Jewish thinking varied. In some instances points of contact were possible. Thus, Plato attained a fusion of religious and philosophical principles which could have been accepted by an educated Jew, had he made up his mind to introduce the categories of rational thought into the dynamic, warm world of religion he had inherited from his ancestors. Jewish Alexandrian literature demonstrated that the attempt to reconcile Hellenism and Judaism on the basis of Plato's doctrine was quite successful, and the synthesis attained by this fusion later served as the philosophical basis for the development of Christianity.[23] However, Plato's illustrious pupil, Aristotle, who stands on the threshold of the Hellenistic Age, represents a turning back from the way towards the East previously opened by his teacher. Although Aristotle accepted a number of Plato's basic metaphysical ideas, his major interest, in contrast to his teacher's, was the exact sciences. The effect is comparable to Greek thought once again turning to the Ionians. At the time, however, it was not mathematics and physics which occupied the center of scientific study but biology. The "liberal arts," too, such as ethics, logic, politics, etc., became the object of philosophical research. Not the creation of a single all-embracing metaphysical doctrine is valuable in Aristotle, but the preparation of the ground for exact research into several branches of science.[24] His numerous disciples followed in his steps. Thus, many essays in botany, zoology, physics, mineralogy, ethics, politics etc., were written in this period — at the beginning of the Hellenistic Age. Greek thought was no longer one single powerful stream; it had divided into numerous different currents. Before Aristotle each individual philosopher had been the creator of a particular philosophical doctrine which reflected the unique characteristics of its founder. After Aristotle less importance was attached to individual thinkers who were supplanted by "philosophical schools." The aim of each school was the elaboration of a complete philosophical system to provide a scientific explanation of the phenomena of the material world, as well as a study of culture and the human soul.[25]

At the beginning of the 3rd century two new schools appeared in Greece which were to dominate the world of Greek, and later of Greek-Roman thought for hundreds of years. These were the schools of the Stoics and the Epicureans. Although both those schools dealt *inter alia* with problems of physics, they did not put forward any original ideas in this domain. Epicurus, for instance, placed the atomic theory, developed much earlier, at the basis of his physical doctrine. These schools were especially preoccupied with problems of man's conduct. How should a man comport himself in order to obtain happiness? By "happiness" both schools understood the avoidance of any activity, in particular political activity. While Epicurus emphasized the importance of pleasure in man's life (meaning not only pleasures of the flesh but also of the spirit), the Stoics' ideal was perpetual spiritual self-improvement. They thus created the image of a sage impervious to all the suffering and misfortunes of life. Thus Greek thought in the Hellenistic Age reflected the change which had occurred in the world of politics: the major interest was shifted from the community to the individual, from the concern for the *polis* to the care of man's soul. Thus again a common link between West and East appears.[26]

Like philosophy, science in the Hellenistic Age also became much ramified. The great scholars of the 3rd and 2nd centuries mainly followed in the steps of Aristotle and his pupils. They carried out detailed research, each in his own field, thus contributing much more than the Ionians to the progress of science. Euclid laid the foundations of geometry which have remained fixed right down to our days. In astronomy, Aristarchus of Samos discovered the heliocentric system which was later forgotten to be rediscovered in the 16th century by Copernicus and Galileo; Eratosthenes established the basic principles of geography and astronomy; medicine and other branches of science made good progress too. The scientific method of research was introduced in all the different fields of science. Basically it was the same method dominating research in our time, i.e., experiment, observation, and a rational approach to everything within the material world. In medicine, for instance, all the ancient Oriental practices of witchcraft and exorcism were excluded from the treatment of illness. Instead, medicine began to rely upon examination of the human body, recording the symptoms, and investigation of the healing qualities of herbs and poisons. Here, too, a large number of different schools and a variety of scientific centers took the place of the individual systems of the classical period.[27]

Eastern man came in contact with the Greek philosopher, physician, engineer, architect, etc., in large centers of Hellenistic culture such as Alexandria in Egypt, or Antioch in Syria. The question repeatedly arises to what degree could the Orient, and in particular the Jewish world, absorb the principles of the Greek spirit without undermining the foundations of the ancestral tradition upon which its religion and ideology had relied from time immemorial.

E. FUSION OF CULTURES

Up to now we have discussed Greek culture in general, without reference to its fate in Oriental lands. Yet all the special qualities of Hellenistic culture developed out of the general historical situation which evolved as a result of Alexander's conquest of the Orient. In the Hellenistic Age, Greek culture was developing against a completely new background and inevitably it was affected by this new Eastern enviroment.

Immediately after the conquest of the Orient, a great number of Greeks rushed into the new lands now opened to them. Soldiers, merchants, artisans, officials, writers, all set out to start a new life in the Hellenistic cities which had been founded in the Eastern countries or to settle in the villages as peasants or craftsmen. As in all periods of emigration, the majority of emigrants were males, especially young and unmarried. These emigrants quite naturally took wives from among the native population. Thus the second generation in the lands of immigration was of mixed blood, Greek and Oriental. This is especially true of the Macedonian army. As has been pointed out in the previous chapter,[28] both Ptolemies and Seleucids settled the Macedonian and Greek soldiers on the land, and in the course of time these military settlers became ordinary peasants. Mixed marriages between soldiers and local women constituted a basic fact in the life of these new settlements, a fact often mentioned in various sources.[29]

The Hellenistic army became the melting pot in which the two different elements first met. Another meeting place was the Hellenistic city. Alexander the Great had already established the population of the newly founded cities from the three elements: Macedonian veterans, Greek mercenaries, and natives. Thus, from the very beginning these cities had a mixed population.[30] It is highly probable that the situation was much the same in the period of the Diadochi, and especially in the reigns of Seleucus I and Antiochus I. A Mesopotamian city was popularly called Antioch ἡ μιξο-βάρβαρος which means "Antioch mixed with Barbarians" and this city was undoubtedly no exception.[31] The fusion of Western and Eastern elements in cities, Eastern since their founding, which adopted the political status of a Greek *polis* was even more effective.[32] Yet the most complete amalgamation, according to the Greek papyri, took place in the villages.[33] Thus, the Hellenistic population of the Eastern lands fated to be the bearer of Greek culture was from the very beginning not pure Hellenic, but a mixture of Eastern and Western elements.

Modern scholars attach special emphasis to the process of Hellenization of the Oriental peoples which they consider as a great cultural achievement of Alexander and the kings who succeeded him. The process of Hellenization undoubtedly continued throughout the whole of the Hellenistic period. What are the nature and the cultural value of that process? How did the Hellenization of the Oriental peoples manifest itself?

In the first place, they acquired a knowledge of the Greek language. Since Greek was the official tongue of the Hellenistic state and of the Greek *polis*, everyone who had recourse to a government office or visited a Greek city on business was obliged to speak this language. However, knowledge of Greek made no inroads among the large masses of the Eastern populations. The villages remained almost completely beyond the range of its influence — a fact of which papyri from Egypt again provide a number of illuminating examples.[34] The large masses of the urban population (craftsmen, workmen, etc.) did not speak the language either; only the thin upper layer of the rich bourgeoisie, linked both economically and politically with the government and with the new Greek population, acquired a knowledge of the Greek tongue.

This knowledge could open the gates of Greek culture to an Easterner, affording him through Greek books the possibility of understanding Greek philosophy, science, mythology, and literature. But the acquisition of Greek culture was not at all easy, and as a matter of fact was achieved by only a few select people. During the whole Hellenistic Age very few names of educated Eastern people attempting to contribute to Hellenistic culture are encountered.[35] More such names appear in the Roman period, i.e. following three centuries of Hellenization and after the Romans had accorded Greek culture special attention. Moreover, papyri from Egypt testify that in the small provincial towns of the land of the Nile, Greek literature was far richer in the Roman period than in the Hellenistic Age.[36]

The Hellenization of Eastern peoples also found expression in the fact that Greek athletics gradually began to take root in the life of the population. Yet again it must be said that this particularly characteristic mark of Hellenism was adopted in the towns only, especially those along the Phoenician coast such as Tyre, Sidon, etc. These were perhaps the most Hellenized among all the Eastern towns; they absorbed large numbers of Greeks and carried on a regular trade with all the Hellenistic lands. It is true that we find Greek educational institutions — *gymnasia* — in Egyptian villages too, but the population there was a mixture of native and Greek-Macedonian military settlers. It is no great wonder that Greek customs penetrated into the remotest villages of Egypt in the wake of these foreign settlers.[37] The participation of the Eastern population in athletics was only slight, for such activities were basically alien to the Eastern spirit. In any case, they lacked the strong inner bonds with other spheres of life which, as we have seen, were so characteristic of Greece proper. It may be said that participation in the games or the establishment of *gymnasia* in the Eastern towns, was a kind of necessary compromise motivated by the wish to be accepted by international Greek society and to gain access to high government officials.

Another compromise concerned the changing of names. Multitudes of Eastern people changed their names for Greek ones (again it must be noted that this applies mostly to the urban and not the rural population) or used both designations simultaneously.[38] The necessity to change one's name may be presumed originally to have been caused by the fact that the Greeks, and especially the government officials, could not remember the alien Eastern names. It was therefore helpful to adopt Greek names in order to enter Greek society more easily. Later, Greek names were included in the local onomasticon (especially among aristocratic families) and became so familiar to the Eastern peoples as to be regarded as a natural phenomenon. The names of gods were altered too; for instance, the Syrian god Baal was called Zeus, Astarte and Isis — Aphrodite, Melkart — Heracles, etc. The alteration of the names of gods was certainly done on the initiative of the Greeks. As early as the classical period it was widely held in Greece that there was no essential difference between a Greek and a foreign god, and that any Eastern deity was in fact a Greek god under a different name.[39] It is hardly surprising, therefore, that the process of equation and adjustment between the Greek and Eastern deities should have been completed in the Hellenistic period, when the two worlds approached each other.

The particular example of changing the names of the gods can supply the key to an understanding of the nature of eastern Hellenization as a whole. Did the Eastern god, when altering his name, change his nature as well? Were the ancient Eastern rituals practised in the temples altered and replaced by Greek ones? Were the priests in charge of a religious cult henceforward appointed from among the Greeks? To all these questions the answer is: no. There is sufficient evidence to demonstrate that the nature of the Eastern god did not change because now he was called "Zeus" instead of "Baal" or "Aphrodite" instead of "Astarte." Religious services were also left in the hands of local priests and continued to be observed according to the laws and customs practised for thousands of years.[40] And since religion was the most important treasure of Eastern civilization, and all other aspects of culture, such as literature, poetry, law, etc., were closely connected with it, it may be concluded that under the influence of Hellenization, cultural life in the East did not change essentially. For instance, juridical concepts hallowed for generations remained as before based upon the local law (especially in matters concerning personal status) and did not easily cede to the concepts of Greek law, completely alien to the spirit of the local population.[41] Thus, the most important and profound aspects of man's life, such as his beliefs, religious cult and family life with its inner laws and traditions, etc., remained rooted in the soil of the East. Only the outer shell was modified in the spirit of Hellenistic customs. Similarly, local tongues were not superseded by the Greek language. While granting the latter priority and recognizing its official function, they persisted in the home and the village. Hence, the process known as "Hellenization of the East" was no more than a shallow penetration of Greek culture into the thin layer of the rich urban population, but not powerful enough to change fundamentally the forms of life and culture of the East.

A few additional words about the fate of the Greek emigrants who settled in the Eastern lands: the number of highly educated people borne on the wave of emigration was not great, and almost all of them settled in the major cultural center — Alexandria. As for the Greeks who penetrated far into Syria and Mesopotamia as far as the borders of India, or settled in the villages of Egypt and Asia Minor, it stands to reason that we should not look for many educated individuals among them. They were mainly soldiers, workers, craftsmen or people without any definite profession, anxious to grasp at the rich opportunities opening to them in the conquered lands. People of this kind were incapable of being the bearers of Hellenic culture, if culture means spiritual and creative life. This is one reason why they were so devoted to athletics, for this side of Greek culture was simple and comprehensible to everyone. Moreover these people did not remain isolated socially. The process of fusion of the Greek and local populations, mentioned above, was in operation as a natural result of mixed marriage in the cities and villages. Greeks living in the villages were the first to yield to local customs; the papyri confirm that before very long Greeks in Egyptian villages drew close to the local population; they called themselves by Egyptian names, spoke Egyptian, and worshipped Egyptian deities.[42] Although there are only a few similar examples from other countries, it seems reasonable to conclude on the basis of various allusions that the situation was not different in the Asiatic lands.[43] Greek cities retained Hellenic culture comparatively longer. The Greek *polis* well understood the danger threatening from the East and different attempts were made to withstand the menace of "barbarization." Sometimes the Greeks flatly forbade intermarriage with the natives (this, for instance, was the case in the city of Naucratis in Egypt). Yet the powers of resistance of the *polis* were not strong enough to win this hard struggle.[44] Easterners from the adjacent areas infiltrated into the *polis* from all sides, as occasional visitors, permanent residents and, finally, as citizens enjoying equal rights with the Greeks. The Greek *polis* in the East was not built in an empty desert but usually stood near some ancient village or Eastern town, and often drew a part of its inhabitants from that town.[45] Close relations with the local population were therefore a natural development, an inevitable phenomenon of everyday life. This means that the Greek population in the East was affected by its surroundings to a greater extent than it was able to exert an influence of its own upon the natives and fulfil its mission of spreading Hellenic culture among the wide masses. It may safely be assumed, too, that the Greek population never dreamed of being the bearer of such an important mission. Its main concern was how to preserve itself against the steady encroachment of its Eastern environment.

The consequences of the cultural situation which developed in the Eastern lands were of prime importance for the development of civilization for many generations to come. Greece was not strong enough to impose its culture upon the East, but at least it succeeded in spreading the Greek language over vast areas together with certain Greek customs (such as athletics), thereby creating a uniform international social group in the large cities of the East, which linked the inhabitants of the East with Hellenism. At the same time, the Hellenistic Age laid the foundations for a real fusion of cultures, and in this fusion the East prevailed over the West. Within the diverse populations composed of Greeks and Eastern peoples there developed beliefs and opinions which had their origin in the spiritual life of both great civilizations and were particularly centered on religious questions. Thus, the Hellenistic Age prepared the ground for powerful religious movements, including Christianity.

Within this world composed of elements of Eastern and Western civilization there also lived and developed Hellenistic Jewry, which was destined to play no small part in establishing means of contact between the two worlds.

PART TWO: HELLENISTIC PALESTINE

CHAPTER III

THE POLITICAL SITUATION FROM 332 B.C.E. TO 175 B.C.E.

by V. Tcherikover

A. SOURCES

THE HELLENISTIC PERIOD in Palestine dates from the summer of 332 B.C.E., when Alexander the Great traversed the country on his victorious march from Phoenicia to Egypt. The end of the early period of Hellenism may be dated to the year 175 B.C.E., when Antiochus IV Epiphanes succeeded to the Syrian throne and opened the way for new political movements and new ideas. This early period of Hellenism is important for many aspects. The Greek language and Hellenistic culture began to strike roots in Palestine. Greek cities were founded along the coast and in the interior, and vital political changes occurred within the country. An analysis of the later Hellenistic political-cultural revolution which took place in Jerusalem, and of the nationalist movement of the Maccabees which developed in reaction to it, makes it very clear that the origins of both these crucial processes are to be found in the preceding period.

Unfortunately, historiographic records of the early period of Hellenism in Palestine are very sketchy. Greek writers touched on the history of Palestine only incidentally, when the political events of the great world were felt there too. Thus Diodorus tells in detail about the battle of Gaza (312) and Polybius describes the war between the Syrian king Antiochus III and the Egyptian king Ptolemy IV in 221–217. Neither of them considers the recorded events as chapters of Palestinian history, but as incidents of general political significance which by chance happened to take place in Palestine. They took even less interest in the fate of the Jews. Greek historians who did mention the Jews included Hecataeus of Abdera, who lived in the period of the Diadochi and was close to the court of Ptolemy I, King of Egypt; unfortunately, however, his writings were not preserved. A few fragments about Jews and Judaism from Hecataeus' works are to be found in Diodorus and Josephus.[1] The material contained in these fragments is of great importance, but insufficient for a full picture of the life of the Jews in that period.

Josephus, naturally, did not ignore the period under discussion, but through no fault of his own he was unable to portray these times in detail for lack of sufficient material in the sources. Up to the time of Ezra and Nehemiah, Josephus' principal material for his great work was derived from the Bible, and from the time of Judah Maccabee onwards reliable sources were again at his disposal — such as the First Book of Maccabees and the writings of the Greek historian Nicolaus of Damascus. As for the period from Alexander the Great to the reign of Antiochus Epiphanes, however, Josephus did not even find a single dependable historical source to serve him as a guide through the darkness. Consequently he garnered stories and legends at random, wherever he could; these included the Hellenistic-Jewish legend about the visit of Alexander the Great to Jerusalem, the Tobiad family chronicles, the story of the translation of the Bible into Greek from the *Letter of Aristeas*, and others. There is no inner connection between one story and another, and if our intention were to fill in the gaps in Josephus, there would be no other way than to follow his example, i.e., to collect historical material from any sources at hand.[2]

Scanty but very valuable information concerning social life in Judea and Jerusalem in the eighties of the 2nd century B.C.E. is to be found in the book of Ben Sira. Ben Sira witnessed important political events (the transfer of power in the country from the Ptolemies to the Seleucids in the years 201–198 B.C.E.), but describing these political events in the country to his readers was not his intention. Nor did he desire to depict social life; he touched on social problems only occasionally, when teaching wisdom and ethics to his readers and disciples. The *Letter of Aristeas*, mentioned above as a source for Josephus, also contains important information about the Land of Israel, Jerusalem and, in particular, the Temple and the manner of worship there. On the other hand the author describes events which took place in the reign of Ptolemy II Philadelphus, although the book itself was written in the 2nd century, B.C.E., i.e., a hundred years after Philadelphus. We cannot always be sure whether what is narrated by Aristeas reflects the political situation in Palestine in the 3rd century B.C.E. or that of the author's own time.[3] We have to be cautious, therefore, in using information drawn from the *Letter of Aristeas* to describe the early Hellenistic period in Palestine.

In the 20th century a new source for research into Palestinian history of the middle of the 3rd century came to the fore. This is the Greek papyri discovered by Egyptian peasants in Faiyum during World War I (1915), which proved to be one of the most important finds in the field of papyrological research. The papyri's deciphering disclosed that they all derived from the great archives (about 1,200–1,300 documents) of a Greek official called Zenon, who served as an agent of Apollonius, Ptolemy II Philadelphus' Minister of Finance. Apollonius appointed Zenon administrator of his large estate in the vicinity of Philadelphia, in the Faiyum. In his archives Zenon kept a great number of accounts, lists, letters, and other documents relating to the life and work on the estate. These archives are of great importance for the historian, since for the first time they afforded an opportunity to study down to the smallest detail the conditions of life and work on Egyptian soil at the beginning of the Hellenistic period. Yet for the historian of Palestine and the people of Israel the archives of Zenon contain items of even greater particular interest. In the year 259 B.C.E., before his appointment as administrator of the Faiyum estate, Zenon had served as a travelling agent of the Minister of Finance, and had, among other places, visited Palestine — at that time a part of the Ptolemaic state. He spent about a year in Palestine and on his subsequent return to Egypt continued to maintain contact with different Palestinian inhabitants. In this way a parcel of about 40 documents accumulated in the archives of Zenon (letters, lists, accounts, contracts, etc.) throw light on life in Palestine during the reign of Ptolemy Philadelphus. A full and detailed account of political and economic life in Palestine should not be demanded of the Zenon papyri; nevertheless, the answers to a number of questions concerning trade with Egypt, the status of Egyptian officials in Palestine, various questions of administration, etc., are now well known thanks to these short and fragmentary documents. They do not refer to historical facts, but they do present a picture of the general background, without which those historical facts would still be quite obscure.[4]

Modern historiography rightly emphasizes the importance of official documents such as royal decrees, laws, regulations, etc. Unfortunately, not a single document of this kind has been preserved among Zenon's Palestinian papyri. However, in 1936, one document from a large collection of papyri in Vienna was published, containing two decrees of King Ptolemy II Philadelphus concerning Syrian affairs. They are 1) a governmental decree ordering the registration of flocks and herds in Syria, and 2), royal regulations laying down certain principles concerning the purchase of slaves in that country.[5] These decrees offer interesting material for an analysis of the political and economic situation in southern Syria under the Ptolemies. In addition, in his account of the conquest of Jerusalem by Antiochus III, King of Syria, in the year 198, Josephus copied two decrees which this king issued concerning the Jews of Jerusalem. The first (*Ant.* XII, 138 ff.) deals with the situation in Jerusalem after the war and the city's reconstruction, as well as with the rights of the Jews under the new Seleucid government; the second (*ibid.*, 145 ff.) relates to problems of religion and worship. This exhausts the list of official documents dealing with Palestine and the Jews in the early Hellenistic period.

These are the sources available for a description of the early Hellenistic period in Palestine. There is no continuous, complete story, but fragments by different authors or odd unrelated documents with no connection between the various authors. Out of these scattered bricks the historian must build a whole edifice — not an easy task, since he must beware of putting extraneous material into the building. Clearly, the description of this period will be more like a reconstruction of historical facts rather than a faithful record of what really happened, and simultaneously with the presentation of authentic information conjecture will have to be resorted to, insofar as it does not contradict the facts and can be useful in helping us understand the pragmatic bond between one fact and another.

B. Alexander the Great in Palestine

In the year 333 B.C.E. Alexander inflicted a decisive defeat upon the armies of the Persian king Darius at Issus, thus clearing the way to Syria and Palestine. The Phoenician maritime towns, such as Aradus, Gebal-Byblos, Sidon, and others, opened their gates to Alexander. Only Tyre resisted the Macedonians but after a seven months' siege it, too, fell to Alexander. From Tyre Alexander proceeded southwards, to be delayed once more, this time by the resistance of Gaza, whose governor, an appointee of Darius, shut the city's gates to him. For about two months, in the course of which he was wounded, Alexander besieged Gaza. After the city's fall he advanced towards Egypt, reaching the first Egyptian town, Pelusium, within seven days. In the meantime the whole of Syria and Palestine had been conquered by Alexander's generals under the leadership of Parmenion, who was in Damascus directly after the battle of Issus (332).

These are the few facts known from the Greek and Roman historians who wrote about Alexander's campaign.[6] There is no hint in these writings of Alexander's visiting Jerusalem, nor of his meeting with the Jews; and since Alexander's historians used to record even the minutest details of his campaign, it is hardly possible that they neglected to chronicle his visit to a city whose religious significance, was considerable, even at that time. It is, therefore, with a certain suspicion that we approach the long and beautiful story in Josephus about Alexander's visit to Jerusalem. Analysis of the story further increases this suspicion.

What follows is Josephus' account of Alexander's meeting with the Jews in Jerusalem (*Ant.* XI, 304–345):

While Alexander was still immobilized at Tyre he sent a letter to the High Priest Jaddua, demanding assistance for his army and offering him an alliance with the Macedonians. The High Priest, however, rejected Alexander's offer with the contention that he was bound by an oath of allegiance to the Persian king and would not violate his word as long as Darius lived. This reply infuriated Alexander and he made up his mind to punish the High Priest and his people as soon as Tyre had fallen into his hands. And, indeed, after the surrender of Tyre and the conquest of Gaza Alexander set out for Jerusalem to carry out his design. Approaching the city, he encamped on Mount Scopus. The Jews were terrified. The High Priest offered sacrifices and addressed a prayer to God, imploring Him to protect His people from the danger threatening them. He then went to sleep. While asleep he heard the voice of God encouraging him not to fear Alexander. God then commanded him to do the following: after decorating the city, the High Priest himself accompanied by all the other priests in priestly attire and all the inhabitants in white festive clothes should open the gates to the Macedonians and go forth to welcome Alexander. And God would protect them so that no harm would befall them. And thus they did. Alexander stood on Mount Scopus, surrounded by Phoenicians and Chaldaeans, and when he saw the approaching festive procession he fell on his knees and prostrated himself before the Divine Name written on the miter of the High Priest, whereupon the Jews cheered Alexander and thronged around him. Surprised, Parmenion asked the king what made him prostrate himself before the High Priest when all men fell down before him. To this Alexander answered: "It was not before him that I prostrated myself but the God of whom he has the honor to be High Priest, for it was he whom I saw in my sleep dressed as he is now, when I was at Dium in Macedonia, and as I was considering with myself how I might become master of Asia, he urged me not to hesitate but to cross over confidently, for he himself would lead my army and give over to me the empire of the Persians." Thereupon, giving his hand to the High Priest, Alexander entered the city, went up to the Temple, and offered sacrifices to God according to the instructions given by the High Priest. There the Book of Daniel was shown to him and the words of the prophet were read out to him, about a Greek who would come and destroy the Persian Empire, and Alexander believed that the prophet had meant him to be this man. In his joy at this prophecy, Alexander asked what he could do for the benefit of the Jews, and the High Priest asked him to allow his people to live according to their ancestral tradition and to keep the years of release; he also requested that the Macedonian permit the Jews of Babylon and Media to follow their own laws. To all these petitions Alexander gave his consent. Before leaving the king said that he would allow any Jew who wished to join him in his campaign to enlist in his army. He also promised to make it possible for those Jews to follow their traditional customs.

It is easy to detect the legendary trends in Josephus' story, and this has been done a number of times by modern historians.[7] According to Greek sources, Alexander arrived at Pelusium after a seven days' march; thus he had no time to go to Jerusalem after the conquest of Gaza. Had he, nevertheless, done so, he would have approached the city from the west and not from Mount Scopus. The Chaldaeans escorting Alexander were entirely the product of the author's imagination, since Chaldaeans were the inhabitants of Babylon and at that time Alexander had not reached Babylon on his victorious march. Parmenion's remarks about the custom of prostration before the king are totally improbable, for Alexander sought to introduce this practice at his court only after crowning himself King of Persia, i.e., about two years later. Opening of the Book of Daniel before Alexander is equally beyond the range of possibility, for the work was written about a hundred and sixty years after Alexander's time. Not only do these various details undermine the historical fidelity of the story, but so does the very approach of Josephus to the description of the meeting between Alexander and the High Priest. Alexander prostrated himself before the High Priest since he saw in him the priest of the Supreme God — the same God who had promised him the victory over the Persians. It follows, therefore, that Alexander acknowledged the God of Israel as the supreme power governing the world. This notion indicates at once the atmosphere in which such ideas originated — the milieu of Alexandrian Jewry at the beginning of the Roman period, when Jewish apologetic literature was at its height. Apologetic writers used to make a point of emphasizing that all the great kings from Alexander down to Julius Caesar paid honor to the people of Israel, its religion and its God.[8] This account too is obviously a legend written in an apologetic spirit, and there is no reason whatsoever to seek even a grain of historical truth in it.

Nevertheless, there is one feature in this legend, as it is recorded in Josephus, which calls for elucidation. Josephus combines his story about Alexander's visit to Jerusalem with a detailed account of Sanballat the governor of Samaria and the erection of the Samaritan temple on Mount Gerizim (*Ant.* XI, 321 ff.). According to Josephus Sanballat appeared before Alexander while the king was still encamped before the walls of

Tyre, and asked his permission to build a temple on Mount Gerizim. With him he brought 8,000 auxiliary troops for Alexander. The Macedonian, having willingly accepted his help, granted him permission to build the temple. The erection of the temple on Mount Gerizim was an act of hostility towards Jerusalem and its Temple, since Sanballat put his son--in law, Manasseh, the brother of the High Priest Jaddua, in charge of it. Manasseh had left Jerusalem out of hatred for his brother and with the firm intention of obtaining the office of High Priest in Samaria (*Ant.* XI, 302 ff.). Sanballat died soon afterward. When the Samaritans learned of the benevolence shown by Alexander to the Jews, they aspired to the same good relations. Accordingly, they invited Alexander to visit the new temple on Mount Gerizim and asked him to grant them all the privileges bestowed upon the Jews. Alexander answered that he had bestowed these favors upon the Jews only. However, he promised to reconsider their request upon returning from his campaign. The story about Sanballat's rule in Samaria and the erection of the temple on Mount Gerizim is unsound, since all these events occurred some hundred years before Alexander's time.[9] Yet the clash between the Jews and the Samaritans in Alexander's reign does seem to be based upon certain historical recollections, since it is repeated in two other independent sources: the talmudic story about Alexander, and the account related by the Greek writer Hecataeus.

A number of peculiar stories about Alexander are extant in the talmudic literature. In general, they are products of the imagination with no elements of historical truth.[10] However, among these stories there is one in Yoma 69a, which is slightly different from a parallel version preserved in the *Scholion*, that is the commentary, on the *Megillat Ta'anit*, which deserves attention. According to the version in the *Scholion* on the *Megillat Ta'anit*, it runs as follows:

> The 21st of the month [Kislev] is the day of Mount Gerizim when mourning is forbidden. On this day the Samaritans[11] asked Alexander of Macedon for the Temple and said to him: Sell us five *kurs* of earth on Mount Moriah. He gave it to them. When they came the inhabitants of Jerusalem went out and drove them away with sticks and told Simeon the Just. He put on priestly vestments and the headmen of Jerusalem with him and a thousand councillors[12] clothed themselves in white and the young priests struck service vessels. And as they walked in the hills they saw torches of light. The King said: What is that? The informers said to him: Those are Jews who have revolted against you. When they came to Antipatris the sun was shining. They came to the first sentry post. They said to

them: Who are you? They said: We are people of Jerusalem and
we have come to welcome the King. When Alexander of Macedon
saw Simeon the Just, he alighted from his chariot and knelt to him.
They said to him: Before this one you prostrate yourself? He is a
mere mortal. He said: I behold the image of this man when I go to
war and am victorious. He [Alexander] said: What do you request?
He [Simeon] replied: Gentiles have misled you and you have
given them the house in which we pray for your kingdom. He asked:
Who are they who have deceived me? He replied: The Samaritans
who stand before you. He said: I hand them over to you. They
pierced their heels and hung them on the tails of their horses and
dragged them over thorns and thistles till they reached Mount
Gerizim. They ploughed and sowed it with horse-beans as [the
Samaritans] had thought to do to the Temple. And the day they did
this they made into a festival.[13]

It is not difficult to see how close this story basically is to Josephus'
account. Only the name of the High Priest Jaddua (who, by the way, plays
no role at all in Jewish history) was replaced by the illustrious name of
Simeon the Just. It is also worth noting that the place of the meeting of
Alexander and the Jews was transferred from Jerusalem to Antipatris. The
interesting point is that in this legend, too, the meeting between them
becomes associated with Samaritan affairs. The description of the city's
destruction, however, belongs not to Alexander's time but to the period of
John Hyrcanus, the Hasmonean High Priest who conquered Samaria,
destroyed its temple and annexed the region to the Kingdom of Judea.[14]
Yet the fact of an encounter between Jews and Samaritans in Alexander's
days remains true.

In the light of these details from Josephus and the talmudic tradition
the short sentence in Hecataeus quoted by Josephus (*Against Apion* II, 43)
acquires special importance: ". . . that, in recognition of the consideration
and loyalty shown to him, [to Alexander] by the Jews, he added to their
territory the district of Samaria free of tribute." We should not, however,
take the whole sentence as historically accurate, since there are no grounds
for thinking that Samaria was annexed to Judea at the time of Alexander.
What is true is that in the reign of the Syrian king Demetrius II, three
Samaritan districts (Ephraim, Lod, and Ramathaim) were joined to
Judea.[15] Therefore how can any credence be placed in the statement that
in Alexander's day the whole of Samaria was already under the rule of
the High Priest? On the other hand, the detailed emphasis on this fact,
repeated in three separate sources, cannot be accidental, and here the grain

of historical truth must be sought. The answer is provided by the Roman historian Curtius Rufus who writes that the Samaritans rose against Alexander and burned alive the Macedonian governor appointed to rule over them. Alexander learned about this when passing through Palestine on his way back from Egypt to northern Syria, and inflicted a heavy penalty on the Samaritans.[16] According to the Christian writer Eusebius a Macedonian colony was founded in Samaria at that time.[17] This is the historical event behind the fabulous stories in Josephus and the talmudic tradition and the obscure words of Hecataeus. Alexander poured out his wrath upon the Samaritans who had betrayed him, but there was no cause for him to be angry with the Jews. In Jewish tradition his different attitude towards the two nations was transformed into a detailed description of hostilities between the Jews and the Samaritans at the time. Again, it is possible that Samaria was for some time put under the supervision of the Macedonian official whose residence was in Judea, and that this administrative measure served as a basis for the garbled information in Hecataeus.

Is it possible to salvage something for history from all these stories and legends? At first sight it would seem that the meeting between Alexander and the Jews in Antipatris (following the talmudic legend) bears the impress of historical truth. It is easy to see why Josephus placed the meeting in Jerusalem, but there seems no reason why Antipatris merits appearing as the center of the action, unless this really was so. However, there are objections. Antipatris did not bear that name in Alexander's time, for it was built as a stronghold only in Herod's reign, not in a vacant spot but on the site of Kᵉfar-Saba — an old Jewish town.[18] The location of the meeting of Alexander and the Jews on the site of Kᵉfar-Saba or near it is convincing, because Alexander went from Tyre to Gaza along the coast, and it was precisely here that the coastal road crosses the road descending from Jerusalem. From elsewhere in the Talmud, however, we learn that it was common at that period to mention Antipatris as a rendezvous whenever Jews had to meet anybody passing through the coastal plain. This would indicate that the mention of Antipatris is conventional and should not be regarded as historical fact.[19] Nevertheless, the possibility remains that the meeting of Alexander and the Jews did take place at Kᵉfar-Saba, since the place actually did serve as the intersection of the coastal highway and the road descending from the mountains to the maritime plain.

But did the Jews meet Alexander at all? They probably did, according to all indications. Judea and Jerusalem must have been conquered by Parmenion or some other Macedonian general while Alexander was still laying siege to Tyre. Can it be assumed that the Jews did not make an effort to appear before Alexander, henceforth their king, when he passed through Palestine on his way to Egypt? Had they not done so they would have made themselves an exception among the peoples inhabiting Syria and Phoenicia, which would surely have provoked the just anger of the king. It can therefore be assumed that soon after the fall of Tyre the Jews sent representatives to welcome the king, and quite probably waited to meet him at Kᵉfar-Saba, the nearest to Jerusalem of all the places through which he passed.

There is another detail which should be taken into consideration. Josephus records that Alexander allowed the Jews to "live according to their ancestral laws." This is the stereotyped formula which is later repeated several times, especially in the Roman period, and signifies the granting of a measure of autonomy to the Jewish nation. In the legend about Alexander however, reference to the "traditional laws" is not reliable evidence of the bestowing of those privileges at that period for the authors of the legend could easily have taken this formula from the historical situation in their own time and transferred it to the period of Alexander. However, considering what is known of the political situation in Palestine in later periods, it is easy to see that the right given to the Jews to live according to their ancestral tradition could well suit Alexander's time and his general policy. The Romans adopted this formula from the Hellenistic kings; Antiochus III, King of Syria, granted such privileges to the Jews at the transfer of power from the Ptolemies to the Seleucids in 198. There is little doubt that he re-affirmed the rights accorded to the Jews by his predecessors, the Ptolemaic kings. Moreover, Judea had already enjoyed a certain autonomy under Persian rule. The known facts about Alexander's attitude towards conquered peoples further support the assumption that he confirmed the autonomous status of the Jews, at least within the same limits as under the Persians. Wherever Alexander appeared, he extended the rights of the natives, gave them a share in the government, and granted them the privilege of practising their ancestral customs. He did so in the cities of Ionia, Lydia, Egypt, and India, so why should it be supposed that he excluded only the Jews?[20] It thus follows that at the meeting with the Jews' representatives Alexander granted the people of Judea, including Jerusalem, the right to "live according to their ancestral laws," and in this way laid the foundations for the development of an independent life of the Jewish people in the future.

C. PALESTINE IN THE DIADOCHI PERIOD

The fate of Palestine in the time of Alexander the Great is obscure. Under Persian rule all the lands west of the Euphrates river had been united into one large satrapy named *Abar Nahara* (i.e., "Beyond the River"). It seems likely that this satrapy was still in existence in Alexander's time, since in general Alexander did not change the administrative structure of the Persian Empire, and certainly not at the beginning of his campaign. In the Persian period the great satrapy of *Abar Nahara* was divided into smaller districts which were also headed by "satraps," such as Nehemiah in Judea, or Sanballat in Samaria. Were these districts still in existence in Alexander's time? It is hard to answer this question, since only a few names of Macedonian satraps in Syria have been preserved in historical literature (such as Arimmas, Menon, and Andromachus), and there is no means of knowing whether each of these satraps governed the entire satrapy or only part of it.[21] The great satrapy *Abar Nahara*, which from now on was called "Syria" or "Syria and Phoenicia," survived after Alexander's death; this follows from the fact that in the two partitions of the satrapies after Alexander's death (the first in 323 and the second in 321), "Syria" or "Syria and Phoenicia" appears as one undivided satrapy, given on both occasions to the same general — Laomedon.[22] There is no information explaining why this man who did not distinguish himself in any way in Alexander's time was awarded such a large, important province. And indeed, in the stormy wars of the Diadochi period, this weak satrap was unable to retain power over a country which from time immemorial had served as a bone of contention between the kingdoms to the north and the south. In 320 Laomedon was forced to relinquish control of Syria in favor of Ptolemy, the satrap of Egypt, who attacked the country with great forces and annexed it to his own satrapy.

The fate of the Syrian territories, including Palestine, in 320–301, faithfully reflects the general situation in the Diadochi period. The country changed rulers five times — in 320, 315, 312, 302 and 301, — and each transfer of power was accompanied by loss of life, destruction of cities, and surely also by the flight of the inhabitants and their transfer from one place to another. The first change (320) apparently took place without much bloodshed. Nicanor, one of Ptolemy's generals, conquered the interior of the country while Ptolemy himself led the operations from the sea. Laomedon, unable to muster sufficient forces against the powerful Egyptian satrap, declined to accept payment from Ptolemy in exchange for his province and was taken prisoner. Later on he succeeded in bribing his guards and fled from the country.[23] There is no reason to think that Ptolemy met with strong opposition on the part of the inhabitants, since officially Alexander's great empire was still a single undivided kingdom, and men such as Laomedon or Ptolemy were merely satraps who governed this or another part of the state by virtue of powers invested in them by the central administration. The change of governors did not, as yet, mean a change in the political situation, and therefore the local population had no special reason to oppose it.

Much more important for Palestine was the change of government which took place in 315, when Antigonus first appeared in the lands of Syria, just as he was about to establish under his own rule a mighty kingdom which later came to include the majority of the territories of Alexander's empire (see above, page 12 f). He came to the lands of Syria not as an appointed satrap, but as an independent ruler. Power over the Mediterranean was an integral part of his imperialistic policy and the conquest of Syria, especially of the Phoenician coast, constituted the first step to control that sea. Ptolemy did all he could to thwart Antigonus' design by stationing garrisons in all the fortresses of Syria, and transferring the Phoenician fleet to Egypt. Antigonus, however, was not a man to retreat in the face of difficulties. He immediately issued orders for the construction of a number of shipyards (three of them in Phoenicia — in Tripoli, Gebal, Sidon, and one in Cilicia) and used the cedars of Lebanon and the forests of the Taurus Mountains to build ships (Diodorus XIX, 58). Then he laid siege to the fortresses of Syria; Tyre fell in 15 months, and by agreement Ptolemy's soldiers who had defended it were allowed to leave (*ibid.*, 61, 5). Jaffa and Gaza, which refused to surrender, were conquered by force and their soldiers distributed among Antigonus' regiments (*ibid.*, 59, 2). In place of Ptolemy's garrisons, Antigonus stationed his own soldiers everywhere. Ptolemy did not dare face Antigonus in open battle but waited for a convenient moment, when the danger to himself and his soldiers would not be too great, before returning to seize power. In 312 he thought he saw his opportunity. At that time Antigonus was not in Syria and military command was in the hands of his son Demetrius. Ptolemy, supported by his friend Seleucus, met Demetrius near Gaza and inflicted a decisive defeat upon him. Demetrius was forced to retreat from the whole of southern Syria (see above, p. 12). However, Palestine did not remain in Ptolemy's hands for long. A few months later he was forced to withdraw again when Antigonus, at the head of a great army, came hurrying from Phrygia to regain what his son had lost. On his way out of the country Ptolemy ravaged the fortified cities — Diodorus (XIX, 93, 7) mentions Acco, Jaffa, Samaria, and Gaza — rendering them useless to his enemy, and this time the country remained in Antigonus' hands for many years.

In 302 Ptolemy joined a large coalition of all the Macedonian kings against Antigonus and conquered Palestine again. His role, it seems, was not only to conquer Syria, but also to participate in the final, decisive battle of all his allies against Antigonus. But extreme caution, verging on cowardice, hindered him from fulfilling this plan. Shortly before the battle of Ipsus false rumors about Antigonus' victories over Seleucus and Lysimachus reached Ptolemy, while he was laying siege to Sidon. He abandoned Palestine and hurried back to Egypt in order to avoid a direct encounter (Diodorus XX, 113). As a result Ptolemy did not participate in the battle of Ipsus, and when the victors came to divide Antigonus' lands, they did not include Ptolemy among those eligible for a share in the booty. The whole of Syria was given to Seleucus. However, when Seleucus appeared in Syria, intending to annex it to his kingdom, he found southern Syria once again in the hands of Ptolemy who showed no disposition to relinquish the country. Seleucus did not allow matters to reach the stage of an open conflict. He did not want to fight a man who had been his friend and had once actually supported him in his war against Antigonus (*ibid.* XXI, 1, 5). Thus, southern Syria remained in Ptolemy's hands. This brings to an end the political changes that took place in Palestine during the Diadochi period.

There is no evidence of the internal situation in Palestine in the Diadochi period, although from several indications it may be assumed that the process of Hellenization had already got under way in these early times. Perdiccas may already have laid the foundations of the Macedonian military colonies in Samaria and Gerasa, either on Alexander's orders during his lifetime or later, when Laomedon was satrap of Syria. There is no doubt that in Antigonus' time a number of Macedonian colonies were founded in Western Palestine and Transjordan, but there is no reliable information about them. Diodorus (XIX, 94 ff.) gives a detailed account of the wars which Antigonus waged against the Nabataean Arabs in the desert and in the vicinity of the Dead Sea, with the aim, apparently, of gaining control of the commercial routes of the incense trade (myrrh and frankincense) from southern Arabia to Syria, and of exploiting the natural resources of the Dead Sea (asphalt). The Arabs, however, courageously defended their freedom and inflicted crushing defeats on the Macedonian army. It may be concluded from Diodorus that Antigonus was forced to abandon the expansion of his dominions in these areas, at least for some time.

Nor are there any reliable sources for the fate of the Jews in the Diadochi period. Only a few remarks by different Greek writers, which were collected by Josephus, have survived. According to Hecataeus of Abdera as recorded by Josephus, in 312, after the battle of Gaza, many of the inhabitants of Syria accompanied Ptolemy to Egypt, abandoning their homes because of the "kindness and humanity" of the king (*Against Apion* I, 186). Among those who went along with Ptolemy, Hecataeus mentions Hezekiah, the High Priest of the Jews, a man some 66 years of age, distinguished as an orator and as a man highly capable in practical matters (*ibid.*, 187). Modern scholars are rather sceptical of this evidence, for Josephus makes no mention of Hezekiah among the High Priests. The name does appear, however, on a coin apparently belonging to that period, but this evidence is not sufficiently reliable.[24] There is, however, no reason to doubt the historical veracity of Hecataeus' records, for the writer was an eye-witness of the events of the time, and in itself the evidence does not contradict the political situation of the period. An interpretation is, of course, called for. The right explanation will probably emerge if it is assumed that among the Jews, as among other small nations situated between two mighty kingdoms fighting for power, there existed two rival parties — one supporting Ptolemy, the second backing Antigonus.[25] After the battle of Gaza the High Priest Hezekiah apparently went over to Ptolemy's camp. Thus, when Ptolemy was about to leave Palestine, while Antigonus was about to conquer the land, Hezekiah and his adherents had no choice but to follow Ptolemy to Egypt. Those who went with him must certainly have belonged to the local aristocracy, since it is not the little man who is apprehensive when power is transferred, but the well-connected and powerful. It is possible that his flight from Jerusalem made an unfavorable impression on his contemporaries, and for this reason they removed the name of Hezekiah from the list of High Priests.

According to Hecataeus Ptolemy appeared in Palestine as a very kind and gracious ruler.[26] However, another tradition based on Agatharchides — a Greek writer who lived in the 2nd century B.C.E. quoted by Josephus (*Ant.* XII, 4 ff.) — depicts Ptolemy as hard and cruel towards the Jews. Agatharchides claims that Ptolemy conquered Jerusalem by a subterfuge, entering the city on the Sabbath when the Jews refrained from taking up the sword, and pretending that his intention was to offer a sacrifice to God. Once inside the city he took it by force and was soon revealed as a harsh master. He also brought many prisoners from Judea to Egypt. This information receives some confirmation in the *Letter of Aristeas*, which also relates that Ptolemy I took many Jewish prisoners to Egypt and sold them as slaves to his soldiers.[27] There seems to be a distinct contradiction between the two aspects of Ptolemy's personality, as presented by Hecataeus and Agatharchides. However, this contradiction only obtains if the conquest of Jerusalem is dated in accordance with Agatharchides' account to 312, the year to which the story of Hecataeus also refers. But there is no need to attribute both stories to the same year. As mentioned above, Ptolemy conquered Palestine four times, and abandoned it on three occasions. Thus, the conquest of Jerusalem may be ascribed not to 312 but to another year. Not 320, for, as already noted above, the population had no sufficient reason at that time to oppose Ptolemy; besides, the sources explicitly state that the conquest of the country was carried out not by Ptolemy but by his general, Nicanor, while Ptolemy was conducting the operations at sea (see above). The situation described by Agatharchides would best fit the year 302. Ptolemy's use of deceit in order to penetrate into the city indicates that the leaders of Jerusalem were not on his side and had closed the gates to him. Nevertheless, there must certainly have been another group interested in a political revolution, whose adherents let Ptolemy in. Thus there were two parties; one in power and supporting the existing government, i.e., Antigonus, and another aspiring to power and inclining toward Ptolemy. The first party may have been stronger so that Ptolemy was obliged to put down disturbances and take many prisoners in order to subdue the Jews. These are, of course, mere suppositions, since the lack of clear evidence does not permit the historian to drawn firm conclusions on this question.

What changes took place in the political situation of Judea and Jerusalem in the Diadochi period? There seems to be sufficient evidence to suggest that this short period considerably advanced the development of Jewish autonomy. In the Persian period various districts of the *Abar Nahara* satrapy were placed under the control of independent governors, and such a Persian administrator ruled in Judea. There is no information of such governors in the Diadochi period; and since the chief satrap was now an independent ruler (even when he was still officially serving as the representative of the central government),it stands to reason that it was in his interest to concentrate all the power in his own hands. The power of the supreme ruler increased all the more when the satraps became kings and considered themselves as rulers with unlimited authority in their own lands. No intermediate office of political importance, comparable to that held by Nehemiah or Sanballat[28], existed between the king (such as Antigonus or Ptolemy) and the local population, which suggests that at least a part of the authority of the Persian governor passed to the High Priest, who from now on served as an intermediary between the monarch and the native population. This assumption is confirmed by a short passage in Hecataeus preserved in Diodorus (XL, 3). Hecataeus notes (*ibid.* 3, 5–6) that there is no king in Judea (he had not heard of Hebrew kings in the past) and that the people's leader is the High Priest, a distinguished personality, and an intermediary between the people and God, who holds the *prostasia*, i.e., the power to represent the people before the authorities.[29] In other words, the High Priest is the man to whom the king or his officers turn when contact with the Jews is necessary. This situation points to a considerable amplification of the concept of political autonomy, or, to use the terminology of the period, of the right of the Jews "to live according to their ancestral laws." During the Diadochi period, the rule of the High Priest (which had begun to take root in Judea and Jerusalem in the first years after the return from the Babylonian Captivity) acquired official political sanction. Later it will be shown that a substantial part of Jewish history in the Hellenistic period is connected with the fate of this rule.

D. Palestine under the Ptolemies

In the year 301, southern Syria, including Palestine, came under the rule of the Ptolemies for the fourth time and remained in their hands for a century. Because of the events of 301, Syria was divided in two, into Seleucid and Ptolemaic areas. In the Roman period, the frontier between northern (Seleucid) and southern (Phoenicia and Coele-Syria) Syria ran by the coast near the city of Orthosia and along the river Eleutherus (Strabo XVI, 2, 2). Since the Romans usually confirmed the situation existing before their conquest, the same city probably also served as a frontier point between the Ptolemaic and Seleucid states.[30] It may be concluded from Diodorus (XVIII, 43; XIX, 57) that Ptolemy I at first intended to conquer the whole of Syria as far as the Taurus Mountains in the north. After the year 301, however, he was forced to content himself with half of the country. Control of the coast as far as Orthosia solved his problem regarding trade, which was perhaps the main motive of his policy of conquest. In ancient times, maritime trade was conducted in small ships which did not dare to cross the sea, but sailed along the coasts so as to be able to enter safe harbors at night or during storms. Ptolemy's control of the coast of Phoenicia afforded him access to the commercial maritime routes from Egypt to Tripolis, whence it was but a short distance to Cyprus, which was also in Ptolemy's hands. Cyprus itself served as a springboard toward several cities on the southern coast of Asia Minor, which belonged

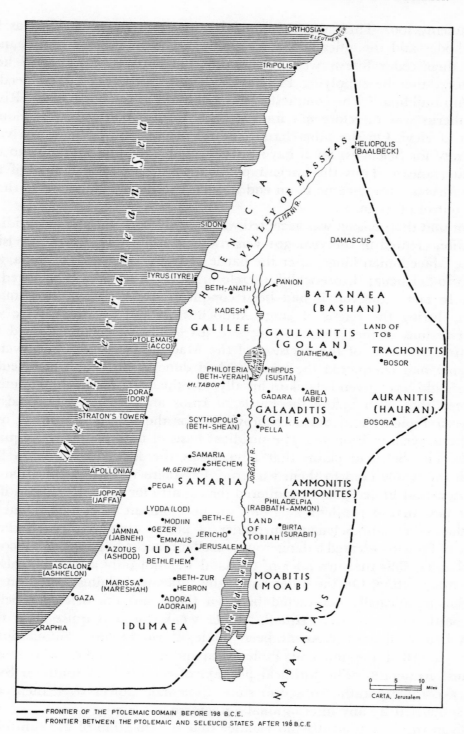

ORTHOSIA

ELEUTHERUS R.

TRIPOLIS

HELIOPOLIS
(BAALBECK)

Mediterranean Sea

P H O E N I C I A

VALLEY OF MASSYAS

LITANI R.

SIDON

DAMASCUS

TYRUS (TYRE)

PANION

BETH-ANATH

KADESH

B A T A N A E A
(B A S H A N)

GALILEE

GAULANITIS
(GOLAN)

LAND OF
TOB

PTOLEMAIS
(ACCO)

DIATHEMA

TRACHONITIS

BOSOR

PHILOTERIA
(BETH-YERAH)

HIPPUS
(SUSITA)

Mt. TABOR

DORA
(DOR)

GADARA

ABILA
(ABEL)

AURANITIS
(HAURAN)

STRATON'S TOWER

SCYTHOPOLIS
(BETH-SHEAN)

GALAADITIS
(GILEAD)

BOSORA

PELLA

JORDAN R.

SAMARIA

SHECHEM

Mt. GERIZIM

APOLLONIA

PEGAI

S A M A R I A

AMMONITIS
(AMMONITES)

JOPPA
(JAFFA)

LYDDA (LOD)

PHILADELPIA
(RABBATH-AMMON)

MODIIN

BETH-EL

JAMNIA
(JABNEH)

GEZER

JERICHO

LAND
OF
TOBIAH

BIRTA
(SURABIT)

EMMAUS

AZOTUS
(ASHDOD)

J U D E A

JERUSALEM

BETHLEHEM

ASCALON
(ASHKELON)

Dead Sea

MOABITIS
(MOAB)

BETH-ZUR

MARISSA
(MARESHAH)

HEBRON

GAZA

ADORA
(ADORAIM)

I D U M A E A

RAPHIA

N A B A T A E A N S

0   5   10
Miles

CARTA, Jerusalem

– – – FRONTIER OF THE PTOLEMAIC DOMAIN BEFORE 198 B.C.E.
——— FRONTIER BETWEEN THE PTOLEMAIC AND SELEUCID STATES AFTER 198 B.C.E

Palestine under the Ptolemies and the Seleucids

to Ptolemy too. Thus, the commercial route from Egypt reached as far as Rhodes and the cities of Greece proper. The mountains of Lebanon with their cedar forests were also within the borders of Egyptian–held territory, thereby supplying Ptolemy with the excellent material needed for ship building.[31] The conquest of parts of Syria to the north of the River Eleutherus was therefore not indispensable from a political or economic point of view. On the other hand, control of northern Syria was a vital necessity for Seleucus, for it gave his enormous kingdom an outlet to the Mediterranean. Thus the ancient political and geographical unit of the *Abar Nahara* satrapy came to an end leaving two hostile kingdoms to share the control of Syria.

Not that this division was accepted willingly by both sides. The juridical situation created in the year 301 was rather complicated. By the decision of the Macedonian kings, after the battle of Ipsus, the whole of Syria was given to Seleucus; theoretically, therefore, southern Syria also belonged to him. In fact, however, it had been conquered by Ptolemy. After many years, during the reigns of kings Antiochus III and IV, there were still repercussions of the events of the year 301.[32] The Seleucids claimed the country by virtue of the decision of the Macedonian kings; and even if Ptolemy had conquered the land, he had done so on behalf of Seleucus and should have given it back to his ally. On the other hand, the Ptolemies claimed that even before the battle of Ipsus an agreement had existed between Ptolemy and Seleucus providing for the transfer of power over southern Syria to Ptolemy. The juridical basis of both claims was equally weak. The Seleucid claim that after Ipsus the Macedonian kings had given the whole land to them was true, but there was no justification for the view that Ptolemy had conquered the country for the Seleucids, as if he were not an independent king but an insignificant ruler dependent on another sovereign. Seleucus' surrender of power over southern Syria in favor of Ptolemy created a dangerous precedent, according to which it could be claimed that the surrender of the land was not only a fact, but also a legitimate action. On the other hand, the Ptolemies' claims, based on the agreement allegedly contracted between them and the Seleucids before the battle of Ipsus, were equally rather weak, for it is quite clear that even had such an agreement been made, it would have automatically been cancelled the moment Ptolemy abandoned his allies who fought against Antigonus. The juridical position of the lands of southern Syria was accordingly rather obscure, since Ptolemaic power over them was not supported by any international agreement.

Given this situation, it is no wonder that the question of the control of southern Syria served as a bone of contention between the two states over a period of about a hundred years. Five times during the 3rd century Ptolemaic and Seleucid armies fought fierce battles, and even though not all the five wars took place in Syria proper, it stands to reason that the power over Syria was the real cause (cf. above, page 61). There is no clear evidence concerning the first three wars, and it cannot be determined whether they affected Palestine directly; but, as will be seen below, the country suffered severely from the fourth and fifth wars.

The Zenon papyri and the two royal decrees recorded in the Greek papyrus mentioned above (see p. 47-8) provide information about Ptolemaic rule in Palestine during the reign of Ptolemy II Philadelphus (285-246). The official name of the country was "Syria and Phoenicia," popularly simply "Syria."[33] The borders of the Ptolemaic state can be defined quite precisely from the Zenon papyri. The northernmost coastal city which they mention is Tripolis on the Phoenician coast (*PSI* 495), situated only a few miles south of Orthosia, which suggests that the frontier between Ptolemaic and Seleucid Syria passed between the two. From another papyrus (*PCZ* 59093) we know that Egyptian officials would visit the Massyas Valley (Μασσύας) between the Lebanon and the Anti-Lebanon ranges. Polybius (V, 45, 8-46, 1) mentions two fortresses situated there in the reign of Antiochus III, and it is likely that the frontier passed near by, perhaps near the ancient Syrian town now called Baalbek, but known in the Hellenistic-Roman Age as Heliopolis. Another papyrus (*PCZ* 59006) tells of a man from Damascus living in Palestine. Although several scholars are inclined to the view that Damascus was under the Seleucids throughout the entire 3rd century, yet strategically and economically the city was linked to Transjordan and the mountains of Lebanon; since these regions (according to the Zenon papyri) were under the Ptolemies, it follows that Damascus, too, lay within the borders of Ptolemaic Syria. The reference to someone from Damascus living in Palestine in 259 is good evidence for this general assumption, since not a single Seleucid city is mentioned in the Zenon Archives. Moreover, the second Syrian War broke out in 258, i.e., one year after these papyri were written, and it is hardly possible that a man from the Seleucid state would have been admitted into the society of Ptolemaic officials at a time when both countries were preparing for war. It may be assumed, therefore, that the northern frontier passed in a south-easterly direction from Orthosia, through Baalbek to Damascus, and thence continued to the desert.[34] As to the eastern frontier, it is quite clear that the whole of Transjordan as far as the desert was under the Ptolemies, since the regions of Hauran, the land of the Ammonites and the land of the Nabataeans, i.e., the whole central and northern parts of Transjordan are mentioned in the Zenon papyri. And if the Ptolemies held Damascus and Hauran, then they must certainly have ruled over Trachonitis and Bashan as well, i.e., the central regions of the country.[35] In summing up, it may be said that Ptolemaic rule in southern Syria embraced the whole Phoenician coast as far as Orthosia, the Lebanon Valley at least as far as Baalbek, and the whole of Western Palestine and Transjordan. The eastern frontier, which passed through the desert, was certainly not fixed.[36]

Palestine had always been a land of transit and, lacking natural frontiers, it was easily accessible from all sides. The Hellenistic period was no exception. Ptolemaic Syria was equally exposed to attacks by Bedouin from the desert, or to invasion by regular Seleucid armies from the north. The security problem caused the Egyptian ruler much concern, and the papyri attest to the existence of a regular Ptolemaic army garrisoned in various parts of the country. The decree of Ptolemy Philadelphus speaks in general terms about "those serving in the army and other settlers in Syria and Phoenicia,"[37] while the Zenon papyri speak of soldiers and a chief of cavalry (ἱππάρχης) in Tripolis (*PSI* 495). This was certainly the regular garrison assigned to defend the northern frontier. The two strong fortresses in the Valley of Massyas mentioned above appear in Polybius only in connection with the events of the year 221, but they may be presumed to have been already in existence at the beginning of Ptolemaic rule in Palestine. The cities of Tyre, Acco, Jaffa, Gaza, and Samaria were already known as strong fortresses in the Diadochi period and it can hardly be wrong to assume that permanent garrisons were stationed there in the days of the Ptolemies. A typical Ptolemaic creation were the *cleruchies*, i.e., settlements of soldiers who cultivated the land while carrying out military duties as a frontier defense force.[38] The Zenon papyri refer to a military *cleruchy* in Transjordan, the center of which served as the capital of the land of the Ammonites (*PCZ* 59003 = *C. P. Jud.* no. 1). Its members were soldiers of different nations designated partly as cavalrymen and in part merely as *cleruchs*. At their head was a local prince, Tobiah, who will be considered in much greater detail later on. Men of diverse military ranks such as "hegemon," "fortress guard," "chief of the guard," and others, are also mentioned in the Zenon papyri, and it is reasonable to suppose that all these officers were appointed from among the members of the *cleruchies* or garrisons stationed in the country.[39] As stated above, the papyri provide only incidental information, from which it is impossible to draw a complete picture of the organization of the Ptolemaic army in

Palestine. In general, however, it may be said that the aim of the Ptolemies was to set up garrisons and military colonies at every vulnerable point in the country, especially along the frontiers, and probably also to disperse them throughout the land, to assure the loyalty of the local population.

Apart from southern Syria, the Ptolemies ruled over a number of other countries such as Cyrene and Cyprus. Each province was headed by a chief administrator with the rank of *strategos* appointed by the government at Alexandria.[40] Were Syria and Phoenicia also ruled by such a *strategos*? Many scholars think so, relying on Polybius, who mentions several Ptolemaic *strategoi* in Palestine.[41] It seems, however, that he had in mind not the regular administrators but the Ptolemaic generals who ruled in Syria during the war. No Syrian administrator is mentioned in the Zenon papyri or in the orders of Ptolemy Philadelphus (recorded on the Vienna papyrus) and this silence encourages the assumption that the office of chief administrator did not exist in the Syrian province. This would not be unreasonable. Syria was not so far away from Egypt as the other provinces, which were separated from the capital by sea or desert, but appeared as a direct continuation of Egyptian territory. It was, therefore, easy to rule it from Alexandria direct. Indeed, the Vienna papyrus mentions the following four different forms in which the decisions of the king concerning Syrian affairs were formulated: orders, regulations, laws, and letters.[42] The Zenon papyri have preserved the correspondence between the Minister of Finance, Apollonius, whose headquarters were in Alexandria, and his agents in Syria. Constant contact was thus maintained between the center of the state and the local officials of the Syrian province, a fact which confirms our assumption that Syria had no need of a special administrator and did not differ in its administration from Egypt proper.

Indeed the whole world of Egyptian officialdom existed in Syria but on a smaller scale. The Vienna papyrus contains important information about the division of the country into districts (*hyparchies*) in each of which there resided an *oikonomos*, i.e., a government official in charge of the economic life of the district.[43] There was also a local *dioiketes*,[44] and remembering that this was the official title of the Minister of Finance in Egypt, we may conclude that the main task of a Syrian *dioiketes* was to deal with financial questions. Again *komarchs* or heads of villages are mentioned, and so are those who "leased the villages" (κωμομισθωταί) and whose function was apparently to collect taxes in them and to forward the money to the king's treasury in Alexandria.[45] Another of Zenon's papyri containing letters to government officials who resided in the city of Maresha (Marissa) in Idumaea (*PCZ* 59015 verso) provides some notion of the number of officials in the districts of Syria. Concerning the affair of the young slaves who were bought by Zenon in Idumaea and later ran away to return to their former masters, Zenon writes five letters to different officials in Maresha requesting them to help his special messenger to take care of this matter. Two letters are couched in very polite terms, and Zenon expresses his readiness to render assistance to the addressees, should such a request be forthcoming. Clearly these persons were high officials, probably the chief of the police and the head of the general administration in Idumaea. To the others, Zenon is less polite and it may be supposed that these were minor officials; and in fact it was precisely these men who were charged with the hard task of actually helping Zenon's messenger and securing the return of the slaves from the refuge to which they had fled.[46] Again, Zenon demands of other officials that they should not require any forced labor (*leitourgia*) of his messenger, since it might hinder him in accomplishing his task. Maresha was a small city in a remote district of Palestine.[47] If, notwithstanding, Egyptian officials were so numerous there, it may well be imagined how great was their number in large commercial cities such as Acco, Gaza, Tyre, and elsewhere. And indeed, government officials were to be found in all these cities, the agents of the Minister of Finance, Apollonius, being especially numerous. From the Zenon papyri it is difficult to determine to what extent the agents of Apollonius were his private agents or official functionaries of the government. In Egypt, under the rule of an absolute sovereign, the difference between a king's official functionary and the private agent of a minister was not clearly defined, any more than the boundary between private and public property was exactly demarcated (see above, page 17). Apollonius' agents in Syria were responsible for buying slaves for the Minister of Finance and sending him presents (ξένια).[48] But in addition, they had an important and responsible role — to organize and improve trade connections between Syria and Egypt. In the year 259, when Zenon resided in Palestine, Apollonius sent numerous agents to Syria for the purpose of visiting various places in the Palestinian region and examining everywhere the possibilities of developing economic life in general, and trade in particular. Zenon, it seems, was the central personality, holding in his hands the organization of the whole undertaking. The Zenon Archives have preserved long lists of agents who crossed the entire country with large caravans, in which at least a hundred men may have been travelling.[49] Some of the agents who took part in these journeys later settled in different cities of Palestine, especially in coastal towns, and there carried out important tasks as tax-inspectors or intermediaries between the Egyptian merchants and the local population. All these facts indicate that the central government in Alexandria paid special attention to the Syrian province and considered it one of the most important regions in the whole Ptolemaic empire.

As stated above, the Ptolemaic government was mainly interested in the development of trade relations between Egypt and Syria. The list of merchandise from Syria which passed through the customs-house of the Alexandrian port provides a picture of the kinds of goods which served as permanent export items from Syria to Egypt; these included grain, olive oil, smoked fish, cheese, meat, dried figs, fruit, honey, dates, etc.[50] The grain trade was organized by the government. Two papyri (*PSI* 324–325) contain the text of a circular letter sent by Apollonius to his agents in Syria concerning merchants engaged in importing Syrian grain into Egypt: the agents were to obtain the price of the grain from the merchants through "the table" (i.e., the government bank) and submit signed documents to the Minister of Finance. They also had to indicate the name of the payer, the amount he had to pay and, in case he paid for another person, to note this as well. Such interference by the Minister of Finance and his agents in trade affairs is very characteristic of a totalitarian state such as Ptolemaic Egypt. The Egyptian merchant could not come into direct contact with the Syrian producer except through the official intermediaries of the Minister of Finance. Syrian grain was quite commonly found in Egypt, although Egypt itself was the richest grain-producing land of all the countries bordering on the Mediterranean and apparently had no need of imports from abroad. Syrian wheat, however, was of superior quality and this, it seems, was the reason for its import into Egypt.[51] Papyrus *PCZ* 59077, refers to the olive oil trade and to the merchants "who came by sea to buy olive oil." They, too, did not receive the merchandise directly from the producers, but through the agents of Apollonius, and they had to pay those agents in cash or provide certain securities. Since the production and sale of oil was a royal monopoly, import of Syrian oil into Egypt must also have been under the strict control of government officials. The papyri give no information about the wine trade, but it is known that Apollonius received wines from his vineyard in Beth-anath in the north of Palestine, and it may be assumed, therefore, that wine was also imported from Syria into Egypt.[52] Palestine was also an entrepôt for the trade in spices, which was almost completely in the hands of the Arabs. Spices from southern Arabia were brought by Nabataean middlemen to Gaza, whence they reached Alexandria. One of the papyri mentions a certain official appointed especially for the frankincense trade, whose residence was in Gaza.[53] However, trade in slaves was the most thriving. Many papyri record the purchase of slaves in Syria by Zenon or his agents, or other functionaries of Apollonius. Especially in demand were young slaves, boys and girls of 7, 9 and 10 years of age, and on occasion such slave children were sent to the Minister of Finance as gifts.[54] The export of slaves from the Ptolemaic state was permitted only to merchants holding a government export licence.[55] There is an account of one of Apollonius' agents who, on his own initiative, tried to transport slaves from Syria but was seized by customs officials in Tyre.[56] This proves that the slave trade was also subject to a certain measure of government control, but on the whole it was freer than the trade in grain or other goods. At any rate, the restrictions of the king's monopoly laws did not apply to it.

Up to now, the political situation of Ptolemaic Palestine, without reference to the fate of the Jews, has been discussed. In fact the 3rd century B.C.E. represents an almost blank page in Jewish history. The Zenon Papyri do contain scattered information, but this is important from a social not from a political point of view. This will be dealt with again in the next chapter. Josephus (*Against Apion* II, 48) relates that the Egyptian king Ptolemy III Euergetes visited the Temple in Jerusalem after the Third Syrian War in order to thank God for his victory. He offered sacrifices according to local custom, and Josephus calls special attention to the fact that the king thanked not the Egyptian gods but the God of Israel. This naive sentence bears witness to the Jewish origin of the narrative's author who, in accordance with the well-known trend of Jewish apologetic literature, was trying to emphasize the particular honor paid by Greek kings to the people of Israel and its God. Another statement which also belongs to Euergetes' time deserves more attention. In *Antiquities* XII, 158 ff. Josephus relates that the High Priest Onias II, an avaricious, intellectually limited individual, refused, out of greed, to submit to the king the regular tax his forefathers had always paid — 20 talents of silver from their own purse (ἐκ τῶν ἰδίων). This refusal angered the king and he threatened that if the High Priest persisted in his refusal, he would send soldiers to settle in Jerusalem and divide the land among them. Joseph son of Tobiah, a nephew of the High Priest, then accused his uncle of avarice. In his opinion, the High Priest's behavior was endangering the whole nation. Joseph also claimed that Onias had received his distinguished office of High Priesthood, and *prostasia* of the people as well, in exchange for tax money it would bring the king. The clash between the High Priest and his young adversary ended in Joseph offering his services as intermediary between the nation and the king, and the people authorized him to go to Egypt as its representative. Thus the office of *prostasia* passed from the High Priest to a private individual (*ibid.*, 167 ff.). This story forms part of the Tobiad family chronicles which are dealt with in the next chapter. Here it need only be noted that the negative characteristics of the High Priest (which sound strange coming from Josephus, who always speaks of the High Priests with great respect) are not the opinion of Josephus but of the author of the chronicles, which Josephus introduced into his book without alteration or criticism. The author of the chronicles describes the High Priest as a greedy, stupid man, in order to emphasize the noble personality of his young rival, Joseph son of Tobiah. It may be assumed, therefore, that it was not only from egotistic motives that Onias decided to betray the Egyptian king. His behavior was certainly also connected with the political situation. Ptolemy Euergetes was at war with the king of Syria (the Third Syrian War) and Onias, for some reason, decided to demonstrate his preference for the Seleucids as against the Ptolemies. It may be assumed, as many scholars do, that this incident occurred in 242.[57] Many details of the story are quite obscure. For instance, the question of the 20 talents of silver that the High Priest had to pay the Egyptian king from "his own purse." This was certainly not the general tax collected in Judea, since the figure seems much too small. It was probably a kind of annual payment by which the High Priest would "buy" his office from the king.[58] The most important information in the story is the mention of the office of *prostasia*, already encountered in Hecataeus (see above, page 60), which empowered the High Priest to represent the Jewish people before the authorities. Thus, this office was in the hands of the High Priest until 242, when a change occurred and the High Priest was relieved of the post as a result of his audacious policy, and it was transferred to another. This fact certainly contributed substantially to the rise of the influential family of the "Tobiads," which appear henceforth as a constant rival of the High Priests' family, the "Oniads."[59]

Information about the fate of the Jews gradually becomes more detailed towards the end of the century. In 221 the young Seleucid king, Antiochus III, made an effort to invade Palestine but was stopped by the strong resistance of the two Ptolemaic fortresses in the Mountains of Lebanon and forced to abandon the attempt. Two years later he renewed his attack, this time with more success. He conquered Tyre and Acco and laid siege to Dor. The negotiations begun at the initiative of the Ptolemies ended in failure[60], and a year later Antiochus resumed his attempts at conquest. In Lower Galilee, the cities of Beth-shean (Scythopolis) and Beth-yeraḥ (Philoteria) and the fortress at the top of Mount Tabor fell into his hands.

Soon, all the fortresses in Transjordan and Samaria surrendered to him. Egyptian rule in Syria seemed on the verge of total collapse. But, in the meantime, Ptolemy IV Philopator made a supreme effort to recruit new forces. In addition to the mercenaries from abroad, he also enlisted in his army soldiers from the local Egyptian population. A decisive battle took place at Raphia, the southernmost point of Palestine. It ended in a total defeat of the Syrian forces. Antiochus was forced to abandon his attempt to conquer southern Syria, and power in Palestine again passed to the Ptolemies.[61]

A small book, known as the Third Book of Maccabees (although it has no connection whatsoever with the Maccabees), the work of an Alexandrian Jewish writer, gives a short description of the battle of Raphia. It makes mention of the particular part played by a Jew, Dositheus son of Drimylus by name, a member of the royal retinue who saved the king from death when the latter's enemies made an attempt on his life (III Macc. 1:2–3). This Dositheus was an Alexandrian Jew who will appear again in the chapters concerning Alexandrian Jewry in the Ptolemaic period.[62] So far as events in Palestine are concerned, III Maccabees contains a detailed description of a visit of Ptolemy Philopator to Jerusalem after the battle of Raphia. According to this description Ptolemy demanded permission to enter the Temple. When the Jews refused, he nevertheless forced his way inside, only to be punished on the spot; he was beaten until his whole body was buffeted "as a reed by the wind," and finally he was knocked down, paralyzed in all his limbs and unable to utter a sound. His friends and bodyguards carried the king out of the danger area and Ptolemy left Jerusalem in a fury and returned to Egypt (*ibid.* 1:10 ff; 2:21 ff). It is superfluous to attempt to prove that the whole story is a myth. If this tale is compared with the parallel account in II Maccabees concerning similar punishment being inflicted on the Seleucid minister Heliodorus, it becomes obvious that this is a mere transfer of the same literary theme from one "hero" to another.[63] The story is clearly a product of the imagination, but this is not to say that Philopator never visited Jerusalem after the battle of Raphia. There is an inscription, written in both Greek and Egyptian, which records visits by Ptolemy Philopator to several cities of the Syrian province after the battle of Raphia, and although the name Jerusalem does not appear, there is no reason to suppose that he excluded just this city from his itinerary. A damaged space in the Egyptian version of the inscription alludes to a certain insurrectionary movement somewhere in Syria and a number of scholars have tried to read into this a hint at events in Jerusalem. However, no definite conclusion can be drawn from this incomplete text, and there is no reliable proof that the myth in III Maccabees in any way reflects historical truth.[64]

To sum up: from what is known of the century of Ptolemaic rule in Palestine, it appears that while the period contained few significant political events, important historical processes, which were to have an effect on the later history of Palestine, were taking place at the time. The mighty upheavals of the Diadochi period, when Palestine changed hands repeatedly, had finally ceased and the country enjoyed a long period of peace and prosperity. The local population accustomed itself to a strong and well-organized government and if this rule sometimes weighed heavily on the people, especially because of its complex bureaucracy, they, nevertheless, did experience a normal administration, following the laws of a very ancient tradition. It is true that the Alexandrian government's main concern was to exploit the land to its own advantage. Nevertheless that same government did issue several decrees showing a sincere interest in the needs of the local population. However, Ptolemaic rule in Palestine was not, in the main, important for political achievement but in the social-cultural sphere. Under Ptolemaic rule Hellenism spread all over the country, new Greek cities sprang up, and a number of Syrian towns adopted the organization of a Greek *polis*, so characteristic of Greek political life. Neither did the Jews remain unaffected by this movement of Hellenization.

E. The Beginning of Seleucid Rule in Palestine

In the year 205 King Ptolemy IV Philopator died, and his son Ptolemy V Epiphanes ascended the throne. The new king was only five years old and, as usual in such circumstances, power became concentrated in the hands of his guardians. Riots flared up in Egypt and the great kingdom's power declined rapidly. The political situation was favorable for its enemies to invade the country. Antiochus III, who still cherished the hope of annexing southern Syria to his kingdom, decided that the right moment had come to renew the war. In 201 he invaded Palestine and quite easily conquered the whole country, except for the city of Gaza, which put up obstinate resistance. The Ptolemaic court made a desperate attempt to rescue the country from Antiochus and placed Scopas of Aetolia, in Greece, one of the most capable generals of that period, at the head of its army of mercenaries. Although Scopas succeeded in reconquering the whole country, at the battle of Panion in the north of Palestine (in the vicinity of Lake Hula) he himself was decisively beaten, forced to retreat and shut himself up in Sidon (in the year 200). In the end, Sidon, too, fell into the hands of Antiochus III, and gradually, in the course of two years, the whole of Ptolemaic Syria passed to Antiochus III, this time for good. From the year 198, the Ptolemies were completely excluded from Phoenicia, Western Palestine, and Transjordan, these countries being permanently transferred to the realm of the Seleucid kings.[65]

The three years' war in Palestine caused direct harm to Judea and Jerusalem. At the beginning of the war Judea must certainly have fallen into the hands of Antiochus, but later on, during the winter months of the next year, Polybius writes (quoted in *Ant.* XII, 135) that it was reconquered by Scopas. Polybius goes on to relate (*ibid.*, 136) that Jerusalem was retaken by Antiochus after his conquest of Bashan, Samaria and the cities of Abila and Gadara; from this it may be deduced that Jerusalem was one of the last cities to fall into Antiochus' hands (perhaps only in 198). Unfortunately, there is no reliable evidence for events in Jerusalem during those fateful three years. Ptolemaic rule had struck deep roots in the country, and it may be assumed that many of the inhabitants of Jerusalem supported the Ptolemies, and had no interest in the sort of political upheavals which usually accompany changes in government. A supporter of the Ptolemies was Hyrcanus the Tobiad, a man of power and influence, who sided with the Ptolemies, fully aware of what he was doing (see p. 93 below). On the other hand, it is natural that the prolonged rule of a foreign power should provoke opposition, and no doubt a party of Seleucid adherents was also to be found among the inhabitants of Jerusalem. The Christian writer Hieronymus bears witness to the factional struggle in Jerusalem and although Hieronymus lived in a later period (the 4th century C.E.), he had at his disposal good historical sources which are no longer available. Hieronymus writes: "While the great Antiochus and Ptolemy's generals waged war between them, Judea, which lay in the middle, was drawn in two opposite directions; some supported Antiochus and others Ptolemy."[66] Then he goes on to say: "When Judea was in Antiochus' hands, Scopas from Aetolia was sent forth... and he waged a fierce war against Antiochus and conquered Judea, and on returning to Egypt, brought along the leaders of the Ptolemy's party."[67] These two quotations indicate the existence of a rift in the Jerusalem population, and severe clashes connected with the changes in the general political situation probably took place between the two parties. Some scholars believe there is a hint at such a conflict in an obscure sentence in the Book of Daniel (11:14), "And in those times there shall many stand up against the king of the south; also the children of the violent among thy people shall lift themselves to establish the vision; but they shall stumble." The sequence of events in chapter II of the Book of Daniel suggests that this verse refers to the period we are dealing with, and clearly implies an attempt at rebellion or agitation among the Jewish population. However Daniel's enigmatic language is difficult to puzzle out.[68] Modern scholars have ventured diverse conjectures in an attempt to find a meaning in this vague sentence; some seeing in the rebels adherents of Antiochus, others of Hyrcanus the Tobiad, while there are investigators who postulate a "Messianic Movement" in the Jewish population. Yet the evidence for all these assumptions is rather weak. Obviously Daniel takes a negative attitude towards the rebels, otherwise he would not call their leaders "children of the violent among thy people."[69] It would seem, therefore, that he had in mind the supporters of the Syrian king (Antiochus Epiphanes) for in his own time the Syrian king was the greatest enemy of the people of Israel. But if indeed the rebels supported Antiochus III, how can their defeat be explained? Antiochus was victorious in this war and, far from being defeated, those who had backed him were rewarded. In short, this interesting passage cannot contribute to historical research, beyond the general information that during the war there was a rift within the population of Jerusalem, that this dissension provoked a rebellion, and that the rebels were defeated.

Much more precise information comes from the decree of Antiochus III, issued in Jerusalem, probably in 198, and preserved in full in Josephus (*Ant.* XII, 138 ff.). In several passages of this document Antiochus mentions the events of that time:

> Inasmuch as the Jews, from the very moment when we entered their country, showed their eagerness to serve us and, when we came to their city, gave us a splendid reception and met us with their *Gerousia* and furnished an abundance of provisions to our soldiers and elephants, and also helped us to expel the Egyptian garrison in the citadel, we have seen fit on our part to requite them for these acts and to restore their city which has been destroyed by the hazards of war, and to repeople it by bringing back to it those who have been dispersed abroad,....... And it is my will that these things be made over to them as I have ordered and that the work on the Temple be completed, including the porticoes and any other part that it may be necessary to build. The timber, moreover, shall be brought from Judea itself and from other nations and Lebanon without the imposition of a toll-charge. The like shall be done with the other materials needed for making the restoration of the Temple more splendid..... And in order that the city may be more quickly inhabited, I grant both to the present inhabitants and to those who

may return before the month of Hyperberetaios exemption from taxes for three years. We shall also relieve them in future from the third part of their tribute, so that their losses may be made good. And as for those who were carried off from the city and are slaves, we herewith set them free, both them and the children born to them, and order their property to be restored to them.

This is a historical document of outstanding importance. Although many scholars of previous generations tried to dismiss it as a Jewish forgery, modern historical research has proved its authenticity beyond doubt.[70] The document contains first and foremost several interesting details about the role played by the Jews at the end of the war. The main Ptolemaic army had left Jerusalem long before, but a garrison remained stationed in the citadel. The citadel was attacked and conquered with Jews actually taking part in the conquest, i.e., at the end of the war they appeared as official allies of Antiochus, King of Syria. They also undertook to supply food for the soldiers and war-elephants, in this way providing real help for Antiochus. We are then told the important detail that the *Gerousia* ("Elders' Council") came out of the city to greet the king. The *Gerousia* consisted of the Jerusalem nobility, and although the members who had supported Ptolemy had certainly fled to Egypt along with the retreating Ptolemaic army, the council as a whole quite probably took a favorable attitude towards the new government. The High Priest, the central personality in Judea in this period, presumably headed the *Gerousia*. In those days the High Priest who ruled Judea and Jerusalem was Simeon the Just,[71] and it is worth noting that he, too, belonged among the adherents of the new government, a conclusion which may be drawn from two statements preserved by two different writers. Josephus attests that in the strife which arose among the Tobiads, Simeon the Just was on the side of the elder brothers, against Hyrcanus (*Ant.* XII, 229); and since Hyrcanus supported the Ptolemies, it follows that his elder brothers and Simeon the Just sided with the Seleucids (see the next chapter). The second testimony is that of Ben Sira, who in his *Book of Wisdom* points out that construction works on a large scale were carried out by Simeon the Just in Jerusalem and the Temple:

> Great among his brethren and the glory of his people
>> Was Simeon, the son of Johanan the priest.
> In whose time the House was renovated,
>> And in whose days the Temple was fortified;
> In whose days the wall was built,
>> [Having] turrets for protection like a king's palace (50:1–2).[72]

There is obvious agreement between this description by Ben Sira and the contents of Antiochus' letter; both passages deal with the destruction of the city and the Temple and the construction needed for their restoration. Since Simeon the Just was a contemporary of Antiochus III, and we do not hear of any wars that might have caused the destruction of the city and the Temple except the war of 201–198, it follows that Ben Sira and Antiochus III were referring to the same event, and this tells us something of great importance about the position of the High Priest. Although the project of restoring the city and the Temple was included in the king's letter to a high Syrian official, it was actually not the official who carried out the construction project but the High Priest. And if the king were willing for Simeon the Just to execute the work of reconstruction, it follows that he accepted the High Priest as a faithful ally and had no doubts of his loyalty to the new government. Moreover, the fact that the king imposed such a task on Simeon the Just points to the power concentrated in the hands of the High Priest. It has been pointed out above that, according to Hecataeus, representation of the people (*prostasia*) was in the hands of the High Priest from the time of the Diadochi period and that in the Ptolemaic period this situation remained unchanged until 242, when as a result of the audacious policy of the High Priest Onias II the office was transferred to Josephus son of Tobiah. So it came about that the transfer of power from the Ptolemies to the Seleucids again enhanced the power of the High Priest. It may be assumed that he was given back the office of *prostasia*, thereby restoring the traditional situation. The High Priest continued to occupy the foremost position in the country in the time of Antiochus Epiphanes as well, in spite of the changes which took place in the functions of his office.

To return to Antiochus' letter: in addition to the measures undertaken to rehabilitate the city after the destruction caused by the war, Antiochus also laid down certain principles concerning national life in the period ahead. He promised that the Seleucid government would contribute large sums to support divine worship in the Temple; he exempted the members of the *Gerousia*, the priests, the scribes (γραμματεῖς τοῦ ἱεροῦ) and the singers (ἱεροψάλται) of the Temple from certain taxes, and granted the whole people the right to "conduct their political life according to their ancestral laws." There is no possibility of explaining fully the matter of tax-exemption. The king mentions three kinds of taxes: the poll-tax, the tax called "crown-tax" (στεφανιτικὸς φόρος or στέφανος) and the salt-tax. It is not known when and by what method the Jews paid these taxes; whether they were the taxes which the Ptolemies had been collecting in Judea and Jerusalem in the course of the hundred years of their rule and the collection of which was now approved by the new government, or whether they were new taxes imposed on the Jerusalem population by Antiochus III in the unsettled period when the city was temporarily occupied by the Seleucid army in 201.[73] Of greater significance is the reference concerning the right granted to the Jews to live according "to their ancestral laws."[74] The assumption was previously made that the Jews were accorded this right by Alexander the Great, and that it was probably confirmed later by the Ptolemies as well. Yet Antiochus' letter represents the first and only official document of the Hellenistic period in which this right was formulated in detail, which prompts the question of what the king had precisely in mind when speaking about the "ancestral laws" of the Jews. Did he mean the laws of the Torah, by which the Jews lived? But did the Greek king have any knowledge of these laws? And how could he grant the people laws he had never heard about? The answer to these questions lies in the fact that the formula of the right given to a nation "to live according to the ancestral laws" or "according to its tradition," is repeated many times in the Hellenistic-Roman period, and not only in relation to the Jews. Other nations and Greek cities as well were given the right to live according to their traditional laws.[75] This is a stereotyped formula of Hellenistic law by which the king granted a certain political unit the right to live according to its traditional law, i.e., to enjoy a limited measure of autonomy. There is no reason, therefore, to assume that Antiochus was interested in the content of Jewish laws. The matter was merely a formality; having found a favorable attitude on the part of the ruling group in Judea, he confirmed the Jewish people's existing political regime. Henceforward, the "ancestral laws" of the Jews were acknowledged by the government in Judea and Jerusalem, and if anybody violated them, the Jerusalem authorities had the right to request the king and his officials for help and protection. Thus, a rather paradoxical situation was created in Jerusalem, in which the Greek king was committed to the defense of the Sabbath rest or the laws of uncleanliness and purity, etc. [76]

Antiochus, then, regarded the matter of "ancestral laws" as no more than a stereotyped formula. However, this was not the attitude of the Jerusalem authorities. They knew exactly what were the ancestral laws by which the Jewish people lived. There is no doubt that the "ancestral laws" corresponded in practice to the Torah, but the concept was, as a matter of fact, much broader. In confirming Jewish autonomy the king clearly had in mind first of all the political pattern of government as practised in Jerusalem, i.e., a theocracy with the High Priest at its head; but it would be fruitless to search for laws confirming theocratic rule in the Torah since there are no references to it: neither the Jerusalem Temple nor the office of High Priest as the highest governmental institution are mentioned. Another example: although in the Torah the Sabbath is emphasized as a day of rest, yet the concept of rest had not as yet received its precise formulation, and the various kinds of work forbidden on the Sabbath had not then been classified and enumerated. Synagogues already existed in the period under discussion, but, as is known, they are not mentioned in the Torah either. It follows, therefore, that the notion of "ancestral laws" comprises not only the "written Torah" but also what we define as the "Oral Law," i.e., all the laws and customs which, though based on the Torah, constituted in this period a separate world which had developed and been molded into fixed practices from the time of Ezra the Scribe onwards. Only the authorized government in Jerusalem could judge which of all these numerous interpretations were fit to be accepted as laws, and which were not; and since power was now concentrated in the hands of the High Priest, it can be seen that the historical process had strengthened the position of this office within the nation and had imparted to it an actual semblance of royal power.

This concludes the analysis of the important document linked to the name of Antiochus III. The publication of this decree marked the beginning of a new era in the life of the Jews. The difficult war years had come to an end and the Jewish people had emerged from the hardships of that time with considerable gains. The nation was on good terms with its new rulers, its internal autonomy was more extensive, and the nation's leader was the High Priest, Simeon the Just, a clever man and an excellent ruler, who willingly accepted the Syrian king as overlord of Judea and Jerusalem. Simeon the Just no doubt found many supporters of his policy among the Jewish nobility. The author of II Maccabees mentions a man called Johanan, probably one of the leading members of the Jerusalem nobility, who negotiated with Antiochus and received royal privileges (φιλάνθρωπα βασιλικά) from him.[77] The nature of these privileges is unknown, but the Jews presumably singled out certain laws for which they thought it necessary to secure the king's special approval. Some thirty years later members of the Jerusalem aristocracy inclining towards Hellenization saw in the Syrian king the supreme patron of their Hellenistic aspirations. However, in the days of Antiochus III there is still a gap between the Syrian government in Antioch and the supporters of Hellenistic reform in Jerusalem. The "royal privileges" were later abolished by Hellenized Jews, thereby proving that their contents accorded with Jewish tradition. The very fact that Simeon the Just, one of the pillars of Jewish tradition in this period,[78] supported Antiochus, is sufficient guarantee that the transfer of power from the Ptolemies to the Seleucids did not introduce any changes into the cultural and religious life of the people. King Seleucus IV Philopator, who ascended the throne of Syria after the death of Antiochus III, was also said to have displayed a favorable attitude towards the Temple and to have contributed considerable sums to maintain its worship, in keeping with the custom during the reign of Antiochus III.[79] Thus the crisis which broke out after the accession of Antiochus IV Epiphanes to the throne did not result from a pre-established Syrian policy, but had deep reasons which must be sought mainly in the process of the inner development of Jewish society itself.

What was Judea's position within the great Seleucid empire? Although its dimensions had considerably diminished in the course of the 3rd century, the Seleucid kingdom remained a mighty realm exercising dominion over very large areas. Within its territory several political units existed which enjoyed internal autonomy, and the royal court in Antioch maintained diplomatic relations with each of them, according to the importance of their position in the state. As described above (p. 62), the authorities at Antioch divided the political units into three categories: cities, dynasts, and peoples.[80] At the head of the "peoples" there were local rulers — princes, heads of tribes, priests, etc. — who, however, did not wield over their populations absolute power comparable to monarchs in their own countries, and who were not strong enough to make the authorities at Antioch show them special consideration. Everything depended on the people's behavior: if it was loyal to the central government, the Seleucid king would be favorably disposed towards it; but if it showed signs of opposition, the king would crush every attempt at rebellion by force. Such was the position of the Jews. Jerusalem was not a Greek *polis*, nor was the High Priest a king. The Jews did not play any significant economic role in the Seleucid kingdom, and their military power was not noticeably strong. Thus within the Seleucid kingdom the political position of Judea was rather weak, and relations between the ruling group in Jerusalem and the Syrian government were dependent on the diplomatic talents of the Jerusalem nobility. Quite probably the heads of the Jerusalem government, and perhaps the High Priests themselves, would often visit Antioch — even before the accession of Antiochus Epiphanes to the throne — in order to secure further confirmation of Jewish autonomy; and it is clear that every political complication and inner crisis could endanger all the political privileges acquired by the Jews in the reign of King Antiochus III. Even their right "to live according to the ancestral laws" could easily be abolished at the king's orders.

CHAPTER IV

SOCIAL CONDITIONS

by V. Tcherikover

A. "Natives" and "Foreigners" in Palestine

THE PRESENT CHAPTER deals with social conditions in Judea and Jerusalem; its aim is to define different social classes among the Jews and to depict the social atmosphere in which the Hellenistic movement developed. It should, however, be borne in mind, particularly in a discussion of the Hellenizing movement, that Judea was only a part of Palestine. The social conditions of Palestine as a whole will accordingly be first discussed.

On this question, the Zenon papyri (see above, p. 47 ff) furnish abundant material. Indeed, without those papyri we would have no conception whatsoever of the social conditions of the population in the country. Of special interest is the factual material depicting the contacts between the local population and foreigners who visited Palestine during Ptolemaic rule. From the time of Alexander onwards Palestine was open to immigrants from Western countries: soldiers, merchants, officials, travellers. People of diverse social classes settled in Palestine or visited it. Through contacts between these people and the native population the important process of the fusion of Eastern and Western elements began to emerge in Palestine, just as it was progressing in every other country conquered by the Macedonians.

In 259 B.C.E., Apollonius, the Egyptian Minister of Finance, sent a large group of his officials and agents to Palestine (see p. 65–66 above). This group broke up into several smaller groups and, with the help of the Zenon papyri, they can be followed on their various journeys throughout the country. One group set out on its journey at Straton's Tower by the sea and passed through Jerusalem and Jericho to Transjordan, then proceeded northwards and returned to the coast, at Acco, after visiting Beth-anath and Kadesh in the north of the country.[1] Another group visited the southern part of Palestine (the papyri mention the cities of Gaza, Maresha [Marissa] and Adoraim [Adora]).[2] People were also sent to Hauran, while

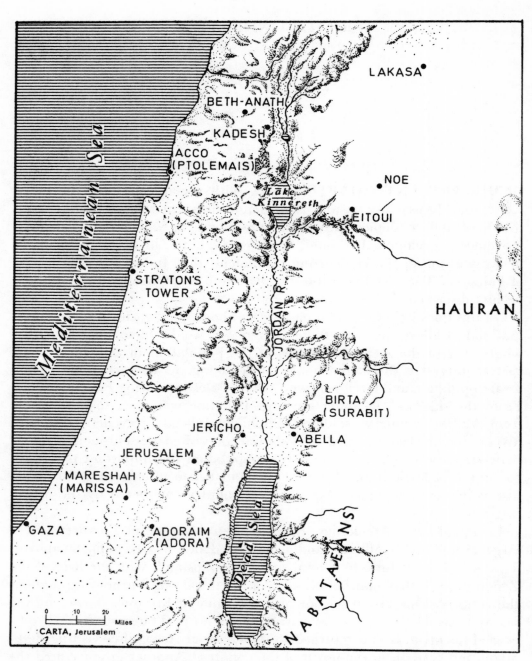

Places in Palestine Visited by Zenon and his Agents

others visited the land of the Nabataeans.[3] Thus not even the remotest corner of Palestine was overlooked by Apollonius' agents on their journeys. And these were not the journeys of small groups. Rather they were large caravans escorted by various attendants and servants: cooks, bakers, grooms, mule-drivers, secretaries, porters, etc. Although individual cases in which these attendants and servants came from Egypt are known, there is little doubt that the majority of them, for instance the coachmen, grooms, and mule-drivers, came from the local population. And, indeed, alongside Greek names attesting to foreign origin, men bearing Semitic names such as Zabeinas, Rabbelos and others are found among the service staff. In a list containing twelve names, Hebrew ones such as Zebulun, Hosea, and Hanan, and the Idumaean designation Kousnatanos[4] appear together with Greek names. It is of course unlikely that such socially inferior members of the local population were accepted as equals by Apollonius' agents, but it may be assumed that they came into close contact with the service personnel from Egypt, learned to speak some poor Greek from them, and became acquainted to some extent with strange Greek customs.

Closer contacts between foreign and local elements may be found in the colonies of Greek and Macedonian soldiers sent from Egypt to Palestine. These soldiers spread in small groups all over the country and it was natural that they seek wives among the local population. It is worth noting that these connections between Egyptian soldiers and local women were not only of a casual and passing nature. An order of Ptolemy Philadelphus, preserved in the Vienna papyri (see above, p. 47), mentions "soldiers and other settlers in Syria and Phoenicia who took wives from among the native girls." If the king found it necessary to mention this fact, it most probably was a natural and enduring practice, even approved by the government. The king's order also explicitly emphasizes that these wives should not be considered slaves (for whom special registration was required). Thus official sanction was given by the king to these mixed marriages.[5] An interesting picture of the fusion of different ethnic elements within a military settlement is provided by one papyrus (*C. P. Jud.* 1) deriving from a *cleruchy* of soldiers in the land of the Ammonites. This papyrus contains a contract of sale of a seven-year old girl by her previous master, a Greek from the island of Cnidus (near the land of Caria in Asia Minor) who is designated as one of Tobiah's men. The buyer is Zenon, acting as a representative of the Minister of Finance Apollonius. Among the local people who served as witnesses to the sale, mention is made of a Macedonian, another witness whose name is obliterated is indicated as a Persian, while a second Persian, also from among Tobiah's men, served as guarantor.

The "Persians" in the Ptolemaic army were actually not of Persian origin but constituted a "pseudo-ethnic" group open to men of different origins (see p. 18 above). Both "Persians" in Tobiah's *cleruchy* were not real Persians. The names of their fathers were Agathon and Hananiah, suggesting that the first was a Greek and the second a Jew. We thus find among the very small number of *cleruchy* members named in the papyrus men from three different nations — a Macedonian, a Greek, and a Jew (who may be assumed to have been a native).[6] As everywhere in the Hellenistic world (and later in the Roman world), the army served as a melting pot in which different nations blended into one uniform mass. It is very likely that the mixed marriages mentioned in Ptolemy Philadelphus' order were an everyday occurrence, especially in such a place as Tobiah's *cleruchy*, where the population had been mixed from the very beginning. The younger generation which grew up in those *cleruchies* was equally close to both worlds. The Hellenization movement could easily find followers among such youths brought up in the atmosphere of international Hellenism, and cut off from any original ancient tradition.

Naturally enough, the Greeks who came from Egypt considered the local population inferior in status. The era of Alexander the Great's romantic policy towards the local inhabitants was over, and the Ptolemies well knew how to differentiate between Greeks and Macedonians — the conquerors — and Egyptians, Syrians, and Jews — the conquered. It was of course always possible to make exceptions for local princes and their retinues, especially if these princes tried to speak Greek and exhibited a desire to entertain close associations with the governing circles. It was not, however, these isolated instances which determined the relations between the Greeks and the natives, but contacts with the large masses of the population. As early as the classical period it was commonly held in Greece that the inhabitants of Eastern lands were actually slaves. Now, when the Greeks took up residence in the East among this very population, it was natural for their prejudice to grow stronger, for they could see with their own eyes the great gulf separating the Egyptian official, imbued with Greek culture and accustomed to conditions of city life, and the local illiterate peasant content with an extremely primitive existence. How much more must this attitude have been strengthened in Palestine. There the Greek official from Egypt found himself in Egyptian–occupied land and accordingly regarded himself as much more independent and powerful than the ordinary official in Egypt itself. This fact explains why the traffic in slaves became the most highly developed branch of trade between Egypt and Palestine. Information about this trade is provided by numerous papyri.[7] Apollonius' agents,

Zenon among them, bought slaves and slave girls, mainly of tender age, to send to Egypt where they were apparently destined to be used as servants on Apollonius' estates. The slave-trade presented an easy way of enrichment, and sometimes Apollonius' agents acted in their own interest and neglected reporting their deeds to the authorities. Papyrus *PCZ* 59093 tells about one of Apollonius' agents, Apollophanes, who decided to export slaves from Syria on his own account, which was prohibited by the government. He brought his live cargo from Gaza to Tyre and transferred it from one ship to another, without saying a word to the customs officials and without obtaining a licence for exporting the slaves. The customs officials got wind of his intentions and confiscated the "merchandise." To save himself, the agent declared that the slaves belonged not to him but to Zenon, calculating rightly that the name of Zenon, the chief agent in Palestine of Apollonius, the Minister of Finance, would make the desired impression on the customs officials, as indeed it did. A man by the name of Menekles, apparently in charge of customs matters in Tyre, helped the minor agent who had fallen into a trap and hushed up the whole affair.[8]

A far more unhappy picture is portrayed in papyrus *PSI* 406 which contains a memorandum, or more exactly, a denunciation, by a man called Heracletus designated as a "coachman" (συνωριστής). This Heracletus was one of the lesser officials who had come from Egypt as attendants of the chief agents. The text of the "memorandum," with some omissions, follows:

> Memorandum to Zenon from Heracletus the coachman with regard to the deeds committed by Drimylus and Dionysius. One girl he [probably Dionysius] delivered to the frontier guard and they fitted her out with all they had at hand. And now she is at Pegai (Πηγαί) with the frontier guard. And the second girl [he] brought from the land of the Ammonites and sold her at Acco (Ptolemais). And the "priestess" [he] brought for the fourth time to Jaffa (Joppa). And he went to Hauran with a slave-girl and sold her for 150 drachmas. And thence [he] came back and deceived the Nabataeans, and when there arose a commotion [he] was brought to jail, and now there are seven days that he is in fetters. And Drimylus bought a girl for 300 drachmas; every day [he and the girl] set out on the road and did excellent business. Doing so they neglected the animals; for every day Drimylus heated two tins of water for his mistress! He sold also the she-ass and the wild donkey. And there are witnessess to these things. As for the rest, if you ask me you will find out the whole truth.

This diverting letter takes us right into the "underworld" of Hellenistic Palestine. Drimylus and Dionysius were no doubt comrades of the coachman Heracletus;[9] one of them is specifically described as a coachman in another papyrus. It was their job to convey Apollonius' agents to various parts of the country and to supply the caravans with grain and other foodstuffs. Instead of doing this, they started a "business" which no doubt brought them greater profits. Quite probably Heracletus himself was a partner in the "business" at first, but having quarrelled for some reason with his partners, a common occurrence in the underworld, he had decided to denounce them. Dionysius and Drimylus specialized in a particular branch of the slave-trade, the traffic in παιδίσκαι, i.e., slave girls. They travelled throughout the whole country, visiting Pegai,[10] Jaffa, Acco, Transjordan, even reaching the land of the Nabataeans, i.e., the frontier of the Ptolemaic province. The young slave girls were made prostitutes, since what else was the role of a girl with the frontier guard if "they fitted her out with all they had at hand"? It may be assumed that the frontier guard was also the keeper of an inn to accommodate travellers, always numerous in the vicinity of the border, and that the girl was appropriately adorned for her "profession." The girl whom Drimylus took out on the road, and with whose help he made a great deal of money, fared no better. The role of the "priestess" who was brought four times to Jaffa is of particular interest. Apparently she was a temple prostitute who was sold to one of the temples of Astarte-Aphrodite.[11] The prices paid for these young slave girls (150 and 300 drachmas) were not high. At any rate they were lower than the prices offered for slaves in Egypt itself, and this chance of easy profits naturally attracted a number of people from among the multitude who came from Egypt to Palestine to practice this vile traffic. It is clear that the local population suffered greatly from the lawless deeds of such men. In fact, the central government in Alexandria found it necessary to intervene for the purpose of introducing law and order into the slave-trade in Syria. The order issued by Ptolemy II Philadelphus, recorded in the Vienna papyrus, commands all persons in Syria and Phoenicia who bought slaves from among the free local population to register them with the *oikonomos* of the district in the course of 20 days from the date of the decree's publication. The slave of a violator of the decree would be confiscated and the offender would also have to pay a fine to the Treasury. Only a slave-owner who at the time of registration could prove that the slave he had bought had not previously been a free man, but a slave, would be able to keep him. At the end, the decree prohibited the purchase of free men under any pretext, except in the case of pur-

chases made by the senior finance official in Syria and Phoenicia who had
the authority to sell debtors to the government. The decree was accordingly
designed to curb the lawless acts of men who had turned the slave trade
into a man-hunt of free people.[12] There is nothing to disprove the assumption that the young slave girls who fell into the hands of Drimylus and
Dionysius had been carried off from Palestinian villages. It is worth noting
that even in cases where the purchase was carried out according to law, i.e.,
by Zenon, the slaves were inclined to run away from their new owners and
return to their former masters. That is what happened with young slaves
($\pi\alpha\hat{\imath}\delta\epsilon\varsigma$) bought by Zenon from two brothers in Idumea, and who escaped when Zenon was about to return to Egypt (*PCZ* 59015 verso).
It is not sure how far the decree of Philadelphus attained its purpose.
Although the Vienna papyrus bears no date, scholars suppose that it
belongs to the end of the sixties, i.e., it preceded the Zenon papyri by
several years. Thus, when Apollonius' agents came to Palestine in 259,
the local population in Syria and Phoenicia was already protected by the
king's decree. Nevertheless, the decree did not prevent Drimylus and
Dionysius from carrying on their activities.

The Zenon papyri also include significant, albeit scanty, information
about land ownership and the condition of the peasants in Palestine. In
Egypt all land theoretically belonged to the king (see p. 16 above). Private
ownership of land was almost inexistent. In Palestine the position was
quite different, since there the Ptolemies had had to take time-honored
local tradition into account. Large areas were in the possession of local
princes whose influence over the population was very strong; to confiscate their lands would no doubt have brought the people's anger down
on the Ptolemaic government. The Greek cities, too, (or those ancient
Syrian towns which were adopting a Greek form of government) possessed
lands adjacent to them. Thus Egypt's "totalitarian" principle was not fully
applicable in Palestine. On the other hand, estates constituting the personal
property of the Persian king or members of his family existed already in
Palestine during the Persian period. Part of these estates, consisting of
forests, vineyards, or orchards and known as *paradeisoi*[13] must have been
taken over by the Ptolemaic king who was now the successor to the Persian
monarch. Additional land, either bought, confiscated or acquired in some
other way by the Treasury, must have been added to the *paradeisoi*. The
Zenon papyri mention an estate in Beth-anath, consisting wholly or
mostly of vineyards, which belonged to Apollonius, and it may be assumed
that this estate was mainly "royal land" presented as a "gift" to Apollonius,
according to custom prevailing in Ptolemaic Egypt (see above, p. 17).

Unfortunately, there is no way of establishing the percentage of Palestinian territory held by the king, the size of the urban lands, nor how much of the land in the country was left in the hands of local princes. Even so, it is clear that the general picture was much more variegated than in Hellenistic Egypt.

The papyri provide some valuable information about Apollonius' estate in Beth-anath.[14] One of the papyri (PSI 554) supplies details about relations between the men in charge of the estate and the local peasants. The chief manager was evidently a certain Melas, one of Apollonius' agents.[15] It appears from the papyrus that Melas and the peasants quarrelled over some wheat which they evidently had to deliver to him. Both sides relied on official documents to support their case: the peasants on a petition they had apparently sent to the king and Melas on his warrant as tax-farmer ($\kappa\omega\mu\omega\mu\iota\sigma\theta\omega\tau\dot{\eta}\varsigma$) of the village. An official with a similar title is mentioned in the Vienna papyrus.[16] The role of these officials was, it seems, to collect taxes from the villages in Syria and hand over the money collected to Apollonius' agents. Unfortunately, the papyrus is badly damaged and the outcome of the quarrel is not known. The same papyrus also refers to another dispute about a quantity of raisins ($\sigma\tau\dot{\epsilon}\mu\varphi\upsilon\lambda\alpha$) which the peasants were supposed to have prepared (apparently for the owner of the estate) and failed to do so. It appears from the text that the peasants spoiled the raisins because of lack of water in the vicinity of the estate. Melas evidently confiscated part of the raisins which were the peasants' own property, thus infuriating them. Melas claimed that many of the villagers owned their own vineyards, and that he had compensated each and every one of them who did not out of his own due. The peasants also complained that Melas had taken too large a share of the fig harvest from them.

The information contained in this papyrus is vague and fragmentary, but it still enables us to reach certain conclusions concerning social conditions among the peasantry. Apparently, they lived on "royal land" which they cultivated under certain conditions. They were required to pay a proportion of their produce or a sum of money either as taxes to the government, or as rent to the landlord. The amount to be paid was fixed by contracts negotiated between the parties. This picture reminds us, in several details, of similar conditions of the peasants in Ptolemaic Egypt, well known to us from papyrological documents. It appears, however, from our papyrus that not all the peasants were tenants of the "royal land". The fact that some of them cultivated their own vineyards is additional evidence that the "totalitarian" principle prevailing in Egypt, whereby the king was the sole owner of all land, did not fully apply in

Palestine. Peasants who lived on their own land enjoyed the right of private property and doubtless maintained the spirit of freedom and independence which had been the ancestral tradition of their families.

Papyrus *C. P. Jud.* 6 is a good indication of the independent position of the rich peasants. The document is of especial value because its "hero" is a farmer with the Hebrew name of Jaddua,[17] which suggests that the action should be placed in Judea, or at any rate in a village with a Jewish population. The papyrus contains a letter from one official, Alexander (evidently a minor Egyptian agent in the village), to another functionary, Orias, apparently his senior. The text of the letter runs:

> I have received your letter, to which you added a copy of the letter written by Zenon to Jaddua saying that unless he gave the money to Strato, Zenon's man, we were to hand over his pledge to him [Strato]. I happened to be unwell as a result of taking some medicine, so I sent a lad, a servant of mine, with Strato, and wrote a letter to Jaddua. When they returned they said he had taken no notice of my letter, but had attacked them and thrown them out of the village. So I am writing to you [for your information].

This letter gives us to understand that there were well-to-do and powerful farmers in Palestinian villages who were not afraid of government officials and even permitted themselves acts of violence against them. We do not know what was meant by the money which Jaddua was to pay to Zenon, whether it was a private debt, a part of his taxes, or some other payment he had to make to the government. Whatever it was, Jaddua quite obviously had no intention of fulfilling his obligations, and, when pressed, resorted to violence. He would hardly have acted so arrogantly towards the representative of the government, had he not been sure of the support of the villagers, although it is also possible that the officials themselves were not disposed to endanger their position by open strife. Alexander's explanation, that he did not go himself because he was ill, sounds very much like a convenient excuse. Quite probably he was simply anxious to avoid an unpleasant meeting with one of the strong men of the village. Jaddua can hardly have been merely one of the minor tenants of the "royal land," for in that case he would surely have been afraid to attack government officials. More likely he was a rich farmer cultivating lands which had been his family's for generations, and who regarded himself as an independent master in his village. The two Idumaean brothers, Kollochutos and Zaidelos, from whom Zenon had bought young slaves, were also no doubt rich local chieftains.[18]

B. The Tobiads

Some of the papyri mentioned above make it clear that there were also Jews among the various peoples of Southern Syria with whom Apollonius' agents came into contact. Hebrew names, such as Hanan and Hosea, appear among the local people who were in touch with the large caravan of Apollonius' agents and their attendants. Jews were members of an Egyptian *cleruchy* in Transjordan charged with defending the frontiers of the country; and as we have seen, some of the rich influential local chieftains in the country were Jews. These instances indicate that as early as the 3rd century the Jews were no longer confined to the mountains of Judea but had spread, perhaps in small groups first, all over the country. The direct result of this process was to bring the Jews into contact with the Greeks in various parts of the country, and presumably even in this early period Hellenism had begun to take root among the Jewish population.

In view of the above it is very important to investigate the history of the Tobiad family, which in a later period played a most prominent part in the process of the Hellenization of the Jews. Ancestors of the family are known as early as the period preceding the Babylonian Exile.[19] Later, Zechariah (6:10 ff.) mentions a Tobiah as one of the leaders of the Exile, in 519. There is more detailed information in the writings of Nehemiah. A Tobiah, whom he derisively calls "the slave, the Ammonite" (Neh. 2:10, 09), was one of Nehemiah's bitterest enemies. Yet it is clear from Nehemiah's own words that this Tobiah was not a slave at all, unless the word "slave" is to be interpreted as meaning "the slave of the King," i.e. a high official of the Persian government. Tobiah was an "Ammonite," that is, a rich prince whose estate was in the land of the Ammonites, in Transjordan. He was a relative of the High Priest Eliashib who arranged a "chamber" in the Temple for him (Neh. 13:4 ff), which means that Tobiah belonged to the Jewish aristocracy and was doubtless of priestly lineage. The palace at 'Arāq el-Emīr in Transjordan, on the ruins of which the name Tobiah is engraved twice, may quite possibly have been erected in the period of the same Tobiah.[20] For another two hundred years nothing is heard about the Tobiads, until another member of the family appears as the head of a military *cleruchy* in Transjordan, appointed by King Ptolemy II Philadelphus. This is known to us exclusively from the Zenon papyri, where his name appears several times.[21] We do not know whether Tobiah had joined the caravan of Apollonius' agents in Palestine, but, in any case, Tobiah's "grooms" are listed among the attendants of the caravan, and this points to the fact that Tobiah had sent his men to assist Apollonius' agents on their journey through the country. And again a Tobiah appears as the head of a *cleruchy* in Transjordan. The inhabitants of the *cleruchy* called themselves "Tobiah's men," or "Tobiah's cavalry." Obviously, the whole colony was named for him and was probably situated on his land. From one papyrus (*C. P. Jud.* 2d) we learn that there was a district in Transjordan called "The land of Tobiah" (ἐν τῆι τοῦ Τουβίου); which lay near another place called Surabit (Σουραβιτ; Hebrew: *Zur Beth Tuvia* [?]). The first syllable "Sur" (Σουρ) is surely a Greek transcription of the Hebrew word *Zur*, meaning stronghold.[22] There is no doubt that this Surabit should be identified with Tyre (Τύρος) mentioned in Josephus (*Ant.* XII, 233) as the residence of Hyrcanus, Tobiah's grandson, at the beginning of the 2nd century B.C.E. Again there is no doubt that this Tyre is the same as the Birta of the land of the Ammonites, mentioned in Zenon papyri as the location of the *cleruchy* of Tobiah's men.[23] Thus a substantial district in Transjordan constituted a kind of small principality, the ancestral domain of this aristocratic family. The fact that the Tobiad family is listed among those Jews who returned from the Babylonian Exile (Ezra 2:59–60; Neh. 7:61–62) plus the important role it played in Jewish history for over three hundred years, is sufficient proof that it was not of Ammonite origin. The family no doubt belonged to the Jewish aristocracy of Jerusalem and it was called Ammonite only because of the location of its lands.

Tobiah's high position is reflected in the Zenon papyri by two letters sent by him (*C. P. Jud.* 4, 5). One is to King Ptolemy Philadelphus announcing a gift of some rare animals (probably intended for the king's zoo in Alexandria). The other is to Apollonius, the Minister of Finance, telling him that Tobiah has sent him, also apparently as a gift, four young slaves (aged seven to ten years) accompanied by a eunuch. Such costly presents to the king and his Finance Minister are evidence of Tobiah's independent position and the close relations he maintained with the royal court at Alexandria.

The very fact that the king had nominated Tobiah as the head of the *cleruchy* in the land of the Ammonites, that is, he had entrusted him with the responsible task of defending the borders of the country, proves how complete was the confidence the Egyptian government reposed in the Jewish prince. It certainly seems reasonable to assume that Tobiah visited the Egyptian capital more than once and was presented to the king. His letters to the king and to Apollonius are written in fluent Greek and in a most polished handwriting. However, this was not Tobiah's own handwriting but that of his Greek secretary, who was also responsible for the Greek text of the letters. It is indeed typical of this Palestinian local prince that such a secretary, or secretaries, should be found in his house, and even more characteristic that he should use in his letter the usual Greek formula "many thanks to the gods" (πολλὴ χάρις τοῖς θεοῖς). This sentence of course was not Tobiah's either, but his secretary's. However, it cannot possibly be assumed that the secretary did not read to Tobiah the exact text of the letter before dispatching it to Alexandria. How could Tobiah, the Jewish aristocrat, permit pagan gods to be invoked in his letter? Clearly, the elements of Hellenism were already making inroads into this family. With the coming of Greek secretaries, Greek tutors must also have come, who instructed Tobiah's sons in the spirit of Hellenism. Greek mythology, and works of Greek literature penetrated into the family, together with pagan forms of greeting and Greek dress and customs. No wonder, therefore, that it was not long before Tobiah's family in Jerusalem hoisted the flag of Hellenization and embarked on a campaign to force the Jewish nation to remold its traditional form of life in the new political and cultural pattern.

If our knowledge of Tobiah comes from fragmentary papyrological sources, the life of Joseph, Tobiah's son, is familiar from the detailed literary account preserved in Josephus (*Ant.* 12:160 ff.). Yet it is precisely this literary element that arouses suspicion. It is easy to see that Josephus does not record true historical events but is repeating a legendary narrative drawn, no doubt, from the Tobiad family chronicles. It is not known when and by whom these chronicles were written but on one point, at least, there need be no doubt. They were not composed as an objective historical record, but to glorify the family "heroes," Joseph and his son Hyrcanus.[24]

To elicit the historical truth behind Josephus' story, it is necessary to subject every detail of his account to a careful, critical scrutiny. Had the documents reached us directly, without his intervention, the task would have been easier. Josephus tends to confuse historical periods. The events of the 3rd century are transposed into the 2nd, and the whole long life-story of Joseph son of Tobiah is presented as though it unfolded itself during the reign of King Ptolemy V Epiphanes, i.e., after the year 198, in which the entire province of Syria was transferred from the hands of the Ptolemies to the Seleucids. This involved Josephus in some curious contradictions while trying to explain how it came about that Palestine was still, nevertheless, ruled by Ptolemy Epiphanes. The detailed analysis to which the legend was subjected by many scholars has proved beyond doubt that the Ptolemy of Tobiad family chronicles was not Ptolemy V Epiphanes but Ptolemy III Euergetes, the son and successor of Ptolemy II

Philadelphus.[25] If this is so, then Joseph son of Tobiah was the son of the Tobiah of the Zenon papyri. Since the father was close to the court of Ptolemy Philadelphus, it was quite natural for the son to make a success of his political career and achieve distinction at the court of Ptolemy Euergetes, the son of Philadelphus. As mentioned above (p. 58), Joseph son of Tobiah evidently made his first appearance in the political arena in 242 when, through his daring intervention in the affairs of Judea, the office of *prostasia* was taken out of the hands of the High Priest Onias III and the Jews were spared the political adventure to which Onias was about to commit them. According to Josephus, Joseph son of Tobiah was a young man at that time (*Ant.* XII, 160), from which it may be assumed that he was born about the year 270, a date which fits in more or less with the end of his career. We know that he left his office of tax-collector as an old man, and that it happened shortly before the Fifth Syrian War, when power in Palestine passed to Antiochus III. However, Josephus' evidence on this chronological question is also contradictory and it must be acknowledged that modern research has not yet reached any definite conclusion.[26]

Although Josephus' account of Joseph son of Tobiah opens with a description of the political strife between him and the High Priest Onias, the sequel to the story does not concern Joseph's political activity but his position as tax-collector in Palestine, on behalf of King Ptolemy. Josephus describes at length Joseph's appearance at the royal court at Alexandria and his proposal to introduce far-reaching reforms into the system of tax collection in the Ptolemaic province of Syria and Phoenicia. According to this account, tax collection in the province had until then been administered by local individuals who had obtained from the king the privilege of serving as tax-farmers in their own city. Here Josephus is certainly accurate, since papyri and ostraca bear witness to the fact that this was the prevailing system in Egypt proper.[27] Joseph son of Tobiah suggested that the office of the petty tax-farmers be abolished and that tax-collection in the whole Syrian province be concentrated in the hands of a single person, namely himself. Although there is reason to doubt the total sum which Joseph supposedly promised to secure annually for the king,[28] it is hardly possible that the financial reform itself was merely a product of imagination. If that were so, there would be no way of explaining how Joseph achieved such fame. He was obviously a man of considerable financial acumen, and his project of concentrating the collection of all taxes in the hands of one person brought order and efficiency into the financial administration and increased the total amount of the tax. That is why the king accepted the proposal and nominated Joseph as head tax-collector for the whole province of Syria and Phoenicia.[29]

Joseph's authority was not confined to financial affairs only. It was to be expected that the Greek cities in Palestine would resist the reform and that force would have to be used to ensure order and maintain discipline. And Josephus indeed records revolts in Ashkelon and Beth-shean (Scythopolis) which were crushed by soldiers whom the king had given Joseph son of Tobiah for the purpose.

A strong ruling hand in Syria and, above all, an increase in revenue were highly welcome to the Egyptian government, especially in view of the severe crisis which the Ptolemaic court was facing during the reign of Ptolemy IV Philopator (from 221 onwards) as a result of Antiochus III's invasion of Palestine (see p. 68 above). In this way, Joseph son of Tobiah, the scion of an ancient Jewish family, a citizen of Jerusalem and a wealthy prince from the land of the Ammonites, became one of the central personages, if not the most important one, in the Syrian province.

Joseph son of Tobiah's brilliant rise to eminence wrought no change in the situation of the Jewish nation under the Ptolemies. It was not as a representative of the Jews that he made his career. Far from benefiting his fellow-Jews, Joseph's activity as a high official of the king can only have harmed them. His actions as head tax-gatherer elicited a considerable animosity in Syria, above all in the Greek cities. He was presumably forced on a number of occasions to take harsh measures against reluctant taxpayers, as he had done in Ashkelon and Beth-shean. Joseph appears as a strong personality, making his way through life on his own, and taking responsibility for his own actions. This was a perfect Hellenistic type prepared to achieve his aims by all possible means, regardless of their moral justification or the sanction of the ancestral traditions of his people.[30]

It was not Jerusalem but Alexandria which Joseph regarded as the center of his political career. Josephus mentions in passing several details which characterize Joseph as an "international" type. For instance, before going to Alexandria, Joseph borrowed money from his "friends" in Samaria (*Ant.* XII, 168) showing that he was indifferent to the traditional, ancient enmity between Judea and Samaria. He presumably had friends at court as well. His principal agent, Arion, who conducted all his financial affairs (*ibid.*, 200–201), lived in Alexandria and certainly maintained contact with all the wealthy and influential circles. Joseph's being a member of the Jewish people did not in any way determine his attitude towards the great world which lay on the other side of the Judean Mountains. As a Hellenist, the borders of his little native country had no significance for him. Any other land where he could rise to riches and high position would suit him just as well.

Obviously, a man of this kind could easily acquire the customs and habits of the Hellenistic world and would feel more Greek than Jew. Tobiah, Joseph's father, had already been an Egyptian official appointed by the king and, as seen above, his house was open to Hellenistic influences. In his son's time the relations between his family and Alexandria became much stronger. Josephus mentions that Joseph, as well as other members of his family, were frequent visitors in Alexandria. We learn, for instance, that Joseph's brother made a visit to Alexandria for the purpose of marrying his daughter to one of the heads of the Jewish community there (*Ant.* XII, 187). Joseph himself dined more than once at the king's table, and it may be assumed that on such occasions he was not too strict about the dietary laws.[31] Moreover, there is an account of his falling in love with a dancing-girl at a banquet, and seeking to make her his mistress (*ibid.*, 187 ff.).

All these stories point to a break-up of the traditional pattern of modest living which Jerusalem Jews had inherited from their ancestors, and to their entrance into the broad and free Hellenistic world. If Josephus writes about Joseph son of Tobiah that he "had brought the Jewish people from poverty and a state of weakness to more splendid opportunities of life," it is clear that he wanted to emphasize the change which had taken place in the life of the Jews as a result of the activities of Joseph and members of his family. It is hardly likely that, having once seen the splendor and abundance of life in Alexandria, which attracted people so much by its external beauty and inner freedom, Joseph would have been satisfied with the modest and humble life prevailing in Judea and Jerusalem. He was certainly the first to open his house in Jerusalem to the extensive influence of international Hellenism, and if already in his father's house there had been Greek secretaries conducting their master's business in Greek, the house of Joseph all the more so served as a center of Greek influence, in all its various manifestations.

C. Hyrcanus the Tobiad and his Brothers

Joseph son of Tobiah was the father of a large family. His first wife bore him seven sons, and another son, Hyrcanus, was born to him by his second wife, who was his niece. The Tobiad family chronicles, which do not spare apocryphal elements in accounts of Joseph son of Tobiah, become pure legend when chronicling Hyrcanus' life. This is so full of imaginary elements that a modern historian has great difficulty in discovering the historical truth concealed in it. Hyrcanus is depicted in the legend as Joseph's favorite son and much cleverer than all his older brothers. The father made no secret of his affection for Hyrcanus, thereby inspiring the older sons with an intense hatred towards their younger brother. The biblical story about Joseph and his brothers patently served the writer as a model for this legend. Nevertheless, undisguised hatred certainly did exist between the older sons of Joseph and Hyrcanus, for the fact is also stressed in other parts of the narrative which do not bear the earmarks of a legend.

The narrative about Hyrcanus centers around the journey to Egypt which he undertook when news reached Joseph that a son had been born to King Ptolemy and that all Syrians of high rank were going to Alexandria to congratulate the king and bring him gifts. Being too old to travel himself, Joseph sent his son instead (*Ant.* XII, 196 ff.). His elder sons, he felt, were not equal to such a delicate diplomatic mission, because they lacked the appropriate education.[32] If the statement about the birth of the Egyptian crown prince is taken as a historical fact, then Hyrcanus' journey to Alexandria occurred in the year 209 or 210, and this date also agrees with the figure for Joseph's age.[33] Parts of the story about Hyrcanus' activities in Alexandria are quite unbelievable. He is said to have offered the king and queen such costly gifts that none of the presents brought by other Syrians of high rank could compete with them. To buy them Hyrcanus spent a third of his father's Egyptian wealth and threw Arion, who had opposed the demands of the young spendthrift, into prison. These stories are not only blatant exaggerations, but they also have no justification in the legend itself, since according to the story Hyrcanus did not pursue any material interest, but only asked the king to write favorable letters about him to his father and brothers.

Yet the same family chronicles relate that Hyrcanus' brothers dispatched letters to the "king's friends," i.e., courtiers in Alexandria who were close to the king, requesting them to kill Hyrcanus (*ibid.*, 218), and when he set out for home his brothers lay in wait for him and tried to murder him. Two brothers fell in the battle that ensued between them and Hyrcanus' men. Clearly, Hyrcanus' activities in Alexandria had a definite goal which was fraught with disaster for his brothers and it is not difficult to deduce what that goal was. He aspired to his father's official position at court and to his father's post as head tax-collector in Syria. This conjecture provides a plausible explanation of conditions in Joseph's home at that time. If Joseph was unable to travel to Alexandria because of his age, then, presumably he had also ceased in fact to act as the head tax-collector, or at least he could be expected to relinquish the office quite soon. The question was: who would succeed to the post and to the large revenues it brought. It would be quite natural for one of the older sons to step forward as the father's heir and indeed, the very fact that the elder brothers could write letters to the "king's friends" in Alexandria proves that there were close connections between them and the court. For Hyrcanus to try to supplant his brothers in this office, which legitimately belonged to them, was an act of extraordinary audacity. Nevertheless he did so, and evidently his attempt was successful for the family chronicles clearly testify that the king had written favorable letters about Hyrcanus to several high officials in Syria (*ibid.*, 220). There is also a highly significant remark that Joseph did not dare show his anger to his youngest son because he "feared the king" (*ibid.*, 221).

Hyrcanus' success in Alexandria occasioned a serious crisis in Judea. In spite of the king's letters, Hyrcanus' brothers were not willing to accept the authority of their young brother, and after two of them had fallen by the hand of Hyrcanus and his men, there can have been little prospect of reconciliation between the two sides. When Hyrcanus appeared in Jerusalem all doors closed to him, and he had no alternative but to leave the city and settle in Transjordan (*ibid.*, 222). A short sentence in Josephus says that after the death of Joseph son of Tobiah the struggle between Hyrcanus and his brothers flared up again, with the majority of the people, as well as the High Priest, on the side of the elder brothers (*ibid.*, 228 f.). Unfortunately the precise date of Joseph's death is unknown, nor is there any information whether it occurred when Palestine was still under Ptolemaic rule, or when power had already passed into the hands of Antiochus III, or perhaps during the war itself. However, in those years every internal quarrel was bound to acquire an international political character. Hyrcanus had purchased his office from the king for a great deal of money and he undoubtedly regarded himself as an Egyptian official, the representative in Palestine of King Ptolemy, like his grandfather Tobiah, and his father Joseph, before him. And if Hyrcanus was on the side of Ptolemy, then his elder brothers surely sought the support of the rival political power which was about to take over southern Syria, i.e., the Seleucid kingdom and its ruler, Antiochus III.[34] The evidence that the High Priest, Simeon the Just, sided with Hyrcanus' brothers also attests to the pro-Seleucid orientation of the brothers, for, as pointed out above, Simeon the Just welcomed Antiochus III on the latter's arrival in Jerusalem.[35] As an adherent of Ptolemaic rule, Hyrcanus could not possibly remain in Jerusalem, and therefore established his permanent residence in Transjordan. How the ancestral estate of the Tobiad family in the land of the Ammonites passed to Hyrcanus is not known; it may have come about by agreement between both family factions, or, most likely, by Hyrcanus' resorting to force. In any case Hyrcanus inherited his grandfather Tobiah's estate, for Josephus mentions his residing in a place called Tyre (Τύρος) near Heshbon, which is easily identifiable with Birta in the land of the Ammonites, the center of the *cleruchy* of the Ptolemaic soldiers under Tobiah.[36] Josephus describes in detail the stronghold Hyrcanus erected there in the form of a splendid palace with large halls for feasting and entertainment built in subterranean caves.[37] Thereafter Hyrcanus spent his life in continuous wars against the Arabs, but the purpose of these wars is unknown — it may have been to extend and strengthen his power or from a need to defend himself against tribes seeking to overrun the whole region. Josephus writes that Hyrcanus held these places for seven years and that he committed suicide after King Antiochus Epiphanes ascended the throne, i.e., about the year 175 (*Ant.* XII, 234 ff.). Here again we are helpless before the chronological enigmas of Josephus. If the assumption about Hyrcanus' retreat from Jerusalem to Transjordan in 200 is correct, then the latter ruled these places not for seven but about twenty-five years. It may be accordingly supposed that Josephus meant only the last period of Hyrcanus' rule in Transjordan, and this short period may have come after Hyrcanus had temporarily achieved a certain position in Jerusalem. II Maccabees relates that at the time of the High Priest Onias III, Simeon the Just's successor, the wealth of "Hyrcanus son of Tobiah" (i.e., Hyrcanus son of Joseph of the Tobiad family) was kept in the treasury of the Temple in Jerusalem, and that the High Priest spoke of Hyrcanus with great respect (II Macc. 3:11). The mists of uncertainty that enshroud this period prevent us from establishing how Hyrcanus finally succeeded in attaining a position in Jerusalem. Did he come to an agreement with his brothers? Did he switch his adherence from the Ptolemies and officially back the Seleucids? Or, was the High Priest Onias III perhaps an adherent of the pro-Ptolemaic policy?[38] There is no answer to these questions and little sense in offering conjectures. One conclusion, however, may be drawn with a fair degree of certainty from Hyrcanus' tragic death. As will be seen below, Antiochus Epiphanes adopted strong measures to strengthen the Seleucid state and maintain its integrity, and Hyrcanus fell victim to this policy. He ruled his estate in the land of the Ammonites not like a rich landowner but like an independent prince or petty king, waging wars at his own discretion and with his own forces against the Arabs of the vicinity.[39] It is thus possible that Hyrcanus aimed at establishing a small independent principality in the frontier region between the two mighty kingdoms, and that the "seven years" mentioned in Josephus is the period during which he appeared to the outside world as an independent ruler.[40] The establishment of such an independent state would certainly not suit Antiochus Epiphanes at all, and after Hyrcanus had realized that he would be forced to submit to the king or else to wage a hopeless war, he took what seemed to him the only way out and committed suicide. The details which Josephus presents about Hyrcanus' last years, his wars and defeats, his splendid palaces and the life of luxury and dissipation he led, all shroud his figure in mystery. Right down to our own time historians have been inclined to attribute far-reaching projects and actions to Hyrcanus, as a means of explaining his strange life.[41] Yet his personality seems strange only when approached from the point of view of Jewish traditional life in Jerusalem. If Hyrcanus is considered not as a Jew but as a Hellenist, then there is no mystery at all, since adventurers of this kind were very numerous both during and after the Diadochi period. Like his father Joseph, Hyrcanus is portrayed as a strong man who broke away from fixed traditions and aspired to a broader, brighter life than the one he saw in his native land. His father's activities had been concentrated in the financial sphere, whereas his own related to political aspirations. And it is here that the key to his failure must be sought. Such daring political projects succeed only if they are backed by large masses of the population, or are carried out by organized, well-trained forces of professional mercenaries. When these basic conditions are lacking, and the attempt to establish an independent kingdom is made in a vacuum, without the necessary support, it is not surprising that it fails even before reaching the stage of realization, nor that the entire structure collapses like a house of cards the moment it comes into contact with harsh reality. A Jewish kingdom was indeed to be established during this period, but not by an adventurer, nor in a remote corner of Transjordan, but as the result of a large scale national movement and in the ancient center of Jewish culture — in Judea and Jerusalem.

D. JERUSALEM SOCIETY

The general social background of the Hellenistic Age in Palestine and the beginning of the Hellenistic influence on Jewish society have been described in previous sections. An attempt will now be made to present on the basis of the meager sources available a general picture of the various classes comprised by Jewish society in Jerusalem.

Josephus (*Against Apion* II, 165) calls the social and political order of the

Jews in that period a "theocracy," i.e., "God's rule," whereas modern scholars justly interpret "theocracy" as "hierocracy," i.e., "priestly rule." The High Priest represented the people before the outside world, and all state affairs, both religious and secular, were concentrated in his hands. The literature of the Hellenistic Age faithfully reflects the strong impression created by the High Priest, and by the priesthood in general, on everyone who came into contact with them. Hecataeus of Abdera gives the total number of priests as 1,500, but this figure is certainly too small. Hecataeus probably meant the priests of Jerusalem alone, but there were also numerous priests living in various villages and estates in the vicinity of the capital.[42] According to Hecataeus, Moses had chosen the most distinguished men and put them at the head of the people as priests, committing into their hands the care of the Temple, its service and the sacrificial rituals. He also appointed them as judges to decide on all important matters and to enforce the observance of the laws and customs. "Therefore," says Hecataeus, "the Jews had never had a king, and the function of representation (*prostasia*) was given to the priest, who excelled all others in wisdom and superior qualities. They call him the High Priest and consider him a Divine Messenger who brings them God's commandments, He is said to transmit God's commandments at assemblies of the people and other meetings, and the Jews show such great obedience to these things that immediately they prostrate themselves before the High Priest who interprets to them [God's words]" (Diodorus XL, 5–6). In Hecataeus' eyes, accordingly, the High Priest appeared as an intermediary between the people and God, and the Greek writer may be applying to the High Priest concepts he had learned from the Egyptian priests.[43] It is worth noting that out of the whole population of Jerusalem Hecataeus took note of only one social group — the priests, which indicates that in his time the priestly class was the only one which could attract a stranger.

A picture resembling the one portrayed by Hecataeus is also presented in a book known as the *Letter of Aristeas*. Although an Alexandrian Jew, the writer assumes the guise of Aristeas, an educated Greek at the court of Ptolemy II Philadelphus, and puts his own sentiments into the mouth of this character.[44] Aristeas' narrative also includes the story of a journey he made from Alexandria to Jerusalem with the object of negotiating with the High Priest. This time it is not a Greek writer describing Jerusalem, but a Jew from the Diaspora, still, the same things that made an impression on Hecataeus aroused the admiration of the Alexandrian visitor. Aristeas describes the city of Jerusalem and Palestine only briefly. The main part of his story is taken up by a description of the Temple and the High Priest, and all the other priests officiating at divine service. Aristeas' description of the High Priest Eleazar and his appearance in the Temple follows:

> We were struck with great astonishment when we beheld Eleazar at his ministration, and his apparel, and the visible glory conferred by his being garbed in the coat which he wears and the stones that adorn his person. For there are bells of gold upon the skirts of the robe giving out a peculiar musical sound, and on either side of these are pomegranates broidered with flowers marvelously colorful. He was girt with a rich and magnificent girdle, woven with most beautiful colors. And upon his breast he wears what is called the oracle, in which are set twelve stones of various species soldered with gold, with the names of the heads of the tribes, according to their original constitution, each of them flashing forth indescribably with the natural color of its own peculiar character. Upon his head he has the tiara as it is called, and on top of this the inimitable miter, bearing engraven in sacred letters upon a plate of gold set between his eyebrows the name of God filled with glory (*Letter of Aristeas*, 96–98).[45]

The divine service performed by the priests in the Temple arouses no less admiration in the Alexandrian Jew:

> In its exhibition of strength and in its orderly and silent performance the ministration of the priests could in no way be surpassed. All of them, self-bidden, carry out labors involving great toil, and each has his appointed charge. Their service is unceasing, some attending to the wood, others the oil, others the fine wheat flour, others the business of spices, and still others the portions of flesh for burnt offering, employing extraordinary strength in this task. For with both hands they grasp the legs of the calves, almost all of which weigh more than two talents each, and then with marvellous deftness they fling them to a considerable height with their two hands, and they never fail of placing the victim correctly (*ibid.*, 92–93) ... Complete silence prevails, so that one might suppose that not a person was present in the place, though those performing the service amount to some seven hundred — besides the great multitude of persons bringing sacrifices to be offered — but everything is done with reverence and in a manner worthy of the great Divinity (*ibid.*, 95).

Aristeas was a stranger in Jerusalem, so it is not surprising that the splendor and magnificence of the Temple should have made so deep an impression upon a Jew coming from afar to prostrate himself before God in the Holy City. Yet it is worth noting that the Jerusalem Jews themselves, though accustomed to the sight of the Temple and the splendor attending the divine service on the great festivals, were also full of a profound admiration for the Temple and all the proceedings within and around it. Reliable evidence of it comes from Ben Sira, who describes the appearance of the High Priest, Simeon the Just, before the people, with genuine enthusiasm:

> How glorious was he when he looked forth from the Tent,
>   And when he came out from the sanctuary!
> Like a morning-star from between the clouds,
>   And like the full moon on the feast-days;
> Like the sun shining upon the Temple of the Most High,
>   And like the rainbow becoming visible in the cloud;
> Like a flower on the branches in the days of the first-fruits,
>   And as a lily by the water-brooks,
> As a sprout of Lebanon on summer days (50:5–8) . . .
>
> When he put on his glorious robes,
>   And clothed himself in perfect splendor,
> When he went up to the altar of majesty,
>   And made glorious the court of the sanctuary;
> When he took the portions from the hand of his brethren,
>   While standing by the blocks of wood,
> Around him the garland of his sons,
>   Like young cedar-trees in Lebanon;
> And like willows by the brook did they surround him,
>   All the sons of Aaron in their glory,
> And the Lord's fire-offering in their hands,
>   In the presence of the whole congregation of Israel.
> Until he had finished the service of the altar
>   And arranging the rows of wood of the Most High,
> [And] stretched forth his hand to the cup,
>   And poured out of the blood of the grape;
> Yea, poured [it] out at the foot of the altar,
>   A sweet-smelling savor to the Most High, the All-King.
> Then the sons of Aaron sounded
>   With the trumpets of beaten work;
> Yea, they sounded and caused a mighty blast to be heard
>   For a remembrance before the Most High.

[Then] all flesh hasted together
　　And fell upon their faces to the earth,
To worship before the Most High,
　　Before the Holy One of Israel.
And the sound of the song was heard,
　　And over the multitude they made sweet melody;
And all the people of the land cried
　　In prayer before the Merciful,
Until he had finished the service of the altar,
　　And his ordinances had brought him nigh unto Him.
Then he descended, and lifted up his hands
　　Upon the whole congregation of Israel,
And the blessing of the Lord [was] upon his lips,
　　And he glorified himself with the name of the Lord.
And again they fell down, [now] to receive
　　The pardon of God from him (*ibid.*, 11–21).

As these accounts indicate, it was the external splendor of the High Priest and the service of the priests which made the greatest impression on every person visiting the Temple. Yet for the priests, the Temple was important not only as the center of worship, but for several other reasons as well. It was also the center of their political power over the people, and it also played an important part economically. Like every other temple of ancient times, the Temple in Jerusalem served as a depository for vast treasures which flowed to it from all over the world. The treasury of the Temple was full of silver and gold, and it was only natural that such a place, protected from the danger of theft and robbery, should also have acted as a kind of bank where various public funds and private persons deposited money for safe-keeping.[46] As to political power, the rights of priests connected with the Temple were included in the concept of "ancestral laws" and were officially approved by the government. Josephus quotes an interesting document from the time of Antiochus III, which contains a "declaration" (πρόγραμμα) forbidding the admittance of strangers (i.e., non-Jews) into the Temple.[47] Together with this declaration Josephus also preserves the contents of another decree which says that it is forbidden to bring unclean animals to Jerusalem, or to breed them in the city, meaning, apparently, the inner city bordering on the Temple. From all this we learn that the Temple was as it were under the special protection of the Seleucid king, who had even pledged monetary contributions for the offerings. Not that the Seleucid king was interested in the Jewish religion and its cult. He only gave official sanction to the situation in force in Jerusalem, i.e., to the absolute power of the priests over the Temple and the city (cf. above, p. 75).

Since the return from the Babylonian Captivity the priests had been divided into families, and to judge from Nehemiah's narrative, many of them lived outside the city of Jerusalem, coming to the Temple only when it was the turn of their family to perform the divine service (cf. above, note 42). It presumably follows that the pattern of life of many priestly families must have been more rural than urban, and that a gap separated the rich Jerusalemite priests from the numerous priestly families living in the countryside. It was no accident that the Hellenistic movement with its aim of introducing far-reaching reforms into the life of the Jewish nation should have arisen among the rich priests of Jerusalem. Nor was it by chance that the nationalist movement found its principal protagonists in the remote village of Modiin, the home of the Maccabees. Unfortunately, historical sources about the various priestly families are lacking, and there is information about only one family: the ruling one — the family of the High Priests known as the "Oniads." According to ancient tradition, the office of High Priest descended from father to son by right of inheritance. In any case, it always remained in the same family. We are familiar with the dynasty of the High Priests from Jaddua, the contemporary of Alexander the Great, down to the Hasmonean period, but there is no concrete evidence that all the names in this list can be accepted unquestionably. According to Josephus, the office of High Priest descended from Jaddua to Onias I (*Ant.* XI, 347) and from him to his son Simeon the Just (*ibid.* XII, 43). After the death of Simeon the Just, power did not pass to his son Onias II, because he was still too young, but to his brother, Eleazar (*ibid.* XII, 44) and after the death of Eleazar the office went to his uncle Manasseh (*ibid.* XII, 157). Only after the death of Manasseh did Onias II take over the High Priesthood. The son of Onias II was Simeon II, a contemporary of Antiochus III, and after his death he was succeeded by his son Onias III. Modern scholars are sceptical about this list because of the obscure passages and even obvious mistakes which it contains.[48] Josephus does not know anything about Simeon's brother, Eleazar, except what he had learned from the *Letter of Aristeas*, where the name of the High Priest is given as Eleazar. But the *Letter of Aristeas* is not a reliable source. It is a kind of historical novel, and it is possible that the writer may well have chosen a fictitious person as his hero, and may not have been referring to any of the High Priests who actually held office in Jerusalem. It is even more difficult to explain the strange fact that the office of High Priest passed to Manasseh after the death of Eleazar. The name is not mentioned in any other source, and we do not know for what reason it was introduced into the list of High Priests.[49] Again, there are good grounds for supposing that Simeon the Just was not Simeon I as claims Josephus, but Simeon II, a contemporary of Ben Sira (cf. below, p. 31 note[35]). If Eleazar and Manasseh are deleted, the following list of six names from the time of Alexander the Great down to Antiochus Epiphanes remains: Jaddua, Onias I, Simeon I, Onias II, Simeon II the Just, and Onias III.

As stated above, the only evidence extant concerns the Oniads, since members of this family were the people's leaders and held power. Abundant evidence also exists about the Tobiads, but they are never referred to as the members of a priestly family, and the part they played in Jewish history is definitely secular. The family of the great Hellenizers to which the three brothers Simeon, Menelaus, and Lysimachus belonged, was also a priestly one, but even its name is doubtful (see Chapter 5 below). Names of priestly families appear in the register of those who had been in exile and returned from Babylon (Ezra 2; Neh. 7), but for us these are mere names, without any significance. Some families, such as that of the sons of Hezir, are known by chance from excavations or through casual mention in historical sources. Yet even in such cases, as that of the sons of Hezir, about whom there is clear epigraphic testimony, nothing is known except the names.[50]

Even less detailed evidence has been preserved of the secular aristocracy. Again there is the long register in Ezra 2 and Nehemiah 7. And once more only names are given. Nevertheless, Nehemiah speaks of "nobles and rulers." These were the rich nobles, the owners of large estates. If they existed in Nehemiah's time, there is no reason to think that they disappeared in the Hellenistic Age. The existence of the *Gerousia*, the Council of Elders, is proof that the nobles ruled the people, since it was an institution of the aristocracy in the cities of Greece as well. It may be assumed that the main revenues of these nobles were drawn from agricultural estates. Nehemiah fought for the rights of the small peasants and freed them from economic bondage to the "nobles and rulers" (Neh. 5:1 ff.), but his reforms were introduced just on a single occasion. Nothing would be known of this reform were it not for Hecataeus, who distinctly asserts that in his time there existed in Israel a law prohibiting small peasants to sell their landed property (Diodorus XL, 7). The existence of such a law indicates that the Jerusalemite nobles sought to amass land at the expense of the small peasants, and that the authorities in Jerusalem sensibly decided to put an end to this process by introducing a special law. It may be doubted whether this law remained in force throughout the whole Hellenistic period, but the fact remains that at the time of the Hasmonean rebellion small peasants constituted the main force of the fighters for freedom. From this it may be concluded that the long struggle between rich estate owners and small peasants ended in a compromise. The bond between Jerusalem and the villages was presumably very strong. Not only did many priests live permanently in the villages; the secular aristocracy, exempt from Temple duties, was even more closely attached to its estates.

In the meantime, new classes arose and gained strength in Jerusalem. According to Josephus, the activities of Joseph son of Tobiah "had brought the Jewish people from poverty and a state of weakness to more splendid opportunities of life," i.e., he had initiated a transformation of the traditional pattern of life by introducing new customs. These customs were undoubtedly borrowed from the Hellenistic world. Moreover, it is also clear that Josephus was talking about men of wealth and authority, the only ones who had established close connections with this Hellenistic world and came under the influence of the new life. It is possible that the first to be carried along by the stream were not the rich landowners but the new classes which emerged in Jewish society together with the rise of Hellenism; these were government officials, tax-collectors and their agents, rich merchants, and others. To use modern terminology, a rich bourgeois class came into being, whose influence was felt for the first time in the period of the Second Temple. Care should be taken, of course, to avoid exaggeration. It should not be assumed, for instance, that the merchants constituted a large proportion of rich Jerusalemites. In the ancient world only trade with overseas countries brought riches, and in Palestine this commerce was not controlled by Jews but by Greek coastal cities such as Gaza, Acco, Tyre, etc. Aristeas (§ 114) writes that the profitable widespread incense trade was in the hands of Arabs, not Jews. As early as the time of Nehemiah trade in foodstuffs (or at least part of it) was the province of Tyrian merchants (Neh. 13:16), and this situation may not have changed by the Hellenistic period. This does not, of course, mean that there were no merchants at all in Jerusalem, but their numbers were probably not large.[51] On the other hand, many undoubtedly made a living from tax-collecting and money-lending. Joseph son of Tobiah and members of his family were the most striking examples of this class of people, but it must be assumed that they had at their disposal numerous agents and attendants, who learned business methods from them and became specialists in money matters. At all times, everywhere, people of this kind were hated by the mass of the population, for obvious reasons. No wonder class enmity between rich and poor became so acute in Jerusalem at the beginning of Seleucid rule (approximately 200–180).

There are several examples of this class hostility in Ben Sira's book. Ben Sira speaks of the rich and the poor as two separate worlds hating one another:

> All flesh loveth its kind
> >And every man his like.
> All flesh consorteth according to its kind
> >And with his kind man associateth (13 : 15–16).

Accordingly, the rich consort with the rich and the poor are drawn to the poor:

> What peace can the hyena have with the dog
> >Or what peace rich with poor?
> Food for the lion are the wild asses of the desert:
> >Even so the pasture of the rich are the poor (*ibid.*, 18–19).

The poor man should avoid approaching the powerful since, if he falls into the latter's hands, it means the end of him. The rich man uses the poor man to his own advantage, but mocks him in times of distress. Only the voices of the rich and the mighty are heard at popular gatherings and rulers' assemblies, and when the poor man dares to open his mouth he is greeted with scorn. There is no hope for a poor man to oppose the rich. Consequently Ben Sira thinks it imperative to preach obedience to authority. In any case, he is careful not to stir up the city masses to rebellion. There is only one way open to the poor — the study of wisdom and moral accomplishment. Although Ben Sira does not explicitly identify the poor with the just and the rich with the wicked, a number of citations in the book convey the impression that only in the poor and the humble does he find the highest degree of morality. And if this is so from the moral point of view, it is equally the case from the point of view of religion, since morals and religion cannot be separated. It is easy to see that men such as Joseph son of Tobiah and his son Hyrcanus, who forsook Jewish traditions for the Hellenistic way of life, were not the ones who evoked the sympathy of the Jewish sage. On the contrary, it was precisely among people of lower rank — who clung to tradition and lived according to their ancestral customs — that Ben Sira found people to whom his ideas would be most readily acceptable.

Unfortunately, evidence concerning the lower classes of the urban and rural population is sparse. Small peasants formed the majority of the populace, and as noted above, their landed property was protected by law against the rapacity of their rich neighbors. But what was the size of their lands? How did they run their economy? How did they cultivate their lands, and how did they provide for their needs? To these questions there are no answers. Nor is there more information about the "urban proletariat," to use a modern term. Various craftsmen are mentioned in Nehemiah and in Ben-Sira, but these details are not enough to provide the entire picture.[52] The fact that in later periods the rabbis showed a predilection for crafts serves as a measure of proof that these elements were already well defined at the beginning of the Hellenistic period. Perhaps it would not be wrong to assume that the majority of the urban population consisted of various kinds of craftsmen. The new forms of life introduced into Judea by Joseph son of Tobiah increased the need of the upper strata of Jerusalem society for the ostentations of a life of luxury and pleasure. It seems reasonable to assume that many of the Jerusalem poor were engaged in manufacturing and perfecting luxury items ordered for the homes of the nobles. Masons, smiths, potters, tailors, and other craftsmen were all able to benefit from the new life developing in Jerusalem as a result of the Hellenization of the ruling classes. Not that this minor economic advance could bridge the gulf dividing Jerusalem society. Wealth and luxury were the share of a few elect only, and the more conspicuous their luxury became, the stronger grew the hatred of the lower classes. Gradually, sharp contrasts developed within Jewish society in Jerusalem. There was the social conflict between the rich and the poor; the political dissension between the supporters of the Seleucid government and the adherents of the Ptolemies; and the cultural and religious differences between the followers of the ancient Jewish tradition and those who were attracted to the new Hellenistic life. It is easy to see that in the first decades of the 2nd century B.C.E. Jewish society in Jerusalem was ridden with profound internal conflicts. A man capable of interpreting the omens of the time could have prophesied the great storm that was soon to break over the heads of the people who lived in Zion.

CHAPTER V

THE HELLENISTIC MOVEMENT IN JERUSALEM AND ANTIOCHUS' PERSECUTIONS

by V. Tcherikover

A. SOURCES

THE SOURCES FOR THE PERIOD of Antiochus Epiphanes and the early Hasmoneans are more numerous than those available for the preceding period (see above, p. 53–6). However, they are just as inadequate for drawing a detailed picture of the events which took place in Jerusalem and Judea at that time, especially since their approach is generally one-sided. Accordingly, the method of conjecture will be applied in reconstructing the historical processes during this period too.

One of the most important sources is the Book of Daniel,[1] which was partly composed at the time of Antiochus' persecutions. Thus it is the sole source which has its origin precisely in the stormy period preceding the appearance of Judah Maccabee. The Book of Daniel, however, is not the work of a historian but the vision of a prophet, or a poet, portraying contemporary events in a lyrical style and a recondite vocabulary. The author of this book was apparently one of the *Ḥasidim*, i.e., a group imbued with an extreme religious-national spirit which regarded not only the Syrian kings in general, and Antiochus Epiphanes in particular, but also all Greeks and Hellenized Jews as the most dangerous enemies of the people of Israel and its religion. A calm and objective record of events should not be sought in a book written during a time of great trials for the followers and defenders of the Jewish religion. It is also far from easy to decipher Daniel's enigmatic language. Only a knowledge of the events of the time derived from a comparison with other sources makes it possible for us to understand the true meaning of various passages in the Book of Daniel. Above (p. 80–8), it has already been pointed out how many different interpretations were given to verse 11:14 of Daniel, which relates to events of the years 200–198. No wonder that the parts dealing with the time of Antiochus Epiphanes also evoked no small number of different and peculiar interpretations. Thus, Daniel's evidence can be accepted only very cautiously, and never without thorough examination. At any rate, no decisive historical conclusions should be drawn from the book's vague statements.[2]

Then there are the Books of the Maccabees. Christian tradition has preserved four books designated by the name "Maccabees." Yet only the first two, I Maccabees and II Maccabees, are true historical works referring to the events of the early Hasmonean period.[3] I Maccabees opens with a very short description of the events of the period from Alexander the Great to Antiochus Epiphanes. This account becomes much more detailed with the appearance of Mattathias the priest and his five sons. The author depicts the period of Judah Maccabee and his brothers, Jonathan and Simeon, and ends with the rule of John Hyrcanus. There are sufficient grounds for supposing that the author lived at the time of John Hyrcanus and wrote his book as an official historian of the Hasmonean court. Certainly all his sympathies are with that splendid dynasty,[4] while in his eyes, enemies of the line, and in particular the Hellenized Jews, are all sinners and transgressors.

Although written in Hebrew and in the spirit of the books of the early prophets, it was preserved only in Greek translation. The author displays considerable familiarity with politics, and has preserved for us some important documents of the period.[5] Scholars rightly consider I Maccabees the most valuable source of the early Hasmonean period. The author reports events simply and without rhetorical embellishment, yet it must be borne in mind that his strong sympathy for the dynasty no doubt influenced his choice of historical material and his approach to it. A historian who makes it his aim to erect a splendid monument to a dynasty so dear to him is unlikely to confine himself to the dispassionate objectivity now demanded — sometimes in vain — of every conscientious scholar.[6]

While historians of our day regard I Maccabees as an excellent historical source, opinions are divided with respect to II Maccabees. The historical problems connected with a study of this book are much more complicated than those of I Maccabees. First and foremost, II Maccabees is not an original work. The author announces his intention of describing the Hasmonean revolt in a single book condensed from the five volumes written about that period by Jason of Cyrene (II Macc. 2:23). We do not know who this Jason was or when he lived, nor is there any knowledge of the exact limits of the period about which he wrote. If the author of II Maccabees is to be trusted (and there is no reason to doubt his explicit statements), Jason depicted only the activities of Judah Maccabee and his brothers in the reign of Antiochus Epiphanes and his son Antiochus Eupator (*ibid* 2:19 ff.). Thus it follows that the great work of Jason ended with a description of approximately the same events as does II Maccabees. The last occurrence mentioned in II Maccabees is the victory of Judah

Maccabee over the Syrian commander Nicanor (161 B.C.E.). Thus, the account of II Maccabees does not even go as far as the death of Judah Maccabee. This does not mean, of course, that Jason also ended his work with "Nicanor's day," and it may be assumed that he did mention the tragic end of Judah Maccabee. However, there is no reason to think that he also wrote about the rule of Jonathan and Simeon, since this assumption would take us beyond the chronological limits mentioned by the author of II Maccabees.[7] From here it follows that Jason's aim differed completely from that of the author of I Maccabees. He is not interested in the whole of the Hasmonean dynasty, but only in the activities of Judah Maccabee, who had apparently deeply impressed him. Since he gives such a full account of Judah Maccabee's deeds, he also finds it necessary to detail the events which led up to the appearance of his hero. An abbreviated account of these events also appears in II Maccabees, which describes the long internal struggle in Jerusalem that preceded Antiochus' persecutions. This short record is of great historical value as a source of information about the Hellenistic reform in Jerusalem and the whole complex of events which served as a pretext for Antiochus Epiphanes' interference in Jewish affairs. These records, written by Jason of Cyrene and transmitted to us by the author of II Maccabees, have aroused the doubts of modern historians, who prefer even today to rely upon I Maccabees rather than draw conclusions from II Maccabees. And, indeed, the narrative of II Maccabees contains many defects, such as chronological confusion, exaggerated descriptions of miraculous deeds, legendary accounts, and so on.[8] Yet, one thing can be said in favor of the author of II Maccabees — he was chronologically close to the events he describes — since Jason of Cyrene, who served as a model for the author, was apparently a contemporary of Judah Maccabee, and may even have taken part in the war under the latter's command. Without such an assumption it is difficult to explain why he devoted such a detailed account to so short a period.[9] His book was written in Greek, which was also the original language of II Maccabees. The book even serves as a fair example of Greek historical writings in the Hellenistic Age.[10] In short, for all its deficiencies, II Maccabees remains an important historical source for the time of Judah Maccabee, while for the period preceding the revolt it is the sole detailed source, without which we would have no idea whatsover of the events which took place in Jerusalem.

There remains Josephus. In recording the early Hasmonean period Josephus follows I Maccabees, and his narrative has no value as an original account. In dealing with the period preceding the revolt of Judah Maccabee, Josephus was not quite up to par as a historian. He read neither the work of Jason of Cyrene nor II Maccabees; or, if he did, there is no hint in his writings that he used these books. However, since there were no other sources at his disposal, he contented himself with a few brief, superficial remarks based on sources which were unknown to him. There are also contradictions between his account of events in the *The Jewish War* (I, 31 ff.) and the version in *Antiquities* (XII, 237 ff.). These contradictions will be referred to later on, when discussing the events themselves.

B. JERUSALEM BEFORE THE HELLENISTIC REFORM

The events which led up to the Hellenistic reform in Jerusalem are complicated and not easy to understand. Our sources, without exception, depict the struggle between the Hellenizers and traditionalists as an attack by transgressors and evil men on the immortality of the Torah. Nowhere in the sources is there any attempt made to present the inner motives of the Hellenizing movement. To understand them, we have to read between the lines. Daniel describes the clash between those who "forsake the holy covenant" (11:30) and those who "are wise among the people" (11:33) as a struggle with a purely religious basis and the description in I Maccabees just about follows the same line. Yet it is clear from II Maccabees that political interests were also involved on both sides. What kind of interests were they? What did each side desire or aspire to? Again, both the author of II Maccabees and Josephus tell us that the background of conflicting interests was the lust for power of the mighty families who ruled in Judea. Thus political, social, and religious motives were intermingled in the short and stormy period preceding the Hellenistic reform. The historian's task is to unravel the inner motives behind the political and ideological programs of the contending factions.

The surprising feature of the developments in Judea and Jerusalem during the twelve years of Antiochus Epiphanes' reign is that the historical process began with trivialities and ended in momentous events which altered the course of Jewish history. The sources tell of minor conflicts between different persons, of struggles between powerful families, of intrigues within the ruling group, etc. Yet these insignificant incidents provoked a deep schism within the nation and at length led to bloody battles between the Jewish nation and the Syrian government. How could this have happened? There is no doubt that right from the beginning, the factors which were to end in upheavals of great historical importance were active among the Jewish population. Since the process began with a struggle between families, the questions should be asked: What social and political interests prompted this conflict? What was the spiritual aspect of each of the great families that took part in the events of that time?[11]

One family, which has been mentioned a number of times in previous chapters, was that of the Oniads — for many generations the holders of the High Priesthood.[12] At first glance, it hardly seems surprising that the High Priest, the head of Temple worship, should have defended the ancestral traditions and the Law of Moses. But the Oniads belonged to the class of the very wealthy and constituted the highest rank of the Jewish aristocracy. It was precisely this group which was most strongly influenced by Hellenistic culture; the emergence of a division among the Oniads, developing against the peculiar cultural background of Jewish society at the beginning of the 2nd century B.C.E., was therefore to be expected. Since the Oniads had been in power for so long there is little doubt that the family would always have defended its rights against any social forces aiming to deprive them of the foremost position in the state.

The family second in rank and influence in Jerusalem society were the Tobiads, whose origins and Hellenistic tendencies have been described above (p. 96–101). Nothing is known of the fate of the sons of Joseph son of Tobiah after control of Palestine passed from the Ptolemies to the Seleucids. Hyrcanus, the youngest son, continued to support the Ptolemies in Palestine, whereas his elder brothers were adherents of the Seleucids.[13] Two of them fell in a battle against Hyrcanus. The fate of the five remaining brothers is obscure, although it may be assumed that by virtue of the education they received in the home of their father, the head tax-collector and a businessman, they became political leaders and businessmen as well. Their support of the Seleucids was certainly advantageous to them at the king's court in Antioch, and just as their father Joseph was a frequent visitor at the court of King Ptolemy, so his sons would certainly have presented themselves occasionally before the Seleucid king in Antioch. They may also have performed various administrative and financial functions, such as tax-collection, etc. The Hellenistic tradition which had already made its appearance in the family at the time of Tobiah, prince in the land of the Ammonites, continued to take root among his descendants. Josephus mentions the Tobiads as the principal factor in the Hellenistic reform during the reign of Antiochus Epiphanes. In *Antiquities* (XII, 240 ff.), Josephus relates that the Tobiads had offered King Antiochus a plan for Hellenistic reform; their intention was "to abandon their country's laws and the way of life prescribed by these and to follow the king's laws and adopt the Greek way of life." They also asked him to allow them to erect a *gymnasium* in Jerusalem. In another place (*War* I, 31 ff.) Josephus gives a brief account of the struggle between the Oniads and the Tobiads without mentioning the Hellenistic reform; yet here, too, says Josephus, the Tobiads found a refuge at Antiochus' court and asked him to interfere in the affairs of Judea. These two passages will be considered again in our study of the political situation which developed in Judea.[14] For the time being, we must only keep in mind that Josephus emphasizes the political status of the Tobiads as the most important factor in all the events which took place at that time in Jerusalem, and notes in particular the significance of their participation in the Hellenistic reform, although officially it was not the Tobiads who carried it out.

The reform was carried out by another family whose name is not even known with any certainty. According to II Maccabees, three brothers — Simeon, Menelaus and Lysimachus — played an important part in the events; Simeon was the first to initiate hostile actions against the Oniads, and Menelaus seized the chair of the High Priest after the Hellenistic reform had taken root in Jerusalem. The author of II Maccabees mentions that Simeon belonged to the tribe of Benjamin (II Macc. 3:4) but this statement is not plausible, since it is hardly reasonable to assume that at that time the people of Jerusalem could distinguish between the descendants of Judah and Benjamin. Besides, as we shall see below, Simeon was a priest and as such could not possibly belong to the tribe of Benjamin. Modern scholars have put forward many different theories about the origins of this family, but so far, no unanimous opinion has been reached.[15] Only one detail is certain about the family of the three brothers, namely, that its members were priests. Evidently the brothers were on good terms with the Tobiads, who were also faithful adherents of the Hellenistic reform.

Now we come to the events themselves. The account in II Maccabees opens with a description of an incident which took place in the reign of King Seleucus IV Philopator (187–175), when Onias III was High Priest. The author of II Maccabees describes Onias' rule as a long period of peace and prosperity which came to an end when a quarrel flared up between Onias and Simeon the "warden of the Temple" (II Macc. 3:4). We do not know exactly what kind of office this was, though clearly it must have been one of the highest positions in the Temple administration.[16] Simeon was apparently not satisfied with his post and also requested the office of *agoranomia* in the city. Again, there is no knowledge what the role of an *agoranomos* was in Jerusalem, the Greek term having had several different meanings in the Hellenistic Age.[17] The High Priest refused Simeon's request whereupon the latter revealed to Apollonius, Seleucid governor of Coele-Syria and Phoenicia, the great riches which, as rumor had it, were kept in the treasury of the Temple in Jerusalem, emphasizing that they by far surpassed the needs of the service in the Temple, and that the king would derive considerable benefit by confiscating them. The matter was brought before the king, and a high Syrian official, Heliodorus, was sent to Jerusalem with an order to appropriate the money. Arriving at Jerusalem, Heliodorus demanded an exact account of all the wealth at the High Priest's disposal. Onias explained that the treasury contained funds for widows and orphans and also certain sums belonging to Hyrcanus the Tobiad, "a man of extremely high position." He claimed that the total amount of money in the treasury was no more than four hundred talents of silver and two hundred of gold and maintained that it would be a great injustice to hand over all this money to the king's treasury. It was money which people had brought to the treasury of the Temple, in the firm belief that that holy place was a repository of complete safety. Onias' claims, however, had no effect on Heliodorus. He resolved to carry out the king's order and confiscate the money. When he entered the treasury, however, a horseman in splendid attire appeared before him accompanied by two strong and handsome young men who seized Heliodorus from either side and scourged him until he fell to the ground in a faint. Only Onias' prayer to God revived Heliodorus, and the Seleucid official hastily returned to his own country (II Macc. 3).[18]

This is the story as told by the author of II Maccabees, and both historical and legendary elements are intermingled in the narrative. No doubt a historical fact lies behind the story: interference in the affairs of the Temple by a high Syrian official as a result of a denunciation received at the king's court. But it is not clear from the narrative what exactly was the subject of Simeon's indictment. As a priest and a high official in the Temple he could hardly have had an interest in the confiscation of the treasures which had accumulated there in the course of many generations. These treasures were not the private property of the High Priest, but a kind of common property at the disposal of the leaders of the Jerusalem theocracy. Evidently Simeon's denunciation related not to all the treasures of the Temple, but only to a certain part of them. Various points in the story make it clear that Simeon's intention was the confiscation of the deposits of private individuals lying in the Temple.[19] The name of Hyrcanus the Tobiad gives the key to the affair. Hyrcanus had been an adherent of the Ptolemies (see above), and was, it may be assumed, openly opposed to the government in Antioch which supported his elder brothers — his mortal foes. Onias III speaks with great respect of Hyrcanus, which indicates that he, too, inclined to the side of the Ptolemies, otherwise why had he accepted the deposit of Hyrcanus' money in the Temple treasury? If Hyrcanus had money deposited in Jerusalem, he would certainly have visited the capital, and it is easy to imagine that these visits would be a source of irritation to the Tobiads who were devoted to the Seleucids. Thus a split on a political basis is evident; Simeon's denunciation was presumably planned with the agreement of the Tobiads with the purpose of removing the pro-Ptolemaic High Priest Onias, whose daring policy appeared to them as fraught with disaster for the ruling aristocracy in Jerusalem. The end of the story is mere legend. Heliodorus was not beaten in the Temple at all; any such action would have been interpreted by the Syrian government as open rebellion and would have caused the dispatch of a Syrian army to Jerusalem. The Seleucid official may have reached an understanding with Onias, and since this agreement excluded the confiscation of the treasure, it appeared to the people as a miracle from Heaven. Yet even if there was some such agreement between Onias and Heliodorus, it did not lead to a settlement of the political situation in Jerusalem, for a short time after the latter's visit to Jerusalem, Simeon again sent a letter to the king, this time openly accusing Onias of plotting treacherously against the government. Onias realized that his position in Jerusalem was growing more precarious and that his only hope was to go to Antioch and present the whole affair to the king. He was unlucky. King Seleucus Philopator had just died, and his brother Antiochus IV Epiphanes had ascended the throne. With the latter's rise to power a new chapter opened in Jewish history.

C. The Hellenistic Reform

Antiochus IV Epiphanes, who succeeded to the throne of Syria in 175, already aroused the particular interest of his contemporaries by his peculiar nature and eccentric behavior, and his personality has continued to attract the attention of scholars down to our own day. On the whole, history has passed an unfavorable judgement on Antiochus, partly based on accounts given of him in ancient times, and summed up by the great Greek historian Polybius in the 2nd century B.C.E.[20] Polybius laid stress on such peculiar facets of Antiochus' character as the pursuit of fame, his friendship with people of mean origin, and his desire to impress people by sudden outbursts of anger or of exaggerated affection, etc. It was said of the king, for instance, that he would visit the public bathhouses and amuse himself by pouring myrrh on the floor and then enjoy the sight of people falling on the slippery surface. Nor did he stand on his dignity, appearing as an actor on the stage or dancing before a multitude of spectators.

Yet along with this eccentricity went great ambitions. Antiochus saw the re-establishment of the Seleucid kingdom as his mission. His education and his views were those of a Western man, for he happened to have spent several years in Rome as a hostage. The customs of Rome and its institutions impressed him greatly, and after becoming king he tried to introduce some of these customs into his capital, Antioch, ill-suited though they were to the spirit of an Eastern state. Antiochus had a good appreciation of Greek culture, too, and made himself famous among the Greeks by the lavish gifts and money he squandered on the erection of public buildings in several ancient Greek cities. Within the boundaries of his own kingdom he regarded Hellenism a strong buttress for his rule, and he willingly granted the rights of a Greek *polis* to ancient Eastern towns.[21]

Some modern scholars see Antiochus as a mad Hellenizer who would not shrink from any endeavor to spread his favorite culture among Eastern peoples. Yet historical research has revealed that nowhere except in Jerusalem did Antiochus abolish the prevailing customs and introduce Greek ones instead. Accordingly, it may be concluded that the notorious persecutions of Antiochus were not the result of his Hellenistic aspirations but had some other motivation. Again, other scholars see Antiochus as a religious reformer, whose aim was, as it were, to create a uniform religion and enforce it over all his kingdom. They even see some external indications of such a religion in the extension of the cult of Zeus Olympius, or rather of the cult of the king himself in the guise of Zeus Olympius. However, there is no corroboration for this assumption in the sources. Moreover, the time was not yet ripe during Antiochus' reign for the creation of a uniform syncretistic religion, like the cults in the Roman Empire 400 years later.[22]

It would be more reasonable to suppose that neither religion nor culture mattered most in Antiochus Epiphanes' life, but that first place was reserved for his imperialistic policy; religion and culture being only the tools of this policy. And, indeed, the Seleucid kingdom badly needed a strong ruler whose aim in life would be the improvement of the numerous defects which had brought the kingdom to a grave crisis. As stated above (p. 26-32), the "East" was the strongest enemy of the Seleucid kingdom, whose disintegration had set in almost on the very day of its establishment. At the time of Antiochus III another important factor had been added to the process of disintegration, i.e., the policy of Rome, which inflicted a decisive defeat on the armies of that king on the battlefield of Magnesia (190). Since then Rome kept vigilant against the restoration of Seleucid power.[23] Thus, Antiochus Epiphanes saw himself completely encircled by enemies. He obstinately fought them all daring even to dream not only of strengthening his kingdom within its present frontiers, but also of extending it at the expense of his weak neighbor, the king of Egypt. It is difficult to say to what extent Antiochus' strange character and his nervousness influenced the realization of his political projects. It is quite possible that his final failure was the consequence not of his personal defects, but of the objective political situation in that period — namely, the powerful reaction of the East to Hellenism, and the hostile policy of the Roman Senate.[24] Within this wide historical framework, embracing an area from the mountains of Iran in the east to the River Tiber in the west, the tragedy of the people of Israel unfolded. The sources of this tragedy originated in two parallel processes: in King Antiochus' general policy on the one hand, and in the people of Israel's own national development on the other.

We do not know what passed between Onias and Antiochus when the High Priest went to Antioch in order to strengthen his shaky political position in Jerusalem. It is clear, however, that Onias was not successful, since he did not return to Jerusalem but was forced, perhaps at the king's command, to stay in Antioch as a man suspected of political designs upon the welfare of the state. In Onias' absence, his brother Joshua, better known by his Greek name, Jason, must surely have substituted for him as head of the Jerusalem theocracy. Jason's subsequent actions were not those to be expected of a brother. The author of II Maccabees relates that Jason presented himself before the king and bought from him the office of High Priest for "three hundred and three score talents of silver, besides eighty talents from another fund" (II Macc. 4:8). For the first time in Jewish history the office of the High Priest had become a matter for bargaining. It is true that prior to this the king's approval had also been mandatory for each new candidate to the High Priesthood. In an Eastern country under an absolute monarchy nobody could hold a high office without the king's approval. Yet King Antiochus III had confirmed the right of the Jews "to live according to their ancestral laws," i.e., had granted them a measure of autonomy. Thanks to this autonomy the office of the High Priest had passed, according to prevailing custom, from father to son within the Oniad family, the sanction of the king having been merely a formality. Now, a new principle was introduced into the transfer of the High Priesthood — the purchase of the office directly from the king. It is true that in this case the purchaser was the brother of the High Priest, and thus the office remained within the same family. Yet it is doubtful whether the removal of Onias necessarily demanded the transfer of his position to his brother, for Onias had a son also called Onias whose claim to the High Priesthood undoubtedly had greater justification in the eyes of the people than that of Jason. Furthermore, once the precedent of buying the office directly from the king had been established, there was no certainty whatsoever that other families would not try to do the same, in which case the High Priesthood would cease to be the ancestral heritage of the Oniads and would be open to every strong and ambitious member of the Jewish aristocracy in Jerusalem.[25]

Yet Jason's principal act was not his buying the office of High Priest, but the use to which he put that office to initiate far-reaching political reforms. The author of II Maccabees adds that Jason promised Antiochus 150 talents more in exchange for a license to build a *gymnasium* and an *ephebeum* for exercise in Jerusalem, and to "register the Jerusalemites as Antiochenes" (II Macc. 4:9). This sentence has been given a variety of interpretations by modern scholars. Some have taken it to mean granting the inhabitants of Jerusalem the same rights as the citizens of the capital, Antioch. Others see in the term "Antiochenes" a corporation of people named for the king.[26] Neither interpretation will bear close scrutiny. The correct explanation is that Antiochus granted Jason permission to transform Jerusalem into a Greek *polis* named Antioch.[27] Indeed, according to II Maccabees this meant neither granting certain privileges to the inhabitants of the city not setting up a small group of royal adherents, but a reform of major significance affecting the life of all the people; for immediately after recording the grant of the license mentioned above, the author of II Maccabees relates that "Jason at once exercised his influence in order to bring over his fellow countrymen to Greek ways of life. Setting aside the royal ordinances of special favor to the Jews (Ἰουδαίοις φιλάνθρωπα βασιλικὰ), obtained by John . . . . , and seeking to overthrow the lawful modes of life, he introduced new customs forbidden by the law," (*ibid.* 4:10 f.). In other words, Antiochus Epiphanes abolished the privileges granted to the Jews by his father, Antiochus III, which were the legal basis of their right to live according to their ancestral tradition. Now, in place of that tradition, the law of the Greek *polis* was introduced. As the first step in establishing the *polis*, the author of II Maccabees mentions the erection of a *gymnasium* and an *ephebeum* — two institutions of Greek education which in the Hellenistic Age served as the most prominent mark of the Hellenistic spirit.[28]

Sports were now to take root in Jerusalem; both I and II Maccabees emphasize the powerful attraction of athletic exercises for the Jerusalem aristocracy, especially among the priests,[29] but unfortunately, our sources give no further details about the implementation of the reform. Jason's first task was probably to draw up the *demos* of the *polis*, that is, to fix the total number of Jerusalem inhabitants who were to be granted the privilege of becoming citizens of the new *polis*. Obviously not all the inhabitants became citizens of the new city of Antioch. Had they done so, it could be said that Jason's aim was to proclaim a democratic regime in Jerusalem, like the one which prevailed in Athens in the 4th and 5th centuries. But the era of democratic rule had passed. In the 2nd century the customary regime in Greek cities was an aristocracy or oligarchy, in which only a limited number of inhabitants counted as citizens of the city.[30] There are sufficient grounds for supposing that the number of citizens in the new Antioch was fixed at about 3,000.[31] Jason's second task was to set up the council which was the main governing body in every Greek *polis*. To this end he probably made use of an institution which already existed in Jerusalem, the Elders' Council or *Gerousia* mentioned in the decree of Antiochus III in 198 (see above, p. 81–2), which served as the body incorporating the leaders of the Jerusalem aristocracy. Since the Hellenistic reform sprang up among this very aristocracy, there is no reason to think that there were many changes in the composition of the *Gerousia* after its enlargement, except for the removal of the men opposing the very fact of the Hellenistic reform.

The Hellenistic reform took place on the initiative of the Jerusalem aristocracy. The number of citizens of the city of "Antioch" was limited and did not embrace all the inhabitants. It is hardly likely, however, that the city of Jerusalem continued to exist side by side with the Greek *polis* as an independent political unit.[32] This conjecture might have been justified had the Temple remained outside the *polis* and continued to be linked to the ancient Jerusalem. But this was not so, either territorially or from a politico-religious point of view. The author of II Maccabees records that the *gymnasium* was built "under the citadel itself" i.e., upon Mount Moriah, in the immediate vicinity of the Temple. Thus there was no possibility of separating the territory of the Greek *polis*, with the *gymnasium* as its center, from the ancient city of Jerusalem and its center, the Temple. Even more convincing is the political aspect. It was the High Priest himself, the head of the Jerusalem theocracy, who had carried out the Hellenistic reform. How could he possibly desire that the Temple should remain outside the *polis*, thereby giving up the revenues and treasures of the Temple and its influence upon the people and leaving the new *polis* without any official urban cult? Again, the fact that many priests took part in the athletic exercises of the *gymnasium* is additional proof that the Temple was closely connected with the new Greek *polis*. On the other hand, there is little doubt that the population of Judea and Jerusalem would not give up their ancient place of worship, which was for them endowed with supreme sanctity. Without the Temple the city of Jerusalem would have lost both the political and the spiritual justification of its existence. It must be acknowledged that the Hellenistic reform did not divide the city of Jerusalem into two parts but transformed the whole of it into a Greek *polis* — Antioch. In this *polis*, however, not every inhabitant counted as a citizen, and not everyone could participate in the general assembly for the election of officials, certainly not everybody could receive a Greek education at the *gymnasium* and the *ephebeum*.

What impelled the Jerusalem aristocracy to carry out this far-reaching political revolution? The answer must be sought not in events in Jerusalem seen in isolation, but in the wider social process taking place in several parts of the Seleucid empire, rooted in the beginning of the Hellenistic Age. As stated above (p. 28–9), the Hellenistic cities were natural allies of the king, since both king and cities feared the possible violence of the Eastern reaction against Hellenism. To be more explicit — it was worth while for the Seleucid king to encourage the big Eastern cities to go over to the side of Hellenism so as to gain the support of the rich bourgeoisie for the central government. For their part, the wealthy classes in these cities were equally interested in close connections with the central government; such contacts promoted the development of trade and enriched the urban upper classes. Each Greek *polis* was linked to other *poleis*, i.e., to the whole state. The geographical horizon of a *polis* was incomparably wider than that of a small Eastern tribe somewhere in the mountains. Even if only for the sake of appearances, an Eastern town had to adopt the political regime of a Greek *polis* and introduce the most conspicuous Hellenistic customs, such as gymnastics, athletic games, etc. Such a superficial adoption of Hellenistic customs was, in general, not too hard to achieve, and it is not surprising that so many Eastern cities transformed themselves into Greek *poleis*. Large cities, such as the coastal towns of Phoenicia or the land of the Philistines had already done so in the 3rd century. At the time of Antiochus Epiphanes it was the turn of the Syrian towns of the interior.[33] From this general point of view, the Hellenistic reform in Jerusalem was part of a broad historical process, and included many of the features common to the social-cultural revolution elsewhere.

Jerusalem had become a Greek *polis*, and there is no doubt that the ruling nobility gained a great deal from this reform. The city was named

"Antioch," after the king, who must certainly have been proclaimed its "founder," thus putting the new *polis* under the direct protection of King Antiochus. The city at once began to participate in the international life of the Hellenistic world. According to II Maccabees (4:18 ff.), Jason sent representatives of the new *polis* to the athletic games in Tyre, held there every fifth year in the king's presence. It may also be assumed, though this is not mentioned in the sources, that the new city was granted the customary permission to mint its own copper coins. These innovations drew Jerusalem out of its remoteness and its inferior status and raised it to the level of other big and rich cities. The path which Joseph son of Tobiah had been the first to tread now became the road of many, and the Jerusalem nobility, its priests and elders, strode confidently along it. Yet along with the promise of prosperity for the city and its leaders, the road also concealed a danger. The nobility was not the only class of people in Jerusalem. The more the reform gained strength, the more widely organized opposition spread among the classes which neither derived advantage from the reform nor approved of its cultural-religious aspect.

For all the great changes they introduced into the political structure of Jerusalem, the reformers did not touch the religious foundations upon which the life of the people had been founded for generations. The sources show little sympathy for the reformers and do not spare them abuse, but they do not accuse them of offence against religion. It may, therefore, be concluded that no changes were introduced in this domain. It is uncertain whether statues of Greek deities were erected in the *gymnasium* (as was the prevailing custom throughout the Hellenistic world) but in any case, it is clear that no statue whatsoever was erected in the Temple. The setting up of a statue in the Temple at the time of Antiochus' persecutions is recorded with great bitterness which suggests that it was an unheard of innovation, the like of which had not been known prior to the persecutions. Any change in the manner of worship or offence to monotheistic purity would without doubt have provoked a revolt among the common people in Judea and Jerusalem, but no such reaction is heard of at the time of the Hellenistic reform. Furthermore, the representatives of the new *polis* sent to Tyre "to carry three hundred drachmas of silver for the sacrifice of Heracles" requested that this money be used for the building of galleys and not for the offering of a sacrifice (II Macc. 4:18 ff.). This shows that the official representatives of the city Antioch-at-Jerusalem rejected the idolatrous cult and remained faithful to the Torah and the customs of Israel. Indeed, the reformers had no intention of uprooting the culture of Israel and introducing the Hellenistic way of life in its stead; their aim was to introduce political and not cultural-religious reforms. Athletics in Jerusalem were a necessary concession to the claims of Hellenism; they were not meant to defile the Jewish religion. From the point of view of Jason and his adherents, Jewish tradition and Hellenism could well co-exist, Judaism serving as the basis of the culture and tradition of Israel, and Hellenism acting as a connecting link between Jerusalem and the outside world. But was this compromise acceptable to the majority of the people?[34]

The first blow against the new regime was struck not by tradition-loving common people, but by the Hellenizers. The Hellenistic reform (as it was carried out by Jason) may have held its ground in the city for quite a long time, if Jason's supporters and Jason himself, had remained at the head of government. Instead, as we have seen, the aristocratic families in Judea were at loggerheads, with the Oniads under attack. Jason was the brother of the exiled High Priest, Onias, and though he supported the Hellenistic movement and assumed leadership of the reform, he must have continued his relations with individuals and families, especially among the priests, who were accustomed to regard the Oniads as the official heads of the people. Such a situation was quite intolerable to the wealthy Tobiad family and to the family of the brothers Simeon, Menelaus and Lysimachus, which undoubtedly had great influence among the Jerusalem priests. The Tobiads offered Menelaus the High Priesthood to supplant Jason. Three years later Jason sent Menelaus to Antioch to deliver a sum of money to the king and report to him on the situation in Jerusalem (II Mac. 4:23). We may conclude, therefore, that Menelaus was already a high official in Jason's time and had probably found support among the Tobiad family.[35] Once in Antioch, Menelaus presented himself before the king, and acted in exactly the same way as Jason had there years before. Just as Jason had removed his brother Onias from the High Priest-hood by offering to pay the king for the office, so now Menelaus displaced Jason. He bought the office of High Priest from Antiochus by offering three hundred talents more than Jason. It may be concluded from the fragmentary narrative in Josephus that a fierce battle between Jason and Menelaus flared up in the city, in which the former was defeated, forced to leave Jerusalem and retreat as far as Transjordan.[36] New men came to administer affairs in Jerusalem and Judea, and, as a result, hitherto un-known methods of governing were introduced into the city.

Menelaus did not belong to the Oniads, and thus, for the first time in many generations, a stranger assumed the office of High Priest. This fact alone sufficed to provoke the enmity of the population. Moreover, the way the new ruler had acquired the office was also strange to the people. The High Priest had merely become an official of the Seleucid king; and succession to the office, like several other priestly offices in the Hellenistic world, ceased to be regulated according to ancestral tradition, but was put on sale and changed hands for money.[37] However, what most angered the people was Menelaus' taking control of the Temple treasury. Menelaus had received his office from Antiochus, but it was clear that the king would support him only provided Menelaus paid the money he had promised — otherwise Antiochus was free to choose another candidate. He therefore considered it necessary to present himself before the king again. Before doing so, Menelaus helped himself to the amount he needed from the Temple treasury. Antiochus was not in his capital just then and one of his high officials, Andronicus, was in charge of state affairs. This man was won over by Menelaus with presents from the Temple treasury. This apparently became known among Jewish circles in Antioch, and Onias, the former High Priest who was living in the city, decided that this was the right moment to take action against Menelaus and accuse him of squandering the treasures of the Temple. Menelaus turned to Andronicus for help. The official tricked Onias out of his hiding place and had him killed. According to II Maccabees, the murder was widely resented in Antioch and even Antiochus himself, decided to punish Andronicus for his evil deeds on his return to the city (II Macc. 4:35 ff.).[38]

In the meantime, matters in Jerusalem became more complicated. During Menelaus' absence, his brother Lysimachus deputized for him; and since it was Lysimachus who, on Menelaus' orders, had actually perpetrated the theft of the Temple treasures, the wrath of the people turned against him. Disturbances flared up in the city and Lysimachus distributed arms among three thousand men upon whom he could rely. This small force, however, was not able to control the rebellious people and Lysimachus himself fell in the battles which raged in the streets of the city. News of the rebellion was brought to the king, who was then in Tyre, and at the same time three delegates sent by the "Elders' Council" (the *Gerousia*) of Jerusalem arrived to lay their case against Menelaus before the king. Yet once again lavish distribution of bribes saved Menelaus. He was acquitted, while the three elders who had come to accuse him were found guilty and condemned to death.[39] Thus, Menelaus continued to rule in Jerusalem with an iron fist and terror, while bribery of the royal officials and obsequious cringing before the king served him in the Syrian capital.

This brings us to the events of 169, when far-reaching political changes in the fate of the Jewish nation occurred, paving the way for the political-religious crisis known as "Antiochus' persecutions." In summing up the events leading up to this year, numerous signs heralding the storm can easily be pointed out. The Hellenistic reform of Jason had abolished the right of the Jews to live according to their ancestral laws, and had changed the previous political organization of the "nation" (ἔθνος) into that of a Greek *polis*. As we have seen, this reform did not introduce changes in religious customs or the service, yet the very fact that the ancestral tradition was no longer protected by the king and that religious practices could be altered by the leaders of the *demos* of the new city of Antioch was an affront to traditionalist circles. One reaction was the emergence of popular leaders from a sect whose members called themselves *Ḥasidim* and regarded devotion to the laws of the Torah their sole aim. Menelaus' policy, which openly permitted the use of sacred treasures for secular purposes and even for bribing the pagan king and his officials, undoubtedly provoked a sharp reaction on their part.

The account in II Maccabees of the course of events from the Hellenistic reform up to 169 attests to a slow but steady rise in the ferment among the population. So many latent conflicts were at work within Jewish society: political differences between the supporters of the Seleucids and the adherents of the Ptolemies, social conflict between the aristocracy and the common people, and ideological conflict between the Hellenizers and the adherents to tradition. The historical process had brought Jewish society to the threshold of a crisis. It needed only the slightest spark for the situation to explode into open war.

D. Apollonius' Persecutions

The political crisis in Judea was linked to the international political situation, particularly the wars between Antiochus Epiphanes and the Ptolemaic kingdom in Egypt. The Ptolemaic court had never relinquished its claim to control southern Syria, taken from it in 198, and continued to dream of reconquering this important area. On the other hand, Antiochus Epiphanes saw the conquest of Egypt as part of a large imperialistic project aiming at the recovery of the power of the Seleucid kingdom, which had greatly diminished after the defeat at Magnesia in 190. Political tension between both states resulted in hostile actions. The sources of that period do not provide a full account of the events, and even the chronology of Antiochus' wars in Egypt is not certain.[40] Nor is the extent of Antiochus' activities and projects in Egypt clear. In his first campaign the king succeeded in conquering the ancient capital of Egypt, Memphis, and in forcing the young Egyptian king, Ptolemy VI Philometor, to acknowledge his sovereignty. The Greek population in Alexandria refused to accept such humiliation, and they replaced Ptolemy Philometor by his young brother Ptolemy Euergetes. When Antiochus attempted to conquer Alexandria he was stopped at the strong walls of the capital and forced to abandon his plan. After Antiochus' return to Syria from his first campaign, the two brothers were reconciled, alien influence was purged, and a nationalist Egyptian policy was restored. In his second campaign (168), Antiochus again conquered Lower Egypt, including Memphis, and laid siege to Alexandria. The Christian historian, Hieronymus, relates that Antiochus placed the crown of the Egyptian kingdom upon his head, and although his evidence seemed rather doubtful to scholars, it has recently been confirmed by a papyrological document attesting that Antiochus was actually recognized as the King of Egypt.[41] Alexandria was not able to withstand a long siege, and Antiochus was already visualizing Egypt as part of his kingdom. But at this point the Romans intervened. An envoy of the Roman Senate appeared in Antiochus' encampment before the walls of Alexandria and transmitted to the king the Senate's request to withdraw at once from Egypt and return to his own land. It was not in Rome's interest that one Eastern political power should become greater than the others; to Rome, an East crumbling and internally divided was preferable to one united under a single strong ruler. When Antiochus answered the Senate's envoy that he would like to think the matter over, the messenger's response apparently made a great impression upon the spectators, for it has come down to us from several sources. With his staff, he drew a circle on the ground around the king and said: "Think it over here." Antiochus dared not openly oppose the explicit order of the Roman Senate; he accepted the offensive demand and at once withdrew from Egypt with all his armies. His attempt to annex Egypt to the Seleucid kingdom thus ended in complete failure.[42]

After his first campaign in Egypt, Antiochus had visited Jerusalem, as usual in need of money. The High Priest, Menelaus, himself led him into the treasury (II Macc. 5:15). Josephus, relying upon his Greek sources, records that Antiochus acted just like an enemy in Jerusalem, robbing the Temple treasury of silver and gold, regardless of the existence of a treaty of friendship.[43] This crude interference in Temple afairs was a hard blow to the national and religious feelings of the Jerusalem population. Yet while Antiochus was victorious in Egypt, the Jews dared not show their bitterness in open hostilities. Moreover, the head of the theocratic government in Jerusalem was Menelaus who had decided to support Antiochus at all costs, since only in Antiochus could he find support for his position in Jerusalem, in view of the hostility and indignation of the population. Antiochus' second campaign totally changed the situation in Jerusalem. False rumors of his sudden death in Egypt apparently gave the signal for the start of disturbances. Jason, the previous High Priest, who had fled to Transjordan after being ousted by Menelaus, left his hiding place and made an assault upon Jerusalem at the head of about a thousand men (II Macc. 5:5). There is no doubt as to the political object of this action. If Menelaus regarded Antiochus as his supporter, then Jason, his mortal enemy, naturally counted on the backing of the Egyptian government. The presumed sudden death of Antiochus offered an ideal opportunity for open revolt against Syria. Fierce fighting flared up in the city between Jason and his adherents on the one hand, and Menelaus and his supporters on the other. This time Jason won and Menelaus was forced to take refuge in the citadel and to hand the whole city over to Jason. II Maccabees, which is the sole source for these events, neglects to describe Jason's rule in Jerusalem, and limits itself to an account of his acts of terror against the population and his complete defeat; he was forced to leave the city and flee again to the land of the Ammonites and from there to Egypt (*ibid.* 5:7–8). The author of II Maccabees does not explain who drove Jason out of Jerusalem. It hardly seems likely that it was Menelaus, for had he been able to re-establish his power in Jerusalem, he would have restored its loyalty to the Syrian king, and this would make the whole account of subsequent events incomprehensible. It may be assumed, therefore, that Jason was confronted with organized opposition on the part of the Jerusalem masses which had once already demonstrated their strength in their rebellion against Menelaus' rule when they had killed his brother Lysimachus. If as a result of these disturbances Jason was forced to leave Jerusalem while Menelaus still remained locked up in the citadel, it follows that the government of the city had been taken out of the hands of the Hellenizers and may even have passed to the leaders of the rebellion, possibly members of the sect of the *Ḥasidim*.

Such an interpretation of events in Jerusalem in 168 explains Antiochus' wrath when rumors of events in the city reached him. Not only had he suffered humiliation from Rome, but now he began to fear that all of Southern Syria would rebel against him and join Egypt, or attempt to obtain political independence under the benevolent protection of the Roman Senate.[44] If Antiochus wanted to preserve the integrity of the state, now was the time to demonstrate his power and energy to the world. Some modern historians have been skeptical about Antiochus' coming to

Jerusalem in person in 168 to crush the revolt; but his appearance was a political necessity, and there is no reason whatsoever to doubt it. Moreover, it is confirmed by the sources.[45] II Maccabees (5:12 ff.) records a terrible massacre carried out by Antiochus in the city, even mentioning a figure of 80,000 persons, allegedly killed in the course of three days. Like every figure in Hellenistic historiography, the number is, of course, exaggerated. Nevertheless, it is clear from the sources that the uprising was put down with much cruelty. Yet one action was not enough to crush the revolt; political measures to prevent the recurrence of such disturbances in Jerusalem had to be taken. Accordingly, a short time after he had left the city, Antiochus sent his general, Apollonius, to Jerusalem to take appropriate steps. In the meantime, it seems, the city was again up in arms for, according to the sources, Appolonius had to enter it by deceit, pretending that his intention was to bring peace to the population (I Macc. 1:29 ff.; II Macc. 5:24 ff.).

Among the measures taken by Appollonius to secure the city's loyalty to the Seleucid king, were two which totally changed the status of Jerusalem: the erection of the citadel known by its Greek designation, *akra*, which was made into the center of the new *polis*, and the dispatching of a *katoikia*, i.e., a colony of foreign soldiers, inside Jerusalem. The introduction of the *katoikia* was a particularly bitter blow. It marked the beginning of mass opposition which very soon turned into a general rebellion. Many examples in Greek and Roman history bear witness that the establishment of a *katoikia*, or *cleruchy*, of soldiers in a quiet town meant its total ruin.[46] Not for nothing did King Ptolemy Euergetes, learning of the rebellious policy of the High Priest Onias II, threaten to send soldiers as settlers to Jerusalem (see above p. 76). And a few years later Lysias — regent and tutor to an infant king — was to repeat the same threat (I Macc. 3:36; II Macc. 11:2). Daniel relates that Antiochus installed in the "fortresses" a people "of a foreign god,[47] whom he shall acknowledge, shall increase glory; and he shall cause them to rule over many, and shall divide the land for a price" (Daniel 11:39); and the author of I Maccabees (1:38) attests that the Jerusalem population fled from the city and that it became a "dwelling of strangers" (κατοικία ἀλλοτρίων). The sources do not specify who those strange settlers were, but they undoubtedly belonged to Antiochus' army, since the main purpose of establishing a *katoikia* was to watch the loyalty of the population, something which could only be done by introducing soldiers into the city. The ethnic origin of the soldiers is quite clear: like the soldiers of other Seleucid kings in the 3rd and 2nd centuries, Antiochus' troops were called Greeks or Macedonians. Actually they did not belong to either of those nations but were recruited from among the peoples of Eastern lands and received military training on the Greek or Macedonian pattern.[48] The soldiers whom Antiochus settled in Jerusalem, with the *akra* as their headquarters, were apparently recruited from among the Syrian population or perhaps even from among the inhabitants of Palestine itself. From time immemorial there had been enmity between the Syrians and the Jews, and it may be supposed that, in addition to the difficulties connected with the very fact of the establishment of the *katoikia*, the Jews now had to endure insults from their new neighbors who were their mortal enemies.

The political situation produced in Jerusalem by Apollonius' repressive measures was not to endure. Consequences soon followed, the first of which was a mass flight from the city. The author of I Maccabees describes the flight in poetic language (1:38 ff.) which aroused the suspicions of modern scholars.[49] Yet II Maccabees (5:27) states that Judah Maccabee, with nine other men, fled from the city immediately after Apollonius instituted his repressive measures, and certainly they were not the only ones. It is true that we need not accept the statement in I Maccabees that Jerusalem was completely depopulated of its permanent inhabitants; however, the fact of the mass flight is quite probable, since (as stated above) the introduction of strange soldiers into a city being always accompanied by acts of robbery and violence on their part. Moreover, old inhabitants of Jerusalem were forced to give up their lands permanently to the new settlers.[50] The author of I Maccabees goes further, testifying not only to the abandonment of the city, but also to the desolation of the Temple (*ibid.* 1:39). Scholars used not to lend any credence to this report and assumed that the story dealt with events taking place after Antiochus' decrees, i.e., a year after Apollonius' repressions. Yet the author of I Maccabees wrote this account before his description of Antiochus' persecutions, and there is not sufficient reason to doubt the accuracy of his chronology. The cause of the Temple's desolation must be sought in the new situation created there as a result of the establishment of the colony of Syrian soldiers. These soldiers certainly had no intention of slighting what they considered to be the cult of a local god, yet, on the other hand, they did not want to give up their own religious customs and their traditional deities. Since their residence was the *akra*, which was also the new center of the *polis* of Antioch-at-Jerusalem, they were obviously regarded as permanent citizens of the *polis*, whether they had obtained full citizenship or were annexed to it as foreigners accorded the status of permanent residents. These new inhabitants of Antioch-at-Jerusalem desired to worship in the Temple the deities who were familiar to them as well; first and foremost the supreme Syrian god Baal Shamin[51] and the Syrian goddess known under different names such as Anath, Allāt, etc. The worship of the god of wine, Dushara, identified by the Greeks with Dionysus, may also have been set up in the Temple.[52] Concurrently with Syrian gods, Syrian customs were also introduced into the Temple. The author of II Maccabees (6:4) attests that the Temple was filled with prostitutes as a result of Antiochus' persecutions, and this is confirmed by evidence in the commentary to M^egillat Ta'anit.[53] The participation of prostitutes in religious rites is not typical of the Greek religion[54] whereas it was a permanent feature in the cult of the Syrian goddess. It follows, therefore, that this custom was introduced into the Temple not as a result of Antiochus' persecutions but some time earlier, just after the establishment of the Syrian *katoikia*. The reaction of the Jews to this invasion of the Temple by strange cults is easy to imagine. For hundreds of years the Temple had been the stronghold of the one unique God of Israel. Is it then conceivable that the mass of the people would have agreed to the transformation of their holy place into a center for the worship of pagan deities? Admittedly, the heads of the *polis* of Antioch-at-Jerusalem — the High Priest Menelaus and his adherents — certainly did not oppose these changes in the Temple, since the slogan of the Hellenizers was: "Let us go and make a covenant with the nations that are round about us, for since we separated ourselves from them many evils have come upon us" (I Macc. 1:11). And though we cannot say that they deliberately sought to do away with the foundations of Jewish monotheism and exchange it for polytheistic cults, yet they had to accept the logical result of the abolition of the Jews' right to live according to their ancestral laws and the transformation of Jerusalem into a Hellenistic city with a mixed population. They must certainly have foreseen the dangerous consequences of the new situation which arose in Jerusalem, but they were powerless and had no choice but to carry out the king's orders without hesitation. The breach within the Jewish nation caused by the Hellenistic reform grew wider until it was on the verge of developing into a bloody encounter between the two sides.

And indeed, war broke out quite soon. Our sources' reports of the Jewish rebellion against the Syrian king open with an account of the Hasmonean family, thereby conveying the impression that before the Hasmoneans there was no movement of rebellion in Judea. This impression is erroneous. It results from the approach of the sources to the events of the time. Both our most important sources, I and II Maccabees, are interested in stressing the idea that hostilities only began with the emergence of the Hasmoneans—

the author of I Maccabees as the official historian of the Hasmonean family, and the author of II Maccabees as a great admirer of the national hero, Judah Maccabee. Neither author wished to mention the movement of rebellion which preceded the appearance of the Hasmoneans, since this would have diminished the glory of the national heroes. However, from the Book of Daniel, written at the time of the persecutions, we learn that there had already been leaders among the people before Judah Maccabee and his brothers. Daniel calls them "they that are wise" and depicts their bitter fate and their sufferings (Daniel 11:33 ff.). Reading between the lines in the Books of the Maccabees, we find that they, too, acknowledge the existence of an insurrectionary movement prior to the appearance of the Hasmoneans. We hear of multitudes fleeing Jerusalem to take refuge in the desert, and it is quite clear that this flight represented not the search for a peaceful life away from the sinful city, but an attempt to organize into groups of freedom fighters and to seek support among the rural population. The multitudes who fled to the desert selected leaders from among the *Ḥasidim*; this conclusion follows from the statement that as soon as the Hasmoneans appeared on the scene, the *Ḥasidim* joined them as an organized fighting group (I Macc. 2:40–42). The author of I Maccabees notes that the "company of the *Ḥasidim*" (συναγωγὴ Ασιδαίων) were "mighty men of Israel" and included all those devoted to the Law. Again, we are told by I Maccabees that various groups of Jews who had hidden in the desert even before the appearance of the Hasmoneans refrained from fighting on the Sabbath day (I Macc. 2:31 ff.). It seems likely that these men who preferred to die rather than profane the laws of the Torah were also *Ḥasidim*.[55] All these examples attest that an extensive movement of rebellion had spread in Judea and Jerusalem, not after Antiochus' decrees, but before them, in a spontaneous response to the transformation of Jerusalem into a "dwelling for strangers" and that the rebel movement was distinctly religious in nature, since at its head stood the *Ḥasidim*, the most zealous devotees of the Torah.

Accordingly, the causes of the strange historical phenomenon known as "Antiochus' persecutions" can now be explained. Students have long found it difficult to understand Antiochus' motives in persecuting the Jewish religion. In the ancient world religious persecution was unknown and it is inconceivable that a Hellenistic king, brought up in the atmosphere of religious tolerance so typical of the Greco-Roman culture, would persecute a strange religion merely because it opposed the principles of his own faith.[56] Even if Antiochus is considered as a man particularly devoted to Greek culture, seeing it as his mission to spread this culture among the backward peoples of the East, that does not explain his persecution of the Jewish religion. Hellenism never denied the existence of other religions nor tried to abolish Eastern cults. On the contrary, it was typical of the Hellenistic culture that it could absorb elements of foreign religions and cults without much resistance. Furthermore, for Hellenists it was natural to respect local cults, since an offense committed against a local deity could provoke his wrath and bring disaster. Therefore, "Antiochus' persecutions" have remained a puzzle in the eyes of modern scholars, and the numerous assumptions they have offered have not succeeded in solving it since they have been wide of the mark.[57] It is, however, not difficult to find the solution if the problem is shifted from the cultural-religious to the political sphere. We have seen above that one of the most important problems in Antiochus' policy was the strengthening of the Seleucid kingdom, both internally and externally. Now, after his shameful defeat in front of the walls of Alexandria, Antiochus strove even more zealously towards this aim. The transformation of Jerusalem from a Jewish city into one with a mixed population was a measure designed to strengthen the power of the Seleucid state at one of its most vulnerable points. The attempt brought a Jewish revolt. This rebellion was supported by a fanatical religious sect which was devoted to its traditional laws and which proclaimed a ban upon anything bearing the mark of Hellenism. The logical conclusion for Antiochus was to crush the rebel movement by a direct onslaught on the hidden force which strengthened the freedom fighters, i.e., the Jewish religion. This initiated a period of suffering and misery for the people of Israel which on the one hand marked the end of the nation's disintegration process, and on the other, the beginning of the people's reunification under the Hasmonean banner.

E. Antiochus' Persecutions

The beginning of the persecutions should be placed in the winter months of 167–6, one year after Apollonius' suppressive measures. Our most important sources, I and II Maccabees, give a general account of the persecutions and dwell only upon a number of details which attracted their attention for one reason or another. None of the sources bothered to give a detailed and systematic record of the persecutions; such an account may have been given by Jason of Cyrene, but his vast work has not survived. The author of I Maccabees prefaces his description with an item of information which raises many doubts as to its historical reliability. The king was supposed to have sent to the whole population of his kingdom a letter saying that "all should be one people and that every one should give up his usages." This sentence serves as important proof for those scholars who regard Antiochus as a Hellenizer or religious unifier. Yet, as stated above (p. 123), there is no adequate evidence to support this assumption, and, accordingly, the sentence should be interpreted as the personal view of the author of I Maccabees, who wanted to present the persecutions as part of a religious reform throughout the Seleucid kingdom.[58] We can place more confidence in the description of the persecutions themselves given in I Maccabees in the following words (1:44–51):

> Furthermore, the king sent letters by the hand of messengers to Jerusalem and to the cities of Judea [to the effect that] they should practise customs foreign to [the traditions of] the land, and that they should cease the [sacrificing of] whole burnt offerings, and sacrifices, and drink offerings in the sanctuary, and that they should profane the sabbaths and feasts, and pollute the sanctuary and those who had been sanctified; that they should [moreover] build high places, and sacred groves, and shrines for idols, and that they should sacrifice swine and [other] unclean animals; and that they should leave their sons uncircumcised, and make themselves abominable by means of [practising] everything that was unclean and profane, so that they might forget the Law, and change all the [traditional] ordinances. And whosoever should not act according to the word of the king, should die. In this manner did he write unto the whole of his kingdom; and he appointed overseers over all the people; and he commanded the cities of Judea to sacrifice, every one of them.

The author of I Maccabees goes on to relate that on the fifteenth day of the month of Kislew, in the year 167, an "abomination of desolation" was set up upon the altar in the Temple; in the cities of Judea high places were set up and altars were built at the doors of the houses and in public places. The scrolls of the Law were burnt, and death penalty awaited those who concealed sacred scrolls in their houses. Ten days after the erection of the "abomination of desolation," a sacrifice was offered upon the polluted altar. Mothers who dared to have their sons circumcised in violation of the king's decree were put to death. The story ends with a general description of the persecutions which severely afflicted the whole people of Israel. II Maccabees adds more details to this general picture. The king sent a special envoy whose mission was "to compel the Jews to depart from the laws of their fathers and to cease living by the laws of God."[59] The Temple in Jerusalem was polluted and consecrated to Zeus

Olympius; it was turned into a place of "riot and revelling" for the gentiles who brought prostitutes into the Temple area. The temple on Mount Gerizim was also consecrated to Zeus. Keeping Sabbath and festivals was forbidden, and instead, the Jews were forced to celebrate each month the king's birthday by offering sacrifices, and to participate in festive processions in honor of Dionysus. The account in II Maccabees also ends with a description of acts of cruelty which accompanied the execution of the king's orders, and a detailed account of the tortures suffered by an old man, Eleazar, one of the head scribes, and of a mother and her seven sons, who all chose a martyr's death rather than transgress the precepts of the Torah.[60]

What were the basic features of the repressive decrees? The sources depict them as the abolition of the rights of the Jews to live according to their traditions and an attempt to force the people to adopt Greek customs. This assumption serves as a basis for the modern trend which regards the legal aspect of the persecution as a) the abolition of the right of the Jews to live "according to their ancestral laws (granted to them by Antiochus III), and b) as the first step towards implementation of the Hellenistic reform.[61] Yet the decree of Antiochus III had already been rescinded in 175, just when the *polis* of Antioch-at-Jerusalem was established by the High Priest Jason. From that year onwards the political and cultural-religious life of the people of Israel was dependent not on the laws of Moses and their official approval by the Seleucid king, but on the decision of the *polis* of Antioch-at-Jerusalem. Nevertheless the *polis*, as we have seen above, did not officially abolish the observance of the precepts of the Torah, merely several Hellenistic customs were added. Thus the Jewish Hellenizers of the city of Antioch-at-Jerusalem cannot be considered as the initiators of the persecutions; and the responsibility of this devolves solely upon the king. Not that the king exceeded his legal authority. According to the basic laws of every Hellenistic state, the king was the prime source of law and justice. It was within his power to sanction the decisions of the cities, yet he could also act independently, at his own discretion, without any consideration for the opinions of the citizens of the *polis*. The present case is a good example of such independent action by the king. We do not know whether the Jerusalem Hellenizers agreed with the king's decrees or opposed them in their hearts, but it is in any case clear that the king did not require their approval, nor did he consider their opinion. Antiochus' decrees (like those of Apollonius before him) were an official act of the Seleucid government. They were published as an order ($\pi\rho\acute{o}\sigma\tau\alpha\gamma\mu\alpha$) issued by the political center of the state, its purpose being to restore Judea's loyalty to the king through the suppression of the rebellious Jewish

religion. It is worth noting that with the appearance of Antiochus Epiphanes upon the historical arena in Judea, the role of the Hellenizers almost
vanishes. From that point two forces confronted one another — the Seleucid
kingdom striving to preserve its integrity and the people of Israel aspiring
to gain wide political and religious autonomy.

The political nature of the persecutions is also evident from the fact that
they were executed by special messengers of the king. The author of I Maccabees speaks (1:44) of officials appointed by the king over all the cities in
Judea whose mission was to force the Jews not only to forsake the precepts
of the Torah but also to accept the new Hellenistic customs. II Maccabees
(6:1) also refers to a special emissary of Antiochus sent for the purpose of
compelling the Jews to abandon their religion[62] and this item (taken no
doubt from Jason of Cyrene) is quite probably true, for it represents an
attempt to concentrate implementation of the persecutions in the hands of
one man, and make it an uniform and better-organized action. It is difficult
to define precisely the geographical area where the anti-Jewish decrees
were applicable. They were primarily directed at Judea, i.e., at Jerusalem
and its environs, since it was there that the rebellion against Antiochus had
broken out. Yet the fact that the name of the deity on Mount Gerizim was
changed to Zeus Olympius and that the people of Shechem, according to
the evidence of Josephus (*Ant.* XII, 257 ff.), hastened to declare that they
were not Jews, despite their common faith, proves clearly that the persecutions were to extend beyond the borders of Judea. On the advice of Ptolemy
son of Dorimenes, the decision was transmitted to the neighboring Hellenistic cities to treat the Jews in the same fashion (II Macc. 6:8). Thus the
struggle against the Jewish religion was about to spread throughout the
country. It stands to reason that total abolition of the Jewish religion was
not the aim *per se* of the persecutions. Antiochus had no intention of
harassing any religion as such. He wanted to suppress it insofar as it
constituted an important political motive in the struggle of the Jews
against the Seleucids. Consequently places which did not take part in the
rebellion did not suffer from the persecutions. The first decree of the king
announcing the persecutions affected only the population of Jerusalem and
the Judean cities. Yet, since the Jewish population in Jerusalem had close
connections with all other Jewish communities in Palestine and the suppression of the traditional customs in Judea certainly caused a ferment in
other Jewish population centers too, there was little doubt that the
persecutions would in the end be felt throughout Palestine.

The decrees themselves served two complementary ends: persecution of
the traditional practices of Israel, and the imposition of Greek customs

upon the people. The first does not require any special explanation. The abolition of the Law of the Torah had a political purpose, for it was a source of inspiration to the rebels. But why the systematic endeavor to impose alien customs upon the people of Israel? King Antiochus was not a fanatical devotee of the Hellenistic religion, believing it to be the only true faith in the world. This was an attitude which developed in Europe in the Middle Ages and was intrinsically connected with the monotheistic religions. It cannot be applied to the Hellenistic-Roman world. Nor do we need to explain the king's wish to force Hellenistic religious customs upon the Jews. He had a number of different reasons for his action, of which the most important are the following:

1. After the establishment of the *katoikia*, Jerusalem became a city with a mixed Syrian-Jewish population, with the Syrian cult already established in the Temple. Thus the king had only to accord official sanction to a process which had already got under way before the publication of the decrees, and to grant the customs of the Syrian religion an official Hellenistic character. Hence the Syrian god Baal-Shamin was transformed into the Olympian Zeus in keeping with Antiochus' special liking for this deity. The festivals in honor of Dionysus were actually those of the Arabian-Syrian god of wine, Dushara, just as the goddess Athena, whose cult now ruled in the Temple, was none other than the ancient goddess Allāt or Anath. The Syrian population of the *akra* did not, of course, oppose the external Hellenization of Syrian cults. Such Hellenization was an ordinary phenomenon all over the East.

2. Hellenistic customs had already taken root in Jerusalem at the time of Jason's reform, and Antiochus was entitled to suppose that the mass of the people would follow them, since they had been introduced into Jerusalem on the initiative of the Jews themselves. It suited Antiochus better to regard the rebels as a small group of religious fanatics, with no deep roots among the people, than to recognize them as the militant vanguard of the whole nation aspiring to gain political and religious freedom. And again, since men like Menelaus were no doubt willing to agree to any measure Antiochus might take to suppress the rebellion, the king could well interpret this support as large-scale popular approval of the suppressive laws.

3. To these two points another may be added: Antiochus' political thinking would naturally lead him to reflect that the place earlier filled by the religion of Israel could not possibly remain a void. Another religion must be substituted and what faith other than the Hellenistic cult could be taken into account? It was the religion of the king, accepted by the cities and the various peoples throughout the great Seleucid kingdom.

Our sources lay particular stress on the cruelty of the persecutions and on the king's personal participation. The same story about a Jewish mother who dared to have her sons circumcized and was therefore put to death in the most cruel way appears in two sources.[63] No doubt many cruelties accompanied the crushing of the revolt, for the hatred of the officials and soldiers for a rebellious people on the one hand, and the religious fanaticism of the rebels on the other, turned the struggle into a war to the death. However, the sources' statement that the king himself took part in the persecutions should not be trusted. The author of II Maccabees, and following him the author of IV Maccabees, have the king presiding over the court before which appeared the victims of the persecutions — such as old Eleazar and the mother with her seven sons. These stories are no more than legends written during the persecutions, or some time after them, to keep up the people's morale and bolster their power of resistance. According to the sources, the order for the persecutions was sent by the king to Judea together with various officials commissioned to carry it out. From this it may be inferred that at that time the king was not resident in Judea and could not therefore have taken part in the oppression. Indeed, just at that moment Antiochus was embarking upon a new and important political undertaking: the re-establishment of the Seleucid kingdom which had been severely shaken by the nationalist movements of the Eastern peoples. He was about to leave Syria for the East, there to put down various rebellions which had flared up and to fight the Parthians. During the campaign the king met his death. Thus, his participation in the harsh suppressive measures against the Jews expressed itself only in his taking the decision to persecute them and their religion. Implementation of this decision was entrusted to others.

This brings us to the end of the period and to the completion of a historical process of great importance. First, individuals, then whole families appeared from among the Jewish nobility all aiming at obtaining for the Jews in Judea a different political organization which should lead them out of their remote corner and put them on the same road as all who stood close to the great Hellenistic world and took part in its turbulent life. Yet this road was bound to conflict with the ancestral traditions of the Jewish people and subject them to foreign customs. The Hellenistic reform turned Jerusalem into "Antioch," a Greek city. As a result, a deep schism developed within the nation, for the common people were reluctant to follow in the steps of the nobility and forsake their ancestral customs. A complex of different factors — political, social and cultural — combined to transform the internal struggle between the two sections of the Jewish population into an open clash between the Jews and the Seleucid kingdom. The appearance of national leaders concretized the opposition of the Jews to the king's policy. So long as those leaders belonged to the *Ḥasidim*, the movement was confined to unorganized and unplanned activities, since the *Ḥasidim* were limited in their warfare by their exaggerated devotion to the laws of the Torah, and consequently refrained from fighting on the Sabbath. With the appearance of the Hasmoneans the struggle acquired the organization it so desperately needed and popular rebellion turned into a stubborn and protracted war with the final aim of emancipating the people from the foreign yoke and establishing a national, independent, Jewish state.

PART THREE: THE WAR OF LIBERATION

CHAPTER VI

THE HASMONEAN REVOLT AND JUDAH MACCABEE'S WAR AGAINST THE SYRIANS

by M. Avi-Yonah

A. The Sources

THE MOST IMPORTANT SOURCE of information about the military activities which preceeded the liberation of Judea from the Seleucid yoke is undoubtedly the First Book of Maccabees. Next in importance is the Second Book of Maccabees, where only in the fifth chapter is to be found a description of the facts which interest us here. Both these books are discussed in the previous chapter (pp. 116–117 above).

A third source are the books of Flavius Josephus (Joseph son of Mattathias), particularly his *Antiquities*. While it is true that Josephus based his work on a summary he made of the First Book of Maccabees, he nevertheless deviated from it, apparently relying on other sources occasionally. In such cases it is up to us to decide where the historical truth lies. The passages in Josephus which interest us here are: *Antiquities*, Book XII, § 265 to the end of the book, and Book XIII, §§ 1–34; and *The Jewish War*, Book I, §§ 31–49.[1]

To these three literary sources must be added a fourth: the topographical structure of the district where the battles of the Hasmonean period took place. While the many forests which covered Judea in those ancient times have long since disappeared, there has been no change in the topography of the hills, valleys, lowlands, travel routes, passes, and other features which necessarily determine where an army can move, camp, and fight. These natural features, combined with what we know of the administrative division of Judea and its neighbors at the end of the Seleucid era, can elucidate a good many points in Hasmonean battles. The technical development of that period was far different from that of today: man was much closer to nature, and was affected by it to a much greater degree. Consequently, topographical conditions, although unchangeable, could yet be utilized properly, ability to do this being the most important quality of any competent commander. For this reason it is necessary to pay particular attention to such data, and to use them to supplement the fragmental tradition of the literary sources, the authors of which either assumed that their readers were familiar with the byways of Judea, or else did not consider such details worthy of their attention.

B. The Beginning of the Struggle: the Revolt at Modiin

According to most of our sources the revolt broke out in Modiin and it was touched off by the priest Mattathias the Hasmonean.[2] Modii is identified with the Arab village of al-Midya, 6.2 miles southeast of Lod. The ancient site is apparently the hill known as ar-Ra's, a little to the south of the village itself, near a place known by the Arabs as al-'Arba'ūn. At the time of the revolt Modiin lay outside the jurisdiction of Judea, as that country was delimited in the Seleucid state; and since later on Modiin undoubtedly came under the jurisdiction of Lod,[3] it can be assigned to that toparchy in those early days as well.

According to I Maccabees (2:17) Mattathias was considered "ruler" (ἄρχων) of the town;[4] most of the later sources, including Josephus (*War* I, 36), confirm the fact that Modiin was the place of origin of the Hasmonean family. It is true that Josephus himself, in *Antiquities* XII, 265, calls Mattathias "a native of Jerusalem," but we may assume that all he meant by that was that Jerusalem was Mattathias' usual place of residence. The First Book of Maccabees (2:1), too, mentions that Mattathias left Jerusalem and went down to Modiin. The fact that he appeared there surrounded by the members of his family, his sons and brothers and that he had property there (*ibid.*, 2:17, 28), proves that Modiin was the family center of the Hasmoneans, even if Mattathias' functions as priest tied him to Jerusalem and the Temple. And in the First Book of Maccabees, 13:25, Modiin is specifically referred to as "the city of his [Simeon's] forefathers."

The spark which touched off the revolt was the coming to Modiin of the "king's officers" dispatched to force the people to sacrifice to idols. Mattathias and his sons fell upon the emissaries and, according to Josephus (*Ant.* XII, 270), the king's officer was killed on the spot together with a few of his soldiers. In the Book of Maccabees his name is not mentioned but in *Antiquities* (XII, 270) he is called Apelles, and in *War* (I, 36) Bacchides.

This was an act of open rebellion against the king. Immediately afterwards Mattathias and his sons fled "unto the mountains" (I Macc. 2:28). The Book of Maccabees does not specify which mountains, whereas Josephus, in *Antiquities* (XII, 271) records that the flight was "into the wilderness" (εἰς τὴν ἔρημον). In *War* (I, 36) he follows the version of the

Book of Maccabees. Actually, there is no real contradiction here between the two versions. The expression "wilderness" in *Antiquities* was shifted to the story of Mattathias' deeds from the narrative of the Sabbath attack by the Seleucid army on the Jews living in caves in the wilderness. In both sources that story follows immediately after the description of Mattathias' flight, which explains how the error crept into *Antiquities*.[5] In fact, the geography of the area precluded a flight to "the wilderness." Anyone seeking a haven in the vicinity of Modiin had no need to cross the watershed and go off into the Desert of Ephraim or the Desert of Judea. At the very edge of the town lay a mountainous area, the mountains of Gophna, which offered an immediate refuge from pursuit.

From the point of view of Mattathias and his sons the most convenient area was that of the mountain ridges which extended between the deep valleys cutting into Mount Ephraim west of the watershed. These ridges rise to an altitude of 2,660 ft., broken up by numerous deep valleys with sharp cliffs jutting out here and there. This area, which lies between the Beth-horon road to the south and the Ramathaim-Timnah-Heres road in the north, is to this day covered with forests; in ancient times the forests were undoubtedly even more plentiful. Mattathias and his sons must surely have been familiar with these mountains, so close to their home. For a foreign army on the other hand, the mountains constituted a formidable obstacle. It may therefore be assumed that Mattathias and his sons beat a successful retreat and that the king's forces either did not pursue them at all, or that they soon despaired of overtaking them.[6]

The news that a center of rebellion had been set up in the mountains of Gophna spread to the villages of Judea and through the desert. The remnants of those who had fled there and had escaped the king's army (see p. 135 above) hastened to join the Hasmoneans (*Ant.* XII, 275; *War* I, 37). Even more important reinforcements came to the rebels from among the *Ḥasidim*, an organized group of opponents to Hellenizing tendencies, who now joined them as "mighty men of Israel," (I Macc. 2:42). Their exact number is unknown, but it probably came to several thousand. The rebel forces now began to move about the country and systematically seize control of the villages in Judea, around Jerusalem. This activity rates only passing references (I Macc. 2:43–47; II Macc. 8:5–7), but it is not to be belittled on that account. It was the Hasmoneans' absolute control over the entire area populated by Jews that enabled them to move freely along internal lines towards an enemy who was operating from outside Judea. It was this control and freedom of movement that enabled them to keep track of the enemy at all times, whereas the latter had to grope in the dark. Obviously, it was easier to gain control of villages with only a few Hellenizers, than of the urban center in Jerusalem, or the provincial towns, where there were many backsliders as well as troops able to protect them. Control of the rural area also provided the Hasmoneans with a territorial base for the future. It is in the nature of a small-scale war based on nationalist-religious aspirations that while rebellion can be suppressed for a time by military invasion, it can not be totally extinguished by external pressure. When the invading army departed, the men of the villages would again place themselves under the authority of the Hasmoneans.

This process of seizing control of Judea lasted about a year, until the death of Mattathias (*Ant.* XII, 279); according to I Maccabees (2:69–70) he died in the year 146 by the Seleucid reckoning, that is, in 165/6 B.C.E. The outbreak of the rebellion should thus be fixed in 167/6 B.C.E., that is about half a year after the desecration of the Temple in the month of Kislew, 145 Seleucid Era — December 167 B.C.E. (I Macc. 1:54). The fact that Mattathias' family interred him with great honor in the burial plot of his fathers in Modiin (I Macc. 2:70; *Ant.* XII, 285) is sufficient proof of the extent to which the rebels were already in control of the Jewish populated towns and villages even outside Judea proper.

In accordance with Mattathias' dying charge, leadership of the rebellion devolved upon two of his sons: Simeon, who "excels in understanding" (*Ant.* XII, 283), was assigned the political leadership although, considering the state of affairs at the time, that function was of only secondary importance. The main task, command of the army, was assumed by Mattathias' third son, Judah, known as the Maccabee (I Macc. 2:65–66).

C. The First Battles. The Blockade of Jerusalem

Of the early years and military training of the new commander next to nothing is known: I Maccabees (2:66) states only that he was "strong and mighty from his youth." It is not clear to what extent the son of a village priest could have demonstrated his prowess in war from his youth. It is after all inconceivable that Judah served in the Hellenistic armies as many Jewish mercenaries had done. The son of an observant family would hardly have done that. Moreover, training in Hellenistic methods of warfare would not have been much help in the guerrilla war that Judah had to wage. Only in the following generation did a Jewish force succeed in facing a regular Hellenistic army on the field of battle; until then, Judah and his brothers were compelled, in the words of II Maccabees

(8:6–7), to "gain possession of strategic positions" and take advantage of the night for military activities.

There is no doubt that the Hasmoneans' seizure of the villages of Judea soon made itself felt in Jeusalem, still ruled by the Hellenizers, the Seleucid army under Sostrates, the officer commanding the *akra*,[7] and Philip, who was in charge of implementing the king's Jewish policy. From the vicinity of Modiin and the mountains to the northeast it was possible to strike at the two main roads linking Jerusalem to the centers of the Seleucid government in the coastal plain, and more important, with Samaria, the seat of the *strategos* in charge of Judean affairs.[8] The roads to the southwest and to the south, to Mareshah (Marissa) and Hebron and to Idumaea, were also subject to rebel pressure. Undoubtedly the Syrian commanders in Jerusalem were most gravely concerned at the severing of the Beth-horon road and the road to Samaria. Their own forces in the city, however, were not strong enough to reopen these arteries. Their first duty was to guard Jerusalem itself and prevent a revival of the Jewish worship which the king had proscribed. Had they split up their forces between the city and the roads leading to it, they might have failed on both fronts and lost control of both the city and the highways. Had they deployed their entire force on the roads they would have endangered the city. On the other hand, time was against them. They were under blockade, and if outside help were not forthcoming, sooner or later lack of food and military supplies would compel them to evacuate the city or surrender. Naturally enough the *akra* garrison appealed for aid to the commanders of the Seleucid army and the king himself. Their appeals were repeated again and again over the years, until the *akra* fell to the Hasmoneans (I Macc. 6:22–27; 7:5–7; 13:21). In the first stage, the Seleucid battles with the Hasmoneans represent a series of rescue operations designed to break through the Hasmonean blockade of Jerusalem and to renew communication with the city. For the most part the Seleucid commanders were acting under the pressure of time, and, accordingly, they chose the shortest road to Jerusalem, which brought them straight up against the Hasmonean forces. This evaluation of the situation provides a key to both the strategy and the tactics used in these battles.

As with most problems of strategy, particularly under the conditions of warfare of the time, the determinant factor was geography. Accordingly the theater of operations in Judea should first be studied. The Jewish-populated area, where the battles were fought, was located along the watershed following the Holy Land's central ridge of the mountains extending southward from Nahal Shiloh (Wadi ash-Sha'ir), a distance of some 37 miles.

Because of the climatic conditions and terrain, most of the settlements in this area lay to the west of the watershed, close to the main road which ran north-south along the ridge. This was the road linking Samaria and Shechem with Gophna, Beth-el, Beeroth, Gibeath-shaul, Jerusalem, Bethlehem, and Beth-zur (3,330 ft.). On either side valleys descend to the deserts of Ephraim and of Judea on the east and the coastal plain on the west. A survey of all the feasible approaches by which a Seleucid army could go up to Jerusalem and break the blockade shows at once that the eastern roads were of no use to them. There are but two roads leading up from Jericho, one via the Beth-el and Ephraim spur, and the other direct to Jerusalem via the ascent of Adummim and the Mount of Olives. Apart from these roads it is hard for armies to move about in the area, and the eastern roads were therefore not used at all by the invaders.

Traffic in either direction on the north-south route also encounters various difficulties, notably because the road lies perpendicular to the course of most of the valleys in the area and the intervening ridges provide excellent positions for a defender. The western routes are by far most convenient although even here the ascent from the coastal plain to the mountain ridges runs between the water courses flowing from the crest of the watershed to the west. These roads sometimes cling to the mountain slopes (e.g. the Beth-horon road), while elsewhere the route at first continues in the valley, climbing only later (as the road in the Valley of Elah or the one from Mareshah to Beth-zur). In either case, the gradient was an obstacle to overcome. In fact, these ascents were the outstanding problems in all the various military campaigns against Judea.

To reach the top of the mountains, the Seleucid armies had to make a long detour through the coastal plain on their way from their centers. Needless to say, these movements were easily visible to Jews living in the coastal plain, who no doubt hastened to inform Judah Maccabee. The Hasmonean forces could move through the hills more rapidly than the heavily-armed Seleucid troops — thanks to the light equipment of the rebels — which more than balanced the disadvantage of their lack of heavy equipment on the battlefield. In the first stages of the war, the Hasmoneans benefited mainly from their superior intelligence network and their use of shorter internal lines of communication. And, of course, they were fighting in their own country, while after each battle the Seleucids had to mobilize new troops and transport them over long distances. On the other hand, both sides were well acquainted with the lay of the land — for occupants of the *akra*, native-born Hellenizers, acted as guides for the Seleucid army on its trek towards the mountains, and they surely knew all the byways of Judea (I Macc. 4:2). But knowledge of the roads could not make up for their lack of information about the movements of the army facing them.

The first action against the Jews was taken by the officer in charge of the eparchy of Samaria. The reason for this lies in the administrative structure of Palestine under the Seleucids. As far as it is known,[9] Judea was then a third-class administrative unit, subject to a second-class unit, namely the eparchy of Samaria. The head of this eparchy as *strategos* and *meridarches* was a certain Apollonius, apparently the same Apollonius who was commander of the Mysian guard (natives of a province in the kingdom of Pergamum in the northwest corner of Asia Minor), serving as mercenaries in the Seleucid army. In this capacity he bore the title *mysarches* (II Macc. 5:24).[10] Apollonius had once been assigned the task of enforcing in Samaria the same religious changes that were now being attempted in Judea. From documents referred to by Josephus, it appears that Apollonius was more successful in his mission than the other officials sent to Judea. The Samaritans pretended to submit to the royal decree and washed their hands of the Jews (*Ant.* XII, 261). Apollonius now organized units from among the "Gentiles" (ἔθνη), apparently Macedonian settlers in Samaria, and mobilized a "great host from Samaria" (απο Σαμαρείας δυναμιν; I Macc. 3:10), an expression which calls to mind the earlier "army of Samaria" of the days of Nehemiah, which was at the disposal of Sanballat the Horonite, also governor of Samaria and an enemy of Judea (Neh. 3:34). It is reasonable to assume that the author of the First Book of Maccabees deliberately used (in the Hebrew original, of course) an expression recalling the plight of Judea in Nehemiah's time and its deliverance in those days. We do not know the number of soldiers under the command of Apollonius; probably it was not large. At least half the Seleucid garrison in the Samaria district was concentrated in Jerusalem; the number of Macedonian settlers in Samaria (and perhaps also in Beth-shean [Scytho-polis], the second Greek city in Apollonius' eparchy, which also included Galilee) was certainly not large enough for extensive mobilization, and the number of Samaritans prepared to join this campaign likewise does not appear to have been very great. With these forces Apollonius proceeded against Judah.

The author of the First Book of Maccabees does not specify the place where the two armies met. All he says (3:11) is that "Judah perceived" the movements of the enemy "and went forth to meet him." The author apparently wishes to indicate that the battle took place outside Judah's familiar territory and perhaps even outside the area of Judea. The site of the battle can be established by considering the route which Apollonius followed. A look at the watershed road southward from Shechem (and roads in those days were not much different from present day routes) shows that after the plain of 'Eyn Soker (Sahl Makhna), which stretches to the east of Mount Gerizim, the road begins to ascend a series of ridges extending from east to west. The first pass, near the village of as-Sāwiya, was still in the district of the Samaritans;[11] while the second pass leading to the village of Lebonah (al-Lubbān) passed at its peak near Anuath Borcaeus, a point marking the northern end of the district of Ephraim (Apharaema, later the Gophna district) which was already then populated by Jews, and was therefore later on joined to Judea (I. Macc. 10:30; 11:34). From that point on Apollonius was therefore under observation by his adversary, thus giving Judah advantage in intelligence. Were it not for the phrase "and [he] went forth to meet him," we might assume that Judah's attack was carried out as the enemy army crossed the mountains at Jeshanah (Burj al-'isāna)[12] along the valley the Arabs today call Wadi al-Harāmiyya — "the robber's brook," no doubt because it lends itself to surprise attack from ambush. A battle at that spot, however, was too dangerous. Victory by Apollonius would have opened the door to Beth-el and the interior of Judea for him. If the enemy had had the same numerical advantage he later enjoyed in the battle of Beth-zur (see below), Judah would undoubtedly have preferred to fight on the border of Judea. However, it appears that Apollonius' army was superior to Judah's neither in strength (we know that Judah had six thousand men [II Macc. 8:1]) nor in training (it, too, had been formed from civilians, not from professional soldiers). For these reasons it may be assumed that Judah attacked Apollonius at the ascent of Lebonah.

It also appears that Apollonius was aware of the deficiences of his army. He put himself at the head of his soldiers in order to spur them on and he was one of the first to fall. With their commander slain, his mixed forces were, of course, completely shaken; many fell and the rest fled. That they were able to escape without being pursued also proves that the battle occurred near the Samarian border. Later sources[13] link this battle with a duel between Judah and Apollonius, but the short version in the Book of Maccabees does not justify this assumption. The Jewish troops benefited greatly from this first victory. On the one hand, the northern border of Judea was secured for quite some time. In addition, the Jews captured a large quantity of booty, particularly weapons, of which they were in great need. At that time, no arms industry existed in Judea. Weapons and military equipment of the Hellenistic period were of high quality, and not

45.
Ptolemaic inscription, Mareshah
(Israel Dept. of Antiquities and Museums)

46.
Samaria inscription
in honor of Sarapis
(Israel Dept. of Antiquities
and Museums)

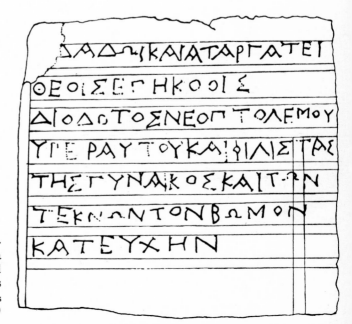

47.
Acre inscription
in honor of Hadad
and Atargatis
(Israel Dept. of Antiquities
and Museums)

48.
Zenon contract papyrus
(Cairo Museum no. 59003)

ΠΕΡ ΒΑΣΙΛΕΩΣ

ΤΟΛΕΜΑΙΟΥΚΑΙ:

ΑΣΙΛΙΣΣΗΣ

ΕΡΕΝΙΚΗΣΑΔΕΛ

ΦΗΣΚΑΙΓΥΝΑΙΚΟΣΚΑΙ

ΤΩΝΤΕΚΝΩΝ

ΤΗΝΠΡΟΣΕΥΧΗΝ

ΟΙ ΙΟΥΔΑΟΙ

49.
Schedia inscription in honor of
Ptolemy III

50.
YHD coin with
name of Ezechias
(Archeological Instit.
Hebrew Univ., Jerusalem)

51.
Ptolemaic coin
struck at Jaffa
(Archeological Instit.
Hebrew Univ., Jerusalem)

52.
Gezer boundary inscription
(Hebrew Union College, Jerusalem)

53.
Gezer "Curse" grafitto

54.
Bene Hezir inscription on tomb
(Archeological Instit. Hebrew Univ.,
Jerusalem)

55.
Hellenistic tower at Samaria

56.
Tomb of Bene Hezir

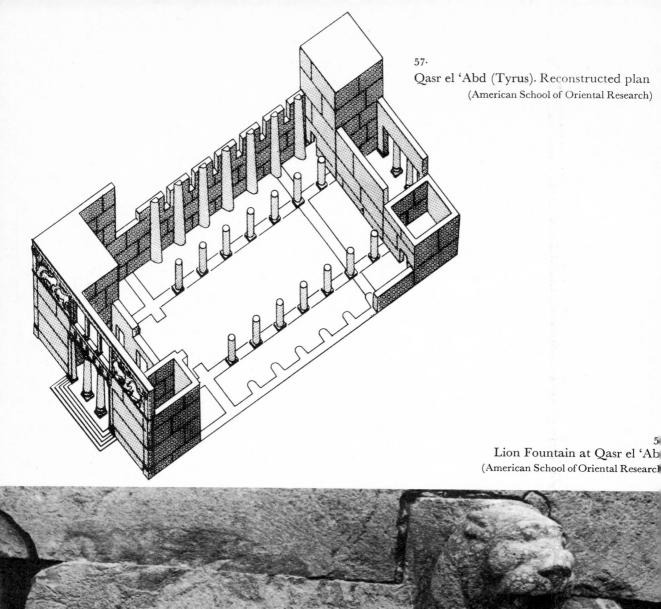

57.
Qasr el 'Abd (Tyrus). Reconstructed plan
(American School of Oriental Research)

5
Lion Fountain at Qasr el 'Ab
(American School of Oriental Research

59.
Qasr el 'Abd. Wall and frieze
(American School of Oriental Research)

60.
Drawing of *menorot*
from Jason's tomb
(Israel Dept. of Antiquities and Museums)

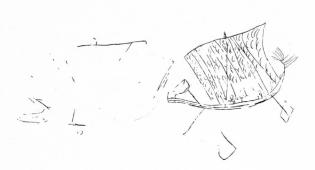

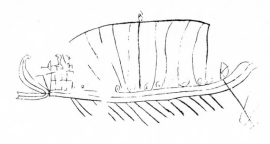

61.
Drawing of naval battle on the tomb wall
(Israel Dept. of Antiquities and Museums)

62.
Jason's tomb. Jerusalem
(Israel Dept. of Antiquities and Museums)

63.
Ruins of Mt. Gerizim temple

64.
Rock cuttings of Acra. Jerusalem

65.
Battlefield near Emmaus

66.
Beth-Horon pass

67.
The Rock of Arbel

68.
The plain of Hazor

69. Maccabbean Wall inside Jerusalem Citadel

70. Hasmonean Tower and Glacis.
Ophel, Jerusalem

71—72.
Hasmonean Walls at Alexandrium and Gezer
(Israel Dept. of Antiquities and Museums)

73.
Hasmonean Wall at Jaffa

74· Seleucid coins showing horn of plenty and anchor
(Archeological Instit. Hebrew Univ.,   Jerusalem)

75· Coin of John Hyrcanus with horn of plenty
(Archeological Instit. Hebrew Univ.,   Jerusalem)

76. Coin of Jannaeus Alexander with anchor and star
(Archeological Instit. Hebrew Univ.,   Jerusalem)

74—76. Seleucid and Hasmonean coins

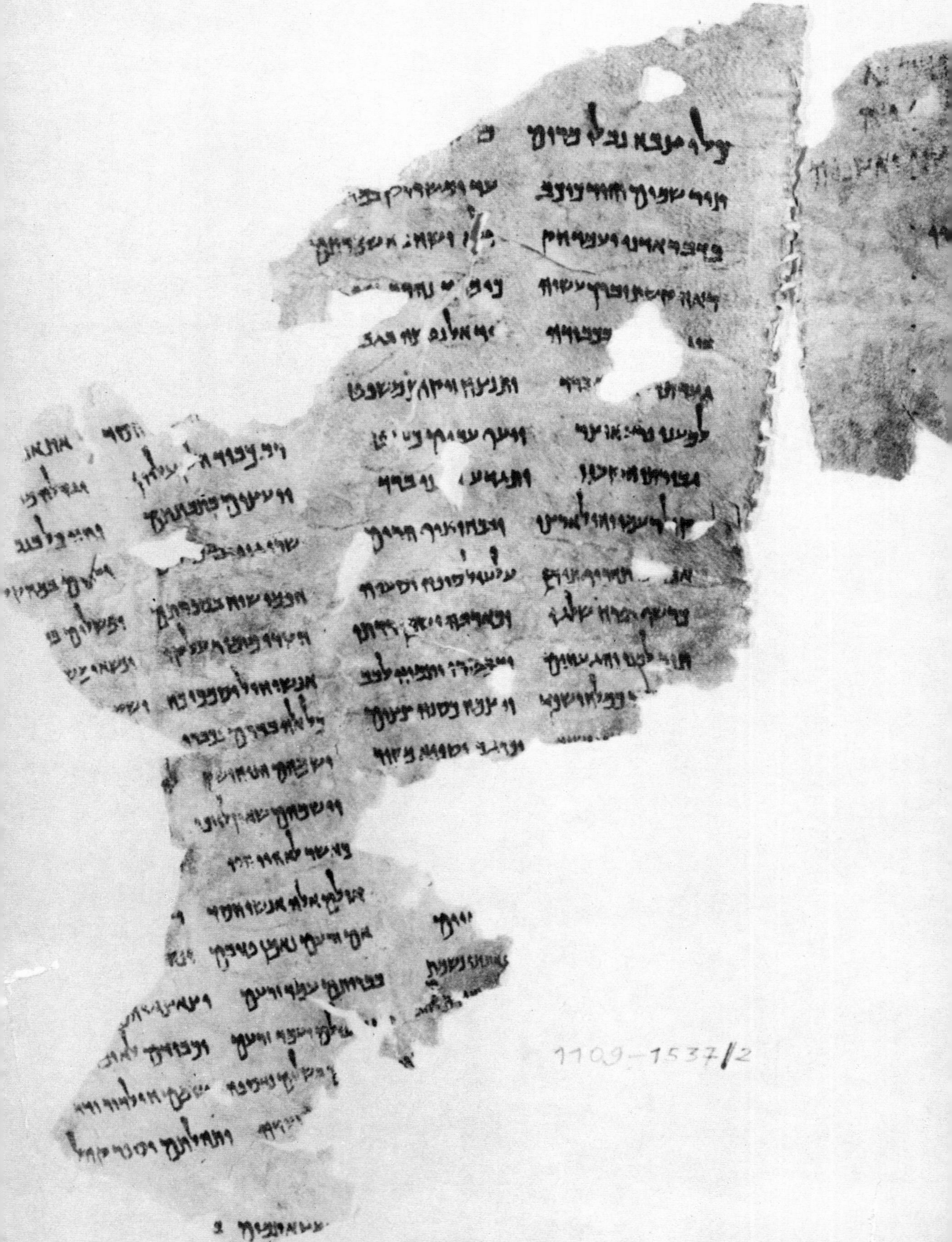

77.
Ben Sira scroll from Masada
(by permission of Prof. Y. Yadin)

ΛΙΗΜΕΡΑΙΜΑΤΤΑ
ΘΙΟΥΑΠΟΘΑΝΙΝ
ΚΑΙΕΠΕΝΤΟΙϹΥΪ
ΑΥΤΟΥΝΥΝΕϹΤΗ
ΡΙϹΘΗΥΠΕΡΗΦΑΝΙ
ΑΚΑΙΕΛΕΓΜΟϹΚΑΙ
ΚΑΙΡΟϹΚΑΤΑϹΤΡ
ΦΗϹΚΑΙΟΡΓΗΘΥ
ΜΟΥΝΥΝΤΕΚΝΑ
ΖΗΛΩϹΑΤΕΤΩΝ
ΜΩΚΑΙΔΟΤΕΤΑ
ΨΥΧΑϹΥΜΩΝΥΠ
ΔΙΑΘΗΚΗϹΠΑΡ
ΥΜΩΝΚΑΙΜΝΗ
ΤΑΙΤΑΕΡΓΑΤΩΝΠ
ΤΕΡΩΝΑΕΠΟΙΗ
ΕΝΤΑΙϹΓΕΝΕΛΙϹ
ΑΥΤΩΝΚΑΙΔΕΞΑ
ϹΘΑΙΔΟΞΑΝΜΕΤΑ
ΛΗΝΚΑΙΟΝΟΜΑ
ΑΙΩΝΙΟΝ
ΑΒΡΑΑΜΟΥΧΙΕΝ
ΠΙΡΑϹΜΩΕΥΡΕΘΗ
ΠΙϹΤΟϹΚΑΙΕΛΟΓΙ
ϹΘΗΑΥΤΩΕΙϹΔΙΚ
ΟϹΥΝΗΝΙΩϹΗΦ
ΕΝΚΑΙΡΩϹΤΕΝΟ
ΧΩΡΙΑϹΑΥΤΟΥΕΦΥ
ΛΑΞΕΝΕΝΤΟΛΗΝ
ΚΑΙΕΓΕΝΕΤΟΚϹΑΙ
ΓΥΠΤΟΥΦΙΝΕΕϹΟ
ΠΑΤΗΡΗΜΩΝΕΝ
ΤΩΖΗΛΩϹΑΙΖΗ
ΕΛΑΒΕΝΚΛΗΡΟΝ
ΔΙΑΘΗΚΗϹΑΙΩΝΙ
ΑϹΙΕΡΩϹΥΝΗϹ
ΙΗϹΟΥϹΕΝΤΩΙΠ
ΡΩϹΑΙΛΟΓΟΝΕΓΕ
ΝΕΤΟΚΡΙΤΗϹΕΝΙ
ΧΑΛΕΒΕΝΤΩΜΑΡΤΥ
ΡΑϹΘΑΙΕΝΤΗΕΚΚΛΗ
ϹΙΑΕΛΑΒΕΝΤΗΝ
ΚΛΗΡΟΝΟΜΙΑΝ
ΑΛΛΕΝΤΩΕΛΕΕΙΑΥ
ΤΟΥΕΚΛΗΡΟΝΟΜΗ
ϹΕΝΘΡΟΝΟΝΒΑ
ΑϹΕΙΑΙΩΝΑϹ

ΗΛΙΑϹΕΝΤΩΖΗΛ
ϹΑΙΝΟΜΟΝΖΗΛ
ΑΝΕΛΗΜΦΘΗΕΙ
ΤΟΝΟΥΝΟΝ
ΑΝΑΝΙΑϹΑΖΑΡΙΑ
ΜΙϹΑΗΛΠΙϹΤΕΥϹΑ
ΤΕϹΕϹΩΘΗϹΑΝ
ΕΚΦΛΟΓΟϹ
ΔΑΝΙΗΛΕΝΤΗΑΠΛ
ΤΗΤΙΑΥΤΟΥΕΡΡΥϹΘΗ
ΕΚϹΤΟΜΑΤΟϹΛΕΟΝ
ΤΟϹΚΑΙΟΥΤΩϹΕΝ
ΝΟΗΘΗΤΑΙΚΑΤΑ
ΓΕΝΕΑΝΚΑΙΓΕΝ
ΑΝΟΤΙΠΑΝΤΕϹΟΙ
ΕΛΠΙΖΟΝΤΕϹΕΠΑΥ
ΤΟΝΟΥΚΑϹΘΕΝΗ
ϹΟΥϹΙΝΚΑΙΑΠΟΛ
ΓΩΝΑΝΔΡΟϹΑ
ΜΑΡΤΩΛΟΥΜΗΦ
ΒΗΘΗΤΕΟΤΙΗΔΟ
ΞΑΑΥΤΟΥΕΙϹΚΟΠΡΙ
ΑΚΑΙΕΙϹϹΚΩΛΗ
ΚΑϹϹΗΜΕΡΟΝΕ
ΠΑΡΘΗϹΕΤΑΙΚΑΙ
ΑΥΡΙΟΝΟΥΜΗΕΥ
ΡΕΘΗΚΑΙΕΠΕϹΤΡ
ΨΕΝΕΙϹΤΟΝΧΟΥΝ
ΑΥΤΟΥΚΑΙΟΔΙΑΛ
ΓΙϹΜΟϹΑΥΤΟΥΑΠΟ
ΛΙΤΑΙ
ΤΕΚΝΑΑΝΔΡΙΖΕϹΘ
ΚΑΙΙϹΧΥϹΑΤΕΕΝ
ΤΩΝΟΜΩΟΤΙΕ
ΝΑΥΤΩΔΟΞΑϹΘΗ
ϹΕϹΘΑΙ
ΚΑΙΙΔΟΥϹΥΜΕΩΝ
ΟΑΔΕΛΦΟϹΥΜΩ
ΟΙΔΑΟΤΙΑΝΗΡΒΟΥ
ΛΗϹΕϹΤΙΝΑΥΤΟΥ
ΑΚΟΥΕΤΕΠΑϹΑϹΤ
ΗΜΕΡΑϹΑΥΤΟϹ
ΕϹΤΑΙΥΜΩΝΠΑ
ΤΗΡΚΑΙΙΟΥΔΑϹΜΑΚ
ΚΑΒΑΙΟϹΙϹΧΥΡΟ
ΔΥΝΑΜΙΝΕΚΝΕ
ΤΗΤΟϹΑΥΤΟϹΕϹΤΑΙ

ΥΜΙΝΑΡΧΩΝϹΤΡΑ
ΤΙΑϹΚΑΙΠΟΛΕΜ
ϹΕΙΠΟΛΕΜΟΝΛΑ
ΩΝΚΑΙΥΜΕΙϹΠΡΟ
ΑϹΕΤΕΠΡΟϹΥΜΑ
ΠΑΝΤΑϹΤΟΥϹΠΟΙ
ΗΤΑϹΤΟΥΝΟΜΟΥ
ΚΑΙΕΚΔΙΚΗϹΑΙ
ΕΚΔΙΚΗϹΙΝΤΟΥ
ΛΑΟΥΥΜΩΝΑΝΤΑ
ΠΟΔΟΤΑΙΑΝΤΑΠ
ΔΟΜΑΤΟΙϹΕΘΝΕ
ϹΙΝΚΑΙΠΡΟϹΕΧΕ
ΤΕΕΙϹΠΡΟϹΤΑΓΜΑ
ΤΟΥΝΟΜΟΥΚΑΗ
ΛΟΓΗϹΕΝΑΥΤΟΥ
ΚΑΙΠΡΟϹΕΤΕΘΗ
ΠΡΟϹΤΟΥϹΠΑΤΕΡΑ
ΑΥΤΩΝΚΑΙΑΠΕ
ΘΑΝΕΝΕΝΤΩΓΚΑΙ
ΜΚΑΙΕΘΕΤΕΙΚΑΙ
ΕΤΑΦΗΕΝΤΑΦΟΙϹ
ΠΡΩΝΑΥΤΟΥΕΝ
ΜΩΔΕΙΝΚΑΙΕΚ
ΨΑΝΤΟΑΥΤΟΝΠΑ
ΙϹΑΚΟΠΕΤΟΝΜ
ΓΑΝ
ΚΑΙΑΝΕϹΤΗΙΟΥΔΑ
ΟΚΑΛΟΥΜΕΝΟϹ
ΜΑΚΚΑΒΑΙΟϹΥΙ
ΟϹΑΥΤΟΥΑΝΤΑΡ
ΤΟΥΚΑΙΕΒΟΗΘΟΥ
ΑΥΤΩΠΑΝΤΕϹΟΙ
ΑΔΕΛΦΟΙΑΥΤΟΥΚ
ΠΑΝΤΕϹΟΙΕΚΟΛ
ΛΗΘΗϹΑΝΤΩΠΡΙ
ΑΥΤΟΥΚΑΙΕΠΟΛ
ΜΟΥΝΤΟΠΟΛΕΜ
ΙΗΛΑΜΕΤΕΥΦΡΟϹ
ΝΗϹΚΑΙΕΠΛΑΤΥ
ΝΕΝΔΟΞΑΝΤΩΛΑ
ΩΑΥΤΟΥΚΑΙΕΝΕ
ΔΥϹΑΤΟΘΩΡΑΚΑ
ΩϹΓΙΓΑϹΚΑΙϹΥΝ
ΖΩϹΑΤΟΤΑϹΚΕΥΗ
ΤΑΠΟΛΕΜΙΚΑΑΥ
ΤΟΥΚΑΙϹΥΝΕϹΤΗ

ϹΑΤΟΠΟΛΕΜΟ
ϹΚΕΠΑΖΩΝΠΑ
ΒΟΛΗΝΕΝΡΟΜ
ΦΑΙΑΚΑΙΩΜΟΙ
ΘΛΑΕΟΝΤΙΕΝΤ
ΕΡΓΟΙϹΚΑΙΩϹϹ
ΜΝΟϹΟΡΕΥΟΜ
ΝΟϹΕΙϹΘΗΡΑΝ
ΚΑΙΕΔΙΩΞΕΝΑ
ΝΟΜΟΥϹΕΞΕΡΕ
ΚΑΙΤΟΥϹΤΑΡΑϹ
ΤΑϹΤΟΝΛΑΟΝΑ
ΤΟΥΕΦΛΟΓΙϹΕ
ΚΑΙϹΥΝΕϹΤΑΛ
ϹΑΝΑΝΟΜΟΙΑΠ
ΤΟΥΦΟΒΟΥΑΥΤ
ΚΑΙΠΑΝΤΕϹΟΙ
ΓΑΤΑΙΤΗϹΑΝΟΜ
ΑϹϹΥΝΕΤΑΡΑΧ
ϹΑΝΚΑΙΕΥΟΔΩ
ΘΗϹΩΤΗΡΙΑΕΝ
ΧΙΡΙΑΥΤΟΥΚΑΙΕ
ΠΙΚΡΑΝΕΝΒΑϹΙ
ΛΕΙϹΠΟΛΛΟΥϹΚ
ΕΥΦΡΑΝΕΝΤΟ
ΙΑΚΩΒΕΝΤΟΙϹ
ΓΟΙϹΑΥΤΟΥΚΑΙ
ΩϹΤΟΥΑΙΩΝΟϹ
ΤΟΜΝΗΜΟϹΥΝ
ΑΥΤΟΥΚΑΙΕΙϹΕ
ΛΟΓΙΑΝΚΑΙΔΙΗΛ
ΘΕΝΕΝΠΟΛΙΟ
ΛΑΚΑΙΕΞΩΛΕ
ϹΕΝΑϹΕΒΕΙϹΕΞ
ΤΗϹΚΑΙΑΠΕϹΤ
ΕΝΟΡΓΗΝΑΠΟ
ΙϹΑΚΑΙΩΝΟΜΑ
ϹΟΘΗΕΩϹΕϹΧΑ
ΤΗϹΓΗϹΚΑΙϹΥΝΗΓ
ΓΕΝΑΠΟΛΛΥΜ
ΚΑΙϹΥΝΗΓΑΓΕΝ
ΑΠΟΛΛΩΝΙΟϹ
ΘΝΗΚΑΙΑΠΟϹΑ
ΜΑΡΙΑϹΔΥΝΑΜ
ΜΕΤΑΛΗΝΤΟΥ
ΛΕΜΗϹΑΙΠΡΟϹΤ
ΙϹΑΚΑΙΕΓΝΩΤΩ

78.
Paragraph of 1 Maccabees, 2:49–
3:11, of the Codex Sinaiticus

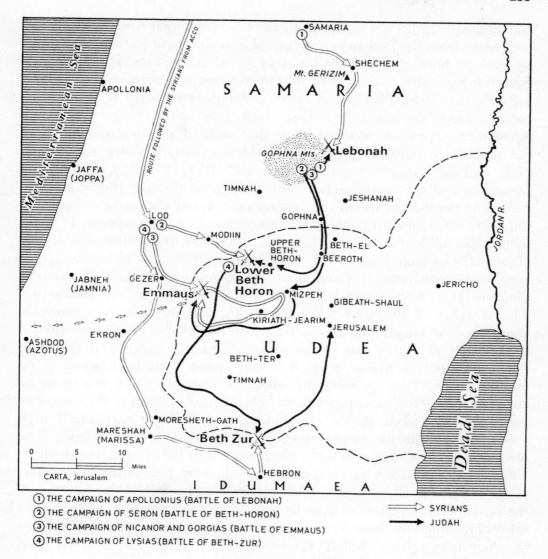

① THE CAMPAIGN OF APOLLONIUS (BATTLE OF LEBONAH)
② THE CAMPAIGN OF SERON (BATTLE OF BETH-HORON)
③ THE CAMPAIGN OF NICANOR AND GORGIAS (BATTLE OF EMMAUS)
④ THE CAMPAIGN OF LYSIAS (BATTLE OF BETH-ZUR)

⟹ SYRIANS
⟶ JUDAH

First Battles of Judah Maccabee

easily manufactured without trained craftsmen. The Jews still fought with the weapons usually found among farmers. Judah Maccabee himself was in need of a good sword; when the opportunity came, he took Apollonius', and it served him for the rest of his life.

News of this victory impelled the Seleucid authorities to take action on a higher level. Suppression of the revolt was no longer the responsibility of the governor of the eparchy but passed to the governor-general of Coele-Syria and Phoenicia, who was in charge of all the areas which Antiochus III had conquered from the Ptolemies and turned into a *strategia* (called a "satrapy" by some authors),[14] one of the 72 satrapies in his kingdom. The position of governor-general was then held by Ptolemy son of Dorymenes (II Macc. 8:8). He had at his disposal an army under the command of Seron, "the commander of the host of Syria" (I Macc. 3:13). Seron had learned from Apollonius' experience of the dangers that awaited an army moving along the mountain roads. He therefore decided to march down the coastal plain and then use the main "public road" (*War.* II, 228; V, 58) linking Jerusalem and the coastal plain, namely the road through the Beth-horon pass. The point from which the army set out is not known, although it is unlikely that Seron left from Damascus, the seat of the governor. It seems more reasonable to assume that his army was concentrated at Acco (Ptolemais), which had served as a royal fortress and mustering point even in Persian times.[15] From there Seron proceeded along the coastal plain as far as Lod, where he turned east toward the Judean mountains. This march took him quite close to Modiin, but the town was probably abandoned as long as he remained in the vicinity. There is no precise information as to the size of his army; from the number of the dead (eight hundred; I Macc. 3:24) it would appear that it consisted of no more than eight to ten thousand men. On the one hand, it cannot be assumed that Seron's troops went on fighting until a tenth of their number had been killed; but, on the other hand, casualties are particularly high when fleeing from an enemy attacking from above — (see below.) The nucleus of Seron's army must have comprised a number of regular units of the king's army, and these were apparently joined by Jew-hating inhabitants of the Hellenistic cities in the coastal plain,[16] and possibly also by some of the Jewish Hellenizers, whom the Book of Maccabees describes as "a mighty army of the ungodly," who joined Seron with the aim of wreaking vengeance on their fellow Jews. Judah Maccabee had undoubtedly also received advance information of the movements of this army; however, the forces at his disposal had been reduced to a dangerous degree after the first battle. It may be true that the *Ḥasidim* had no part in this battle, as *Josippon* (4, 20) states. In any case, the Jewish force concentrated in Upper Beth-horon was so small that the soldiers lost courage when they saw Seron's army leave Lower Beth-horon and begin its ascent of the mountain (I Macc. 3:17). However, words of encouragement from Judah revived their spirit and they launched a sudden attack (εἰς . . . . . ἄφνω) on the enemy. The site of the battle can be determined from the topographical features of the Beth-Horon pass. The village of Lower Beth-horon lies at an altitude of

1,310 ft. Above it, the road continues on a ridge which climbs between two streams to the upper village, 2,024 ft. above sea level. From there, the shoulder narrows progressively to a hill 2,180 ft. tall, after which the ascent becomes easier until it reaches 2,206 ft., the heights of Ramallah-Beeroth.

Judah must have camped in the upper village, from which he could watch the entire ascent (I Macc. 3:17). It is very likely that when he saw the enemy advancing, Judah fell back to the hill. Two reasons would favor such a withdrawal. If Judah saw the enemy, the enemy may have seen him and his men, and in that case the unexpected retreat would account for the subsequent element of surprise which is emphasized by the author of the First Book of Maccabees. It also appears that the surprise came precisely because Seron and his men ascended without hindrance as far as Upper Beth-horon and accordingly supposed themselves safe from any ambush. The unexpected attack from the hill took them completely by surprise.[17]

According to our source, eight hundred of the enemy fell; Josephus mentions (*Ant.* XII, 292) that Seron, too, was killed in this engagement, and that his death threw the deployment of his troops into disarray. This story sounds like fanciful repetition of the account of the battle against Apollonius, where the foreign commander also fell; but that in itself does not discredit it. Seron's name does not appear in the description of subsequent battles, which strengthens Josephus' testimony.

The soldiers who fled from the battle made their way to "the land of the Philistines" (I Macc. 3:24), that is, the district of Idumaea which included Ashdod and the other former Philistine cities. In contrast to the description of the battle against Apollonius, our source in this case emphasizes the fact that Judah pursued the enemy "unto the plain" (I Macc. 3:24) without of course actually entering the coastal plain, since this was dominated by the royal fortresses. The difference between the battles of Lebonah and Beth-horon may be explained by the fact that in the first case the armies were fighting on the border of Jewish and Samarian territory, and any pursuit would have brought Judah Maccabee and his men into a hostile country, whereas in the battle of Beth-horon the enemy had penetrated quite deeply into Jewish territory, and the pursuit took place in the foot-hills of an area populated by Jews, even though formally it was not yet part of Judea itself.

This second defeat further undermined the position of the soldiers and civilians in Jerusalem, who once again called upon the king for help. Antiochus himself was at that time setting out for a campaign in Persia[18] leaving affairs of the kingdom west of the Euphrates in the hands of Lysias, one of his "friends and relations" whom he had appointed viceroy with authority from the Euphrates to the Egyptian border (I Macc. 3:32).[19] In the spring of 165 B.C.E., the king set out on his campaign, leaving the suppression of the revolt in Judea in the hands of his deputy.

In the view of the author of I Maccabees (3:34–36), this was one of Lysias' main tasks, and for this purpose he was given half the Seleucid army and "the elephants," that is, the bulk of the kingdom's military might. A more objective approach suggests that this activity, important as it was, still did not occupy a central place in the affairs of the Seleucid kingdom. In any case, Lysias did not tackle the job himself but assigned it to the above mentioned governor of Coele-Syria, Ptolemy son of Dorymenes. According to the First Book of Maccabees (3:38–40), three generals — Ptolemy, Nicanor and Gorgias — set out on the conquest of Judea. However, Ptolemy's name does not recur in this connection, and the version of the Second Book of Maccabees is more reliable on this point. According to II Maccabees (8:9), Ptolemy named Nicanor son of Patroclus as the commanding general, and assigned to him an experienced mercenary commander as an adviser. This man was Gorgias, who perhaps served as a sort of chief-of-staff. As to the numbers of the army, the account of Jason of Cyrene again appears to be the most reliable one. According to that source Nicanor's army numbered no fewer than twenty thousand men, whereas the First Book of Maccabees speaks of forty thousand infantry and seven thousand cavalry. Since this is the first time such exaggerated figures are encountered, it should be made clear at once that they are not at all plausible. When the Seleucid kingdom was much stronger, at the time of Antiochus III, all the Seleucid and Ptolemaic forces were mobilized for the decisive battle near Raphia (in 217 B.C.E.), and Polybius[20] gives the strength of the Egyptian forces as 75,000 soldiers (including 25,300 Egyptian and Lybians) and lists 68,000 in the Seleucid army (including 38,500 Syrians). The figures in I Maccabees are further suspect because of their similarity to the number of Arameans killed by David according to I Chron. 19:18: "the men of seven thousand chariots, and forty thousand footmen."[21] But even if we take the lower figure and subtract from it the auxiliary forces accompanying the actual fighting troops (whom we also met in the previous battles, except that this time they were Idumaeans and inhabitants of the Philistine coastal plain; I Macc. 3:41), it still leaves Nicanor with a sizeable military force, greater than Judah's.

The two previous attempts to enter Judea from the north and the north-west, which had ended in defeat, convinced Nicanor and Gorgias to give preference to an invasion from the west. To that end they advanced with their army to Emmaus and camped among the hills (the biblical "Lowland" [Shefela] according to I Macc. 3:40). Strategically, three alternatives were available to them: to stay put, to advance in a single column, or to divide up their army. In the first instance they would indeed keep their army intact, but they would not accomplish their object: the liberation of the blockaded Hellenizers and soldiers in the *akra* of Jerusalem. The second possibility was to round up their whole army and proceed towards Jerusalem. Since, following Seron's defeat, the Beth-horon road appeared the most dangerous, they were left with the alternative of the road which today leads from Sha'ar Haggay to Jerusalem: first along the Valley of Nahshon (or one of the parallel ridges to the north or south) and then along the plain to Kiriath-jearim. From there it would be an easy matter to advance to Mizpeh (an-Nabī Samwīl [see below]) and to Jerusalem via Mount Scopus. Of course, during the ascent in the Valley of Nahshon, or by one of the routes leading up to Kiriath-jearim or to Mizpeh, they might be attacked by Judah Maccabee; but in view of their great numerical advantage this choice was perhaps the best. Nevertheless, Nicanor and Gorgias chose the third possibility. Gorgias took five thousand foot soldiers and a thousand cavalry and in the middle of the night set out to make a surprise attack on Judah's forces, while Nicanor remained in camp with the rest of the army (I Macc. 4:1–2).

The reason for this decision was information about the massing of the Jewish army, brought by the people of the *akra*. Judah Maccabee was well aware of the danger threatening from the strong military concentration encamped at Emmaus, i.e., already in Judean territory (*ibid.*, 3:42). He thereupon decided to muster all his forces (in contrast with the handful that had fought with him at Beth-horon). As the place of assembly he chose "Mizpeh, over against Jerusalem for in Mizpeh there had been aforetime a place of prayer for Israel" (*ibid.* 3:46). On the basis of this verse many commentators[22] identified Mizpeh with Tell an-Naṣba, north of Jerusalem. However, three points may be noted with reference to this view: first of all, the identification of Tell an-Naṣba with Mizpeh is not that certain.[23] Second, such a concentration would have left the road to Jerusalem open to the enemy. True, Abel has rightly pointed out[24] that at Tell an-Naṣba Judah would have commanded both the road coming from the north and the Beth-horon road. But then the question arises, why was it necessary for him to defend these roads if the enemy was poised at Emmaus, at the head of an entirely different road? And we know that throughout the Hasmonean War Judea's intelligence service was most efficient. Third, to say that Tell an-Naṣba is "over against Jerusalem" is doubtful; for the Mount Scopus ridge separates and conceals this place from Jerusalem. For all these reasons, it appears more likely that the place where the troops were massed was elsewhere. The name Mizpeh, "Watch-point," was indeed quite common in Judea and Israel. The most suitable location for this Mizpeh is the hill known in Arabic as an-Nabī Samwīl (2, 903 ft. above sea level), one of the highest points on the approaches to Jerusalem and from which one can view both the city itself and the ridges leading to it.[25] According to II Maccabees (8:16), the Jewish force consisted of six thousand men, organized into units of tens, fifties, hundreds, and thousands (I Macc. 3:55). This was a natural division; it is to be found in the Pentateuch in civil affairs (Ex. 18:21, 25; Deut. 1:15) and partly also in the military establishment (Num. 31:48; II Kings 1:9 ff; 11:4, 9; I Chron. 27:1). Nor did they forget "the officers of the people" (I Macc. 5:42), who constituted a sort of military police.[26] Josephus (*Ant.* XII, 301) emphasizes that the organization was "according to the ancient custom of their fathers."[27] According to the Second Book of Maccabees (8:21–22), on the other hand, the army was divided into four forces of 1,500 men each, headed by Judah himself and his brothers Simeon, Joseph, and Jonathan. Thus the two sources are contradictory. Furthermore, we do not know of a brother of Judah by the name Joseph; and perhaps there was also a commander by the name of Eleazar (II Macc. 8:23). However, these contradictions can be reconciled with the aid of references in the First Book of Maccabees (5:56) regarding the commanders Joseph ben Zechariah and Azariah (see below). It thus seems more likely that the full complement of the Hasmonean army was divided into six groups of 1,000 men each. Four of them were commanded by the Hasmonean brothers (with the exception of Johanan) and the remaining two by Joseph and Azariah. At the head of his fully organized army, Judah proceeded to a camp south of Emmaus, perhaps on the 1,030 ft. high hill north of the present-day village of Mᵉsillat Ziyyon. The small valley concealed to the south of this hill was well-suited for a camp. An observation point at the top of the hill overlooked the opposite ridge, at the foot of Emmaus, where the enemy was encamped. We should also note that in this campaign Judah avoided the error of his adversaries, and instead of splitting up his army, kept it intact as a unit.

Gorgias received a report about the concentration at Mizpeh from the men of the *akra*, and was prompted to undertake a night expedition with the latter serving as guides (I Mac. 4:1–2). The high proportion of cavalry in this unit indicates his desire to insure the mobility of his troops, particularly in view of the superior quality of the Hellenistic cavalry (*ibid.* 4:1). After marching through the darkness, Gorgias arrived at Judah's camp at Mizpeh, only to find it empty and with the camp fires still burning to deceive the enemy (*Ant.* XII, 306). On the mistaken assumption that Judah was fleeing from him, Gorgias began to search for the Jews in the hills — apparently along the ridges extending south of Mizpeh — but in vain. On leaving the mountains around noon, he beheld the Emmaus camp already abandoned and going up in flames.

The attack on the Seleucid detachment which had remained at Emmaus was carried out by Judah in accordance with sound rules of strategy. He succeeded in attacking the enemy while the latter's forces were divided. And the attack was carried out by half of his strength, three thousand men, the remainder being kept in reserve against the sudden appearance of the enemy units moving about among the mountains. The Jewish army was not equipped with defensive armor, and the quality of their swords was not to their liking. In addition, the enemy camp was heavily fortified and surrounded with mounted watches. Obviously, the Greeks were on guard against a surprise attack, but the Jews had the advantage of the timing of their onslaught: in the early morning, when an army's watchfulness and fighting spirit are generally slacker. Indeed, the surprise was complete. When they saw the advancing Jews, the Seleucid troops left the camp, but were immediately attacked, even before they had time to form a phalanx. The commander, Nicanor, escaped this time, but his army was routed. The soldiers who made their escape reached Gezer, the large royal fortress which guarded the western approaches to Judea. The pursuit continued as far as "the plains of Idumaea" (I Macc. 4:6-15).

The province called Idumaea, and populated by Idumaeans (the biblical Edomites) who had wandered in after the destruction of the First Temple, occupied an area in southern Judea, but it had at first not included territory in the coastal plain. The Seleucids converted it into one of their eparchies and expanded it to comprise the cities of Ashdod (Azotus) and Jabneh (Jamnia). The author of I Maccabees emphasizes this fact by mentioning the two cities in the same verse.

During the chase Judah gave a good demonstration of his ability as a commander and the level of discipline he had been able to introduce in his army. He ordered the pursuit halted and the booty left alone, in view of the approach from the rear of the Greek army headed by Gorgias. Keeping in mind the difficult task confronting a commander trying to keep an army of irregulars from hoped-for booty (particularly considering the poor equipment possessed by the Jewish army, as already mentioned), the power of Judah's personality can be appreciated. The pursuit was discontinued and the soldiers turned about. The vanguard of Gorgias' army was at once discerned by guards at the top of the mountain, apparently on the northern ridge of Sha'ar Haggay, at an altitude of 1,256. However, beholding the rest of the Seleucid army in retreat, their camp at Emmaus in flames, and the Jewish army in front of them drawn up for battle, Gorgias withdrew to the plain of Philistia, no doubt bypassing Emmaus from the south (I Macc. 4:16–20). It was obvious to him that with the bulk of his army defeated, he had no prospect of winning with the rest, particularly against an enemy arrayed for battle. Had the Jewish army been scattered while pursuing the enemy, matters might have been different. The source does not mention Gezer in connection with this retreat, and Gorgias may have chosen the Nahal Sorek road to Ekron (Khirbat al-Muqanna'). Thus the third battle for the approaches of Judea ended in the same manner as the previous two.[28]

Now, as after each of the other defeats, the problem of the continuing rebellion in Judea was dealt with at a still higher echelon in the Seleucid administration. Instead of leaving the matter in the hands of the governor-general of Coele-Syria, the viceroy Lysias decided to deal personally with this messy business and to lead his army against Judea. Regarding the size of the army, neither of the sources can be relied upon.[29] The First Book of Maccabees (4:27) attributes to Lysias sixty thousand infantry and five thousand cavalry, while the Second Book of Maccabees (11:2, 4) speaks of eighty thousand foot-soldiers, thousands of cavalry and eighty elephants. None of these figures is plausible in view of what has been said above concerning the size of the Seleucid armies in general. Similarly, no conclusion is possible from the figures of the dead (5,000 in I Maccabees and 12,600 in II Maccabees). It suffices to state that the Seleucid army was undoubtedly larger than Judah's, perhaps three times as numerous. On the other hand, the number given for Judah's soldiers in this battle (10,000) can be accepted as reasonable. After his victory near Emmaus, many additional volunteers probably joined him, and their number may well have risen to four thousand.

Lysias drew up an ingenious plan of campaign, showing that he had learned from the experience of the previous battles. Like his predecessors he made no attempt to use any of the roads on which Judah Maccabee had already been victorious. His army was too small (which is also evidence of the exaggeration in the figures mentioned above) to allow him to attack Judah from two directions, although this would, no doubt, have been the most effective way of breaking the blockade of Jerusalem and putting down the rebellion. Instead, Lysias chose to attack from a new direction. True, he could also have used a road in the southwest which lay south of the Emmaus road, beginning at Mareshah and skirting Moresheth-gath to the Valley of Elah, and thence to Jerusalem, near Azekah or Beth-ter. But experience had proved that in the mountain passes and on the roads between them the Seleucid army could expect an ambush, a tactic in which Judah Maccabee would have had the advantage. Lysias, or his advisers, decided to take the army up on to the ridge of the watershed, instead of along the dangerous mountain roads in a hostile country. In this maneuver they could take advantage of the fact that the southern Judean mountains were in the hands of the friendly Idumaeans. Accordingly, the Seleucid army massed at Mareshah, and from there marched to Hebron, without Judah Maccabee being able to stop them.[30] From Hebron the road followed the watershed about 3.7 miles north to the Judean border, and by continuing on the same route Lysias could reach Jerusalem from the south without endangering the army.

In this way, Lysias' army arrived at the border fortress of Beth-zur (Khirbat Tubayqua). The city fell without resistance.[31] At that moment Judah and his men were in real danger. The enemy was only a day's march from Jerusalem, and had he succeeded in breaking through, all Judah's previous efforts would have been in vain. To meet this threat, Judah assembled the entire force of ten thousand men at his disposal. Assuming that the population of Judea was then 400,000–500,000,[32] it would appear that about 2.5 per cent of the inhabitants joined his force, a very high rate for a volunteer army. Unfortunately, there are practically no details of this battle in our sources (I Macc. 4:34); the description in II Maccabees (11:10–11) is legendary, but from Josephus' comment that it was the enemy's vanguard units that Judah engaged killing five thousand of them (*Ant.* XII, 314), we gather that the main body of Lysias' army did not take part in the encounter at all. In any event, this battle determined the political outcome. Lysias recognized that victory could not be achieved on the field of battle and agreed to negotiate. Eventually the king's agreement[33] to a compromise was received. The rebels were granted an "amnesty"; the Jews obtained permission to live in accordance with their own laws, as before, i.e., the situation was restored in accordance with the charter issued by Antiochus III.[34] The royal letter embodying the compromise, issued on October 15, 164 B.C.E., was sent to Menelaus, the last High Priest before the desecration of the Temple. In December of the same year Judah and his men seized the eastern hill of Jerusalem, together with the Temple Mount, and during the first days of Hanukka restored the Temple service. In accordance with the agreement with the Seleucids, they left the western hill with the *akra* in the hands of the Hellenizers and the king's garrison. The initial stage of the battle had ended with the attainment of the first and original object of the rebellion: the restoration of the freedom of worship and the cessation of religious persecution.

D. CONTINUATION OF THE FIGHT OUTSIDE JUDEA

The success of the Jewish revolt resounded throughout the neighboring countries, where it sparked off attacks on the Jews scattered throughout these lands. Prompted by the need to save their brethren in this "Diaspora," Judah and his brothers embarked on a series of military actions even after the conclusion of the "agreement" with the king — a fact which testifies to the anarchy already prevailing in the Seleucid kingdom. These actions differed in character from the battles just described. In Judah's previous operations the initial objectives had been to defend Judea from invasion, and only in the course of the fighting did the Hasmoneans take the offensive. Now, Judah's troops were embarking upon a series of lightning actions aimed at liberating the scattered Jewish communities from the hands of their enemies, and in many cases also at evacuating them to Judea. In these actions speed and mobility were the vital qualities. At the same time, the forces at Judah Maccabee's disposal in these battles were limited by his need to leave a good part of his troops in Judea itself, in case the Hellenizers or the king's army should renew their activity. It turned out, however, that the very smallness of the number of fighting men who could be spared for battle beyond Judea's borders was a factor making for speedy action. When it came to problems of intelligence, knowledge of the terrain, and information about the enemy's movements, the Hasmoneans were undoubtedly aided by Jews living in the neighboring countries, to whose rescue they were hastening. They also obtained important assistance from the Nabataeans, a semi-nomadic Arabic tribe which had seized biblical Edom when its inhabitants had left for southern Judea. The Nabataeans managed to retain their independence despite all the efforts of the Hellenistic kings to subdue them;[35] being enemies of the Seleucids, the Nabataeans gladly extended a friendly hand to Judah Maccabee, rendering him assistance mainly in two spheres. First of all, the Nabataeans guided the Jewish troops in their desert territory, thus enabling them to carry out surprise attacks at various points (I Macc. 5:25–27). Second, the tents of the Nabataeans served as a haven for the women and children of the fighting men and a storage point for the booty that Judah and his men accumulated in their campaigns.[36]

The first campaign was directed against "the children of Essau in Idumaea, at Akrabattine" (I Macc. 5:3).[37] This double specification of the locale of the events has led to a difference of opinion among scholars. Some place the events in Idumaea, and identify the Akrabattine of the verse with the biblical "ascent of Akrabbim" (Num. 34:4), in the south-eastern Negev. It should be noted, however, that this identification of the ascent of Akrabbim west of the Arabah is not at all certain; second, even if we accept this identification, the ascent of Akrabbim would be outside the area of the Idumaeans, which (following the southern border of the kingdom of Judah at the time of the destruction of the First Temple) ended at Nahal Beer-sheba and Nahal Malḥata. In the third place, the source mentions the Idumaean encirclement of the Jews in the same areas; and it is too much to assume, even if we expand the area of Jewish settlement remaining in Idumaea (according to Neh. 11) to the farthest possible limit, that there were such settlements south of Beer-sheba. For all these reasons the besieged Jewish settlements must be sought in the Akrabattine district, southeast of Shechem. In the days of the later Hasmoneans this district was joined to Judea [38] which proves that a Jewish settlement did exist there; and it may well be that certain Idumaeans seized areas in this district. Judah went to Akrabattine, defeated the enemy, and took a large quantity of booty. It is worth noting that, contrary to his actions in Galilee and Gilead (see below), he did not evacuate the Jews, just as he did not remove the Jews living in the land of the Tobiads in Transjordan.[39] In both cases, the Hasmoneans apparently felt themselves strong enough to defend the Jews of these areas bordering on territory settled by a Jewish population.

The second campaign was designed to ease the situation of the Jews of Transjordan. Jewish habitation there had not come to an end even with the destruction of the Temple, and it developed anew under the protection of the House of Tobiah. Their main enemies were "the children of Baean" (υἱῶν Βαιαν; I Macc. 5:4), the reference apparently being to the in-habitants of the Baal-meon district,[40] south of Jewish Transjordan. They were aided by the Ammonites (inhabitants of Rabbath-Ammon [Philadel-phia]) who apparently retained their hatred of the Jews since the time they had been subject to the rule of the Tobiads. They were also helped by Timotheus, governor of the Gilead district. Whereas in the First Book of Maccabees (5:6 ff.) we find a very vague account of these battles, the Second Book of Maccabees (8:30; 10:24 ff.; 12:2) provides some illuminat-ing details. According to the first source, the "children of Baean" ambushed

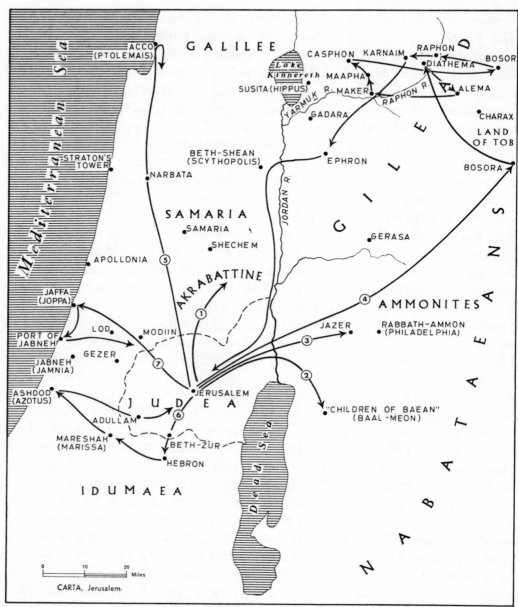

① THE CAMPAIGN IN AKRABATTINE
② THE CAMPAIGN AGAINST THE "CHILDREN OF BAEAN"
③ THE JAZER CAMPAIGN
④ THE CAMPAIGN IN GILEAD
⑤ SIMEON'S CAMPAIGN IN GALILEE
⑥ THE CAMPAIGN IN IDUMAEA
⑦ THE CAMPAIGN AGAINST JAFFA AND JABNEH

Judah's Campaigns outside Judea

the Jews, possibly with the purpose of cutting Judah off from the Nabata-eans. Judah Maccabee overran their land and succeeded in shutting them up in their fortresses to which he set fire. The reference is undoubtedly to the fortresses and observation towers which had existed in Moab and Ammon as far back as the time of the Israelite kingdom.[41] In the Second Book of Maccabees, (8:30–33) mention is made of a later battle with Timotheus, the conquest of the fortresses, and the killing of the leader of the Arab tribes (phylarch, apparently the "head of the tribe" of "the children of Baean"), who was one of the chief enemies of Israel. The campaign ended with the conquest of Jazer, on the border of Jewish Transjordan (the modern Khirbat aṣ-Ṣār; I Macc. 5:8).[42]

After the early battles east of the Jordan, Judah was forced to expand the field of his activities northward. Disturbing reports reached Jerusalem about the situation of the Jews in Gilead and Galilee. In Gilead (the reference is to the Seleucid district Galaaditis, which includes Bashan and Golan, and not the biblical Gilead),[43] the Jews were compelled to take refuge in their fortress, Diathema (I Macc. 5:9). Scholars are divided as to the location of this fortress. Some, relying on the version רמתא in the Aramaic translation of the Book of Maccabees, have fixed the location at Tell ar-Rāma in the vicinity of Arbel, i.e., in Gilead proper;[44] but Abel's view, which identified this fortress with Tell Ḥamad in the heart of Bashan,[45] seems to have more in its favor. Timotheus laid siege to this fortress. At the same time the Jews who lived in the land of Tob were under attack too (I Macc. 5:13); the reference is not to the area of the House of Tobiah, but to the district of Tob which is also mentioned in the Pentateuch (Jud. 11:3–5), and which is apparently located near Bosora.[46] At the same time, reports of the concentration of the men of Acco, Tyre and Sidon and "all Galilee of the Gentiles," against the Jews of Galilee (I Macc. 5:14–15) were also received. Judah set out for Gilead with eight thousand men, while his brother Simeon headed for Galilee with three thousand. Since we know that the other two commanders, Joseph ben Zechariah and Azariah remained in Judea, and since it is not likely that the Hasmonean brothers withdrew more than half their men out of Judea, it may be assumed that they had 22,000 men at their disposal at the time, about half the force it would have been possible to mobilize in Judea.

These two campaigns were not designed to conquer territory, but to evacuate the Jews scattered among hostile gentiles. Simeon commanded the smaller force, both because of the shorter distance he had to cover, and because his enemies lived in cities lacking the support of the organized military power of a Seleucid governor. He managed to win a number of battles, apparently in Western Galilee, and pursued his enemies as far as the gates of Acco, without, however, attempting any attack on the city. Upon his return, he evacuated the Jews of Western Galilee, as well as the Jews of the Narbath district,[47] and brought them with him to Judea. The Jews of Eastern Galilee, on the other hand, stayed where they were. They were far from the Greek cities, and were protected by the mountains, the Jordan, and Lake Kinnereth. The description of the campaign of Bacchides (see p. 176ff. below) confirms that they were still there at a later period. They were in due course to serve as a basis for the rapid Judaization of Galilee in the time of the third generation of the Hasmoneans.

Judah's campaign (on which he was accompanied by his brother Jonathan) was longer and more dangerous. He was careful not to decome involved with the Greek cities of Transjordan founded by the Seleucids, which remained loyal to the king. Instead, he infiltrated among them and, in a three days' march, advanced into the desert. There, his army encountered the Nabataeans who informed Judah of what was happening in Gilead. The Jews had evidently been imprisoned in most of the cities of Gilead, such as Bosora, Bosor, Alema, Casphor, Maker and Carnaim.[48] Judah's sudden appearance, coming to Gilead as he did from the south (i.e., from a completely unexpected direction) facilitated his liberation campaign, which also bore a punitive aspect. Obviously, the small and scattered cities of Bashan and Golan could not withstand the powerful force advancing against them. The first city to fall was Bosora, whose inhabitants seem to have been particularly guilty of oppressing the people of the land of Tob. Judah conquered the city, had the men executed, and burned the place down (I Macc. 5:28).[49] In this manner he broke through the chain of the enemy's fortified cities, and in a night march, advanced right up to the fortress of Diathema — a distance of approximately 31 miles — where the Jews were under attack. The fact that the Jewish forces could march such a distance in one night and attack the enemy at dawn is excellent testimony to the mobility and fighting qualities of Judah's men.

The attack on the forces concentrated at Diathema — which Judah and his men came upon in the morning light — was carried out by the standard method of surprise assault against a fortress; arrows and stones were shot over the battlements, forcing the defenders to abandon their positions, while the attackers used ladders to scale the walls (I Macc. 5:30). Judah divided his army into three sections and to the sound of trumpets and war cries attacked the enemy from the rear. The surprise was complete, and the vanquished sustained heavy losses. The First Book of Maccabees (5:34) speaks — with some exaggeration — of about eight thousand dead.

From Diathema, located in the center of Bashan, Judah launched a series
of punitive campaigns in various directions. At first he turned southward
to Alema, with the intention perhaps of opening the way to the Jews of
Tob, who were massed in the vicinity of Charax, south of Alema (II Macc.
12:17). From there he turned to Maker (I Macc. 5:36) which lies in the
Yarmuk valley; a campaign which may have been designed to secure his
line of withdrawal to Judea and to threaten the city of Gadara — a dangerous Greek fortress which dominated the mountain heights. From Maker
Judah turned northward and conquered Maapha[50] (Khirbat Naaf'a). He
then continued in the same direction and took Casphon[51] on the other side
of Nahr ar-Ruqqād. This move, too, was apparently designed to prevent
intervention from the city of Susita (Hippus), which was situated west
of the Jewish settlements. The next place mentioned in our sources is
Bosor on the boundary of Trachonitis, at the eastern edge of the area then
settled by Jews.[52] This series of marches to the south and west was
calculated to gain enough time to permit the Jewish inhabitants to assemble
prior to their evacuation. But it was from the north that the danger came.
Timotheus apparently received reinforcements from Damascus, together
with a force of cavalry recruited from among the desert nomads (II Macc.
10:24). His forces appeared in Judah's rear during the latter's campaign
along the borders of Trachonitis.[53] From its base in the fortified city of
Carnaim, the king's army advanced to the banks of the Raphon brook
(Nahr al-Iḥrayr). The figures given in II Macc. 10:31 for the size of this
army (once over 20,000 and elsewhere 120,000!) are much exaggerated,
particularly if we recall that Judah could field only the eight thousand men
he had brought with him, plus perhaps a few thousand Jewish inhabitants
of Gilead. From the First Book of Maccabees (5:38–39) we learn that
Judah also saw to it that the enemy's movements were reported to him,
and had sent spies (no doubt local residents who were familiar with the
area) to the enemy camp. Timotheus apparently thought that Judah
would not dare to cross the river, which gave him some protection, and
planned to cross to the other side himself. But Judah beat him to it. Leading
his troops, he waded across the water, routed the enemy, and seized their
base in the temple of Astarte at Carnaim (I Macc. 5:44). Timotheus'
Arab allies surrendered separately and sued for peace with Judah, present-
ing him with a gift of cattle. Judah agreed, in the well-founded hope
that these desert inhabitants would continue to serve him in the future
(II Macc. 12:10–12).

Following the victory at the Raphon brook, the time for the evacuation
had come. Judah assembled the Jewish inhabitants of Gilead into a long

caravan including men, women, and children, whose presence in large numbers precluded any notion of returning by the route he had taken on his march there through the desert. The Jews, therefore, had to force their way through the mountains of Gilead, across the territory of Gadara. This task was made easier by Judah's previous victories, which had sown fear before him. The only city in his path to venture offering resistance was Ephron (aṭ-Ṭayyiba; I Macc. 5:46–51) which was stormed, captured, and destroyed. The caravan continued on its way, crossing one of the fords of the Jordan. In the great plain of Beth-shean the Jews received a friendly welcome (II Macc. 12:29),[54] though it appears that the caravan did not go through the city but immediately turned southward along the Jordan and proceeded towards Jerusalem. The First Book of Maccabees does not specify the route followed by the Jews from Beth-shean to Judea, but the Second Book of Maccabees (12:29) gives the distance they covered as about 600 furlongs (54 miles). On this information the road leading from Beth-shean to Judea across Samaria is excluded. First of all, it is about 74.5 miles long. Second, it passed by the city of Samaria, a Greek town hostile to the Jews, and later, through the land of the Samaritans, who were not over-friendly to Israel either. More probably, Judah had the caravan proceed from Gilead via the Jordan plain along a road, about 55.9 miles long, which is more compatible with the 600 furlongs mentioned in the source.

The caravan entered Jerusalem to general rejoicing;[55] although joy was mixed with concern in view of the situation which Judah and Simeon found upon their return to Judea. The commanders whom they had left there — Joseph ben Zechariah and Azariah — had not obeyed Judah's orders. He had ordered them not to attack Judea's enemies, but they had disobeyed him and gone ahead with an assault on Jabneh. The author of the First Book of Maccabees (5:57 and 62) attributed their action to personal ambition and the hope of fame, and regards them incapable of success because they were not "of the seed of those men" (that is, of the Hasmonean family), into whose hands the salvation of Israel had been entrusted. Josephus (*Ant.* XII, 352) marvels at Judah's foresight in forbidding them to give battle. The prohibition was probably issued with the idea in mind that with the Jewish forces dispersed in three directions, it was no time to provoke a new enemy. On the other hand, the decision to attack Jabneh was probably taken in response to the hostile attitude to the Jews living there, which is also mentioned in II Maccabees, 12:8–9. In any case, Joseph and Azariah became involved in a fight with Gorgias, (Nicanor's adviser in the battle of Emmaus) who now occupied the post of governor of the eparchy of Idumaea. They were defeated, and lost two thousand of their men. Judah's return restored the balance of power. He launched a new series of campaigns with an attack on Jaffa and the port of Jabneh (II Macc. 12:3–9), which he burned together with the ships that were at anchor there. The people of Jaffa had drowned the Jews of their city in the sea, and the inhabitants of Jabneh had planned the same atrocity. Judah then turned inland towards the mountains of Idumaea. He fortified Beth-zur (I Macc. 4:61; 6:26), attacked and destroyed Hebron (*ibid.* 5:65), crossed the area of Mareshah, where he again defeated the enemy army[56], reached the outskirts of Ashdod, then returned to Judea, encamping at Adullam (II Macc. 12:38). The description of the battle with Georgias near Maresha for once supplies an accurate figure for the armies which Judah fought: Gorgias commanded three thousand infantry and four hundred cavalry, (*ibid.* 12:33). The same account suggests that the evacuation of the Jews of Gilead was also intended to strengthen the forces fighting under Judah.

E. RENEWAL OF THE BATTLES IN JUDEA

In 164 B.C.E., Antiochus IV died during his campaign in Persia. His son, Antiochus V, inherited the throne while still a boy; the viceroy Lysias ruled in his name as regent. In the belief that this transition period was an opportune moment to remove the threat of the *akra* from the Temple and unite the city of Jerusalem, Judah blockaded and began to besiege this fortress of the Hellenizers; however, for lack of technical knowledge in the construction of siege engines and ramps, the investment progressed haltingly.[57] The blockade was not complete, and the defenders were able to send to the king for help. Lysias assembled an army whose numbers as given in I and II Maccabees are no less exaggerated than in other places. According to the first source (6:30), there were 100,000 infantry, 20,000 cavalry, and 32 elephants, and according to the second (13:2), 110,000 infantry, 5,300 cavalry, 22 elephants, and 300 chariots.[58] Two points, however, are clear: this was a strong force, perhaps the bulk of the Seleucid army, and it included the main weapon of the Seleucid army: elephants specially trained for war. Seleucus Nicator, the founder of the Seleucid dynasty, had won the battle of Ipsus with the help of these animals and therefore they constituted the most important, though not the decisive weapon, in the wars of the Diadochi. Apparently, the Seleucid army this time planned an all-out fight on the battlefield. Otherwise it is difficult to understand why they took along the elephants, whose task was to break into the enemy's phalanx and open the way for the foot-soldiers and cavalry. The problem, of course, was how to draw Judah onto the battle-field without laying the king's army open to ambushes, in which the Jewish forces excelled. Even during their march to Judea the Seleucid commanders were made aware of Judah's talent for night attacks, when a small group fell upon the king's camp in the vicinity of Modiin (II Macc. 13:14–17).[59] The lesson of past battles was not lost on the Syrians, and they knew better than to risk the ascent to Jerusalem from the north or west. They, therefore, repeated the strategy adopted by Lysias three years earlier and crossed through friendly Idumaea, reaching Beth-zur, which they besieged. While it is true that Judah fortified this town, ex-cavations[60] have proved that the fortifications were not particularly strong; they came nowhere near the strength of Hellenistic fortresses (e.g., the fortress of Samaria).[61] The besieged inhabitants fought courageously, burning the siege engines with which they were attacked. Judah, for his part, tried to send in supplies to the defenders (II Macc. 13:20); but his efforts failed, partly owing to an act of treachery in the Jewish camp. The position was now quite serious. Since the conquest of Beth-zur could open the way to Jerusalem to the king, Judah decided to lift the siege of the *akra* and to make his camp at Beth-zacharia, about 6.2 miles north of Beth-zur. The appearance of the Jewish army in this area, on the one hand hindered continuation of the siege of Beth-zur, but on the other, opened the way for the Seleucid commanders to engage Judah in battle an eventuality to which they had been looking forward and preparing for. The king set out with his army at daybreak, and the two armies joined battle. The clash seems to have taken place in a valley in the vicinity of the present day Kᵉfar 'Eẓyon.[62] The detailed description of the elephants in the Seleucid army in I Maccabees, 6:34–37, shows what a great impression these animals made on the Hasmonean soldiers. The elephants were placed in the center of the battle-line, protected on both sides by cavalry, which also protected the flanks of the phalanx marching behind the elephants and the infantry interspersed with the horse. From a distance, the formations could be seen advancing in two directions: the one in the plain headed straight up towards the Jewish positions, while the second force circled along the mountains, thus threatening to surround the Jews. Even though Judah attacked the king's army with courage, and his brother Eleazar sacrificed his life when he killed one of the elephants (thinking it was the king's), the Jews were defeated in this battle. While I Maccabees (6:47) describes the battle simply as ending in a retreat,[63] the bitter truth appears in Josephus (*War*, I, 45): the vanquished Judah was compelled to evacuate Jerusalem and to withdraw to the Gophna mountains, that is,

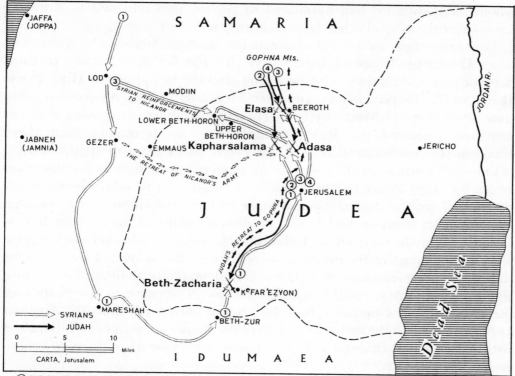

① THE CAMPAIGN OF LYSIAS (BATTLE OF BETH-ZACHARIA)
② THE FIRST CAMPAIGN OF NICANOR (BATTLE OF KAPHARSALAMA)
③ THE SECOND CAMPAIGN OF NICANOR (BATTLE OF ADASA)
④ THE CAMPAIGN OF BACCHIDES (BATTLE OF ELASA)

Last Battles of Judah Maccabee

the same hilly area used as a haven by his father, his brothers, and himself
at the beginning of the revolt. The garrison of Beth-ẓur was forced to
surrender.[64] The king banished the defenders from the city, stationing a
Seleucid garrison and a group of Jewish Hellenizers in their place. From
Beth-zur, the royal army advanced towards Jerusalem, and finally, after
five years of struggle, liberated the people of the *akra* from their long
blockade. Most of the Jewish forces scattered. However, for all their
military success, the king's advisers realized that they must not repeat the
mistakes of Antiochus IV. They contented themselves with effecting a
breach in the wall of the Temple Mount, in order to preclude the possibility
of the Jews once again fortifying themselves within it, but they did not
interfere with Jewish worship. When they received the news that Philip,

whom Antiochus IV had appointed as regent, had returned to Antioch, Lysias and the king also left Jerusalem to make their way there.

This campaign completely changed the strategic balance in Judea and when Demetrius I ascended the throne (in 162 B.C.E.), Judah's position deteriorated still further. The new king decided to appoint a High Priest again, to fill the post left vacant after Menelaus had been executed some time previously (II Macc. 13:3–4). He sent Bacchides, the governor of the provinces "beyond the River" (Euphrates), to Jerusalem, and there Eliakim-Alcimus was annointed High Priest. Since from the point of view of lineage his fitness for the post was not open to question, he was recognized as lawful High Priest by the *Hasidim* (I Macc. 7:13), who constituted a substantial part of Judea's armed forces. In their opinion, it was enough that religious freedom had been established; political liberty and independence were not their goals. Judah had therefore to continue the struggle with a small part of his previous forces, which he mobilized from among those who were anxious to achieve complete political liberation. Before leaving the country, Bacchides made a show of strength in the vicinity of the mountains of Gophna, where Judah had entrenched himself. Arriving at Berzetho,[65] Bacchides took vengeance on people accused of collaborating with the rebels, then departed from Judea, leaving part of the army there to support Alcimus.

The turning point in the political situation after the defeat at Beth-zacharia and the installation of a High Priest loyal to the king was also felt on the battlefield. Up to this point Judah had operated on internal lines and his enemies on external lines, i.e., he had been able to reach the place of battle by the shortest route and to arrive there before the enemy. Now he was confined to the northwestern corner of the Judean mountains and could expect to be the target of a punitive campaign from Jerusalem. The area at his disposal had shrunk, and the number of his soldiers had diminished. But Judah and his men were not lacking in courage. They relied on the justice of their cause, and continued to fight in the hope that the Seleucid commanders and the High Priest who accepted their authority would sooner or later commit political and religious blunders, which would once again alienate the majority of the people, and thus restore the fighting unity which had characterized the first stages of the struggle.

That is exactly what happened. Alcimus tried to introduce changes in the interior arrangements of the Temple, leading to a gradual removal of the partitions between Jews and non-Jews, thus arousing the ire of the *Hasidim*. At the request of the High Priest, the king once again sent Nicanor, who was acquainted with the country and the Jewish manner of fighting since the time of the battle of Emmaus. Nicanor at first attempted to make peace with Judah, or at least pretended that he wished to do so, but at the same time he tried to take him prisoner. The effort failed, and fighting flared up again.

In this campaign, Nicanor's intervention was first of all to open the Beth-horon road to the movement of his army. After the Seleucid victory at Beth-zacharia and the conquest of Beth-zur, the roads leading from Jerusalem to the south had been open to the king's army, but not the short road westward to the coastal plain, nor the northern road. It was precisely the Beth-horon road that linked Jerusalem most conveniently to the supply bases and fortresses along the coastal road. It is thus easy to understand why Nicanor wanted to open the roads to the west which, owing to their proximity to the mountains of Gophna, where Judah was encamped, were in constant danger of being cut off. Nicanor therefore left Jerusalem with most of the garrison stationed there, and as he passed Kaphar-salama (Khirbat Salamiyya, northwest of Gibeon on the Beth-horon road) Judah attacked him and routed his army. Judging by the number of dead given in the source — only 500 (I Macc. 7:31–32)[66] — and considering the customary exaggeration concerning the size of the enemy forces, it may be assumed that Nicanor's army had consisted of several thousand men. Judah could take on such a relatively small force, even though his army had shrunk to three thousand men.

Although the victory was not a decisive one, it raised Judah's spirits. Furthermore, Nicanor's contemptuous attitude towards the priests and other inhabitants of Jerusalem aroused widespread anger and brought the masses of the people back into the rebel camp. Meanwhile, Nicanor planned a combined operation which was designed to make up for his earlier failure to open the Beth-horon road. He succeeded in leaving Jerusalem and reaching Beth-horon, where he set up his camp. Simultaneously, other Syrian forces came up from the coast to join him. With his troops thus strengthened, all he had to do to achieve his strategic goal was to return with his united forces to Jerusalem. On the way he had to pass near the village of Adasa, (I Macc. 7:39–44),[67] south of the road, and there Judah's men fell upon him. The Jewish forces did not number more than three thousand men (that is, the troops of Judah, Simeon, and Jonathan), all that remained of the whole army. Nicanor's army was three times as great,[68] but the surprise attack was successful. The first to fall in the fighting was Nicanor (I Macc. 7:43),[69] and his death decided the fate of the battle. His troops began to flee and, since the Jewish forces were attacking from south of the road, they were unable to head towards Jerusalem; Nicanor's beaten army had to take the difficult mountainous track in the direction of the royal fortress of Gezer, where they sought refuge. This road apparently took them along the Chephirah ridge, between the Valley of Chephirah and the Valley of Beth-hanan, and then past Emmaus, towards Gezer. The retreat went on for a whole day. On their way, Nicanor's soldiers were pursued by the inhabitants of the villages, alerted by Judah's trumpet calls (I Macc. 7:45–46). Over a distance of 22 miles the army of Nicanor was attacked throughout the entire day, the bands of retreating soldiers being chased in utter confusion. In the end, Nicanor's entire army was destroyed, though it is hardly likely that not a single man escaped, as I Maccabees would have it. The stereotype "and there was not one of them left," used there may be understood simply as indicating a complete rout. Whatever the precise situation, this victory substantially undermined Alcimus' position and that of the king's men in Jerusalem. Judah and his party were once again a political and military power, a fact which found expression in the support promised them by Rome, the the enemy of the Seleucids (I Macc. 8).

F. Judah Maccabee's Last Battle

Nicanor's defeat led to an immediate and vigorous reaction on the part of Demetrius I, who was personally requested by the High Priest Alcimus to intervene on his behalf. Once again he sent Bacchides, his best commander, to Judea together with "the right wing" of his phalanx, the picked troops of the Seleucid army (I Macc. 9:1). On their way from Damascus to Jerusalem the Syrians passed the fortress ("Mesiloth") of Arbel in Galilee, near Lake Kinnereth, where they slew many of the inhabitants (I Macc. 9:2). The fact that Bacchides found it necessary to take punitive action against the population of this place shows, first of all, that even before Galilee was joined to Judea it had many courageous Jewish inhabitants and, second, that the occupants of this fortress, famous zealots at the time of Herod, had excelled in their patriotism even before then. In the spring of 160 B.C.E., approximately one month after the defeat of Nicanor, the Syrian army reached Jerusalem. Its haste testifies to the king's assessment of the gravity of the situation. From Jerusalem the Syrians marched against Judah. Bacchides encamped on the eastern outskirts of the Gophna mountains at Beeroth (al-Bīra; I Macc. 9:4),[70] a village which, lying on the main road, assured easy communication with his base in Jerusalem. According to I Maccabees, the Syrian army consisted of twenty thousand foot-soldiers and two thousand cavalry, i.e., a force approximately equal in strength to the army fielded by Nicanor at the battle of Emmaus. Judah was encamped opposite, at a site called Elasa (Ελασα; according to other manuscripts: :Ακεδασα, Αλασα). Ruins named al-'Asha have been found near Ramallah, and it has been suggested that this was the location of Judah's camp.[71] Faced with this desperate contest Judah may have decided to conduct a rearguard action; which could explain the statement in I Macc. 9:6 that only eight hundred men remained with him, i.e., the force under his personal command (one thousand men minus the customary pre-battle loss). However, the description of the battle does not justify the figure mentioned in the source. The author's wish to explain away the defeat of the national hero by the paucity of his troops is understandable, but it was impossible to continue a protracted battle on two flanks with eight hundred men against twenty thousand and even to inflict a partial defeat on the enemy.

The problem of the positions of the combatants depends on the identification of "Mount Ashdod" (Αζωτου ὄρους), mentioned in most manuscripts. If we accept Abel's view that the name of this mountain should be corrected to Αζωρου and identified with Mt. Hazor (Baal Hazor, Tell 'Aṣūr 3,333 ft., 1.8 miles north of Ephraim),[72] this would mean that the battle was fought with the Jews facing east and the Syrians facing west. But if we accept Yeivin's theory[73] that the reading here should be ασηδωθ του ὄρους, i.e., the "slopes of the mountain," meaning the slopes of the Judean mountains to the west, then the situation was just the reverse — the Syrians faced east and the Jews, west. This conjecture, which indeed seems more plausible, suggests other deployments. Judah had camped west of Berea and Bacchides may have hoped to cut him off from his base in the mountains of Gophna, and accordingly established his line between the Jewish force and the mountain slopes. In a parallel fashion, Judah attempted to draw up his troops between Bacchides and the road linking the Syrian army to its base in Jerusalem.

Either way, the attack was launched by the Syrian army, which was eminently stronger. The phalanx was arranged in two masses, with each flank protected by cavalry. At the head of the phalanx were the slingers and archers as well as a vanguard of picked men whose task it was to harass the enemy's battle-line before the phalanx struck. In his attack Bacchides apparently tried to repeat the tactic employed by the Syrians at Beth-zacharia: one part of his army carried out a frontal attack while another section tried to outflank the enemy and to attack him from the rear. Judah endeavored to withstand the assault by dividing his men into two groups. He himself, at the head of the left wing, thrust back the Syrian right flank. Bacchides indeed retreated to the mountain slopes, but without losing control of his army; the commanders of his second force also displayed great military acumen. Once they had put the Jews facing them to flight, they did not pursue them, but diverted their attack to Judah's rear, while the withdrawing right flank under Bacchides now turned and began to attack Judah from the front. Judah and his men had no choice but to fall heroically in battle (I Macc. 9:14–18). Thus, Judah's own war came to an end. His brothers Jonathan and Simeon buried him in Modiin, but they could not hold their position in the mountains of Gophna and moved with their followers to the Judean Desert — the traditional haven of fugitives ever since the time of King David — and from there they continued the struggle.

G. Conclusions

With the death of Judah Maccabee the revolt seemed to have ended in utter failure; Seleucid governors were in control in Jerusalem and throughout Judea, while only a handful of rebels stood fast in the Judean Desert. But, as is usually the case with national movements rooted in the vital needs of a people, the factors which were in the end to lead to the Hasmonean's victory were still operating. And less than ten years after the death of Judah, his brother Jonathan ruled as High Priest and governor of Judea.

Despite a natural esteem for the heroism and sagacity of the early Hasmoneans, the historian cannot ignore the objective historical factors which were likely to cause the collapse of the forces arrayed against the Jews. One of these factors was the political weakness of the Seleucid government — a weakness which sprang from two causes: one external, the other internal. The external cause was a consequence of the efforts made by the Romans to undermine the Hellenistic kingdoms. At the end of the third century B.C.E., after their victory over Carthage, the Romans had emerged as the strongest military power in the entire Mediterranean basin. Their defeat of Antiochus III in the battle of Magnesia in Asia Minor (190 B.C.E.) had severely shaken the structure of the Seleucid kingdom. It was precisely the desperate efforts of Antiochus IV to strengthen his kingdom from within which — owing to the juxtaposition of internal and external strains customary in the history of declining kingdoms — led to the revolt of the Hasmoneans and hastened the decline. The second weakness derived from the internal structure of the kingdom. Like all absolute kingdoms lacking a written constitution, the Seleucid monarchy was entirely in the hands of

an autocratic ruler. Since the occupant of the throne was — in theory and
to some extent also in practice — omnipotent in the state, various members
of the dynasty were constantly striving to seize power. The fact that
Antiochus IV was crowned as the heir of his brother Seleucus IV while
the latter's son, Demetrius I, was being held captive in Rome, provoked a
serious split within the royal family itself. Two factions arose in the dynasty,
and their struggle for the crown lasted right up to the actual dissolution of
the kingdom and its conversion by Pompey into the province of Syria, in
64 B.C.E. The presence of an external enemy seeking to exploit the weakness
of the Seleucid dynasty, combined with civil war within the country, were
of great help to the Jews. For one thing, they could obtain assistance from
the Romans. Moreover, on at least two occasions, the Greek commanders
were compelled for reasons of internal policy to discontinue their campaign
in Judea and sign an armistice of sorts, or even a real agreement. To these
two factors a third should be added: an erroneous appraisal of the true
feelings of the Jewish people. Here, the culprits were to be found not
among the king's officials, but among the Jewish Hellenizers themselves.
Of course, these were the circles which were close to the government and
spoke its language. The officials had contact mainly with such people and
tended to accept their views. But, in fact, their opinions were those of a
minority far removed from reality. In this sense, the Hellenizers, who
misled "the king's men," cut off the branch on which they were sitting.
It was their mistaken assumption that the majority of the people would be
prepared to accept the fusion of religions as proposed by Antiochus, and
that only a minority of benighted fanatics would oppose it, which doomed
all the political and military activity of the Seleucids and their officials in
Judea to failure. Even before the death of Antiochus IV, the king's commanders had realized their error and made haste to initiate negotiations
with the rebels through the High Priest Menelaus, the main spokesman of
the Hellenizers. Although this was a defective instrument, they did achieve
their object, at least in part.

At this stage, the possibility of achieving some reconciliation between
the rival sides still existed, and this brings us to one of the factors which
worked to the detriment of Judah and his men. It must be admitted that,
in a certain sense, the supporters of the Maccabees were also divided, except
that this division stemmed not from personal reasons, but from dissimilar
aims and differing evaluations of the situation. Alongside Judah Maccabee
and his brothers there stood the *Ḥasidim*, who had been fighting the battle
of the Lord; but — in contrast with the open or hidden ambition of the
Hasmoneans to achieve political liberation — the *Ḥasidim* aimed only at

the purification of the Temple and the restoration of worship there. This difference in aims was unimportant so long as the oppressive government opposed both the political and religious objectives equally. But the moment the royal advisers took the revolutionary step of agreeing to the purification and rededication of the Temple, even appointing a ritually acceptable High Priest for the Jews, Eliakim-Alcimus, they succeeded in splitting the Hasmonean camp and won an advantage in the struggle, the influence of which was felt for a long time. If they, nevertheless, failed to liquidate the separatist tendencies among the Jews and permanently turn Judea into an obedient province of their kingdom, this failure was a result of the logic of historical development, which they could not control. Our sources, in the manner of ancient historiography in general, attribute the event to conflicts between personalities, but in point of fact the clash of interests between the Seleucid command (represented by Nicanor) on the one hand, and the priesthood and the nation, on the other, was unavoidable. Moreover, the memory of common victories in the past could heal the breach between the Hasmoneans and the *Ḥasidim* at any moment, in the event of some new affront on the part of the Seleucid governor — a situation which could easily be inferred from many of the actions of the king's officials at a time when the kingdom was struggling for survival. Under the circumstances, political opposition was likely to revive with all its military consequences.

In considering the struggle from the point of view of military history, the customary distinction must be made between problems of strategy and tactics, that is, between the general running of the war and the methods adopted on the battlefield. It is true that these two aspects dovetail, and that there is no value in tactical efficiency if the strategist does not achieve superiority in the field and, by the same token, there is no hope for a commander who attains strategic superiority without insuring tactical success on the battlefield. In the strategic sense, the two sides operated according to different prineiples which grew out of their special position. At the beginning of the struggle, when battle was being waged over the approach roads to Jerusalem besieged by the rebels, the Seleucid commanders were aiming at a quick solution (a "lightning war"), while Judah Maccabee was more interested in a protracted war. If these opposing intentions are grasped, the methods adopted will also be understood: on the one hand, attempts were made to invade Judean territory from various sides, on the other, a battle was fought over the mountain approaches. Judah's advantage lay in his use of shorter internal communications which enabled him to reach all points before the invading army. Under the circumstances, the Seleucid commanders had no choice but to act as they did. The limited number of soldiers at their disposal prevented them from carrying out coordinated assaults from many sides — even though that method of warfare was no doubt the proper one against an enemy fighting on internal lines. Nor can we ignore the fact that in the end they achieved their military goal — the liberation of the *akra's* inhabitants from the blockade, though it is doubtful whether after Seron's defeat at the Beth-horon pass there was any point in trying to break through the Emmaus road rather than advance immediately by the safer Mareshah road. Proof that the Seleucid commanders learned their tacticdl lesson is the fact that in the second battle for Beth-zur they did nor repeat previous mistakes. After the approach to Jerusalem was opened, everything changed. On the defensive in the mountains of Gophnu, Judah desired a quick victory in order to regain control of Jerusalem and prevent the Hellenizers from establishing a base there. The king's commanders, on the other hand, now had a chance to organize themselves in the city and to open the roads leading to it. From a strategic point of view, Nicanor's activities werɔ well-planned, especially his march to Beth-horon for the purpose of linking up with the army coming from the coast. His final defeat was also due to tactical conditions. In the same way, Bacchides defeated Judah Maccabee in battle but was later trounced in small-scale fighting, where it is difficult for regular troops to win. On the other hand, it must be recognized that Judah's strategic leadership was without blemish, considering the defective military instrument at his disposal.

Tactically, the position was the reverse of the strategic one. On the battlefield, the Greek commanders were interested in slow action, and the Jews in a quick decision. The reason for this was the superiority of the trained soldiers over the irregulars under conditions prevailing in ancient time. Battle in those days turned into a series of duels between swordsmen, in which, of course, the experienced fighter had the advantage. Conversely, the Hellenist army, and the phalanx in particular, lacked flexibility: its striking power was effective mainly on unobstructed, level ground. On hilly, rough terrain, and with no time to form properly, the phalanx disintegrated. Judah's tactical skill was evidenced by his ability to draw the enemy into a position in which both the elements of terrain and of surprise would work to the advantage of the Jews. The first was made possible by the geographical features of the Judean Mountains, and the second, by his superior intelligence. Since the villagers were always on his side, he possessed complete information about the enemy's movements, whereas the Greek commanders were mostly groping in the dark. Only during the battle for Beth-zacharia did conditions change for the worse and the enemy managed to fight on more or less level terrain. The advantage of surprise again aided Judah in his encounters with Nicanor, but in the battle of Elasa the unfavorable conditions of the battle of Beth-zacharia were repeated, coupled with the diminution of the forces at Judah's disposal.

Of course, the Jews' weak point was the absence of a regular army whose presence in battle could be relied on. The number of Jewish combatants was at first very small, then it steadly increased until the great battles of Emmaus and Beth-zur. It declined again during the course of the war, especially after the defeat at Beth-zacharia and the Syrians' entry into Jerusalem; it rose temporarily during the battles against Nicanor, and dropped to a minimum in the battle of Elasa. Obviously, it was difficult for a commander to conduct a war without knowing the size of the forces available to him. On the other hand, the Jewish forces do not seem to have suffered from other shortcomings which tend to afflict irregular armies: lack of discipline and internal dissension. From time to time the *Ḥasidim* abandoned the fight; but on the battlefield the Hasmonean army displayed exemplary discipline. Evidence of this is the halt, on orders, of the pursuit to Gezer after the battle of Emmaus, when the pursuers relinquished the chances of considerable spoils and re-grouped for battle. The absolute unity of action among the Hasmonean brothers should also be noted. Although they sometimes acted separately and at considerable distances from one another, complete unity of view prevailed among them. That this unity was not always conspicuous among the lower-ranking officers is proved by the conduct of the local commanders during Judah's absence in Gilead.

Looking at the conclusion of the war it is easy to point to the factors which led to the liberation of Judea from a foreign yoke and the establishment of an independent state, which later extended its power over the entire country. Such an objective approach, however, need not blind us to a subjective appreciation of the courage of Mattathias, Judah, and his brothers at the time of the revolt. They could not know the final result; and if they nevertheless chose the way of freedom they did so out of devotion to national-religious values which was to serve as an example to succeeding generations.

CHAPTER VII

THE FIRST HASMONEAN RULERS: JONATHAN AND SIMEON

by J. Klausner

A. THE ACCESSION OF JONATHAN AND THE RENEWAL OF HOSTILITIES (161–153 B.C.E.)

IN THE YEAR 160 B.C.E. Judah Maccabee fell in battle, and it appeared that all his victories and heroic deeds would go for nothing and Judea's political and religious situation would revert to what it had been in 162 B.C.E., at the beginning of the reign of Demetrius I. Once again the Hellenizers held power in Jerusalem, upheld by the spears of the troops of the Syrian king, commanded by Bacchides. The High Priest was Alcimus (Eliakim), maintained in office by the grace of Bacchides. Once again the rich and the privileged among the "repudiators of the covenant" came to the fore, and all those who had opposed them, particularly the followers of Judah, were hunted down and destroyed.

But some of the Hasmoneans' adherents remained steadfast in their loyalty, and the more courageous joined together in a small band and chose Jonathan son of Mattathias as their leader. Mattathias' will had designated Simeon, the oldest of the brothers, to succeed Judah, but differences appear to have arisen between Simeon and Judah. Accordingly, the group turned to Jonathan to lead them. The choice was a happy one. Jonathan proved to be a courageous warrior, even though he was not the adored hero that Judah had been. Victorious in many battles, nevertheless it was not as a military commander that Jonathan excelled. Rather was he outstanding in his grasp of the political situation and in his uncanny ability to exploit a situation to his advantage. During the eighteen years of his rule he gradually led the Judean state towards independence.

At first, Jonathan's small band was naturally unable to fight the Syrians openly. As his father Mattathias before him, Jonathan had to launch his liberating operations with hit-and-run tactics. Now and then, he would swoop down on small Syrian detachments, or on the Jewish Hellenizers in villages and towns outside Jerusalem, where his opponents were not very strong or numerous. On one occasion Bacchides pursued Jonathan and his men into the wilderness of Tekoa, east of Bethlehem. The Jews planned to leave all their possessions in the land of the Nabataeans who, unlike the other Arabs, were friendly to the Hasmoneans (I Macc. 5:25, 9:35), and sent a small detachment under Jonathan's brother, Johanan, the third living son of Mattathias, to escort the property to the Nabataean cities. Near Medeba in Transjordan, the Arab tribe of the sons of Ambri[1] attacked and killed Johanan and his men and plundered all the property. To avenge the blood of his brother and his comrades Jonathan fell upon the sons of Ambri as they were celebrating the wedding of one of the leading tribesmen, and not only recovered their own property but even seized a good deal of booty. But of Mattathias' five sons only two were left.

Meanwhile, Bacchides crossed the Jordan in pursuit of Jonathan and his band in order to put an end to their raids. Advancing on them as they were returning from their battle against the sons of Ambri, he blocked their way near the fords of the Jordan and tried to force them to fight. Knowing that his troops were no match for the larger and stronger Syrian army, Jonathan avoided the encounter by ordering his men to swim across the Jordan at a point some distance from the Syrians (ca. 160 B.C.E.). Bacchides was aware of the fact that in Judea the Hasmoneans could count on large numbers of devoted adherents to join Jonathan. Accordingly, he hastened to fortify the towns of Jericho, Emmaus, Beth-horon, Beth-el, Timnah, Pirathon (above Wadi Kelt in the northeast) and Tekoa,[2] and stationed a Syrian garrison in each of them. In addition, he strengthened the garrison of the *akra* which was controlled by the Hellenizers, and fortified Beth-zur, on the road to Hebron, and Gezer, on the road to Jerusalem. Finally, he took hostages from among leading Jewish families suspected of Hasmonean sympathies and imprisoned them in the *akra*.

A short time later, during the month of Iyyar 159, Alcimus acted in a way that aroused widespread anger among the people. Although not an extreme Hellenizer, he began to tear down the balustrade separating the inner and outer courts of the Temple,[3] a wall which was regarded as the "works of the prophets."[4] Soon after inaugurating the work, according to I Macc. (9:55–56), Alcimus was stricken with apoplexy, his body became paralyzed, and he died in great pain. In the Midrash[5] there is apparently an ancient tradition that "Yaqim [Alcimus] of Ẓᵉrudot" (or "Ẓᵉrorot") died seeking repentance.

For seven years after Alcimus' unnatural death (159–153 B.C.E.), there was no High Priest in the Jerusalem Temple. These are the seven years without a High Priest to which Josephus refers on one occasion when he speaks of the period between Alcimus and Jonathan son of Mattathias

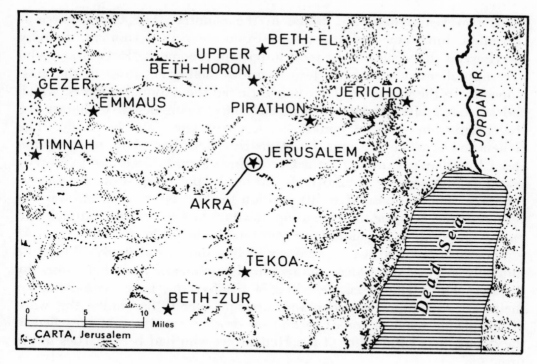

Bacchides' Fortifications

(*Ant.* XX, 237). In another place (*ibid.* XIII, 46), however, Josephus says that Jonathan donned the garments of the High Priest "four years after the death of his brother Judah — for there had been no High Priest during this time." The source of this contradiction lies in the fact that according to Josephus (*ibid.* XII, 413), Alcimus died, "having been High Priest for four years," immediately after Nicanor was killed. Judah then acceded to the High Priesthood. Further on, Josephus states (*ibid.* XII, 434), that Judah Maccabee "had held the High Priesthood for three years when he died." It is these three years that Josephus subtracted from the seven years which elapsed between Alcimus and Jonathan. It is then more accurate to say that there was no real High Priest in Jerusalem "for seven years."

After Alcimus' death, Bacchides departed from Judea, taking along the special force which he had brought with him, apparently relying on the garrisons he had left in the various cities. He may also have thought that the situation would quiet down with the death of Alcimus, who had been a cause of friction between the nationalist party and the Hellenizers.[6]

For two years there was peace in the country. The Greek garrison prevented Jonathan and his troops from entering Jerusalem, thereby carrying out the wishes of the most important among the Hellenizers, who were apprehensive about the Jerusalemites' inclination towards the Hasmoneans. In the meantime Jonathan gathered the nationalist forces, which had scattered after Judah's death, and once again began to harass the Hellenizers wherever he could, his force growing all the while. The Hellenizers sent deputations to Demetrius and Bacchides to complain about Jonathan's hounding of the Greek king's loyal subjects and to propose that the suppression of the rebels should not be put off in order not to give Jonathan time to consolidate his position further. Now, while he was not yet too strong, was the time to swoop down on him in a surprise attack and put an end both to the nationalist movement and to the revolt.

These words found a receptive ear in Bacchides, and in 158 B.C.E. he suddenly swept into Judea, taking the Hasmoneans and their allies by surprise. The Hellenizers, the allies of the Syrians, gave assurances, for their part, to capture Jonathan and turn him over to Bacchides, But word of this pledge reached Jonathan and his brother Simeon, and they fled to the desert, first killing fifty of the Hellenizers who had been parties to the promise.[7]

Jonathan built a fortress in the desert, in an oasis called Beth-basi in I Macc. (9:62)[8] and Bethalaga by Josephus (*Ant.* XIII, 26). Bacchides laid siege to the place, but putting Simeon in charge, Jonathan quietly slipped out of the bastion with a small detachment of troops and struck at the small Arab tribes which had aided Bacchides. Then he passed through the towns and villages of Judea enlisting new troops. Thus reinforced, Jonathan returned to attack Bacchides, who was still besieging Simeon. Bacchides' troops turned about to repel the attackers, whereupon Simeon and his men emerged from the fortress and fell upon the Syrians from the rear. The two brothers did not score a decisive victory, but by now Bacchides had lost all enthusiasm for this war on behalf of the Hellenizers. It was clear that these allies of his monarch had no roots in the nation and that most of the people supported the Hasmoneans. By disparaging the nationalist party the Hellenizers were endangering the position of the Syrian army in Judea. Angry at having been thus misled, Bacchides ordered a number of Hellenizers killed. When Jonathan learned of this, he dispatched a peace offer to Bacchides, who was agreeable. They exchanged prisoners and promises not to continue fighting one another. Bacchides left garrisons in the fortresses he had built, and taking hostages from among the leaders of the nationalist party and imprisoning them in the *akra*, he returned home. Jonathan did not go to Jerusalem: he had given his word that he would not fight the Syrians, and Jerusalem — and the *akra* in particular — were protected by a Syrian garrison. He went to Michmas to the north, two hours' distance by foot from Jerusalem.

For five years (158–153 B.C.E.) the country again knew peace. The Hellenizers and the aristocracy ruled in Jerusalem, with the aid of the foreign garrison. Outwardly, Jonathan submitted to the Syrian king, but secretly he continued to enlist fighting men from among loyal Jews, and as soon as he felt himself sufficiently strong, "Jonathan began to judge the people; and he destroyed the ungodly out of Israel" (I Macc. 9:73).[9] He resorted to such measures for the Hellenizers were opposed both to freedom of religion and to the liberation of the nation. Their goal went counter to the spirit of the people, nor were they aware of the times in which they lived. They did not realize how shaky Syria's political position was, nor how easily the situation might be exploited to free Judea from the foreign yoke. The Hasmonean party was fully aware of these possibilities and that realization won them the hearts of the masses — a fact none knew better than Jonathan son of Mattathias. Thus it came about that during these five years of tranquillity the Hellenizers grew progressively weaker, while the nationalist-religious party steadily gained ground. Once a persecuted opposition party, the Hasmoneans now became the ruling popular party. And, after Judah Maccabee, no one contributed more to this transformation than Jonathan.

B. POLITICAL UPHEAVALS IN SYRIA. JONATHAN HIGH PRIEST AND RULER OF JUDEA (153–147 B.C.E.)

Beginning in 153 B.C.E. the Syrian throne was occupied by a succession of kings-for-a-day of the Seleucid dynasty, each of whom achieved power by revolt and murder. This situation was obviously to the advantage of the Hasmoneans, whose political fortunes rose steadily, until the complete national liberation of Judea was achieved over a period of slightly less than ten years (153–141 B.C.E.).

In 153 B.C.E. the Syrian throne was claimed by a youth of lowly origin, Alexander Balas, who gave himself out as a son of Antiochus IV Epiphanes. He was supported in his claim by Attalus II, King of Pergamum, as well as by Ptolemy VI Philometor, King of Egypt, and Ariarathes VI, King of Cappadocia. The pretender went to Rome with the object of persuading the Senate to recognize him as Antiochus' son and the legitimate monarch of Syria. As a way of adding to the confusion in Syria, in line with the principle of "divide and rule," the Senate acknowledged Balas' royal origin, although everyone knew the truth.

Recognized by Rome as king, Alexander Balas arrived in Syria, ready to do battle with Demetrius Soter. The latter's unpopularity with the Syrian people improved the pretender's prospects of winning the throne. And indeed, Demetrius soon found himself in difficulties. He appealed to Jonathan for help in his war against Balas, even allowing him to mobilize troops in Judea for the purpose. In return for Jonathan's military assistance, Demetrius promised to release the leaders of the nationalist-religious party still held hostage in the *akra*. Happy at the turn of affairs, Jonathan hurried to Jerusalem. Demetrius kept his word and freed the hostages, whereupon Jonathan conquered the city except for the *akra*, and strengthened the Temple Mount. Most of the garrisons which Bacchides had posted in the fortresses returned to Syria, leaving only those in Beth-zur and the *akra*. Jonathan was quick to change the municipal leadership of Jerusalem, repaired the walls of the city (I Macc. 10:11), and generally took measures which accorded with the wishes of the religious-nationalist party.

Learning of the inducements Demetrius was offering Jonathan, Alexander Balas was not slow to make his own bid for Jonathan's support by offering him the highest possible privilege in Judea: he appointed Jonathan to the High Priesthood. As High Priest, Jonathan was also ethnarch. To indicate Jonathan's high rank, Balas sent him a robe of purple and a wreath of gold. On the Festival of Tabernacles in the year 153 B.C.E. a priest of the Hasmonean line officiated as High Priest in the Temple for the first time.[10] With this, the High Priesthood passed from the descendants of Zadok, who had kept the office in their hands for over 800 years. At the same time the Hellenizers ceased to exist as a party. They were replaced by the Sadducees, while the *Ḥasidim* were supplanted by the Pharisees and the Essenes. Jonathan, the representative of the religious-nationalist party, became the religious and political head of the nation, and along with the leadership of the state, the High Priesthood passed to the Hasmoneans.

The fact that neither Demetrius nor Alexander Balas made any overtures to the Hellenizers, then the actual government party, but made all their offers to the religious-nationalist party which was fighting foreign rule, religion, and culture, is eloquent testimony to the deep roots of the religious-nationalist party among the people. On the other hand, the wealthy Hellenizing faction attracted by Greek culture had little in common with the masses. Moreover, the religious-nationalist party possessed a popular leader, the scion of a simple priestly family, beloved by the majority of the nation as their liberator from a foreign faith and foreign political oppression.

Learning of the concessions granted to Jonathan by Alexander Balas, Demetrius tried to win Jonathan back by an abundance of inducements of his own.[11] He promised to exempt the Jews from the poll-tax, salt tax, and crown tax,[12] one-third of the grain tax and half of the fruit tax, to turn the *akra* over to Jonathan, and to free without ransom all Jews captured by the Syrians during the war who were now scattered throughout the Syrian territories. He was prepared to concede that payments of taxes and other debts falling due on Sabbaths and Jewish holidays, and even on the New Moon, which in the time of the Temple was a half-holiday, be deferred to the following weekday; to cede three districts in Samaria to Judea, and exempt them from the payment of taxes, to contribute a large sum of money from his treasury for the needs of the Temple, and to appropriate the income from the port of Acco for the same purpose. Demetrius also offered to cover the expenses of constructing the wall of Jerusalem from the royal treasury; and to admit into the king's army 30,000 Jewish soldiers, with Jewish commanding officers, chosen from among the troops, who would be granted the right to observe the Sabbath and Jewish holidays as well as the dietary precepts of the Jewish religion. They were also promised other privileges.

Such extravagant promises both in nature and quantity led Willrich, Wellhausen and Schürer to conclude that Demetrius' letter is either a complete forgery or, at the very least, an exceedingly free rendering by the author of I Maccabees. It is, nevertheless, quite possible that in view of his critical situation, Demetrius really did make these lavish promises with every intention of breaking them as soon as his position improved.[13] This, Jonathan well understood. A discerning statesman, he was certain that Demetrius had no hope of success in his war against Balas, for he was hated both by his own people and by the countries adjoining the kingdom of Syria. Accordingly, Jonathan chose to cast in his lot with Alexander Balas; and he had no cause to regret his decision. In 150 B.C.E. Demetrius was defeated by a coalition of monarchs, and Alexander Balas became king of Syria.

To make his throne more secure once he was king, Alexander turned to Ptolemy Philometor, King of Egypt, and asked for the hand of his daughter Cleopatra in marriage. Philometor agreed, and the royal wedding took place at Acco in great splendor. King Alexander invited Jonathan to the festivities and received him with great honor, to the displeasure of the

Hellenizers. The faction was still ensconced in the *akra* and most probably retained representatives in many centers of Judea, although Jonathan had driven them out of most towns (I Macc. 10:12–14). The Hellenizers sent emissaries to Alexander Balas at Acco to complain about Jonathan, denouncing him as the enemy of the Syrians and their allies. But Alexander paid no attention to them and conferred even greater honors on Jonathan. He seated him on his right hand, had him dressed in purple robes, and appointed him *strategos* and *meridarches* i.e., commander of the army and civil governor of Judea (and perhaps of all of Palestine) as a Syrian vassal. Thus, Jonathan become tantamount to an autonomous ruler in Judea; only the Syrian garrison in the *akra* remained, to indicate that supreme power still lay in the hands of the Syrians. Jonathan did not ask Alexander to remove this garrison for fear the Syrian king would suspect him of wishing to free himself entirely of Syrian rule.

C. The Expansion of Judea. Jonathan's Capture by Tryphon

With Jonathan both military and civil ruler in Judea, Syrian suzerainty there became practically nominal. The Hellenizers lost all influence, and internal affairs were entirely in the hands of the Hasmoneans. But a statesman like Jonathan could not content himself even with this. It was his ambition to sever Judea from Syria altogether, and to turn little Judea into a great Jewish state. For the first goal, the time was not yet ripe. Moreover, in those days of constant upheaval in Syria, the Syrian yoke was hardly felt, and Judea's subjection became little more than a formality. More important was the second aim; and here Jonathan was helped by the instability in Syria and the changes taking place in the Seleucid dynasty. Not that external events were the main cause and the Hasmoneans simply knew how to make the most of them for the needs of their people. Rather, a new situation had been achieved by the people of Judea as a result of demographic, economic, and cultural developments which had been taking place since the days of Ezra and Nehemiah. Out of that new position an inner driving force had emerged and been strengthened which made it possible for every turn of external events to be exploited to meet internal, national needs. Without this internal power, the sequence of events in Syria in the days of the Hasmoneans would have yielded no more benefit to the Judean state than had the confusion which prevailed in Persia between the death of Cambyses and the succession of Darius I to the throne, or the quarrels between the Diadochi and the Epigoni after the death of Alexander the Great. The events were not a fundamental cause, only an immediate one. Circumstances merely hastened developments which were bound to occur even without them.

What the state of Judea and its people lacked most was an outlet to the Mediterranean. Up to the time of the Hasmoneans the Jews, who had advanced in agriculture and in civilization, had remained landlocked in their small country. With no outlet to the sea they could not export any of their produce by way of the Mediterranean. All the ports of Palestine were controlled by foreigners — those in the south by the Greeks, and those in the north, by Tyre and Sidon. A national need — both political and economic — to gain control of the coastal cities had been ripening over the years. Now, political events helped to satisfy it.

The political changes took place in rapid succession. Alexander Balas' reign was without incident for only three years (150–147 B.C.E.). He was a weak and licentious ruler who failed to win the affection of the Syrian nation and its subject peoples, an omission which was exploited by Demetrius II, son of Demetrius I, who in 147 B.C.E. laid claim to his father's throne. The governor of Coele-Syria, Apollonius Taos,[14] transferred his allegiance to Demetrius. Jonathan remained loyal to Alexander Balas and as a result fought a battle against Apollonius from which he emerged victorious. Then Jonathan stormed the coastal area, drove the Syrian garrison out of Jaffa and defeated Apollonius' army near Ashdod, while Ashkelon opened its gates to him without a fight. Victorious and laden with booty, Jonathan returned to Jerusalem, where as a mark of gratitude for his military help, Alexander Balas sent him a golden bracelet (πόρπη), and also turned Ekron and the surrounding area over to Judea. The Hasmonean conquest of the ancient Philistine cities along and near the coast had begun.

Jonathan's loyalty to Alexander Balas is convincing testimony that the success of the Hasmoneans stemmed not merely from the·disorders in Syria or from Jonathan's diplomatic acumen, but from the internal strength of the Jewish people in their land. For this time, Jonathan was not acting as a far-sighted statesman: in his loyalty to the bungling Alexander Balas he stood alone. Balas was deserted not only by Apollonius Taos, his military commander, but even by his father-in-law Ptolemy Pilomhetor, who, with the aim of uniting the crowns of Egypt and Syria on his own head, gradually conquered most of the cities of Syria. He dared not seize all the Syrian states immediately, for fear of Rome,[15] which would not permit any Near Eastern potentate to grow too strong. With this in mind, Ptolemy took his daughter back from Alexander and gave her to Demetrius II, thereby making it appear that his conquests in Syria were all for the sake of his new son-in-law. In fact, Ptolemy was apparently looking forward to the day when he would rid himself of Demetrius as well. Of course, Ptolemy became an enemy of Jonathan, who was allied to Alexander. Nevertheless, when Ptolemy passed through Ashdod and the Greeks there complained to him that Jonathan had demolished their temple and destroyed their land, Ptolemy took no action. By this time, it would seem, Jonathan was a power to be reckoned with.

Ptolemy marched with a large force against Alexander Balas, Demetrius' rival, and both armies met in the valley of Antioch, on the Oenoparas river. Just part of Alexander's army was involved in the struggle against Demetrius, only those troops whom Alexander had taken with him to put down a revolt in Cilicia. The rest of the army remained at Antioch, and along with the local population, defected to Demetrius II. It is thus hardly surprising that Alexander Balas was defeated. He then fled to Arabia, where he was murdered by Zabdiel (I Macc. 11:7; Zabeilus according to Josephus, *Ant.* XIII, 118), the commander of the local Arab soldiery who sent his head to Ptolemy Philometor. Ptolemy, undoubtedly, planned to betray Demetrius — the man for whom he had ostensibly been fighting and whose rightful inheritance he sought to restore, but before he could carry through his plans, he died of wounds received in battle. In 145 B.C.E. Demetrius II Nicator (the Victorious) became king of Syria.

In spite of Demetrius victory, Jonathan still hoped to finish what his brother Judah Maccabee had begun and make Judea completely independent. To this end he laid siege to the *akra*, still held by the Greek garrison and by the Hellenizing Jews. This aroused the wrath of Demetrius Nicator, who sent a stern demand to Jonathan to lift the siege and report to him immediately at Acco to account for his insolence. Jonathan was undismayed. He did not lift the siege. Nevertheless, reluctant to become embroiled in open war with the king of Syria, he reported to him at Acco together with a number of Judean dignitaries and priests and brought him gifts of gold, silver, expensive garments, and other costly articles. The Hellenizers presented themselves before Demetrius at the same time and repeated the complaints about Jonathan which they had made in the days of Alexander Balas. But Demetrius knew Jonathan's great power because of the people's backing. Ignoring the protests of the Hellenizers, who, he realized, had no deep roots in the nation, Demetrius received Jonathan with great honor and confirmed him in the High Priesthood, military command, and civil governorship of Judea. In return for a contribution of a lump sum of 300 talents of silver from Jonathan to the royal treasury, Demetrius annexed to Judea three districts of Samaria: Ephraim,[16] Lod, and Ramathaim.[17]

The *akra*, the siege of which had so angered the king, was not mentioned at all on this occasion. Apparently Jonathan did lift the siege and the Syrian garrison remained there as a symbol of that country's suzerainty over all of Judea. In Renan's view,[18] Jonathan lifted the siege even before going to Acco, and the account of his compliance with the king's order (I Macc. 11:23) should read: ἐκέλευσε [μὴ] περικαθῆσθαι ("he command-ed that the citadel should [not] continue to be besieged"); this would explain why the matter of the *akra* was not raised at all at Acco. However that may be, the Syrian king was satisfied with Jonathan's behavior, and for Judea the acquisition of the three new districts was a matter of great importance. With Jonathan confirmed as the effective ruler of the country under the formal suzerainty of Syria, the end of the road to Judea's indep-endence was in sight.

In Syria, revolts against the throne multiplied. Alexander Balas' former commanding general, Diodotus Tryphon of Apamea, now appeared with Alexander's young son, Antiochus VI, who had been brought up in the home of an Arab by the name of Malchus (*Ant.* XIII, 131). In the year 143/2 B.C.E. Diodotus proclaimed him king in place of Demetrius II, hoping that once Demetrius was out of the way he would get rid of the boy, whose father after all was an impostor, and would himself assume the throne — exactly the hope Lysias had cherished during the reign of Antiochus IV, and Ptolemy Philometor, at the time of Alexander Balas. Tryphon based his hopes of deposing Demetrius II on the fact that he was hated not only by the people of Antioch for his cruelty and capriciousness but, even more important, by his own soldiers. They were bitter against Demetrius because after defeating Alexander Balas with an army composed of both Syrian conscripts and mercenaries, he had failed to pay his soldiers and had discharged all Syrians from the army, preferring to rely on foreign troops. In the Syrian capital of Antioch, open rebellion flared up against Demetrius. This afforded Jonathan the opportunity of demanding the removal of the remaining troops garrisoning the *akra* and Beth-zur. Sorely pressed, Demetrius acquiesced, but on condition that Jonathan send him a Jewish contingent to save him from his rebellious subjects in Antioch. Jonathan sent 3,000 soldiers, who quashed the rebellion in short order. Thus, some thirty years after Antiochus Epiphanes had appeared at the gates of Jerusalem at the head of his armies to crush the revolt of the Jews against the desecration of all they held sacred, the armies of the Jewish High Priest arrived at the gates of Antioch to put down the rebellion of the Antiochenes against their cruel king. Times and historical circumstances had indeed changed.[19]

Jonathan's troops saved the throne of Demetrius Nicator. But Demetrius showed no gratitude to the Jews. As soon as he was freed of the rebels, he went back on his promise to remove the Syrian garrison from the *akra*. In the meantime, however, many of Demetrius' troops, none of whom had been paid, deserted and went over to Tryphon, who was acting as regent for the young Antiochus. With their help Tryphon conquered Antioch. In Antiochus' name, Tryphon immediately confirmed everything that Demetrius had promised Jonathan. Moreover, again speaking for the young king, he appointed Jonathan's brother Simeon *strategos* (military and civil governor) of the area from the "Ladder of Tyre" to the Brook of Egypt (Naḥal Miẓraim; in Arabic: Wadi al-'Arīsh). Thus, Simeon also became the actual ruler of parts of Palestine lying outside the confines of Judea, even though formally they remained under Syrian suzerainty. The Hasmoneans had taken another great step towards their goal of expanding the boundaries of little Judea to those of the Greater Land of Israel of the days of David and Solomon. To this end, Jonathan also tried to obtain from the Syrian king dominion not only over the three districts of Samaria already mentioned, but also over the region of Philistia containing the coastal cities of Judea and Samaria, of economic importance to the Jews as an outlet to the Mediterranean.

Since Demetrius had failed to keep his word, Jonathan and Simeon abandoned him and allied themselves with Tryphon. In the name of the young Antiochus they conquered Ashkelon, which opened its gates to them, then marched on Gaza, which resisted and had to be taken by storm by the Jewish forces. Jonathan and Simeon made hostages of a number of the city's notables and took them to Jerusalem. In the capital they conducted themselves as sovereign rulers in every respect, although ostensibly acting in the name of the king of Syria.

With the southern coastal cities secured, Jonathan and Simeon launched an attack on the northern cities, on the outskirts of Upper Galilee. There, Demetrius' troops caught Jonathan's forces in an ambush in the valley of Hazor and dealt them a heavy blow. But Jonathan's two generals, Mattathias ben Absalom and Judah ben Chalfi (or ben Chapsaios),[20] quickly recovered, counter-attacked and routed the Syrians pursuing them as far as Kedesh-naphtali. Jonathan and his men then returned to Jerusalem with considerable booty which the retreating foes had jettisoned in their flight. Around this time Simeon forced the Syrian garrison at Beth-zur to surrender and abandon the fortress and posted a Jewish garrison there. There may be a hint of this important event in *Mᵉgillat Taʿanit* which says that the 17th day of Nisan became a holiday because of "the seizure of the tower of Shur" (the fortress of Beth-zur).

To buttress his rule in Palestine and free it altogether from the Syrian yoke, Jonathan sent two ambassadors to Rome — Numenius son of Antiochus and Antipater son of Jason (as in the days of Judah Maccabee, the nationalist-religious party again sent emissaries with Greek names) for the purpose of strengthening the alliance his brother Judah made with Rome. Emissaries were also sent out to conclude treaties of friendship with Sparta and other countries. The Jewish ambassadors to Sparta recalled the fact that Areus, a former king of the city (undoubtedly Areus I, who reigned from 309 to 265 B.C.E.), had sent a message of friendship to Onias, the High Priest.[21]

Smarting under his defeat at Hazor, Demetrius mobilized a large army to take revenge on Jonathan, who marched out to meet him at Hamath, north of the mountains of Lebanon. Apparently Jonathan's army was much larger than that of Demetrius; at any rate, the Syrians lost heart and fled from their positions during the night. Jonathan then attacked and defeated the Arabic tribe of Zabadeans in the Lebanese mountains, who had evidently joined forces with the Syrians against Judea, and made off with booty. According to Derenbourg,[22] there is a hint of this event in the following ancient *barayta*: "On the 17th of that month [Adar], the Gentiles had risen against the remnants of the scribes in the country of Chalcis, in Beth-Zabdai, and there came salvation,"[23] but Schürer doubts that this is the incident referred to.[24] From here Jonathan went on to Damascus, traversing the entire country.

While Jonathan was engaged in conquering the land, Simeon was busy making himself master of the maritime towns. He conquered Jaffa, Judea's natural port, and stationed a Jewish garrison there. Another garrison was stationed in the city of Hadid, in the Coastal Plain west of the Mountains of Judea, near Lod and Modiin (I Macc. 12:33 ff.).[25] Meanwhile, Jonathan returned to Jerusalem, summoned the "elders of Judea," and proposed that the city wall which he had previously built be fortified, and that a high wall be erected between the city and the *akra* to cut off the Syrian garrison and Jewish Hellenizers from the Jerusalem markets, thus preventing them from stealing into the city to buy food, and consequently force them to surrender. Clearly, Jonathan and Simeon were preparing to proclaim the independence of the Judean state, and were doing their utmost to annex as much of Palestine as possible to Judea. And a large Jewish army, strong enough to pit itself against the mercenaries of the kingdom of Syria, torn asunder by the fighting between rival claimants to the throne, stood at their command.

Tryphon may have been aware of all this. His plan was to take the crown for himself as soon as he could get rid of young Antiochus, the son of

Alexander Balas, for whom he was ostensibly acting as regent. But fear of Jonathan inhibited Tryphon from carrying out his design (I Macc. 12:39–40). According to Graetz,[26] Jonathan was loyal to the memory of Alexander Balas and the devoted champion of the rights of Antiochus. Tryphon may also have feared that Jonathan would take advantage of his *coup d'état* to throw off the Syrian yoke altogether. In either case, Tryphon sought some stratagem to do away with Jonathan, who appeared to constitute a serious threat as his armies increased and his influence grew stronger.

Anxious to win a decisive victory, Tryphon appeared at Beth-shean at the head of a large army. But Jonathan's forces were just as strong, numbering 40,000 men. Knowing that he had no hope of defeating so great an army, Tryphon resorted to treachery.

He received Jonathan with all possible ceremony assuring him that he had no intention of fighting the Jews and had brought along his army only for the purpose of according Jonathan the full military honor that was his due. Somehow or other, Jonathan was duped into dismissing his large army, and sent the bulk of his troops back to Judea, leaving only 3,000 men, of whom he sent 2,000 to garrison Galilee. The remainder he retained as a guard of honor. With this tiny force of 1,000 men Jonathan accompanied Tryphon and his whole army to Acco. Once there, Tryphon's soldiers killed Jonathan's escort to the last man, and Jonathan himself was taken alive as a hostage.

D. Assumption of Control by Simeon. Tryphon's Attempt to Conquer Judea. Jonathan's Murder

With Jonathan his prisoner, Tryphon quickly advanced on Judea, convinced that now that the Jews were without their leader, he would have no trouble in defeating their army and conquering the entire country. But Simeon hurried to Jerusalem, where he summoned an emergency assembly of the people and promised to follow in the steps of Jonathan (I Macc. 13:2 ff.). The people accepted Simeon as their leader "instead of Judah and Jonathan thy brethren" (*ibid.* 13:8). Simeon lost no time in taking action: he fortified the walls of Jerusalem, mobilized a new army — every sword-bearer in Judea — and continued the siege of the *akra*.

Simeon also despatched the military leader Jonathan ben Absalom to conquer Jaffa, whose previous conquest (see above) seems to have been only a temporary one, designed to prevent the city from falling into the hands of Demetrius' men, hostile to Jonathan. The idolatrous inhabitants were now expelled and Jews settled in their place (I Macc. 13:11). This

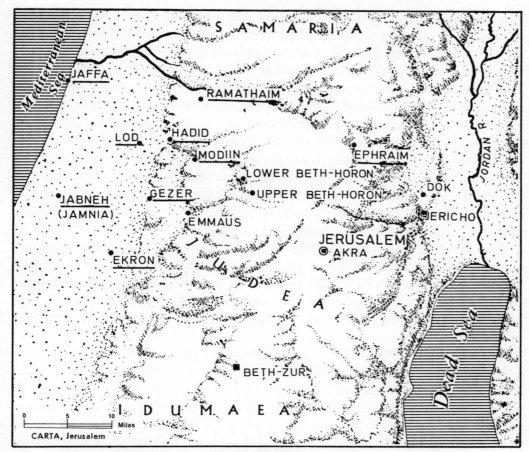

SYRIAN FORTRESSES IN JUDEA CONQUERED BY JONATHAN AND SIMEON
LOD   AREAS AND CITIES ADDED TO JUDEA UNDER JONATHAN AND SIMEON

Judea under Jonathan and Simeon

had been the first action by a Hasmonean ruler to Judaize Palestinian cities outside Judea. Thereafter it became the rule for the Hasmonean fighters to Judaize every idolatrous city they conquered if it was located within the borders of the kingdom of David and Solomon and had had idolatry imposed on it when the kings of Assyria, Babylonia, Persia, or of the Hellenistic states held sway in Israel. The Hasmoneans believed the Jews were morally justified in recovering their patrimony which had been forcibly seized by strangers.

The Hasmonean Judaization campaign began in Jaffa, because since ancient times the city had been a prominent port, from which ships sailed not only to Egypt, Tyre, and Sidon, but even as far as Tarshish.[27] And the Jews needed an outlet to the sea in order to reach the civilized countries of the time. To be sure, the Jews were not yet primarily traders: the great majority were farmers. But they had no direct access to world markets for their grain and fruit crops. Only through ports seized by the inhabitants of the Greek cities in the south and the Hellenized Phoenicians in the north could they send their produce to market or obtain the goods of countries across the sea. But the foreign inhabitants of the coastal cities collected taxes on all imports and exports passing through their ports. Under these conditions Judea had no hope of achieving economic prosperity and Jonathan began secretly and by degrees to try to win back all the coastal cities of Palestine. Simeon took the last step. He began to Judaize the coastal cities, beginning with Jaffa, the port nearest Jerusalem.

The Hasmoneans undoubtedly fought the Syrian kings for religious-national and political reasons; but very soon they became aware of the people's economic needs which were being felt even at the time of Joseph son of Tobiah and his son Hyrcanus. As the hour of liberation approached, the economic aspect of the war of independence assumed greater prominence.

With Jonathan still in his custody Tryphon proceeded from Acco with a large force. At Hadid he was met by Simeon's army, and once again Tryphon tried to trick his adversary. He sent messengers to Simeon to inform him that Jonathan had been taken prisoner because of his failure to pay the customary tribute upon his appointment; if Simeon would deliver one hundred talents of silver and turn over Jonathan's two sons as a guarantee against rebellion, Tryphon would release Jonathan. While Simeon sensed that this was a ruse, he was afraid of being accused of refusing to redeem his brother in order to make himself ruler of Judea. He accordingly sent the money and the two boys to Tryphon.

As Simeon had anticipated, Tryphon did not release Jonathan. The people besieged by Jonathan and Simeon's army in the *akra* sent pressing appeals to Tryphon to come to their aid. Tryphon made an attempt to invade Judea from the south by way of Adoraim (Adora) in Idumaea. But, most unusual for that subtropical climate, snow fell in the night blocking Tryphon's line of advance and compelling him to divert his army and march in the direction of Gilead (winter 143/2 B.C.E.).

Furious at the failure of his plans, Tryphon had Jonathan executed and buried in the city of "Bascama" (or "Basca"),[28] and it appears that he killed Jonathan's two sons as well. That left as Jonathan's only remaining offspring a daughter married to Mattathias ben Simeon Psellus (the

Stammerer), from whom the historian Josephus was descended, as he relates in the autobiography appended to his *Antiquities*. Simeon recovered Jonathan's remains and re-interred him at Modiin, the burial place of his ancestors. Above the sepulcher, where he also had a crypt quarried for himself, Simeon erected a monument,[29] so high that it was visible from the sea. Its seven pillars (representing his father and mother and the five brothers) were decorated with carved designs of various weapons (symbolizing the wars of Mattathias and his sons) and ships (an allusion to the Hasmoneans' ambition to achieve an outlet to the sea for Judea).

The entire nation mourned deeply for Jonathan. With his death the Jews had lost a great statesman and accomplished diplomat, who, with his sound grasp of Syria's position, had known how to exploit its political quarrels with Egypt and with mighty Rome.

Politically, Jonathan had indeed achieved much. Judah Maccabee had bequeathed him only a small band of enthusiasts inspired by the ideals of religious liberty and political liberation and spurred on by the ambition of extending the borders of small Judea. Jonathan turned this band into a people. From the leader of a small band he became the head of a nation, and from a hunted rebel, High Priest, commander of a national army, and almost the independent ruler of his country. Furthermore, Jonathan began the transformation of little Judea into the Greater Land of Israel; ostensibly in the name of the Syrian king, he conquered practically all the cities of the Syrian Greeks and Hellenized Canaanites in Judea and Galilee. He was also concerned about the country's economic life which he sought to improve by securing an outlet to the sea. It appears too that he was responsible for transforming the *Hever ha-Y^ehudim* into a national council to head the nation, enact its laws, and supervise its religious, political, and economic affairs. Jonathan thus paved the way for the complete liberation of Judea. All that remained for his brother Simeon to do was to proclaim Judea's independence and to obtain confirmation of this from the king of Syria.

E. COMPLETE LIBERATION OF JUDEA

After Jonathan was killed, it was obvious that the people would recognize Simeon son of Mattathias as their leader, for he had acted as such from the day Tryphon captured Jonathan. Naturally enough Simeon set himself against Tryphon, the betrayer and murderer, especially after this "regent" did away with young Antiochus VI and assumed his throne (142 B.C.E.). Simeon entered into negotiations with Demetrius II. In return for a certain amount of gold which Demetrius badly needed for paying his mercenaries, and because he feared Simeon might ally himself with Tryphon, the Syrian ruler agreed to confirm in writing what already was a fact: the complete independence of Judea. On the 27th day of Iyyar, 142 B.C.E., after receiving a silver wreath and a golden palm branch from Simeon, Demetrius II even agreed to release Judea from the payment of annual tribute to Syria, on condition that Simeon sign a treaty with him against Tryphon. And the official historian of the Hasmonean dynasty proclaims with a flourish: "In the one hundred and seventieth year [of the Seleucid era] was the yoke of the heathen taken away from Israel. And the people of Israel began to write in their instruments and contracts: 'In the first year of Simeon the great High Priest and captain and leader of the Jews'" (I Macc. 13: 41–42). And to mark the discontinuance of the payment of tribute to Syria, the 27th of Iyyar was declared a holiday: "On the 27th of that month [Iyyar] the crown tax was remitted from Judea and Jerusalem."[30] In other words they eliminated the payment of the gold wreaths, the form in which subject peoples used to pay tribute to the Syrian king, which Simeon had also sent to Demetrius.

Once free of Tryphon and assured of Demetrius' willingness to recognize Judea's complete independence (end of 143 or beginning of 142 B.C.E.), Simeon made haste to induce the Jews of Alexandria to recognize the significance of Judea's liberation from foreign dominion by celebrating the *Ḥanukka* festival, proclaimed by Judah Maccabee after his decisive victory.[31] For Simeon realized even then that the Hasmoneans had achieved a tremendous feat which ought to be perpetuated as a holiday for generations to come. On that holiday all the Jews in all the lands of their dispersion should rejoice at the restoration of the second free Kingdom of Israel, following the Kingdoms of Judea and Israel in the days of the First Temple. This was the first holiday universally observed by Jews which is not prescribed by the Torah; accordingly, work is permitted, but there are special readings from the Pentateuch, a special prayer (*'al-ha-nissim*) is recited, and the *Hallel* liturgy praising God is chanted.

With Judea's independence officially recognized, Simeon lost no time in expanding the independent state. His first goal was to gain control of the city which would secure his position in Jaffa—Judea's outlet to the sea and the economic key to Jerusalem. That city was Gezer, dominating the mountain passes in Judea which linked Jaffa to Jerusalem. Simeon laid siege to the city and conquered it. He evacuated its idolatrous inhabitants, apparently because he was convinced that they could not be trusted, settled in their place "men who observed the Law," and posted a Jewish garrison there under the command of his son John (Hyrcanus), whom he named commander of Judea's armed forces.[32]

In the same period Simeon apparently also conquered Jabneh (*Ant.* XIII, 215).[33] He then undertook the conquest of the *akra* where, for close on thirty years, the Hellenizers — "lawless men" and "repudiators of the holy covenant" — had been entrenched, a constant thorn in the side of Jerusalem. So long as the *akra* remained in the hands of the Syrian garrison, the victory of the nationalist party was inconclusive and Judea's independence incomplete. It should be noted that although Demetrius agreed to release Judea from all signs of subjection to Syria, the foreign garrison did not leave the *akra*. Either the Syrian king no longer had full control over the army as a result of the frequent struggles between pretenders to the throne, or Demetrius deliberately failed to remove his garrison in order to hold a whip over the Hasmoneans. Simeon had to take the *akra* by force. He besieged it until hunger forced the garrison to surrender. Simeon then allowed the people inside the *akra* and the foreign garrison to leave the fortress. On the 23rd day of Iyyar, 141 B.C.E., Simeon's forces entered the *akra* with drums, zithers, and palm branches and singing hymns of thanksgiving; this date was subsequently proclaimed a holiday. *Mᵉgilat Taʿanit* states that "On the twenty-third of the month [Iyyar] the people of the *akra* departed from Jerusalem."[34] Josephus relates that Simeon had the *akra* razed to the ground and the hill on which it stood levelled (*Ant.* XIII, 215). This account is true, except that the work was carried out in the days of John Hyrcanus.[35] Had it happened at the time of Simeon, this would surely have been reported in I Maccabees, whose author was careful to include every praiseworthy and notable act of the early Hasmoneans. All that is related there, however, is that Simeon fortified the Temple Mount more than it had been before, and that he dwelt there.[36]

F. SIMEON'S RULE

The rule of the first independent prince of the Hasmonean dynasty inaugurated a period of well-being. The author of I Maccabees uses an exalted style to describe this period, employing many of the flowery expressions used in the Book of Kings to describe the period of Solomon. And it is noteworthy that at the head of all of Simeon's glorious and heroic deeds, the author of I Maccabees places the conquest of Jaffa, Judea's outlet to the sea: "And in addition to all his [other] glory [was this that] he took Jaffa for a haven, and made it a place of entry for the ships of the sea" (I Macc. 14:5). The great political and economic importance of the conquest of Jaffa was fully realized by the early Hasmoneans. This is no mere conjecture, but is based on what is clearly stated and stressed in I Maccabees, written close to the time of Mattathias' sons. Even Strabo says: "The Jews who reach the sea use Jaffa as a harbor."[37]

Simeon also applied himself to improving the administration of domestic affairs. He reinforced law and justice in the land which for thirty years of constant war and disorder had been torn asunder by ánarchy. He seems to have made life difficult for lawbreakers among the remaining Hellenizers. But, otherwise, he was apparently a venerable and wise ruler who avoided unnecessary harshness, as is evidenced by his treatment of the inhabitants of Jaffa and of the *akra*. The period of his leadership was marked by peace and tranquility, security and happiness. It is described by the author of I Maccabees (14:6–15) in a passage of sonorous rhetoric, not free of hyperbole, but true in its essentials:

> He enlarged the borders of his nation,
> And ruled over the land.
> And he gathered together many that had been in captivity,
> And he ruled over Gezer and Beth-zur and the *akra*.
> And he took away uncleannesses therefrom,
> And there was none that could resist him.
> And they tilled their land in peace;
> And the land gave her increase,
> And the trees of the plains their fruit.
> Old men sat in the streets,
> All spoke together of the [common] weal,
> And the young men put on glorious and warlike apparel.
> For the cities he provided victuals,
> And furnished them with defensive works,
> Until his glorious name was proclaimed to the end of the earth.
> He made peace in the land.
> And Israel rejoiced with great joy.
> And each sat under his vine and his fig tree,
> And there was none to make them afraid;
> And no one was left in the land to fight them
> And the [foreign] kings were discomfited in those days.
> And he strengthened all that were brought low of his people;
> He sought out the Law,
> And put away the lawless and wicked.
> He glorified the sanctuary,
> And multiplied the vessels of the Temple.

Such words generally reflect the end of an era — usually one of wars and upheavals; they express the gratification that comes with the attainment of a great and lofty goal achieved with so high a toll in blood. The great majority of the people of Judea took satisfaction in the victory of the religious-nationalist party, in the throwing off of the Syrian yoke, and in their new freedom, the like of which they had not tasted for some four hundred years. It is their satisfaction which is echoed in these florid phrases, permeated by the spirit of the Scriptures.

And the people gave expression to their pleasure in a highly significant act. Up to that time the Hasmoneans had been self-appointed rulers. No one had elected them; no one had commissioned them. They came from a small town, from a family of common priests. The legitimate dynasty was the House of David, which had disappeared, or the House of Zadok, which had been exiled. Remnants of the House of David still survived in Babylonia and members of the House of Zadok still lived in Egypt. Only through the pressure of events had the sons of Mattathias supplanted these two dynasties. The time had come for an overt act by the people to confirm the rule of the Hasmoneans.

On the 18th day of Elul (end of August, beginning of September), 141 B.C.E., in the third year of Simeon's *de facto* leadership, a great assembly (συναγωγὴ μεγάλη) of priests and leaders of the nation convened (I Macc. 14:28). This was the "Great Assembly" acting as a political body, a function it periodically fulfilled. The Assembly confirmed Simeon son of Mattathias the Hasmonean as High Priest, commander of the army, and ethnarch of the people, "for ever, until a faithful prophet should arise." That is, for all future generations. The office was to be handed down from father to son, until the Prophet Elijah should appear and re-establish the kingdom of Messiah son of David. This resolution was engraved on tablets of brass, which were placed in the Temple Court.

This singularly important document begins with a review of the accomplishments of the Hasmonean brothers, and particularly of the great deeds of Jonathan and Simeon. At the end of the first verse, or the beginning of the second verse of the document (I Macc. 14:27, Rahlf's ed.; 14:28, Sweete's ed.), the Greek words ἀρχιερέως μεγάλου. (High Priest) are followed by an obscure compound word, or perhaps two baffling words: ἐν ασαραμελ. *Saramel* has variously been explained as *Ḥazar ʿam El* (חצר-עם-אל — Ewald) or *ʿAzar ʿam El* (עצר-עם-אל — Geiger). But Derenbourg[38] conjectures that the word ἐν was erroneously added by a copyist, the word itself being *Sar ʿam El* (שר-עם-אל); a compound Hebrew word corresponding to the Greek ἡγούμενος (bishop) or ἐθνάρχης (prince of the people, leader of the people).[39] The title "king" was not bestowed on Simeon.[40]

Recognition of a hereditary princedom of the Hasmonean dynasty by the people of Judea was significant internally. From then on Simeon not only headed the *Ḥever ha-Yᵉhudim*, as had the priests of the House of Zadok, but also the army and the civil administration of the state. It was but one short step to the kingship of the Hasmonean dynasty.

But at a time when Rome was already brandishing its sword over the head of the kings of Syria, Simeon also needed external recognition — that of Rome. To Rome he therefore dispatched Numenius, apparently accompanied by his comrade Antipater. The two ambassadors whom Jonathan had previously sent there bore as a gift a gold shield weighing a thousand *mane*. The Senate in Rome gave the Jewish envoys a friendly reception and issued orders to the kings of Egypt, Syria, Cappadocia, and Parthia, to a number of Greek and Asiatic islands (Delos, Samos, Cos, Rhodes, and Cyprus), to the states of Lycia and Pamphylia, and to various free cities (Halicarnassus in Caria, Sicyon in Greece, Aradus in Canaan, Cyrene in Africa, and others) not to violate the borders of the Jews, Rome's allies, and to extradite criminals from Judea.[41]

Simeon also renewed the alliance with Sparta, again employing the same two envoys, Numenius and Antipater. This action was unavoidable in those Hellenistic days. For politically and culturally, Rome and Hellenism ruled the world, and no new government could last unless it made its peace with them. Only by putting down the Hellenizers at home and by compromise with the nations abroad could the new dynasty of princes endure.

Thus, by the confirmation of the Great Assembly of the Jews and the approval of the Roman Senate, Simeon (and with him the entire Hasmonean dynasty) was firmly installed on the princely throne in Judea where he could sit in peace, and concern himself with the happiness of his people and the material and spiritual well-being of his land. As agriculture flourished and the maritime trade through Jaffa's port prospered, the home of the prince was filled with all the fine possessions of royalty.[42]

G. Antiochus VII Sidetes' Endeavor to Restore Control over Judea. Simeon's Murder

However, at a time when Syria was in a state of upheaval it was impossible even for a peace-loving leader to rule long without incident.

As already mentioned, Tryphon deposed the child Antiochus VI and declared himself king in his place (142–138 B.C.E.). Whereupon Simeon allied himself with Demetrius II. But Demetrius was captured by Mithridates I, of the Arsacid dynasty, while fighting the Parthians,[43] and Antiochus VII Sidetes, a brother of the captive king, assumed the throne (138–129 B.C.E.). He proclaimed himself king in Seleuceia, with the aid of Cleopatra, wife of the captive Demetrius, who was afraid that Tryphon might do away with her and her sons, the true heirs of Demetrius (*Ant.* XIII, 222). Antiochus VII planned to go to war against Tryphon, but before doing so, he hastened to send a letter of friendship to Simeon "from the isles of the sea" (Rhodes) in which he proclaimed Judea free, confirmed to Simeon all that Demetrius had granted, and gave him, or confirmed, the right to strike his own coins (I Macc. 15:5 ff.) — all this on condition that Simeon became his ally against Tryphon. Simeon, who hated Tryphon, the betrayer and murderer of his brother and his nephews, did join Antiochus VII, and when the latter set out against Tryphon and laid siege to the coastal fortress of Dor, Simeon sent two thousand soldiers to his aid, as well as gold and silver. But Antiochus was confident of achieving victory over Tryphon without external aid, and he did not accept Simeon's soldiers nor the money. In the meantime, envoys from the Greek cities which Jonathan and Simeon had captured probably came to him with complaints that Simeon had devastated the Philistinian cities and had conquered towns which did not belong to Judea. Meanwhile, Tryphon escaped from the fortress of Dor to Apamea, where he was again besieged, and eventually killed (138 B.C.E.).

No sooner was Antiochus VII rid of his rival Tryphon, than he sent an official by the name of Athenobius to Jerusalem to protest against the destruction caused by the Jews outside the borders of Judea and to demand that Simeon restore to Syria not only Jaffa, Gezer, and all the other conquered cities outside the borders of Judea, but the *akra* in Jerusalem as well. However, if Simeon were unwilling to return all these cities he was given the choice of paying a thousand talents of silver for them. Simeon replied that all the cities he had conquered outside Judea were the inheritance of the Jews, unjustly conquered by foreigners and now restored to their true owners (I Macc. 15:33–34). He added, however, that in order to avoid a war with the king of Syria he was prepared to pay one hundred talents of silver for Gezer and Jaffa, Jerusalem's outlet to the sea; as for the *akra*, that indisputably belonged to Judea and there were no grounds for demanding payment. Athenobius said nothing in reply and reported Simeon's answer to Antiochus. The latter then sent an army under Cendebaeus to make war on Judea and bring it once again under the Syrian yoke.

Cendebaeus invaded Judea, encamped at Jabneh, and fortified Gederah.[44]

Not far from the camp of the Syrian commander, at Gezer,[45] separated
only by the valley of Sorek, were the headquarters of John, Simeon's son,
commander of the Judean army. John notified his father of the invasion,
and Simeon, an old man by now, appointed his two sons, Judah and John,
to conduct the campaign against Cendebaeus. The two brothers had
20,000 foot-soldiers as well as cavalry, which the Jews had apparently not
possessed previously. John reached the valley of Sorek, impassable because
of the high waters from the winter rains. The soldiers were afraid to cross on
foot, but when John plunged into the stream, they followed suit. Near
Modiin, so dear to the sons of Mattathias, a fierce battle took place.
Cendebaeus sustained a heavy defeat, but Judah was severely wounded,
leaving his brother John to pursue the fleeing Syrians.

This was the only battle in which the Jews engaged during Simeon's
time. In his old age Simeon dwelt in peace and judged his people. A wise
and alert ruler, he would travel around the country to ascertain the
people's needs and introduce necessary social, political, and economic
measures.

In view of the peace and quiet which prevailed in Judea in Simeon's
time, it might have been hoped that the last of the five brothers would
die peacefully. But it seems to have been preordained that all the sons of
Mattathias should die by violence.

Simeon had a son-in-law, Ptolemy son of Abubus, whom he appointed
military commander of the plain of Jericho. A man of wealth and inordinate
political ambition, Ptolemy conspired to murder Simeon and his sons and
make himself ruler of Judea. He may have contracted an alliance for this
purpose with the king of Syria, who could not forget the rout of the Syrian
army by Simeon's sons and was seeking to subjugate Judea to Syria once
again. While Simeon was travelling through the country on an inspection
tour in the month of Sh⁰vat, 134 B.C.E., together with his wife and two of
his sons, Mattathias and Judah, Ptolemy prepared an elaborate banquet
in their honor at the fortress of Dok (I Macc. 16:15 ff.)[46], the modern
'Ayn ad-Dūk, near Jericho. During the meal, after the High Priest and his
wife and sons had drunk freely of the wine, Ptolemy killed Simeon and his
two sons[47] and took Simeon's wife (his mother-in-law) hostage. Then he sent
murderers to Gezer to kill John Hyrcanus as well, and he himself marched
to Jerusalem, which he hoped to conquer with the aid of the king of Syria.
Informing the Syrian king of the murder of Simeon and his sons in a letter,
Ptolemy requested military aid to enable him to carry out his design; to
sit on Simeon's throne and subjugate Judea to Syria once again. But a man
loyal to the Hasmoneans, hastening to John to apprise him of all that had

befallen his father, his two brothers, and his mother, managed to reach Gezer before the hired assassins. John was thus able to capture the would-be murderers, after which he hurried to Jerusalem, which he reached before Ptolemy and his army. The people of Jerusalem welcomed the only heir of Simeon the Hasmonean and prevented Ptolemy from breaking into the city. John Hyrcanus then assumed the High Priesthood as heir to his father.

PART FOUR: THE HEYDAY OF THE HASMONEAN STATE

CHAPTER VIII

JOHN HYRCANUS I

by J. Klausner

A. War with Antiochus Sidetes

JOHN HYRCANUS assumed the High Priesthood in 134 B.C.E., after the murder of Simeon the Hasmonean by the latter's son-in-law, Ptolemy son of Abubus. John's first action was to proceed against his father's murderer. Ptolemy, after an unsuccessful attempt to enter Jerusalem, returned to the fortress of Dok, where he had murdered Simeon.[1] John laid siege to Dok, but when he attempted to storm the fortress, Ptolemy had Simeon's widow, whom he was holding captive, brought up to one of the walls, had her beaten and tortured before her son's eyes and threatened to kill her if John persisted in his attack. The mother urged her son to disregard her torture and even the risk that she might be killed and to avenge the murder of his father and two brothers. But John could not bear to see his mother's suffering, and he therefore lifted the siege intermittently, resuming it after each interruption. This, of course, drew out the siege, and meanwhile the sabbatical year approached, making it difficult to find enough food for the army. John Hyrcanus was accordingly compelled to lift the siege. Taking advantage of the opportunity, Ptolemy, after murdering John's mother, fled to Rabbath Ammon (Philadelphia), which was ruled by the dynast Zeno Cotylas.

But no sooner was John free of Ptolemy, than Judea was invaded by Antiochus VII Sidetes who had apparently made use of Ptolemy to further his design of destroying the Hasmoneans. Antiochus' attack occurred in the very first year of John Hyrcanus' rule (134 B.C.E.).[2] The king reached Jerusalem after ravaging whatever Judean territory he passed through and immediately laid siege to it with John Hyrcanus and his army inside the city. Jerusalem was well fortified, but as the siege dragged on, provisions began to run out, and John was forced to expell all non-combatants from the city. But Antiochus, who had encamped near the wall and thrown up embankments and blockhouses around the city, refused to admit the evacuees into his camp and did not permit them to leave the area between the blockhouses. These unfortunates were compelled to wander about between the wall and the blockhouses, targets not only for the arrows shot by both sides but victims of hunger as well. Even on the New Year and the Day of Atonement the evacuees were not admitted to the city; it was only on the eve of *the* festival of the year, the Feast of Tabernacles, a few days later, that John Hyrcanus permitted them to return. In fact, shortly before the holiday, John has asked Antiochus for a truce during the seven days of the festival. Antiochus not only agreed, but even sent bulls with gilded horns for sacrifice, as well as spices for the Temple incense.[3] The protracted siege was apparently becoming burdensome to him. Antiochus was also concerned about the approach of the rainy season after the Feast of Tabernacles and, in addition, he was anxious to make peace in order to be free to march against the Parthians (see below). John Hyrcanus regarded Antiochus' reverent attitude towards the Temple as a good omen, and he sent emissaries to him to negotiate a peace settlement. Antiochus put the question before a meeting of his advisers. Some of his Greek counselors urged him to follow the example of Antiochus IV: outright destruction was the only solution for the Jews because of their "separateness" (ἀμιξία; *Ant.* XIII, 245), which was considered a criminal attitude towards the whole of mankind. Judaism must be cut out root and branch, as Antiochus Epiphanes had tried to do. Antiochus Sidetes, however, was inclined to accept the view advanced by the majority of his advisers, namely that since all the rebellions of the Jews had had their origin in the Jewish religion, it would be expedient to assure the Jews religious liberty, that is, they should be granted internal autonomy but kept subjugated politically. Antiochus thereupon informed John Hyrcanus that he had no intention of suppressing the Jewish religion,[4] and this paved the way for continuing the peace talks, for it guaranteed what was then regarded by the Jews as the matter of greatest consequence — the preservation of their religion. But the political terms laid down by Antiochus were very harsh. He insisted that Judea once again become a Syrian vassal, paying an annual tribute as well as a special tax for Jaffa and Gezer, which had been captured by Simeon, the father of John Hyrcanus. Furthermore, he demanded that the Jewish army surrender its arms to him and that John Hyrcanus admit a Syrian garrison into Jerusalem. In short, Antiochus wanted to return Judea to its position in the days of Judah Maccabee, after the conquest of Beth-zur by Lysias. Nevertheless, John Hyrcanus agreed to all of these severe terms, with the exception of the last: the return of a Syrian garrison to the confines of Jerusalem. He justified his refusal on religious grounds: it was forbidden to allow a non-Jewish garrison into Jerusalem because of the prohibition against mixing with Gentiles (*Ant.* XIII, 247). On the other hand, John Hyrcanus undertook to demolish the city walls[5] (or perhaps only the battlements of the walls),[6] to turn over hostages — including his own brother — and to pay five hundred talents of silver, three hundred of them immediately. To obtain this sum, as well as to pay the mercenaries whom he had been forced to employ in order to maintain at least the relative independence of Judea, John Hyrcanus opened the tomb of David and took from there three thousand talents of silver,[7] of which he paid three hundred to Antiochus. The remainder he used to hire an army of foreigners — consisting of Pisidians and Cilicians, but not of Syrians, who hated the Jews (*Ant.* XIII, 249). John Hyrcanus was the first of the Hasmoneans who imitated the kings of Syria by hiring mercenaries, in addition to the Jewish army which, like his father Simeon and his uncle Jonathan before him, he had at his disposal.

B. Antiochus Sidetes' Campaign Against the Parthians. Civil War in Syria

Once again Judea became a vassal of Syria. But this time there was no foreign garrison in Beth-zur or in the *akra*; Jaffa and Gezer remained under the rule of John Hyrcanus; and the prince of autonomous Judea maintained an army of Jewish and mercenary troops. The days when the Persians, the Ptolemies, and the Seleucids ruled over Judea did not return. Antiochus contented himself with this limited success because he was anxious to set out against the Parthians. As a Syrian vassal John Hyrcanus was obliged to ally himself with Antiochus in this war and to furnish him with a Jewish auxiliary army and supplies. Antiochus was not unappreciative of John Hyrcanus' aid. He treated the Jews with respect and granted them a variety of privileges, particularly when it came to religious matters, which had been the reason for their revolt. The historian Nicolaus of Damascus, who was Josephus' source for everything pertaining to the political history of the period of the Hasmoneans and of Herod's reign, relates that Antiochus tarried for two days on the banks of the Lycus river "at the request of the Jew Hyrcanus because of a festival of his nation on which it was not customary for the Jews to march out." And Josephus goes on to explain this puzzling statement of Nicolaus (since no holiday in Palestine — not even the New Year in ancient times — was observed for two successive days on which travelling was forbidden) by pointing out that in the year in question the *Shavu'ot* festival fell on a Sunday, and travelling was forbidden both on the holiday itself and on the Sabbath which preceded it (*Ant.* XIII, 250–252). The episode is of interest for several reasons.

First of all, it indicates that even though the government in the time of the Hasmonean princes had become more or less secular, the laws of the Torah were observed to such a degree that even in time of war, and even in a gentile environment, the Jews were capable of delaying the movement of a large army, and a gentile one at that, in order not to have to travel on the Sabbath or on a holiday. Furthermore, it would appear from this incident that at that time, even before the outbreak of the controversy between John Hyrcanus and the Pharisees which led to his joining the Sadducees, the *Shavu'ot* festival was already pointedly observed on Sunday ("on the morrow after the Sabbath"), in accordance with the practice of the Sadducees then and of the Karaites to this day.

In any event, John Hyrcanus was a Syrian vassal (although it was a less demanding vassalage than in the days before the Hasmonean revolt) for five, or at least four, years (134/3–129 B.C.E.). But it was not long before he rid himself of the Syrian yoke as new unrest and revolts broke out in Syria.

No sooner had Antiochus Sidetes launched his campaign against the Parthians than the King of Parthia produced Demetrius II, whom he had been holding captive, and put him forward as a rival to Antiochus Sidetes, his brother. Antiochus was killed soon thereafter and Demetrius II once again became King of Syria (129–125 B.C.E.). Demetrius, who had old scores to settle with the Ptolemies, prepared to attack Ptolemy VII Physcon, King of Egypt. This induced Ptolemy to set up a rival to Demetrius, Alexander Zabinas (from the Aramaic *Z'vina*, "the Bought One," as he was called by the people, because rumor had it that he was a redeemed slave). Zabinas was an Egyptian of mean origin, whom Ptolemy presented as an adopted son of Antiochus Sidetes or as a son of Alexander Balas.[8] Zabinas defeated Demetrius near Damascus, following which the latter fled to Acco, and from there he went by boat to Tyre, where he was killed on arrival. For a short time (125–122 B.C.E.) Alexander Zabinas was regarded as the sole ruler of Syria, and John Hyrcanus signed a treaty with him: no longer was he to be a vassal of the Syrian king, but his ally. But Zabinas was soon challenged by the son of Demetrius II, Antiochus VIII Grypus Aspendius (122–113 B.C.E.), who defeated Zabinas and killed him (according to another version, Zabinas committed suicide) in 122 B.C.E. But Antiochus Grypus faced trouble from within his own family. His half-brother, Antiochus IX Cyzicenus, son of Antiochus Sidetes, waged war on him and for two years (113–111 B.C.E.) was in control of all of Syria. This Antiochus was similar in character to Antiochus Epiphanes. But the power of the Syrian kingdom declined during his reign, and John Hyrcanus had little reason to be afraid of him; Cyzicenus, on the other hand, was in constant fear of his rival, Antiochus Grypus, who had wrested back most of the country from him in 111 B.C.E.

C. JOHN HYRCANUS' GREAT CONQUESTS AND THE ALLIANCE WITH ROME

This period of constant change in Syria — when the occupants of the throne replaced one another in rapid succession, most of them being murdered by their rivals and relatives — was taken advantage of by John Hyrcanus to expand his country's borders. He ceased paying tribute to these temporary kings, nor did he provide them with an auxiliary army: "he . . . no longer furnished them any aid either as a subject or as a friend" (*Ant.* XIII, 273).

At the same time, John Hyrcanus tried to fulfill the great object which Judah and Jonathan had worked for: to expand the boundaries of Judea. Independent, heavily populated, abounding in fresh vigor, eager for action, and full of daring after the military victories and the national revival, Judea burst eastward toward Transjordan, northward toward Shechem, and southward toward Idumaea. The first conquest of John Hyrcanus was that of Medeba, in Transjordan, in the land of Moab.

Following this, John Hyrcanus set out against the Samaritans, whom the Jews called Cutheans during the Second Temple period — an allusion to the biblical account (II Kings 17:24–41) which describes them as a mixture of Jews who assimilated among the gentiles Shalmaneser[9] had brought "from Babylon and from Cuthah." Ever since, the land of the Samaritans, which is referred to in the Talmud and the Midrash as "a strip of [land inhabited by] Cutheans,"[10] or "the Cuthean Patch"[11] has been disparagingly called "the land of the Cutheans," because since the exile of part of the Ten Tribes from their land the Jews considered Samaria an obstacle to their development. Its population, which was not gentile, but neither was it pure Jewish, interrupted the contiguity of independent Judea and all of Galilee, which was no longer the "district of the nations," since many Jews had also settled there.[12] Jonathan therefore endeavored to conquer this "land of the Cutheans." He took Shechem and Mount Gerizim and destroyed the temple of the Cutheans, which had stood for about two hundred years; but he did not coerce the Cutheans into adopting the Jewish religion. The conquest of Samaria was essential, for otherwise it would have remained a foreign stronghold in the middle of Palestine. And if the Jews had not conquered *all* of Palestine, their patrimony, they would have been stifled within the narrow boundaries of little Judea.

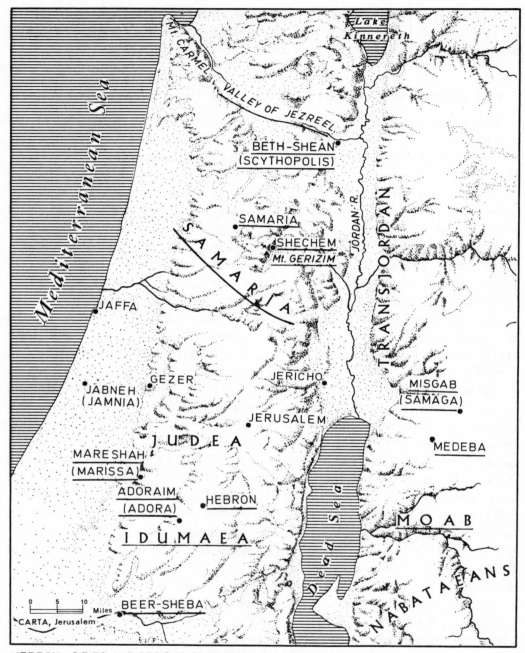

HEBRON CITIES AND REGIONS CONQUERED BY JOHN HYRCANUS

John Hyrcanus' Conquests

The temple of Mount Gerizim likewise had to be razed, since it was in competition with the Temple in Jerusalem, that having been the object of its construction from the very first. During the persecution of Antiochus Epiphanes, the Samaritans had falsely denied that they and the Jews worshipped the same God and dedicated their temple to Zeus, calling themselves "Sidonites of Shechem."[13] In the days of Alexander the Great, they had claimed to be descendants of Ephraim and Manasseh, Hebrews but not Jews.[14] When convenient, then, they denied both their people and their God. Accordingly, John Hyrcanus considered it necessary to destroy this temple. The people of Judea felt so strongly about the necessity of destroying the Cuthean temple, which had been a foe of Judaism and a rival to the Temple in Jerusalem, and their hatred of their brethren, the Ephraimites, had become so intense (although, as a matter of fact, only a sprinkling of Gentiles had intermingled with them) that the 21st day of Kislew, the day this temple was destroyed, was declared a holiday: "The 21st of the month [Kislew] is the day of Mount Gerizim. Mourning is forbidden."[15]

After the conquest of Shechem, John Hyrcanus marched against Idumaea. First he conquered the Idumaean cities of Adoraim (Adora) in the Hebron area and Mareshah (Marissa) near Beth-guvrin, both of which had constituted a danger to Judea even at the time of Judah Maccabee and his brother Jonathan, for it was easy to attack from the direction of Idumaea. John Hyrcanus did not treat the inhabitants of the Idumaean cities as his father Simeon had acted towards the inhabitants of Jaffa. He did not expel the idolatrous residents and instal Jews in their place, but gave them a choice between embracing Judaism or leaving the country. The Idumaeans, who were attached to their homeland, chose the former, and henceforth became Jews in every respect. Actually, these Idumaean cities which John Hyrcanus conquered and Judaized were the cities referred to as "the South of Judah" during the period of the First Temple or, simply "the South" in the days of the Second Temple and the period of the Talmud.[16]

After John Hyrcanus' occupation of Shechem he had no choice but to take Samaria, the Cuthean city second to Shechem in size. Either because of his age or since as High Priest he could not leave Jerusalem for an extended period, he sent his two sons, Antigonus and Aristobulus, to lay siege to Samaria. The Samaritans appealed for help to Antiochus IX Cyzicenus,[17] who came to their aid. But Aristobulus defeated him and pursued him as far as Beth-shean, after which he returned to resume the siege on Samaria. The Samaritans again called upon Antiochus for assistance. Aware that he was no match for the Judean army, Antiochus turned to Ptolemy Lathyrus, who then shared the throne of Egypt with his mother, Cleopatra. Ptolemy sent Antiochus about six thousand men, against the wishes of his mother. Antiochus invaded Palestine and deliberately laid waste the country in order to compel the Jewish army to come to the defense of the Judean cities and thus raise the siege of Samaria. According to Josephus (*Ant.* XIII, 279), he failed in this object, since many of his men fell in an ambush laid by the Jews and he was compelled to retreat to Tripoli. But there are grounds for thinking that this was not the case and that Antiochus Cyzicenus succeeded in conquering Judean fortresses, ports, and cities and in posting a garrison in Jaffa. Be that as it may, Antiochus himself was unable to aid Samaria in her distress. He went to Tripoli and left the war against the two sons of John Hyrcanus in the hands of his Greek generals, Callimandrus and Epicrates. Callimandrus engaged the Jews in battle and was defeated. Epicrates, who fortified himself at Beth-shean, surrendered the city to the two brothers, either in return for a bribe[18] or because the city was captured by the brothers in an assault, together with "the whole country south of Mount Carmel," that is, the entire Valley of Jezreel (*War* I, 66). After a siege of a full year, with hunger rampant in the city, Samaria too was captured. Incensed over the long siege and the city's appeal for help to the Greeks, which had cost the Jews much blood, John Hyrcanus not only had Samaria razed to the ground but, according to Josephus (*Ant.* XIII, 281), also "left it to be swept away by the mountain-torrents" (εἰς χαράδρας). Apparently, he diverted the aqueduct into the city itself.

The surrender of Beth-shean and the conquest of the Valley of Jezreel, as well as the capture of Samaria, are also mentioned in *Mᵉgillat Taᶜanit*: "On the fifteenth and on the sixteenth of the month [Siwan] the people of Beth-shean and the people of the Valley [of Jezreel] was banished . . . On the twenty-fifth of the month [Marḥeshwan] the walls of Samaria were captured."[19] And in the commentary on *Mᵉgillat Taᶜanit*[20] there is even an allusion to the diversion of the aqueduct, although the reference is garbled: "When the first Exile returned, they went to the patch of the Cutheans, but they did not let them [settle]. They came to Sebaste [the name of Samaria from the days of Herod] and they settled it, and they surrounded it with walled cities, and many towns of Israel were close to it, and they called it the towns of *navrakta*" (*navrakta* is Syrian for "the pool"). This apparently is the aqueduct or the rushing torrent which John Hyrcanus diverted into Samaria, in order to make it unfit for settlement.[21]

The references in *Mᵉgillat Taᶜanit* make it possible to fix the day and the month of Samaria's conquest (and also the day and the month of the conquests of Beth-shean and the Valley of Jezreel): the twenty-fifth of the month of Marḥeshwan. Fixing the year is more difficult. The *terminus a quo* is the rule of Antiochus Cyzicenus in the valley of Lebanon (beginning 111 B.C.E.), and the *terminus ad quem* is the co-rule of Ptolemy Lathyrus and his mother Cleopatra (up to 107 B.C.E.). This important event thus occurred between 111 and 107 B.C.E. And it was important, because together with the Valley of Jezreel John Hyrcanus also conquered a portion of Galilee, as will be seen below.

While Antigonus and Aristobulus were locked in battle with Antiochus — so Josephus relates (*Ant.* XIII, 282) — John Hyrcanus was offering a sacrifice in the Temple and heard a voice saying "his sons had just defeated Antiochus." On leaving the Temple he revealed this to the people, and it turned out to be true. The same story is to be found in the Talmud and the Midrash: ". . . it has been taught that Johanan the High Priest, heard a Voice issue from within the Holy of Holies announcing, 'The young men who went to wage war against Antioch [read Antiochus] have been victorious' . . . They noted down the time [when the Voice spoke] and it tallied,"[22] that is, it turned out that at that very moment they had won the victory.

The Book of Ben Sira[23] says:

> For two nations, doth my soul feed abhorrence,
> (Yea), and (for) a third, which is not a people;
> The inhabitants of Seir and Philistia,
> And that foolish nation that dwelleth in Shechem.

These three peoples, which were most hated by and most dangerous to the people of Judea, were subdued by John Hyrcanus. There is also reason to believe that he conquered Lower Galilee too.[24] At this time he rebuilt the walls of Jerusalem which he had been compelled by Antiochus Sidetes to tear down (or whose battlements he had been forced to destroy).[25]

In order to strengthen his political position and consolidate his great conquests John Hyrcanus did what all his Hasmonean predecessors had done: he sent an embassy to Rome to confirm the treaty between the two countries and to persuade the Roman Senate to bring influence to bear on Antiochus, King of Syria, to return the Judean cities and ports he had occupied. The Roman documents which contain the replies of the Senate to the Jewish emissaries are cited in two places in Josephus. A passage in *Antiquities* (XIII, 260 ff.) mentions the request of the Jews "that Jaffa and its harbors and Gezer and Pegae[26] and whatever other cities and territories

Antiochus [not further identified] took from them in war, contrary to the decree of the Senate, be restored to them, — and that the soldiers of the king be not permitted to march through their country or those of their subjects, and that the laws made by Antiochus during this same war contrary to the decree of the Senate be annulled." The Jews also asked the Romans to "send envoys to bring about the restitution of the places taken from the Jews by Antiochus and to estimate the value of the territory ruined during the war." The Senate replied that it would grant Hyrcanu's request.

A second passage in *Antiquities* (XIV, 247 ff.), quoting the decree of the people of Pergamum, erroneously includes an order of the Roman Senate to the effect that "King Antiochus, son of Antiochus, shall do no injury to the Jews, the allies of the Romans; and that the fortresses, harbors, territory and whatever else he may have taken from them shall be restored to them; and that it shall be lawful for them to export goods from their harbors and that no king or people exporting goods from the territory of the Jews or from their harbors shall be untaxed except only Ptolemy, king of Alexandria, because he is our ally and friend; and that the garrison in Jaffa shall be expelled, as they have requested." These are the two documents referring to the war which one of the Seleucid Antiochuses waged against the Jews in John Hyrcanus' time.[27] Both documents refer to John Hyrcanus I and not to Hyrcanus II, who was a Roman vassal and against whom Antiochus would not have been able to fight without permission from Rome. And the documents show that the Hasmonean prince was trying to improve both the political and the economic situation by securing decrees from the Roman Senate, which greatly desired weakening Syria by making use of the Judean State, which had been torn away from it.

D. THE LAST DAYS OF JOHN HYRCANUS

John Hyrcanus I ruled Judea for thirty years. During this period he liberated a large part of Palestine, subjugated the hostile neighbors and even contracted a treaty of alliance with Rome. There was every reason to expect that the people would be satisfied with his rule, and part of the nation doubtlessly esteemed and admired him. But only a part. Toward the end of his life a breach occurred between the High Priest and the Pharisees (the matter is discussed in detail below).[28] Most of the people sided with the Pharisees and rebelled. John Hyrcanus, however, quickly crushed the revolt and his final years were spent in peace. He died at a ripe old age, showered with honors, and a magnificent mausoleum was erected on his grave, which even at the time of the destruction of the Second Temple was known as "the Tomb of Johanan the Priest." Not without reason was he favorably referred to even in the Talmud, although he had become a Sadducee. The following *mishna* in the tractate Yadayim (4, 6) testifies to the high repute in which he was held by the Sages: "The Sadducees say: 'we complain against you, o ye Pharisees, because you say that the Holy Scriptures render unclean the hands, but the books of Hamiran [Homer] do not convey uncleanness to the hands.' R. Johanan ben Zakkay said: 'Have we nothing against the Pharisees excepting this? Behold they say that the bones of an ass are clean, yet the bones of Johanan the High Priest are unclean," for "proportionate to the love for them, so is their uncleanness." The great *tanna*, R. Johanan ben Zakkay could find no more striking parallel to illustrate the absolute antithesis between the utterly base and the altogether lofty than to contrast the "bones of an ass" with the "bones of Johanan the Priest." And he employed this parallel in replying to the Sadducees, despite the fact that John Hyrcanus "in the end became a Sadducee."

CHAPTER IX

JUDAH ARISTOBULUS AND JANNAEUS ALEXANDER

by J. Klausner

A. Judah Aristobulus I (104–103 B.C.E.)

JOHN HYRCANUS left a wife and five sons, Judah Aristobulus I, Antigonus (whose Hebrew name is not known), Jannaeus (Jonathan) Alexander, Absalom, and a fifth son whose name has been lost. In order to make peace with the Pharisees and their partisans, John Hyrcanus laid down in his will that the offices of prince and High Priest be separated, with his widow holding the secular office and his eldest son, Aristobulus, serving as High Priest. However, Josephus relates that Judah Aristobulus imprisoned his mother and caused her death by starvation, imprisoned two of his brothers and, not content with ruling as prince, assumed the title of king. Josephus writes: "and he was the first to put a diadem on his head, four hundred and eighty-one years and three months after the time when the people were released from the Babylonian captivity and returned to their own country" (*Ant.* XIII, 301).

Josephus then spins a gripping yarn, which he undoubtedly found in a book by some Greek historian with a passion for tales of miracles, or in a Hebrew book of legends; it is difficult to distinguish fact from fiction in his story. Aristobulus — according to the narrative — permitted only Antigonus to share in the government. And since Aristobulus fell seriously ill shortly afterwards, Antigonus assumed command of the army, and going off to war, returned victorious. The queen, Aristobulus' wife, and her faction were assailed by the fear that the healthy and victorious Antigonus who undoubtedly had also the support of the army, would usurp the throne and do away with the ailing Aristobulus, his wife, and all their supporters. They thereupon concocted a story that Antigonus was conspiring to kill his brother and seize the throne. When Antigonus, arrayed in his armor, returned in triumph to Jerusalem for the Feast of Tabernacles, to the cheers of the populace, the sick king was struck with jealousy and suspicion (stimulated by the whisperings of the queen and her adherents) that his brother would come to him armed in order to kill him. Aristobulus accordingly summoned his brother to come to him unarmed, and ordered his bodyguard to slay Antigonus if he came bearing weapons. But the queen bribed Aristobulus' messenger to tell Antigonus that his ill brother wished to see him splendidly arrayed in his armor, as befitted a victorious hero. Antigonus did just that, and was killed by Aristobulus' bodyguards. According to Josephus, this deed had been foretold by an Essene by the name of Judah. Aristobulus was soon seized by remorse for what he had done to his brother, his illness was aggravated and he began to cough up blood. One of his servants who was carrying this blood away slipped on the very spot where the stains made by the innocent blood of Antigonus were still visible. Thereupon an outcry went up in the royal household, and Aristobulus learned what had happened. This exacerbated his illness, and he died shortly afterwards. This is the story related picturesquely and in great detail by Josephus (*Ant.* XIII, 304 ff.; *War* I, 73 ff.).

All these accounts from beginning to end, from the killing of the mother by starvation to the murder of Antigonus, suggest highly-imaginative fiction. The two Sadducee kings of the Hasmonean dynasty — Judah Aristobulus and Jannaeus Alexander — had many enemies both among the Jews and among the Greek writers. The crown on the heads of the Hasmoneans aroused the ire of the Pharisees and their sages, for only a scion of the House of David could be king. Furthermore, Aristobulus was a philhellene, and Strabo, on the authority of Timagenes, praises him and says that he had a kindly nature.[1] Aristobulus' Jewish political enemies apparently fabricated stories ascribing all sorts of cruelties to him, as they also did with respect to Jannaeus Alexander.[2] As for the Greek historians, they hated the Hasmonean rulers for having destroyed the Greek cities in Palestine, and referred to them as a "kingdom of robbers." They were therefore ready to believe any tale spread by the Greek enemies of the Hasmonean kings. The whole episode about the deep remorse felt by Judah Aristobulus which hastened his end shows the confusion which troubled Josephus, when confronted with the account of the cruelty attributed to the ill king on the one hand, and by the testimony of Timagenes that he "was a kindly person and very serviceable to the Jews," on the other.[3]

Judah Aristobulus I reigned just one year (104–103 B.C.E.). On his coins, which bear only Hebrew inscriptions,[4] there is no mention of kingship (just as on those of his father and grandfather), and Strabo even writes that the first of the ruling High Priests in Judea to assume the crown was Alexander, that is, Jannaeus. Here Strabo erred, because he did not consider a one-year reign, and he was not aware that the first coins of

Jannaeus Alexander made no mention of kingship either.[5] The coins of Judah Aristobulus I, on which a cornucopia is engraved, only bear the inscription יהודה הכהן גדול וחבר היהודים ("Judah the High Priest and the *Ḥever ha-Yᵉhudim*").

However, Judah Aristobulus became an admirer of Greek culture, as Josephus testified and as would also appear from the praises showered on him by Timagenes. There are also grounds for believing that it was during his reign that the *Ḥever ha-Yᵉhudim* began to be called by the Hebraicized Greek name "Sanhedrin."

This philhellenism raises some questions. After all, the Hasmoneans achieved greatness only as a result of their struggle against the Greeks and against Greek religion and culture. How, then, could Aristobulus I, the third generation of Mattathias' descendants, have become a phil-hellene? But it should be kept in mind that even his father John had added the foreign "Hyrcanus" to his Hebrew name, and that his sons, too, have Greek names (Aristobulus, Antigonus, Alexander) in addition to their Hebrew ones. The movement in the direction of Hellenism had thus already begun in his father's time and it was connected with the rapproche-ment with the Sadducees. The secular ambitions of the Hasmonean dynasty, combined with the political circumstances of the times made this development inevitable. However, the fact that only a Hebrew inscription appears on the coins minted by Judah Aristobulus leads to the conclusion that Hellenization in the spirit of Jason and Menelaus is not involved here.

This conclusion is strengthened by a great deed of Judah Aristobulus — the single important political act known of his brief reign. He (or, more correct, his brother Antigonus at his command) fought the Itureans, conquered part of their land, and compelled those of them who wished to remain in their homeland to accept Judaism and circumcision, as John Hyrcanus, his father, had offered the Idumaeans. Apparently the only territory in the north of Palestine that was in the possession of John Hyrcanus was Samaria and the southern part of Galilee — Lower Galilee (we know that his son Jannaeus was brought up in Galilee [*Ant.* XIII, 322]). To this area Judah Aristobulus added the northern part of Galilee — Upper Galilee — and possibly also an area in Transjordan.[6] The Itureans ordi-narily lived near Lebanon, but in that period they had apparently spread southward to Upper Galilee. Thus did Judah Aristobulus complete the conquest and the Judaization of Galilee.[7] Possession of northern Palestine yielded to the Kingdom of Judea the transit duties paid by the caravans transporting merchandise of all kinds between the lands of the Euphrates and Tigris and Arabia, Egypt and the seaports across Upper Galilee, by way of what is the modern Daughters of Jacob bridge and the Valley of Jezreel. Only most of the coastal cities of Palestine still remained in Greek hands — a fact which harmed Jewish trade considerably. Their conquest and Judaization was the task of Judah Aristobulus' successor, his brother Jannaeus Alexander.

B. JANNAEUS (JONATHAN) ALEXANDER, 103–76 B.C.E.

After Aristobulus' early death, his widow, called by Josephus Salome (Σαλώμη an abbreviation of Sh°lomẓiyyon) and whom the Greeks designated by the name Alexandra, released his three brothers from prison. She appointed as king the eldest brother, who was also the most capable. This was Jannaeus (ʼΙανναῖος), who was also know as Alexander (Josephus first refers to him as Jannaeus; his name is thus Jannaeus Alexander rather than Alexander Jannaeus).[8] Since the name of Jannaeus' widow who succeeded him to the throne after his death was Salome (Sh°lomẓiyyon) Alexandra, most scholars conclude that she had been Judah Aristobulus's wife and had married his brother Jannaeus Alexander after her husband's death; Jannaeus entered into a levirate marriage because Judah had died childless. However, a number of objections have been raised to this view: (a) Josephus says that this only Jewish queen of the Second Temple period died at the age of 73 (*Ant.* XIII, 430). If the seven years that she reigned by herself and the 27 years that her husband Jannaeus sat on the throne are subtracted from this figure, this would make her 39 when Jannaeus became king. But Jannaeus died at the age of 49, meaning that he was 22 when he ascended the throne. This would make Salome seventeen years older than he. (b) Josephus does not say explicitly that Judah Aristobulus' widow married Jannaeus. (c) It is doubtful whether a High Priest would be permitted to enter into a levirate marriage with the widow of a High Priest, since the High Priest is instructed by the Torah: "And he shall take a wife in her virginity. A widow, or one divorced, or a profaned woman, or a harlot, these shall he not take; but a virgin of his own people shall he take to wife" (Lev. 21:13–14). (d) Hyrcanus II, the son of Jannaeus and Salome Alexandra, was over 80 years old when he was killed by Herod in 30 B.C.E. (*Ant.* XV, 178). Thus, Hyrcanus was born in 110 or 109 B.C.E., six or seven years before Jannaeus became king and prior to the death of Judah Aristobulus. The scholars are therefore divided over the question whether Jannaeus married his brother's widow or another woman whose name was also Salome.

The former view seems more acceptable. The evidence contradicting "a" will be discussed below. "b" is of no consequence; Josephus does not state the general implications to be inferred from his narrative. Nor is point "c" at all substantial; at the time of Jannaeus the rules of levirate marriage were not strictly observed and the injunction against the levirate marriage of a widow to the High Priest was not applied; the verse from Ezekiel (44:22) "but they [the priests] shall take . . . a widow that is the widow of a priest" was sanctioned instead. As to "d," Josephus was mistaken in the age of Hyrcanus II; for if it is held that he was born in 110 or 109 B.C.E., his father Jannaeus would then have been only 15 or 16 years old at the time (Jannaeus became king at the age of 22, in 103 B.C.E., as stated above), and while this is not impossible it was unusual even in ancient times and even in the East. The same applies to the age of Salome; Josephus erred when he wrote that she died at the age of 73, which would mean a difference of 17 years between her and Jannaeus. Again, this is not impossible, but it would have been most unnatural for a young king to marry a widowed queen close to middle age. This may be the reason why Josephus does not say explicitly that Salome Alexandra married Jannaeus.[9]

From the coins minted by Jannaeus, a large number of which are still extant today, it is clear that his Hebrew name was not Johanan, as was previously thought by many scholars, but Jonathan. These coins are of two types. The first, the earlier one, which was minted before Jannaeus came into outright conflict with the Pharisees and before he became an autocratic king and abolished the *Hever ha-Y'hudim* (see below), was similar to the coins minted by his father, John Hyrcanus, and his brother Judah Aristobulus. Like his brother, he did not mention his royal title on these coins. The coins bear the inscription יהונתן (יונתן) הכהן הגדול וחבר היהודים in Hebrew only and in ancient script. Shortly afterwards, however, he minted — being the first to do so — coins with inscriptions in both Hebrew and Greek which included the word "king": Ἀλεξάνδρου βασιλέως — המלך יהונתן. There was no longer any mention of the High Priesthood. More and more, the later Hasmonean kings tended to imitate the kings of the gentiles.[10]

In addition to the cornucopia (which also appears on the coins of John Hyrcanus I and Judah Aristobulus I) the coins also bear a ship's anchor — an allusion to Jannaeus' ambition to conquer the coastal cities of Palestine and develop the maritime trade of the young kingdom of Judea.

Whereas the Talmud refers to the successor of Judah Aristobulus as *Yannai* and Josephus calls him Jannaeus (Ἰανναῖος) the coins only bear the name Jonathan (יהונתן or ינתן). The Hebrew *Yannai* is the diminutive or the hypocorisma for Jonathan.

According to Josephus, Jannaeus put to death one of his two brothers whom he suspected of having designs on the throne, while the second, who preferred to live a quiet life, he honored as the king's brother, then an important title. This, too, would seem to be apocryphal, on a par with the stories about Judah Aristobulus' murder of his brother. If Jannaeus had acted in this manner immediately after assuming the throne, Josephus would surely not have praised the "moderation" ($\mu\epsilon\tau\rho\iota\acute{o}\tau\eta\varsigma$) which he displayed at the beginning of his reign (*Ant.* XIII, 321; *War* I, 85).

Directly after becoming king, Jannaeus turned to war. He was aware of the vital importance of completing what his predecessors had begun, that is expanding his rule over all of western and a considerable part of eastern Palestine. There were the political and national aspects — the restoration of a patrimony to its heirs. But an economic factor was also involved. As yet only part of the coastal cities were in the hands of the Jews. And this hindered the development of commerce in "Greater Judea" as well as the general development of the young kingdom, the bulk of whose revenue should have come from export and import duties necessary for maintaining an army of conscripts and supporting contingents of mercenaries.

After the conquest of Galilee it was considered particularly necessary to annex to Judea what was then the key to Galilee, Acco (Ptolemais), and Jannaeus laid siege to the city. The inhabitants of Acco thereupon turned for help to Zoilus, dynast of the cities of Dor and Straton's Tower (later Caesarea), but the latter was unable to drive Jannaeus away. They then appealed to Ptolemy Lathyrus, who had been deposed from the Egyptian throne by his mother, Cleopatra, and had become ruler of Cyprus. Ptolemy came to the aid of Acco with an army of 30,000 men by way of Sycaminum (near Haifa), and Jannaeus was forced to lift the siege. Jannaeus proposed peace to Ptolemy, who indicated his willingness to form a friendly alliance with him. Meanwhile, however, Jannaeus secretly called on Cleopatra for help against her son, who was at war with her. When Ptolemy learned that Jannaeus had tricked him, he was furious and marched against the kingdom of Judea: he invaded Galilee, and one Sabbath day conquered the city of Asochis, near Sepphoris. Failing to conquer Sepphoris itself, he deployed his forces against Jannaeus, who opposed him with 50,000 (or 30,000, according to another view) men near the city of Zaphon (Asophon) in Transjordan (Josh. 13:27), known in some rabbinic sources as 'Amatu or Ḥammᵉthan.[11]

When Ptolemy's men crossed the Jordan the Jews struck them a heavy blow. But Ptolemy's Greek commander, Philostephanus, succeeded in driving a wedge between the right and the left wing of the Jewish forces and defeating both one after the other. The Jews fled and Ptolemy's troops gave chase, striking them down "until their swords became blunted with killing and their hands were utterly tired." Josephus (*Ant.* XIII, 344) relates that according to some reports, 30,000 and according to Timagenes, 50,000 of them were killed.

Ptolemy then drove through all of Judea. Conquering and devastating cities, towns, and villages, he advanced as far as the Egyptian border. Citing Strabo and Nicolaus of Damascus, Josephus writes (*ibid.*, 345–347) that in the course of this advance Ptolemy committed great atrocities, in order to intimidate the Jews.[12] However, his successes near the boundary of his mother's kingdom aroused her jealousy and fear: might he not try to depose her just as she had done to him? She accordingly marched against Ptolemy with a large army under the command of two Jewish generals, Hilkiah and Hananiah (Ananias), sons of Onias the High Priest who had fled to Egypt at the time of the persecutions of Antiochus Epiphanes. The two commanders, imbued with love, which they later revealed (see below), for the religious and national homeland, fought Ptolemy and forced him to flee to Gaza. Practically all of Judea was now in Cleopatra's hands, and it was quite natural for her to conceive of annexing the country to Egypt. But Hananiah (Hilkiah had met his death during the pursuit of Ptolemy) dissuaded the queen from adopting this course. "I would have you know," he told her, "that an injustice done to this man will make all us Jews your enemies" (*Ant.* XIII, 354). The Jews then constituted a powerful force in Egypt and Hananiah, too, apparently possessed considerable influence. Consequently, Cleopatra followed his advice and contracted an alliance with Jannaeus after receiving from him at Beth-shean (Scythopolis) many "gifts," i.e., a heavy one-time tribute. She then returned to Egypt with her army. Thus did Egyptian Jewry save the throne of the Hasmoneans and the freedom of Judea. It is worth noting that the Hasmonean dynasty was so dear to all Jews that even the High Priests of the House of Zadok, whom the Hasmoneans had displaced, by now accepted the situation and sided with the Hasmonean monarchy.

No sooner was Jannaeus free of both Ptolemy and Cleopatra than he went to lay siege to the cities of Transjordan, which were the bearers of Greek culture in Palestine and were hostile to Israel and to Judaism. For the young Jewish kingdom could not develop peacefully so long as it did not possess these rich commercial cities. Jannaeus realized this and, to begin with, marched against Gadara, the important city of the Decapolis, near the Yarmuk river (also frequently mentioned in the Talmud), the modern Umm Qays, whose beautiful ruins have been preserved.[13] He took the city as well as the strong fortress adjoining it which is known in the Talmud variously as Ḥameꜩtan deꜩgeder, Ḥammta, or Ḥammat geder.[14] Jannaeus then turned his attention to the coastal cities of the south. He conquered the ports of Raphia, Anthedon[15] and, after a whole year's siege, also the large and well-fortified city of Gaza which, according to Josephus (*Ant.* XIII, 362 ff.), he had his soldiers plunder because he was angered by the protracted investment (96 B.C.E.). However, the objective historian will treat with caution the accounts of the heroism of the Gazaeans and of Jannaeus' cruelty in this city, since Josephus derived all his information from a Judeophobian Greek source partial to Gaza. Little by little all the cities in Palestine, which the gentiles had wrested from the Jews from the time of the destruction of the First Temple passed to the Hasmoneans. This turn of events brought about a tremendous change in the entire economic structure of Judea; commerce — transit trade and maritime trade alike — now became one of the principal economic branches in Judea alongside agriculture and crafts. In this way, small Judea became a sea-trader after retrieving large coastal cities and a number of important ports which had previously been held by the Canaanites in the north and by the Greeks or the Hellenized Philistines in the south and east. The Hasmonean rulers now began to collect import duties, which yielded substantial revenues, and a period of prosperity set in. But for both internal and external reasons this prosperity did not last long.

C. CIVIL WAR IN JUDEA

No sooner did Jannaeus win a respite from his foreign wars than he was faced with the wrath of the Pharisees.

Jannaeus' great victories and conquests undoubtedly raised his stature in the eyes of the masses. But they also had a negative result: they brought the king into ever-closer contact with the Hellenized Syrians and, consciously or not, he learned the ways of the Hellenist kings. The process of Hellenization, which had already begun in the days of John Hyrcanus and Judah Aristobulus accelerated, and Jannaeus' ambition to be sole ruler, on the pattern of the Hellenist "tyrants," became more intense. Apparently at this time Jannaeus dissolved the *Ḥever ha-Yeꜩhudim*. There is evidence of this in Jannaeus' coins, which make no mention of the *Ḥever ha-Yeꜩhudim* or Jannaeus' title of High Priest; all that is inscribed is "King Jonathan" (יהונתן המלך), plus a Greek inscription: "of King Alexander." Autocracy, then, on the one hand, and ever growing Hellenization, on the other.

Another important fact was held against Jannaeus. For a good many years he had uninterruptedly been involved in fierce and protracted wars, and the blood was not dry on his hands. Yet it was he who held the office of High Priest and he who in the Temple served the holy and faultless God, who came to be regarded as purely spiritual by the majority of the people and was referred to by the abstract names of "Heaven" and "the Place."

In the wake of his battles and victories Jannaeus had become more and more secular, and thus he gradually drew closer in spirit to the Sadducees, who had abrogated a number of the rigid interpretations which the Pharisees had given to the Law where these were not explicitly stated in the Torah; and little by little the Pharisees and their "innovations" became an object of his mockery. Josephus (*Ant.* XIII, 372) cites an instance when Jannaeus, standing beside the altar on the Feast of Tabernacles and about to offer the sacrifice of the festival, was pelted with citrons by rebellious Jews shouting "son of the captive woman" and declaring that he was unfit to serve as High Priest (the same stigma that Judah ben Gᵉdidya applied to John Hyrcanus according to the *barayta* in Qid. 66a). There is a reference to this story in the Mishnah which makes it clear what caused the sudden anger of the people against Jannaeus, except that the Mishnah does not call the king by name: "To [the priest] who performed the libation [on the Feast of Tabernacles] they used to say, 'Raise thy hand'; for on a certain occasion a certain man poured out the water over his feet, and all the people pelted him with their *ethrogs*."[16] The Tosefta relates: "Once there was an incident with a Boethusian, who poured the libation water over his feet, and all the people pelted him with their *ethrogs*, and the horn of the altar became damaged and the Temple service was cancelled that day, until they brought a lump of salt and placed it upon it so that it should not be seen to be damaged."[17] The same episode is recounted in a *barayta* of the Babylonian Talmud[18] which speaks of "a certain Sadducee" instead of a "Boethusian," of "handful of salt" instead of "a lump of salt," and says "it was stopped up" instead of "and they placed it upon it." The reference most probably is to Jannaeus, the Sadducee king. Flushed with victory, he had permitted himself to mock a custom of the Pharisees which had no basis in the Mosaic Law. The Sadducees maintained that the libation was not prescribed in the Torah, and Jannaeus, who sided with them, wished to strengthen this view by putting it into practice. But the people would not allow the Sadducees to act in accordance with their opinions in the Temple, nor were the Pharisees afraid of actively opposing even the king himself.[19] Thus it came about that the people, who were adherents of the Pharisees, dared to reply to the insult to a Pharisaic custom by an extremely sharp affront to the king. Jannaeus did not ignore the offence to his honor, and sent his army against the people — undoubtedly his Pisidian and Cilician mercenaries. According to Josephus, Jannaeus' troops killed some six thousand Jews that day, which is surely a highly exaggerated figure. And in order to keep the people from coming too close to the High Priest, Jannaeus had a wooden barrier erected around the altar. This incident occurred in the eighth year of Jannaeus' reign, around 95 B.C.E.

The people's outbreak was suppressed with a strong hand. But the use of force created pent-up hatred, which found an outlet at the first opportunity. And this opportunity was not long in coming.

King Jannaeus continued to wage war and conquer. He overran Moab and Gilead, and razed the city of Ḥamat-geder, a previous conquest of his which had rebelled against him. But in his campaign against Obedas I, king of the Nabataean Arabs, Jannaeus fell into an ambush in a rocky defile. After sustaining a serious defeat he fled to Jerusalem with the remnants of his army. The people had not forgotten Jannaeus' conduct that Feast of Tabernacles and, under the command of Pharisee extremists, they openly rebelled against the defeated king. The revolt lasted for six years (roughly, 90–85 B.C.E.), during which time Jannaeus fought his people with Jewish troops as well as with foreign mercenaries. According to Josephus, (*Ant.* XIII, 376; *War* I, 91) "no fewer than 50,000 Jews," lost their lives in this civil war. Even if this figure appears exaggerated, it is certain that the Jews suffered numerous casualties in their war against their king.

Jannaeus fought the Pharisees a long time and defeated them again and again. But victory over his own people brought little satisfaction to a man who aspired to real conquests. Time and again, therefore, Jannaeus sought to make peace with the Pharisees, but in vain. Once after one of his victories he again tried to make peace with his people (*War* I, 91). He sent to inquire under what terms they were prepared to end their hostility to him. What did the Pharisees actually want of him? The answer was curt: His death! (*Ant.* XIII, 376; *War* I, 92). So great was the hatred borne him by these fanatic defenders of a religion which had turned into state policy.

Finally the Pharisee extremists took an unpardonable step — they called upon Demetrius III (Eukairos), King of Syria, to help them against their own king, no doubt promising that Judea would become a Syrian vassal provided they were granted autonomy in religious matters, as had been the case prior to the Hasmoneans. It may be assumed that it was not

Pharisee leaders such as Judah ben Ṭabbay or Simeon ben Sheṭaḥ who were guilty of this deed, but demagogues who wrapped themselves in the cloak of Pharisaism — those "hypocrites who ape the Pharisees," whose "deeds are the deeds of Zimri but they expect a reward like Phinehas" of whom Jannaeus warned his wife.[20] This strange breed of Pharisee will again be encountered in the camp of Pompey, when they try to abolish the Hasmonean kingdom and restore the state of affairs which prevailed in the times of the Ptolemaic and Seleucid dynasties: internal autonomy under the leadership of a High Priest who would be a vassal of Rome instead of Egypt or Syria. This type will be met yet again in the palace of the Emperor Augustus begging him to abolish the Herodian kingdom and to subjugate Judea to the Roman proconsul in Syria. To be sure, the Pharisees thought they were justified in doing what they did: in the first place, in their eyes religion came before the state, and even before national freedom, which cannot exist simultaneously with the tyranny of a dictator; and, second, the Jewish king himself was fighting his people with the help of an army of foreign mercenaries — why then should they be forbidden to make use of the assistance of a gentile king? The treason of the Pharisee extremists occurred in 88 B.C.E.

Demetrius Eukairos, naturally enough, did not hesitate very long, but was quick to launch an attack on Jannaeus. The Syrian army was joined by many Jews — men rebelling against their king and betraying their country – bringing its strength up to 40,000 infantry and 3,000 cavalry, while Jannaeus had only 6,200 infantry mercenaries,[21] in addition to 20,000 Jewish infantry,[22] who remained loyal to their king, and only 1,000 cavalry. Both sides conducted propaganda among the enemy soldiers: Eukairos tried to persuade Jannaeus' Greek mercenaries to defect to him, while Jannaeus attempted to win back the Jewish soldiers in Eukairos' army — but in vain. The encounter between the two camps took place near Shechem. Jannaeus was unable to withstand the overwhelming impact of the enemy and fled to the mountains with the remnants of his army.

A sudden change then occurred: the Jews in Eukairos' army regretted their action against their king. And before long 6,000 of them joined Jannaeus. Eukairos' victory over Jannaeus had cost him dear; in addition, he feared the Nabataean king Obedas, to whom Jannaeus had returned those parts of Moab and Gilead which he had previously conquered, in order to win Obedas to his side. Eukairos accordingly withdrew and went back to his own country (*Ant.* XIII, 379 ff.).

But the die-hards among the Pharisees continued to fight their monarch even after 6,000 of their comrades had deserted them, and Jannaeus defeated them in a pitched battle. They retreated to the unidentified city of Bethoma or Bemeselis,[23] which Jannaeus captured after siege, taking their most prominent men to Jerusalem as his prisoners. In the capital, Jannaeus had 800 of them crucified, after their wives and children had been butchered before their eyes in the center of the city, while Jannaeus gave a feast for his concubines at the very spot, all of them gorging themselves and taking pleasure in the horrible tortures suffered by the Jews on the crosses. For this act of cruelty the Jews called Jannaeus the "Thracian" (Thrakidas), i.e., the murderer. This deed so terrified his opponents that 8,000 of them fled from Judea and did not return during the lifetime of Jannaeus Alexander. This is the account given by Josephus (*Ant.* XIII, 383; *War* I, 98).

The Talmud, too, refers to these deeds. There (in the uncensored editions) mention is made of Jannaeus killing the Sages[24] and of the flight of two of them, Joshua ben Peraḥya and Simeon ben Sheṭaḥ. Of Judah ben Ṭabbay, the partner of Simeon ben Sheṭaḥ, both of whom are mentioned in Mishnah Avot as a "pair,"[25] we are told that the people of Jerusalem wanted to appoint him *Nasi* (president of the Sanhedrin) and that he therefore fled to Alexandria;[26] the reason for the flight was undoubtedly Jannaeus' persecution of the Pharisees, which made it dangerous for a Pharisee to be *Nasi*. About Simeon ben Sheṭaḥ there is a Talmudic legend which says that Simeon proposed to the king to provide him with a sum of money with which to buy sacrifices for 150 of the 300 Nazirites who came to Jerusalem to offer sacrifices needed to absolve them from their vows, promising that he, Simeon, would buy the sacrifices for the remaining 150. Later, Jannaeus learned that Simeon ben Sheṭaḥ had not bought the sacrifices at all, but had absolved the Nazirites of their vows by means of a hermeneutic interpretation. Simeon then fled the country to escape the King's anger. Simeon returned to Jerusalem at the request of some Parthian emissaries, who had visited Jerusalem and asked for the venerable Sage. He then explained to Jannaeus that he had acted properly with respect to the Nazirites: Jannaeus had given them of his money while he, Simeon, had given them of his learning. Simeon even sat between the king and the queen, in accordance with the passage in the Book of Ben Sira: "Esteem her [learning], so she shall exalt thee and seat thee between princes." And when Simeon was asked to recite grace, he did so in a strange manner: "Let us say grace for the food which Jannaeus and his companions have eaten," for he himself had not eaten; and only when he too was offered something to eat did he say: "... for the food that we have eaten."[27] All this, of course, is mere legend, and the only historical kernel that can be extracted from it is that Jannaeus and Simeon ben Sheṭaḥ were not on good terms, to the point where Simeon was even forced to flee from the king's wrath, as had been the case with Joshua ben Peraḥya (apparently, at the beginning of the rebellion against Jannaeus) and Judah ben Ṭabbay (after the suppression of the insurrection). But the legend also provides the information that Simeon ben Sheṭaḥ "sat between the [Sadducee] king and the [Pharisee] queen."

The stories of Josephus concerning Jannaeus' cruel deeds are also nothing but legends. First of all, the figure 800 for those who were crucified (all of them leading rebels) and the figure of 8,000 who fled are enough to arouse suspicion (the number of those fleeing being exactly ten times the number crucified). Secondly, crucifixion was not a Jewish form of punishment, and until the period of Roman rule in Judea this cruel type of death is not found in Judea at all.[28] Thirdly, the name "Thracian," with which the Jews dubbed Jannaeus seems strange coming from Jews, and Graetz was already perplexed by it.[29] Josephus obtained his information on Jannaeus from Pharisee and Greek sources. The former hated him for his Sadducaism; the latter had an aversion for Jews in general and Jannaeus in particular for having conquered idolatrous, Hellenistic cities in Palestine, as related above. For this reason they invented all sorts of lies about Jannaeus (as they did about his brother Judah Aristobulus) and attributed to him the cruelest of acts, which he did not do. There is no doubt that he avenged himself on the Pharisees, who embittered his life and caused him to lose the fruit of his great victories in Transjordan and refused to make peace with him under any condition save his death. But it may be said with certainty that he did not commit the acts of cruelty which Josephus ascribes to him.[30]

Eventually, however, Jannaeus seems to have made peace with the Pharisees by restoring the *Ḥever ha-Yᵉhudim* to its former role. There is evidence for this from the last years of his reign (80–78 B.C.E.) similar to the evidence from its beginning (103–98 B.C.E.) — coins engraved only in Hebrew with the words "*Ḥever ha-Yᵉhudim*" (חבר היהודים) and not bearing either the Hebrew inscription "King Jonathan" or the Greek legend "of King Alexander."[31]

D. JANNAEUS' FINAL WARS AND CONQUESTS

After putting down the revolt of the Pharisees, Jannaeus gained a respite with regard to internal affairs. But Judea, weakened by the civil war, almost fell into the hands of the kings of Syria and of the Nabataeans. When Antiochus XII Dionysus set out to fight the Nabataean king, he

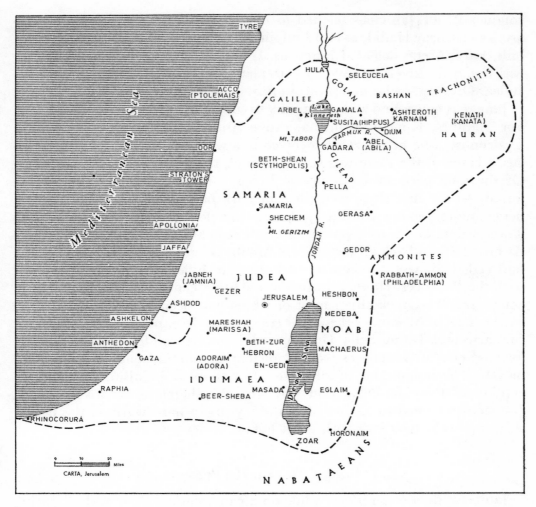

Jannaeus Alexander's Kingdom

invaded Judea on the way. In his weakened position, Jannaeus did not feel up to opposing the Syrian king in open warfare. But in order to block his penetration of the interior of the country he dug a deep trench and constructed a kind of wall fortified with wooden towers along the entire route from Jaffa to K'far Saba, later called Antipatris,[32] according to Josephus. Antiochus Dionysus, however, burned the towers and destroyed the wall and proceeded on his way to the lands of the Nabataeans. There he was killed in battle against Aretas, King of the Nabataeans, who became ruler of Damascus as well. Aretas then attacked Judea, too, in an effort to conquer it, for Jannaeus seemed to be a most dangerous rival. The two armies met near Hadid, east of Lod, in the coastal plain west of the Judean hills,[33] and Aretas defeated Jannaeus. It appears, however, that the victory was not a decisive one, and Aretas made peace with Jannaeus and left Judea. Once again Jannaeus was in firm control of his kingdom.

Jannaeus now found an opportunity to complete the conquest of Palestine. For Tigranes, King of Armenia, drove Antiochus (the son of Antiochus Cyzicenus), who had become involved in a war with Aretas, out of Damascus.[34] None of the three was strong enough to check Jannaeus' conquests. Of the four parts of Palestine — Judea, Samaria, Galilee, and Transjordan — the first three were in Jannaeus' hands, only Transjordan still being under foreign control. Jannaeus therefore turned his attention to Transjordan, and waged war there for three years (roughly, 83–80 B.C.E.). At first, he won back all the cities of Moab, Gilead, and Hauran, which he had ceded to Aretas, when he had been in difficulty because of his war with the Pharisees. He then turned to the other centers of Transjordan and conquered the Greek cities, most of which had been founded in Palestine by the heirs of Alexander the Great (the famous Decapolis or "ten cities").[35] Jannaeus took Dium, Pella, Gerasa, and Seleuceia and finally the naturally fortified city of Gamala as well as ancient Philoteria, south of Lake Kinnereth. The inhabitants of all these cities adopted Judaism, with the exception of those of Pella, and this city was therefore destroyed. When Jannaeus returned in victory after three years of hard warfare, the people this time welcomed him with great honor.

E. JANNAEUS' DEATH. HIS PERSONALITY

Jannaeus died of an illness while on a campaign in Transjordan, during the siege of the fortress of Ragaba.[36]

Josephus writes that shortly before his death Jannaeus advised his wife to conceal his demise from the soldiers until the fortress had been captured. Then, on her return to Jerusalem crowned with victory, she should make concessions to the Pharisees and thus win their hearts. At the same time, she should deliver to them the corpse of their enemy, the king, for them to do with as they liked. They would then certainly not dishonor the body, first, because she had appeased them and, second, out of respect to the queen, who was devoted to them. The queen followed Jannaeus' shrewd advice, and the Pharisees buried him with great honors (*Ant.* XIII, 400 ff.).

But these "historical" facts smack of popular legend. The kernel of truth they contain is that the queen did not make public the news of the king's death until after the conquest of the city in order not to undermine the morale of the soldiers besieging it. The queen may also really have informed the Pharisees that in his last days the king had changed his attitude towards them for the better. And the Pharisees, for their part, may have realized that with all his faults this Hasmonean had been a great man who had brought considerable benefits to his people. They may finally have seen that he had been motivated only by the good of his people and of his land. He had Judaized all the cities which he conquered. During the great rebellion against him, he had sought peace from his enemies even after vanquishing them. He restored the *Ḥever ha-Yᵉhudim* which he had previously dissolved. No defeat he suffered at the hands of the Gentiles brought about the renewed subjugation of Judea: he always managed to extricate himself from difficulties and to add new conquests to old. Jannaeus, the Sadducee, even wrote a Torah scroll, in which the Ineffable Name was written in letters of gold: "It was related of the Torah of Alexandros [undoubtedly Jannaeus, who had become wealthy from the spoils of war], in which all the *azkarot* [Divine Names] were written in gold, and the matter came before the Sages, and they said: Let it be hidden away!"[37] His heart, then, was not cool toward the Torah (the written Torah, of course, not the Oral Law). And he honored both "the Pharisees and the non-Pharisees," regarding only "the hypocrites" as dangerous. After his death, when the hatred and the envy had faded away, the devout straightforward Pharisees recognized his great deeds and many of his virtues. To be sure, a king who engaged in battle all his days, a king who had angered the Pharisees with his contempt for the water libation hardly made the ideal Jewish king. But neither was Jannaeus the cruel tyrant depicted by his enemies among the Greeks and the Pharisees.

F. Political and Economic Results of Jannaeus' Reign

In attempting to evaluate the results of Jannaeus' reign it must be pointed out that he completed what had been begun by Simeon son of Mattathias and was continued by John Hyrcanus and Judah Aristobulus.[38] All the coastal cities from Dor to the Egyptian border (including Rhinocorura, south of Raphia) became Israelite cities. In the north, Jannaeus' kingdom extended as far as Seleuceia, not far from the Ḥula. He was in possession of the entire Decapolis (with the possible exception of Rabbath-Ammon [Philadelphia]): Beth-shean (Scythopolis), Gadara, Susita (Hippus), Dium, Pella, Gerasa, Abel (Abila),[39] Kenath (Kanata; the modern

Qanawāt in the Hauran region); in Transjordan in addition to Hauran he controlled Bashan, Golan, Trachonitis, Gilead, Moab, and virtually the whole land of the Ammonites; in the south, he extended his control to rich commercial cities such as Gaza, Anthedon, Ashdod, Jabneh and Raphia; he was also in possession of Gezer, Jaffa, Apollonia (Arabic: Arsūf), Straton's Tower, Dor, Gamala, Seleuceia, Heshbon, Medeba, Horonaim, Eglaim, Zoar, Ashteroth-karnaim, Adoraim (Adora) and Mareshah (Marissa).[40] Up to the time of the Hasmoneans the wealthiest cities in Palestine, which had become rich from their lively foreign commerce, were non-Jewish cities hostile to the Jews. Galilee was mainly the "district of the nations," Transjordan was more Arab-Greek than Jewish, Samaria was an intervening "strip of Cutheans," Idumaea was pagan. Even parts of Judea itself had fallen into the hands of foreigners and its most important cities belonged to the Greeks. Had the situation continued, there is no doubt that Judaism would have remained a religion confined to a small corner of the globe and would hardly have been in a position to leave its imprint on the world; most likely it would have been engulfed by Greeks, Syrian Canaanites and Arabs. Jannaeus put an end to this state of affairs after his grandfather, father and brother had little by little taken steps to alter it. It was he who made all of Palestine Jewish.[41]

Jannaeus Alexander's accomplishments in strengthening the Judean state were so important that it is no mere chance that the Talmud refers to practically all of the Hasmonean kings as "Yannai." For Jannaeus was preoccupied not only with expanding the borders but also with fortifying the country. He built the fortress of Machaerus on the southern border of Transjordan facing Arabia.[42] And it is almost certain that it was he who constructed the powerful Jewish fortress with the ancient name of Meẓad or Meẓada (Masada in Greek) on the western shore of the Dead Sea not far from En-gedi. Josephus credits "Jonathan, the High Priest" with having built the fortress, but this is erroneous, since the territory over which Jonathan son of Mattathias held jurisdiction did not extend to Masada at all. Josephus apparently confused Jonathan-Jannaeus, the king, with Jonathan son of Mattathias because of the similarity of the two names and because they were both High Priests. At the beginning of his reign, as noted above, Jannaeus also had his coins inscribed only with the Hebrew legend, "Jonathan, the High Priest." Hölscher also ascribes to Jannaeus the fortress Alexandrion, on Mount Sarṭaba,[43] but in the opinion of S. Klein, this fortress was built by Salome Alexandra, which explains why it was called Alexandrion in Greek, and in Hebrew Sheʿlomey, a diminutive of Sheʿlomẓiyyon.[44] In any case, Jannaeus constructed powerful fortresses facing Moab and Ammon, Cuthean Samaria, and Arabia. And it was undoubtedly Jannaeus Alexander, and not his father John Hyrcanus, who built the palace of the Hasmoneans, which afforded a splendid view of the city and of the Temple.[45] In addition, the right-angled building in Hebron known as the Cave of Machpelah, already mentioned in the *Book of Jubilees* and in the *Testaments of the XII Patriarchs*,[46] was erected by Jannaeus. The excellent gravestones on the outskirts of Jerusalem, near the Bucharan quarter, which are known as the Tombs of the Sanhedrin, may also have been erected in Jannaeus' time. The tomb of Johanan the High Priest, mentioned above (p. 221), was certainly built by his son Jannaeus since Judah Aristobulus, who reigned before his brother Jannaeus, occupied the throne for only one year and was ill during that entire period.

A report concerning a splendid work of art fashioned at Jannaeus' order has also been preserved. This was a golden vine weighing 500 talents, resembling an entire garden which attracted the attention of all who beheld it and was accordingly called "delight" ($\tau\epsilon\rho\pi\omega\lambda\dot{\eta}$). The geographer Strabo saw this vine in Rome in the temple of Jupiter Capitolinus with the inscription Ἀλεξάνδρου τοῦ τῶν Ἰουδαίων βασιλέως ("of Alexander, King of the Jews"). Jannaeus' son, Aristobulus, made a gift of the vine to Pompey (*Ant.* XIV, 36).[47]

Both the Talmud and Josephus display great interest in spiritual and religious matters. But presumably not much was accomplished in this sphere in Jannaeus' time, because the 27 years of his reign were a period of heavy warfare. The Sadducees heading the government were more concerned with political and military matters than with the people's spiritual life. Most of the regulations which Simeon ben Sheṭaḥ introduced, undoubtedly belong to the reign of Queen Salome, Jannaeus' successor. Nevertheless, a good number of the Hebrew apocryphal books, which have survived in Greek, Syrian, Ethiopian and even in Armenian and Slavic translations may be ascribed to Jannaeus' time. Furthermore, Jannaeus' tremendous political exploits also led to great spiritual achievements: Judaism (i.e., the culture-religion of the Jewish nation) was thereby rendered a force bent on expansion and capable of competing with the faith and culture of the Syrian Greeks and the Hellenized Canaanites.

The economic consequences of Jannaeus' reign are of the utmost importance.

It is a point of dispute among scholars whether the *Letter of Aristeas*, designed to portray the genesis of the Septuagint, belongs to the period of Simeon the Just (Schürer's opinion) or to Jannaeus' (the view of Herzfeld, Wendland, and others). The latter theory appears more acceptable. First of all, the nostalgia for the Judean theocracy expressed in the *Letter of Aristeas* shows that the book was written when such a state was a thing of the past — and this would be true in Jannaeus' period and not in the time of Simeon the Just, when the country's chief temporal ruler was still the High Priest and not a king who was also High Priest. Second, the author of the *Letter of Aristeas* presents an economic picture of all Palestine and not of Judea alone, which would have been only natural had the book been written in the days of Simeon the Just.[48] Third, the political and economic descriptions in the book give no special indications of foreign rule in the country.[49] In any case, the picture it does portray accords with the period of the Hasmoneans' undivided sovereignty:

> For the country is large and good, and some parts, those in Samaria so-called and those adjacent to the Idumaeans' country, are level plain, but others, in the center, are mountainous, and unremitting attention to agriculture and care of the soil is essential for these latter parts to obtain crops in plenty also. Since such attention is given, the whole of the aforementioned country is cultivated in various ways and with abundant yield (*Letter of Aristeas*, 107).

And the author of the *Letter* continues:

> The diligence of their agriculturists is indeed great. Their country is plentifully wooded with numerous olive trees, and rich in cereal crops and pulse, and also in vines and honey. Date palms and other fruit trees are beyond reckoning among them. They have plentiful cattle of all varieties, and their pastures are lush. Hence, they recognized that the rural districts required a dense population, and they laid the city and the villages out in proportion. A great volume of spices, precious stones, and gold is brought into the region by the Arabs. For the country is adapted for commerce as well as agriculture, and the city is rich in crafts and lacks none of the things imported by sea. It also has harbors well situated to supply its needs, those at Ashkelon, Jaffa, and Gaza, and likewise Acco, which was founded by [Ptolemy] the king" (*ibid.*, 112–5).[50]

All this clearly proves that not only agriculture, but commerce, too, was highly advanced in liberated Palestine. Jannaeus' main purpose in conquering all the coastal cities was simply to continue the effort launched by his grandfather, Simeon son of Mattathias: to provide the country with an outlet to the sea. Not without reason was Jannaeus the first also to engrave an anchor, the emblem of maritime power, on the coins he struck.[51] And, in fact, it was only during Jannaeus' reign that the Jews began to be a nation of traders competing with Sidon and Tyre. Contrary to Herod, Jannaeus did not draw the people away from farming, but he did attract them towards commerce. And by facilitating the export of the produce, he made agriculture more profitable. Thus where previously only Jews who had cut themselves off from their country and gone abroad (e.g. to Alexandria or Rome) engaged in commerce, beginning with Jannaeus' time the Jews became traders in their own land as well. A consequence of this new commerce was an increase in the country's population, since trade can support a greater number of people than agriculture. Were it not for Jannaeus' economic policy the Jews would probably not have become a majority in their own country. The expansion of Judea's boundaries and the conquest of the seaports enabled the Jews to export their agricultural produce through adjacent free ports, thus alleviating the struggle for existence and furthering the population increase; the Jews became a majority in practically all the districts of Judea. It can almost be said that as a result of this Israel changed from a small community to a nation creating spiritual values of universal significance. In this sense the secular Hasmonean king furthered the development of spiritual Judaism — not consciously, to be sure — more than a number of recognized spiritual leaders.

CHAPTER X

QUEEN SALOME ALEXANDRA

by J. Klausner

A. The Hebrew and Greek Names of Queen Salome

LIKE HIS FATHER John Hyrcanus, Jannaeus Alexander also commanded that he should be succeeded by his wife. But whereas John Hyrcanus' will was not carried out, that of Jannaeus was: his wife became queen of Judea. As High Priest, she named Hyrcanus, her eldest son.

The full Hebrew name of the sole ruling queen of the Hasmonean line is neither Sh°lomit nor Shalma, as various scholars have thought, but Sh°lom-Ziyyon (שְׁלוֹם־צִיּוֹן) which became Sh°lomẓiyyon[1] (שְׁלוֹמְצִיּוֹן), Shalom (שָׁלוֹם), and Sh°lomey (שְׁלוֹמִי) in the vernacular. In Greek, this Hebrew name is found in the form Σαλώμη and also Σαλίνα (*Ant.* XIII, 320). In Talmudic literature she is called Sh°lamtu,[2] Sh°lamẓu,[3] Sh°lamẓa,[4] and Shalminon,[5] but the version closest to the true Hebrew name is Shelẓiyyon (שלציין) or as two words Shel Ẓiyyon (של ציין).[6]

The short form of the name Sh°lomẓiyyon is, apparently, Sh°lomey (שלומי), like the name of the fortress mentioned in Talmudic literature;[7] in Greek the fortress is called Alexandrion, like the Greek name of Queen Salome.[8] And it is surprising that this queen, whose entire policy was Pharisaic, engraved only a Greek inscription on the coins she struck: βασιλὶς Ἀλεξάνδρα — Queen Alexandra; only on a single extant coin which may be from her period is the Hebrew letter ת visible, which most scholars guess is simply a remnant of the world מלכת (queen); but even this conjecture is doubtful.[9]

B. Salome's General Policy. The Rise of the Pharisees

Josephus refers to Queen Salome as "a woman who showed none of the weakness of her sex . . . . . . inordinately desirous of the power to rule . . . . ." And to avoid any possible misunderstanding, he adds: "For she valued the present more than the future, and making everything else secondary to absolute rule, she had, on account of this, no consideration for either decency or justice" (*Ant.* XIII, 430–431). In a previous passage, however, he says: "She permitted the Pharisees to do as they liked in all matters, and also commanded the people to obey them; and whatever regulations, introduced by the Pharisees, in accordance with the tradition of the fathers (πατριαν παράδοσιν), had been abolished by her father-in-law Hyrcanus, these she again restored. And, so, while she had the title of sovereign, the Pharisees had the power. For example, they recalled exiles, and freed prisoners, and, in a word, in no way differed from absolute rulers" (*ibid.* 408–409). This obvious contradiction can only be explained by presuming that the two conflicting statements have their origin in two different sources: a Jewish-Pharisee source in defense of Salome and a Greek source hostile to the Jews (or a Jewish source aimed against the Pharisees). It seems that in all that concerns government of the country during Salome's reign the Pharisee sources are more reliable.

In any case, during Salome's reign the aristocratic Sadducees were gradually removed from the Sanhedrin and replaced by Pharisees, and the Sadducee book of decrees was abolished. Abrogation of the Sadducee ruling that the *Shavu'ot* holiday always be observed on a Sunday (i.e., giving a literal interpretation to the biblical "from the morrow after the Sabbath") apparently dates from this period. An allusion to this has been preserved in the Talmudic tradition. Four holidays were proclaimed to commemorate the triumph of the Pharisees over the Sadducees: "On the fourteenth of Tammuz, *Sefer ha-G*e*zerot* [The Sadducee book of decrees] was set aside [mourning is forbidden];[10] "on the twenty-fourth of the month [Av] we returned to our laws,"[11] i.e., the Pharisees once again judged in accordance with their laws and not those of the Sadducees; and "on the twenty-eighth of Ṭevet the Assembly [the Sanhedrin] sat in judgement,"[12] i.e., the Pharisees entered the Sanhedrin in place of the Sadducees.[13] And, finally: "From the eighth of the month [Nisan] until the end of the holiday [Passover] the Feast of *Shavu'ot* was restored — mourning is forbidden."[14] The connection between the eighth of Nisan and Passover is to be found in Josephus: " . . . at the time when the people were assembling for the feast of unleavened bread, on the eighth of the month Xanthicus [Nisan]" (*War* VI, 290). In those days the two weeks from the new moon of Nisan until Passover were apparently regarded as belonging to Passover. And as for the "restoration" of the *Shavu'ot* festival to its former glory, Derenbourg has already pointed out[15] that the expression "was restored" (אתותב in the Aramaic original) proves that *Shavu'ot* had previously been observed in accordance with the opinion of the Sadducees, and that its observance was later "restored" to conform to the interpretation of the Pharisees. As a matter of fact, we know that in the days of John Hyrcanus, who was still a vassal of Antiochus Sidetes and as such was required to assist him in his war against the Parthians, Antiochus halted for two days on the banks of the Lycus river "at the request of the Jew Hyrcanus because of a festival of his nation on which it was not customary for the Jews to march out" (*Ant.* XIII, 251). And since in those days no holiday in Palestine was observed for two successive days (not even the New Year), Josephus, who cites Nicolaus of Damascus as his source for this episode, had to explain that in the year in question *Shavu'ot* fell on a Sunday, so that the Jews could not travel either on the holiday itself nor on the Sabbath which immediately preceded it. For at that time the quarrel between Hyrcanus and the Pharisees had not yet broken out.[16] The restoration of the Pharisaic laws toward the end of Jannaeus' reign and at the beginning of Salome's can also be inferred from the end of the ancient *barayta* about John Hyrcanus' break with the Pharisees: ". . . all the Sages of Israel were massacred, and the world was desolate until Simeon ben Sheṭaḥ came and restored the Torah to its pristine [glory]."[17]

That the Pharisees "recalled exiles" is also alluded to in the Talmud. There[18] we read that "When King Jannaeus put the Rabbis to death . . . R. Joshua ben P'raḥya fled to Alexandria" and "when there was peace" between the Pharisees and the Hasmoneans he returned to Jerusalem. Closer to the historical event is the account in the Jerusalem Talmud[19] that Judah ben Ṭabbay fled to Alexandria and people of Jerusalem wrote: "From great Jerusalem to little Alexandria! Until when will my betrothed dwell among you while I sit here melancholy!" And, the Talmud goes on to say, Judah ben Ṭabbay (who is mentioned in the Mishnah as Simeon ben Sheṭaḥ's "colleague"[20]) came back to Jerusalem by boat. This return no doubt occurred during the reign of Queen Salome, when the Pharisees "recalled exiles," according to Josephus. It would also appear that Simeon ben Sheṭaḥ, who had also fled Jannaeus' wrath over the "subterfuge" of the Pharisees regarding the sacrifice needed to absolve the Nazirites from their vows (see p. 233 above), returned at this time.[21]

Since the entire internal leadership of the state was in the hands of the Pharisees, how was Salome's "love of power" manifested?

The answer to that question is: in everything pertaining to external affairs.

The Pharisees were apparently not concerned with diplomatic and military affairs, fortification of the country's boundaries, and similar matters. These were matters which the queen reserved for herself — and she may have deliberately turned over domestic affairs to the Pharisees to preclude their interference in foreign matters which she regarded as much more important and to which she paid much attention. Josephus writes that "the queen took thought for the welfare of the kingdom and recruited a large force of mercenaries [in accordance with the custom of the day] and also made her own force twice as large, with the result that she struck terror into the local rulers round her and received hostages from them" (*Ant.* XIII, 409). And elsewhere he says of Salome: "She . . . doubled her army, besides collecting a considerable body of foreign troops; so that she not only strengthened her own nation, but became a formidable foe to foreign potentates" (*War* I, 112).[22]

But foreign and domestic affairs are of course inter-related, particularly in Judaism, where everything requires the sanction of the Torah. The Pharisees demanded the removal of the Sadducees from leadership on the grounds that they had proved poor advisers to Jannaeus and that it had been on their counsel that he had executed many Pharisees. Salome gave the Pharisees a free hand in all matters relating to their political opponents. One of Jannaeus' principal advisers, Diogenes the Sadducee, was sentenced to death by a Pharisee court, and a good many other prominent Sadducees were executed together with him. The Pharisees also looked askance at the mercenary army because these foreigners had proved a bastion for the king whenever he had acted in a manner alien to Judaism. At that time, however, every nation, large or small, possessed an army of this sort, and Salome expanded the one she had inherited from Jannaeus. But the commanders of the mercenary battalions were all Jews. It was they who made the war plans, and the soldiers obeyed their orders, so that this army of mercenaries could constitute no danger to state security.

These Jewish commanders now turned to Aristobulus, the second son of Jannaeus and Salome, who resembled his father in his love of battle if not in political wisdom, and complained to him that the queen had forgotten all the accomplishments of the Sadducees as the leading generals in her husband's wars. Now their very lives were in jeopardy because of the Pharisees' desire for revenge. If the queen did not alter her negative attitude toward the Sadducees, they would prefer to relinquish their positions and serve as mercenaries in the army of Aretas, King of the Nabataeans; he would appreciate their heroism in battle. At any rate, in order to remove them from constant danger the queen should send them to the fortresses of Judea far from Jerusalem.

Aristobulus spoke harshly to his mother. He argued that the fact that it was not he who was the king was an injustice since his military prowess entitled him to the crown; he complained of the wrong done him; Hyrcanus, his brother, had at least obtained the High Priesthood, but he — nothing at all. As for the request that the fortresses be turned over to the Sadducee generals, the aim from the outset had been to make use of them as a base from which to fight against his brother and his old mother when the time came, as later actually happened.

The queen heard the argument of her younger son on behalf of the army commanders and handed over to them the small fortresses in Judea. But she was apprehensive about handing over to men who were so close to Aristobulus the three most important fortresses — Hyrcania, Alexandrion, and Machaerus — where her treasures and equipment were kept (*Ant.* XIII, 417).

C. SALOME'S LAST DAYS

Toward the end of Salome's reign, Ptolemy the son of Mennaeus, King of Chalcis, grew more powerful and threatened Damascus.[23] He thus became a dangerous neighbor of the Judean kingdom. Salome, who was apprehensive about this development, sent Aristobulus to frustrate Ptolemy's designs on Damascus. In so doing, she may have wished to occupy him in an external war so that he would forget his domestic demands. But Aristobulus failed in this mission (*Ant.* XIII, 418). Some time later, Tigranes, King of Armenia, marched against Damascus and conquered it, after which he proceeded towards the Judean border and laid siege to Acco (*ibid.*, 419).

Aware of her inability to fight so powerful an enemy as Tigranes seemed to be, the queen sought to avoid a clash. She therefore sent Tigranes gifts and asked for peace. Tigranes agreed, not so much because he was influenced by the presents as he was by the rumor he had heard that the Romans, under Lucullus, who was then pursuing Mithridates, King of Pontus, had attacked Armenia. Tigranes was forced to return to his own country; and peace returned to Judea.

But it was only in her foreign relations that Salome enjoyed peace. Within, calamity struck at the end of her life. When the queen was afflicted with the illness from which she was never to recover and Aristobulus realized that after her death the Pharisees would support Hyrcanus, his elder brother who was legitimately High Priest and who was a man of peace and devoted to the Pharisees, he raised the banner of rebellion — not so much against his mother as against the Pharisees and their ally Hyrcanus. The fortresses which were in the hands of the Sadducee generals,

Aristobulus' supporters, came under his control one after another. He was now ready to attack the three strongest fortresses, held by men loyal to his mother and brother. Within a short period, he mobilized an army in Lebanon and Transjordan and conquered 22 cities in Judea in two weeks. The Pharisees and the elders committed to neither party who tended to go along with the Pharisees appealed to the ailing queen. She told them that they still possessed three important assets: a strong nation (the majority sympathetic to the Pharisees), a large army, and a rich treasury. Old age and sickness made her unable to lead them in battle against Aristobulus and the Sadducees. She did, however, imprison Aristobulus' wife and children as hostages in the citadel called "the Baris" (later Antonia). She died shortly thereafter at the age of 73 (or perhaps 63) in the year 67 B.C.E., after a reign of nine years.

D. ECONOMIC AND SPIRITUAL SITUATION DURING SALOME'S REIGN. SIMEON BEN SHEṬAḤ

The talmudic literature is lavish in its description of the bright economic situation in Palestine in the days of Queen Salome: "It is told that in the days of Simeon ben Sheṭaḥ and Queen Salome rain fell on Sabbath nights [when Jews did not venture out on the roads] until wheat grew to the size of kidneys, barley to that of olive berries, lentils to that of gold *denarii*."[24] There were evidently many years of plenty in those days. And in addition to the enrichment of the people as a result of the good crops, Jannaeus Alexander's victories had resulted in an accumulation of booty in gold, silver, and precious stones. The numerous coastal cities which now came under Judean control also yielded considerable gold and silver in customs duties on all the imports and exports, and many rulers of small states and semi-independent cities paid tribute to the Hasmonean monarchs. All this enriched the entire country. Wheat, oil, wine, fig-rolls, balsam, and other products were sent from Judea, Galilee and Transjordan to lands near and far, and they brought considerable material blessing to the little country which had so greatly expanded. Were it not for this abundant wealth accumulated in the days of Jannaeus and Salome, the land would not have been able to endure the taxes and spoliation by the Romans, from the time of Pompey's conquest, nor would the Hasmoneans have had sufficient funds to conduct a protracted hard war for thirty years against one another, and against the Romans and Herod who did their bidding.

Regarding spiritual matters, it should be noted to begin with that all domestic matters of the state were in the hands of the Pharisees. These were headed by a great personality, original in his views and a man of numerous achievements — Simeon ben Sheṭaḥ. Of the events of his life little is known and even this consists of legends.[25] But it is only about a great man that wondrous legends take shape in the consciousness of the people, and such stories contain something of history. The Talmud[26] regards the queen, Jannaeus' wife, as the sister of Simeon ben Sheṭaḥ. In any case, there is little doubt that in Jannaeus' days, and even more so during the reign of Salome, Simeon ben Sheṭaḥ was very close to the Pharisee queen. He treated her as a brother, guiding her in all her deeds to the advantage of the Pharisees — and this may be the origin of the legend that he actually was her brother. There is hardly any doubt that it was Simeon ben Sheṭaḥ who urged his "colleague" Judah ben Ṭabbay, to return from Alexandria to Jerusalem (see p. 244 above). Nor are there any grounds for doubting that it was Simeon ben Sheṭaḥ who gradually replaced the Sadducees in the Sanhedrin with Pharisees.[27] It may have been he, as *Av bet din*, and Judah ben Ṭabbay, as *Nasi*, who dealt firmly with the Sadducees and who were responsible for the complaint of the army commanders to the queen, through Aristobulus, that they were being repressed (see p. 245 above). Allusions to this firm hand are also to be found in the talmudic literature. There is an Aggadic tradition which says:

> Once Simeon ben Sheṭaḥ sentenced to death one false witness against whom an alibi had been established. Judah ben Ṭabbay then said to him: 'May I not live to see the consolation if you did not shed innocent blood. For the Torah said: You may sentence to death on the evidence of witnesses, and also, you may sentence witnesses to death on the basis of an alibi. Just as there must be two witnesses giving evidence, so also must there be two against whom an alibi is established.'[28] But elsewhere we find the opposite: "R. Judah ben Tabbay said: 'May I [never] see consolation [of Israel][29] if I did not have one *zomem*-witness[30] done to death to disabuse the mind of the Sadducees, who used to say that *zomemim* [found guilty] were put to death only after the [falsely] accused person had [actually] been executed.' Said Simeon Sheṭaḥ to him: 'May I [never] see consolation [of Israel] if you have not shed innocent blood because the Sages declared that witnesses found to be *zomemim* are not put to death until both have been proved as such.' Forthwith did Judah ben Ṭabbay take upon himself a resolve never to deliver a decision save in the presence of Simeon ben Sheṭaḥ.[31]

It would appear that the first version is the one to be preferred.

In any case, "in order to disabuse the mind of the Sadducees" one of the two leading scholars of the time took human life. Extremism of a like nature is also revealed in the story that Simeon ben Sheṭaḥ hanged eighty women for witchcraft in Ashkelon "because the times called for it."[32] However, it is difficult to accept this story as being historically true, for Ashkelon, even if it was in the possession of the Jews in the days of Jannaeus and Salome,[33] was in their hands only a short time. Derenbourg[34] may have been right in his conjecture that. the talmudic tale confuses Simeon ben Sheṭaḥ with Simeon son of Mattathias, for during the time of Jonathan and Simeon, the sons of Mattathias, who were virtually free rulers in Ashkelon, that city was in the hands of the Jews for a much longer period.[35]

The story of the hanging of the witches is connected with another tale. The relatives of the hanged women wished to take revenge on Simeon ben Sheṭaḥ, and they hired false witnesses to testify that his son had committed a deed punishable by death, "and he was sentenced to death." The witnesses then felt remorse causing the death of an innocent person, and they appeared in court and acknowledged that they had given false testimony. Simeon ben Sheṭaḥ wished to reverse the verdict, thus contradicting the ruling of the Pharisees that "once a witness testifies, he cannot testify again." His son said therefore: "Father, if you wish deliverance to be brought about through you, make me the threshold for the Law to pass over me."[36] And he mounted the scaffold, the father himself ratifying the death sentence against his innocent son, so that the interpretation of the Pharisees be carried out.

Perhaps it is only the legend that connected this horrific story with the hanging of the witches. But the entire tale, in both its parts, is quite in keeping with the spirit of Simeon ben Sheṭaḥ. This devout Pharisee fought the Sadducees with all his power on behalf of the Pharisaic views, and in order to establish their principles he was even capable of sacrificing his son. The Talmud had a reason for saying, "Simeon ben Sheṭaḥ had heated hands." This sharp statement can apply not only to the death sentence on his son, but also to his harsh treatment of the Sadducees when he wielded power during the reign of Queen Salome.

This most prominent among the Pharisees of his time, though *Av beth din* in the Great Sanhedrin and in constant contact with the royal court, lived a life of poverty. According to Talmudic tradition, he made a living from dealing in flax and consequently had to do a great deal of walking on the roads. The Talmud tells moving stories about his moral integrity;[37] his high political and social moral standards are illustrated by the following episode, which bears all the earmarks of a historical event:

> A slave of King Jannaeus killed a man. Simeon ben Sheṭaḥ said to the Sages: 'Set your eyes boldly upon him and let us judge him.' So they sent the King word, saying: 'Your slave has killed a man.' Thereupon he sent him to them [to be tried]. But they again sent him a message 'Thou too must come here, for the Torah says [Ex. 21:29] If warning has been given to its owner [teaching], that the owner of the ox must come and stand by his ox.' The King accordingly came and sat down. Then Simeon ben Sheṭaḥ said: 'Stand on thy feet, King Jannaeus, and let the witnesses testify against thee; yet it is not before us that thou standest, but before Him who spoke and the world came into being, as it is written [Deut. 19:17], 'Then both the men between whom the controversy is, shall stand . . .' 'I shall not act in accordance with what thou sayest, but in accordance with what thy colleagues say,' he answered. [Simeon] then turned first to the right and then to the left, but they all [for fear of the king], looked down at the ground. Then said Simeon ben Sheṭaḥ unto them: 'Are ye wrapped in thoughts? Let the Master of thoughts [God] come and call you to account!'[38]

Here we see in all his moral stature the great Pharisee who, like a prophet of old, has no fear of the wrath of a powerful and victorious king, and for whom the Torah and justice take precedence over the honor of kings and the danger of vexing them. He mocks the cowardly "great ones of the nation" as persons "wrapped in thoughts" who dare not oppose the king's will, yet find it difficult to contravene a biblical injunction. He sharply rebukes these timorous members of the Sanhedrin with a telling phrase in the classical style.[39]

E. SIMEON BEN SHEṬAḤ'S GREAT ORDINANCES

Simeon ben Sheṭaḥ is mentioned in the Talmud as the author of several reforms in Jewish life. Among these were the improvement of the position of the Jewish woman and reforms in Jewish education. The social position of women in any land is evidence of the country's cultural state. And the same is true of education. During the reign of the Hasmoneans, steps were taken to improve both of these. As far as women are concerned, the Talmud says Simeon ben Sheṭaḥ instituted the woman's marriage contract [Kᵉtubba].[40] There are certainly grounds for assuming that the *kᵉtubba* preceded

Simeon ben Sheṭaḥ. First of all, a marriage contract similar to the customary Jewish *kᵉtubba* has been discovered among the Aramaic papyri of Elephantine.[41] Second, had the *kᵉtubba* been instituted at the time of the Hasmoneans, a time of strong national sentiments, it would have been drafted in Hebrew rather than Aramaic.[42] Third, in the tractate 'Eduyyot of the Mishnah and in the Tosefta to the same tractate[43] the School of Shammai quote parts of the *kᵉtubba* in Hebrew — and it is most unlikely that the passage was translated from Aramaic, for the Mishnah and the Tosefta are careful to bring quotations in their original language; indeed, we find in the same tractate that a testimony given by Jose ben Jo'ezer of Zereda is brought in Aramaic.[44] It thus follows that the *kᵉtubba* was in existence even prior to the period of the Hasmoneans, when Aramaic was the second official language in the Persian kingdom,[45] but that Simeon ben Sheṭaḥ introduced changes and reforms for the woman's benefit in order to make it more difficult for a man to divorce his wife. This, in fact, is implied in the Talmud itself: "It was then ordained that the amount of the *kᵉtubba* was to be deposited in the wife's father's house. At any time, however, when the husband was angry with her he used to tell her, 'Go to your *kᵉtubba*.'[46] "It was ordained, therefore, that the amount of the *kᵉtubba* was to be deposited in the house of her father-in-law.[47] Wealthy women converted it into silver, or gold baskets,[48] while poor women converted it into brass tubs. Still, whenever the husband had occasion to be angry with his wife he would say to her, 'Take your *kᵉtubba* and go!' It was then that Simeon ben Sheṭaḥ ordained that the husband must insert the pledging clause, 'All my property is mortgaged to your *kᵉtubba*."[49] Simeon ben Sheṭaḥ's intention in instituting this reform was to make it difficult for the husband to pay the marriage settlement and thus be rid of his wife — a reform the significance of which in family life is obvious. This regulation was connected with another one: "At first they used to give merely a written undertaking in respect of [the *kᵉtubba* of] a virgin for two hundred *zuz* and in respect of that of a widow for a *maneh* [one hundred *zuz*] and consequently they grew old and could not take any wives [because women refused to marry under such precarious conditions] when Simeon ben Sheṭaḥ took the initiative and ordained that all the property of a husband is pledged for the *kᵉtubba* of his wife."[50] There is reason to believe that the terms *niksey-mᵉlog* and *niksey zo'n barzel* (property which a woman brings to her husband's house: the former is not included in the *kᵉtubba*, the husband enjoys its usufruct only and is not responsible for it; for the latter he is responsible), which are so original and cast in such living language, also date from the time of Simeon ben Sheṭaḥ. This eminent scholar drafted the laws to the woman's advantage connected with these terms, even though the legal concepts they incorporated were developed through Roman influence.

In general, the status of women in Judea was improved under the Hasmoneans. The legend about "the mother and her seven sons" during Antiochus' persecutions shows that the nation knew how to appreciate the dignified and patriotic stand taken by the Jewish woman. Mention should also be made of the fine relationship depicted in the Book of Tobit between Tobit (the father) and his wife Anna, between Tobiah (the son) and Sarah, and between Raguel and Edna, whom he calls "my sister," just as the "beloved" calls his love in the Song of Songs.[51] All this is reliable evidence that the general attitude towards women took a turn for the better in Hasmonean Judea. The position of Queen Salome constitutes further proof of this. Also worthy of note is the fact that not a single Hasmonean king had more than one wife, in contrast to Herod, for example, who took many. The regulations which Simeon ben Sheṭaḥ introduced regarding the woman's k'tubba simply lent religious and juridical sanction to this satisfactory situation which already prevailed in fact.

Just as Simeon ben Sheṭaḥ was concerned with the problems of women and of the family, so, too, did he put his mind to education.

According to the Talmud, Simeon ben Sheṭaḥ deserves credit for the regulation that "children must go to school (beth sefer)."[52] The Hebrew expression beth sefer[53] is so current among Jews that it may come as a surprise to hear it is not found in the Bible, but first appears in the Talmud and Midrash. But the word is so Hebraic in spirit and form that it is impossible not to conjecture that it was coined, at the latest, during the Hasmonean period, when the Hebrew language developed and was enriched in vocabulary and concepts. It is therefore likely that the word beth sefer was created by Simeon ben Sheṭaḥ together with the institution itself. From the days of Ezra the Scribe to the Hasmonean times, each father ordinarily taught his sons Torah in order to fulfill the injunction "And shou shalt teach them diligently unto thy children" (Deut. 6:7); it was also customary for the hazzanim (superintendents) not only to serve as the spokesmen of the congregation in prayer, and as sextons and Torah readers in the synagogue too, but to teach the young children Scripture as well — either going from house to house or gathering the children for this purpose in the synagogue. References to this method of teaching are still to be found in the Book of Ben Sira (51, 13 ff.). However, in the peaceful days of Queen Salome, the Pharisees, who conducted all the internal affairs and who, according to talmudic tradition, "used to count all the letters of the Torah,"[54] saw to it that the knowledge of the Law was disseminated in the nation by means of public schools. Since in the period of Jannaeus and Salome, the leader of the Pharisees was Simeon ben Sheṭaḥ, it was probably he who established the Jewish school in its popular form. It is true that we find in the Babylonian Talmud a statement which ascribes the founding of schools "in each district and each town" to Joshua ben Gamala,[55] apparently to be identified with the High Priest Joshua ben Gamaliel who held this office shortly before the Great War with the Romans. Basing himself upon this statement, Schürer[56] even disputed the tradition preserved in both the Babylonian and Jerusalem Talmuds that it was Simeon ben Sheṭaḥ who instituted the ruling that "children must go to school." However, the statement referring to Joshua ben Gamala should be understood as meaning that Joshua ben Gamala only expanded Simeon ben Sheṭaḥ's general ruling, by decreeing the establishment of schools "in each district and each town."[57]

The importance of Simeon ben Sheṭaḥ's ruling for Jewish education can hardly be over-estimated. Not without reason does the ancient *barayta* praise him in such glowing terms: "And the world was desolate until Simeon ben Sheṭaḥ came and restored the Torah to its pristine [glory]".[58] Philo of Alexandria could say that the Jews learn their laws "even from the cradle"[59] only because of the reform which Simeon ben Sheṭaḥ had carried out in Jewish education.

The Talmud ascribes to Simeon ben Sheṭaḥ the promulgation of still another ruling — that glassware should be subject to the laws of ritual impurity.[60] But elsewhere, the Talmud attributes this regulation to Jose ben Joʿezer and Jose ben Johanan, while ascribing to Simeon ben Sheṭaḥ the regulation applying the laws of ritual impurity to metal utensils.[61] The Jerusalem Talmud[62] attributes this regulation jointly to Judah ben Ṭabbay and Simeon ben Sheṭaḥ. The Babylonian Talmud[63] links the decree to an incident involving Queen Salome: "It once happened that Queen Shelẓiyyon made a banquet for her son and all her utensils were defiled. Thereupon she broke them and gave them to the goldsmith, who melted them down and manufactured new utensils of them. But the Sages declared: They revert to their previous uncleanness." These "Sages" were undoubtedly Judah ben Ṭabbay and Simeon ben Sheṭaḥ.

Since both Judah ben Ṭabbay and Simeon ben Sheṭaḥ sat at the head of the Great Sanhedrin it is but natural that they were preoccupied with matters of law and justice, and that most of their sayings, too, dealt with these subjects: "Judah ben Ṭabbay said: 'Do thou not [as a judge] play the part of an advocate; whilst they [i.e., the parties in a lawsuit] are standing before thee, let them be regarded by thee as if they were [both of them] guilty, and when they leave thy presence [after] having submitted to the judgement let them be regarded by thee as if they were [both of them] guiltless.' Simeon ben Sheṭaḥ used to say: be thorough in the interrogation of witnesses, and be careful in thy words, lest from them [i.e., from your words] they learn to utter falsehood."[64]

The brief period of Pharisee rule in the peaceful days of Salome did not pass without important results for the survival of the nation and its spiritual development. On the other hand, there were no significant political consequences insofar as the expansion of the country's borders or the ending of the party strife between the Pharisees and the Sadducees was concerned.

CHAPTER XI

DOMESTIC POLITICS AND POLITICAL INSTITUTIONS

by A. Schalit

A. The Hellenistic State

THE HASMONEAN KINGDOM differed in one fundamental respect from the Hellenistic kingdoms of the East: the latter were established by adventurous individuals who succeeded in gaining control of foreign countries by force. The conquerors regarded these countries as their private domain, possession having been acquired by conquest. Every Hellenistic kingdom was "a land conquered by the spear" ($\delta o \rho i \kappa \tau \eta \tau o \varsigma \ \gamma \tilde{\eta}$), and the law of the spoils of war applied; the conquering victor was the sole master. This was the source of the fundamental characteristic of the Hellenistic kingdom. The kingdom was built around the personality of the king as the center to which all peripheral forces gravitated. The Hellenistic king was all-powerful, his word was law, and no one could refuse him. The Hellenistic system of government cannot be regarded as an actual continuation of the ancient Oriental system of Babylonia, Assyria, and Persia, in which the inhabitants—the nobles and the common people—were regarded literally as the slaves of the king. It resembled that of the ancient East in that it too regarded the conquered people resident in the state, if not as the king's slaves, then in any event as subjects who were required to pay taxes without the king having any legal obligation whatsoever to them. An exception to this rule were the inhabitants of the Greek and Macedonian cities who enjoyed special privileges. They were considered "freemen" and were bound to the Hellenistic king by a "treaty." These cities constituted a *polis* in the midst of a "barbarian" environment which lacked any rights at all.

Such was the Hellenistic state in theory — but in practice it was not so. The king often disregarded the "freedom" of the Greek-Macedonian cities in his kingdom, and imposed his rule on their inhabitants, particularly in straitened circumstances when he required their financial and military assistance. Thus, the entire administration of the Hellenistic state was in effect concentrated in the hands of the king. The officials were the king's functionaries, and the army was personally bound to the monarch by a contract of hire; any sign of disobedience on the part of the soldiers was tantamount to a violation of the contract with their employer. Obviously, a really direct relation existed only between the king and the highest officials and military leaders. The lower officials and officers were subject to the authority of their superiors, so that administration was carried out by a hierarchy composed of many different links. The administrative hierarchy of Ptolemaic Egypt is known to us down to the last detail from the thousands of papyri which have been preserved, and give us a very clear idea of the complex structure of that Hellenistic kingdom. The structure of the other Hellenistic kingdoms appears to have been simpler, even though documents of great importance about them are scanty. However, as far as fundamentals were concerned, the internal composition of all the Hellenistic states was uniform, since all of them emerged from the empire of Alexander the Great and all of them, except Macedonia, were erected on the ruins of the ancient kingdom of Persia, which left its mark on them.[1]

B. The Political and Legal Institutions of the Hasmonean State

In discussing the governmental system of the Hasmonean state we have to disregard most, if not all, of these features. The Hasmoneans could not wield power on the absolutist pattern of the Hellenistic rulers. The earliest extant information on Hasmonean power indicates its nature and extent. Simeon, the last surviving son of Mattathias, was invested with power by "The Great Assembly" (ἐκκλησία μεγάλη) which convened in Jerusalem on the eighteenth day of Elul in the year 172 of the Seleucid era, that is at the end of summer, 141 B.C.E. This solemn ceremony was performed "in a great congregation of priests, and people and princes of the nation and of the elders of the country" (I Macc. 14:28). The document which recounts this important event specifies the powers granted to Simeon (I Macc. 14:41–46) as follows:

> And the Jews and the priests were well pleased that Simeon should be their leader and High Priest for ever, until a faithful prophet should arise; and that he should be a captain over them, to set them over their works, and over the country, and over the arms, and over the strongholds, and that he should take charge of the sanctuary, and that he should be obeyed by all, and that all in-

struments in the country should be written in his name, and that he should be clothed in purple and wear gold; and that it should not be lawful for anyone among the people or among the priests to set at naught any of these things, or to gainsay the things spoken by him, or to gather an assembly in the country without him, or that any [other] should be clothed in purple, or wear a buckle of gold; but that whosoever should do otherwise, or set at naught any of these things, should be liable to punishment. And all the people consented to ordain for Simeon that it should be according to these words.

These details may provide a key for understanding the legal institutions which, in part, existed even before the Hasmonean revolt and which developed in the course of the rebellion, until the appointment of Simeon. The first question we must ask is: the document mentions "the people." To whom does the word "people" refer? Whom did they represent in the Great Assembly? What was their relation to the other groups who participated in the inaugural ceremony?

It should be emphasized, to begin with, that the rebellion involved the majority of the people, that is the masses of simple farmers who went out to fight for religious freedom, and who bore the brunt of bloody battles and sacrifices over a period of many years. If only for this reason, it would appear that the masses were justified in demanding to participate in the official institutions as one of the political factors of the nation. And, indeed, at the great national assembly of 141 B.C.E., at which the official legal status of the Hasmonean family was laid down, we find the "people" as one of the elements agreeing to the appointment of the new High Priest and ethnarch.

The document cited speaks of λαός (the people). What does this concept imply? It would appear that this expression which is mentioned alongside ἱερεῖς (the priests), indicates that part of the people distinct from the priests. In other words, λαός in the document refers to the totality of non-priests, that is, the laymen, designated to this day as "the Israelites." From the religious aspect these two groups, the priests and the Israelites (ἱερεῖς καὶ λαός), constituted the entire nation and together formed an integral body within the National Assembly.

Along with these two groups, mention is made of ἄρχοντες ἔθνους. The concept ἔθνος is undoubtedly a *terminus technicus* as used in Hellenistic public law; it indicates the nation, the community as a body politic.[2] For the ἄρχοντες in the document are simply the leaders of the people invested with political and legal authority, and just as the two previous groups represented the people as a religious entity, the ἄρχοντες represented them from the political and legal aspects. In other words, this group was the representative of the nation as a body politic.

The fourth group which participated in the Great Assembly was composed of the elders of the country (πρεσβύτεροι τῆς χώρας). The elders represented the people based on its division into clans.

Who was included in the three aforementioned bodies which comprised the Assembly? In the first, consisting of priests and Israelites, as noted above, the priests belonged simply by virtue of their being of the seed of Aaron performing divine services. This, however, did not hold true in the case of the Israelites. Not every layman in Israel was qualified to express an opinion concerning the laws of religious worship; for this, professional knowledge was necessary. Therefore, only scholars of the Law came under consideration as members of the body within the National Assembly, in which various religious questions were decided after long debates requiring of the participants a knowledge of the various fields of *Halaka*.

The second body, that of the princes of the nation, which represented the people as a politico-juridical entity, was constituted with a different view in mind and in accordance with a different principle. This body, principally concerned with the actual government of the state and the conduct of foreign relations, could function properly only if its members were men of social and economic pre-eminence and with political experience. Accordingly, most of the men in this body probably came from distinguished and wealthy families with a generations-old tradition of governing.

The third body was composed of representatives of the families, that is, of the elders heading the clans.

Thus, it emerges that the National Assembly of 141 B.C.E. was composed of four different classes of the people in Judea: (a) priests, (b) scholars of the Law, (c) representatives of the distinguished and wealthy families, (d) the elders of the clans. These four classes, organized in three distinct bodies, constituted the National Assembly at the time of Simeon and the constitutional foundation of the Hasmonean state which then came into being.

The document in I Maccabees sums up Simeon's powers as follows (I Macc. 14:47): "And Simeon accepted [hereof], and consented to fill the office of High Priest, and to be captain and ethnarch of the Jews and of the priests, and to preside over all of them."

Simeon's powers thus embraced: a) the religious authority, i.e., the High Priesthood; b) the military authority, i.e., command of the army and the security of the nation and the country; and c) the political authority, i.e., supreme rule and leadership of the nation.

Two of these functions — the High Priesthood and the leadership of the people — were ancient ones. The High Priesthood in the new shape it assumed in the Second Temple period had emerged very shortly after the return from the Babylonian exile; the leadership of the people as part of the authority of the High Priest is known as far back as the beginnings of Ptolemaic rule in Palestine, its origins undoubtedly going back to the fourth century B.C.E., at the end of the period of Persian power.[3]

Leadership of the people in the time of the Ptolemies was called προστασία τοῦ λαοῦ and the High Priest who exercised it was known as προστάτης τοῦ λαοῦ. At the end of the period of Ptolemaic rule in Palestine the leadership of the people passed to Joseph son of Tobiah.[4]

The military power came into being in the days of the Hasmonean revolt. In those stormy times it was, undoubtedly, the most important power of all. Judah Maccabee held it until his death. The political power was then of necessity indissolubly connected with the military power, since only Judah was in a position to negotiate with the Syrian enemy. Politically and militarily it was also logical for Judah to conduct the negotiations with the Roman Senate concerning a Roman-Judean treaty. After Judah's death both of these powers passed on to his brother Jonathan, and when Jonathan was appointed High Priest all three powers were concentrated in his hands. By virtue of the decision of the National Assembly of 141 B.C.E. they were all bestowed on Simeon. It is generally accepted that the text of the Assembly's resolution given in I Macc. 14:25 ff., preserves the original Hebrew term for the political power which Simeon wielded. Simeon is called σαραμελ or ασαραμελ, which is taken to be the Greek translation of the Hebrew title Sar 'am El. This assumption is, however, completely wrong.[5]

The foregoing gives us to understand that Simeon was the ruler of the people and governed for their sake. As High Priest he was required to negotiate with that body in the Assembly which represented the people on religious matters, i.e., with the priests and the Israelites. As military commander Simeon had to maintain relations with the representatives of the tribes and clans, i.e., with the elders of the land, since the clans, and particularly the large agricultural families that lived in villages and small towns, were required to provide soldiers for the military commander. And as the political leader Simeon had to consult with the "princes of the nation" who were the representatives of the nation as a body politic.

The three bodies mentioned appeared before the High Priest as the aggregate representation of the nation. This three-fold, all-embracing representation is, it may be assumed, the *Ḥever ha-Yᵉhudim* (tentatively translated "the Commonwealth of the Jews"), inscribed on the Hasmonean coins, beginning with John Hyrcanus.[6]

From the time of Simeon the Hasmonean, the *Ḥever ha-Yᵉhudim* served as the governing body which decided questions of religious worship in the Temple, the issue of war and peace, and matters pertaining to the political, constitutional, and legal leadership of the nation and the country. Thus Simeon and his successors were indissolubly bound to the constitutional basis of their power. In other words, government by the Hasmonean line meant the rule of the ethnarch jointly and parallel with the *Ḥever ha-Yᵉhudim*. Cutting the ties between the Hasmonean ruler and the *Ḥever ha-Yᵉhudim* would have been tantamount to undermining the constitutional basis of Hasmonean rule. The latter, under such circumstances, would thus have become illegal in the sense that overthrowing it would have become a religious duty.

In 141 B.C.E. all the above mentioned sections of the nation assembled in order to confer authority on Simeon in a binding official ceremony. The strict interpretation of the obligation which Simeon assumed on that occasion was that he would do nothing contrary to the wishes of the *Ḥever ha-Yᵉhudim* and without consulting it. In this context the term signifies the ruling body in its full complement, convened in the Great Assembly. The full *Ḥever* was presumably convoked when matters extremely vital to the nation and country were under consideration, when emergency political or military decisions had to be taken, or fundamental religious questions settled. At such times the ruler did not hesitate to summon a general assembly of the *Ḥever ha-Yᵉhudim* from the entire country.

Government, however, consists not only of making decisions in times of periodic crises, but also in day-to-day matters. Consequently, it was essential to create a governing body less unwieldy than the *Ḥever ha-Yᵉhudim*, but with full powers, equal to those of the complete body. The need gave rise, apparently as early as the time of Simeon the Hasmonean, to a new governing body which in the talmudic sources[7] is called the Court of the Hasmoneans. This Court was not intended to displace *Ḥever ha-Yᵉhudim*. That large body remained even after the establishment of the Court of the Hasmoneans as the supreme governing body alongside the Hasmonean High Priest. There is evidence for this in the coins of the High Priests of that dynasty until Hyrcanus II on which *Ḥever ha-Yᵉhudim* is inscribed next to the name of the High Priest.[8] The new conclave came to meet the urgent need for a governing body, limited in size, to sit alongside the High Priest and take the place of the cumbersome *Ḥever* in dealing with day-to-day affairs; its decisions possessed full legal validity as if they had been laid down by the full *Ḥever ha-Yᵉhudim* meeting in a Great Assembly.

The composition of this Court is a perplexing question. One point should be clear: since the Court of the Hasmoneans was designed to fulfil the function of a reduced *Ḥever ha-Yᵉhudim*, its structure had to parallel that of the *Ḥever*. This had to be so since it was not a court in the limited sense of the word, adjudicating only upon religious matters or just in civil cases. Rather, it performed all the executive functions of the *Ḥever ha-Yᵉhudim*, in the religious, military, political, and administrative spheres. It is thus reasonable to assume that the Court of the Hasmoneans was a facsimile of the *Ḥever ha-Yᵉhudim*. The designation, "Court of the Hasmoneans," shows that it was constituted by the Hasmonean High Priest and ethnarch. Consequently, the Hasmonean ruler could determine the character of the constitutional body to which he was bound, and adapt and even subordinate it to the political line he found desirable.

It would appear, however, that Simeon did not abuse this possibility. Everything that we know of him and his rule indicates that in his time neither unity nor peace were disturbed either in the full *Ḥever ha-Yᵉhudim* or in its component part. Simeon was very popular with all groups of the people because in governing he remained faithful to the terms stipulated at the National Assembly of 141 B.C.E. Evidence to it is the paean extolling Simeon by the author of I Maccabees, 14:4–15.[9] The first Hasmonean ethnarch not only did not try to usurp the prerogatives of the members of the *Ḥever ha-Yᵉhudim* and its bodies, but he even maintained an equilibrium among them. These efforts of his were expressed, it seems, in the fact that he fixed an equal number of members for all three aforementioned bodies of the Court of the Hasmoneans. The nature of this number seems to have been preserved in an authentic tradition of the Mishnah. According to this tradition, a Small Court (*Beth Din Qaṭan*) numbered three, five, or seven members, a Small Sanhedrin (*Sanhedrin Qᵉṭana*) twenty-three, and the Great Sanhedrin (*Sanhedrin ha-Gᵉdola*) seventy-one.[10] The basic number was probably seven. If that is the case, then a Small Sanhedrin consisted of twenty-one members (three times seven) in addition to the president (*Nasi*) and his deputy (*Av Beth Din*).[11] The Great Sanhedrin consisted of this number multiplied by three, i.e., sixty-nine, plus a president and his deputy, so that altogether the Great Sanhedrin comprised seventy-one persons.[12]

These arrangements, which are cited in the Mishnah, appear to be ancient. We shall probably not err if we attribute them to Simeon the

Hasmonean, and regard them as an important link in the general structure of the independent Hasmonean state which arose in his time. The most important achievement in Simeon's domestic policy was undoubtedly his creation of the young state's administrative and legal machinery, for only thus could it be put on a firm footing and overcome the chaos which had prevailed during the long years of war. Simeon's first step was to fix, unequivocally and firmly, the relative strength of the forces in the Court of the Hasmoneans, since this institution fulfilled the function of the full *Ḥever ha-Yᵉhudim*. This could only be done by stabilizing the number of members of each of the elements which constituted the Court. In the above-cited tradition, preserved in the Mishnah, we find an echo of the decision of Simeon the Hasmonean; we have every reason to assume that he set the number of members in each of the bodies of the Court of the Hasmoneans at twenty-three, adding to their total the president of the court and his deputy to make the entire Court consist of seventy-one members. This Court was the supreme authority in the state, with powers to make decisions in all important matters. It was also called the Great Court (*Beth Din ha-Gadol*). The activity of this Supreme Court made it unneccessary to convene the *Ḥever ha-Yᵉhudim* in its full national composition. Only in extraordinary situations, such as when the country and the nation were in danger, or when cardinal religious matters were involved, was the National Assembly, i.e., the *Ḥever ha-Yᵉhudim* in its full complement, asked to hand down a decision, as was the case in the year 141.

A central government does not normally deal with matters of mere local importance. Such affairs require a special governmental arm, and Simeon met this need by establishing small courts of twenty-three men in the cities, and of seven (or five, or even three) in the small towns. He himself was accustomed to visit various places and to see to it that things were properly run.[13]

As the Hasmonean state developed at home and in its foreign relations, far-reaching changes occurred in the central body of Hasmonean power. First of all, the ancient and original Hebrew name of the governing body — the "Court of the Hasmoneans" — practically disappeared and only a faint memory of it has been preserved in the two talmudic passages quoted above.[14] The other Hebrew name — *Bet Din ha-Gadol* — also began giving way to the Greek name συνέδριον Hebraicized as "Sanhedrin." This new name for the governing body of the nation appears for the first time in our non-Hebrew sources during Herod's reign: young Herod was summoned to appear before the Sanhedrin in Jerusalem to answer for the murder of Hezekiah the Galilean and his comrades (*Ant.* XIV, 168–76).

But there is every reason to believe that the name was not introduced into Judea only in the days of Herod. It was doubtlessly employed by the government and the people beginning with the period of Simeon's successors, perhaps already in the time of John Hyrcanus. This was when Hellenistic influence began to leave its imprint on the politics of the Hasmonean dynasty, and various Hellenistic concepts with respect to the army and public administration began to penetrate in growing numbers the Jewish body politic. However, inasmuch as the Hasmonean kingdom, despite Hellenistic influences in various spheres, remained Hebraic in its general internal structure and its administrative character, as will be seen later, the name *Beth Din ha-Gadol* was presumably not entirely supplanted by the Hellenistic term and the two designations remained in official use until Herod's power was firmly established. Evidence of this may be found in the fact that even the name *Ḥever ha-Yᵉhudim* did not fall into disuse but appeared regularly on the coins struck by the Hasmoneans until the end of the dynasty and ceased to exist together with it.

It may be assumed that insofar as the Hasmonean High Priests failed to convene the *Ḥever ha-Yᵉhudim* in its early sense as the Great National Assembly (ἐκκλησία μεγάλη), and the *Beth Din ha-Gadol* (the initial "Court of the Hasmoneans") began to function in its stead and perform its full legal function (see above), the name *Ḥever ha-Yᵉhudim* came to be applied to the *Beth Din ha-Gadol*. In the course of time the two terms became synonymous. The two names apparently served different purposes, even though both of them referred to the central government of the nation: to the outside world the central governing body of the Hasmoneans was designated as *Ḥever ha-Yᵉhudim* (in negotiations with foreign states and on coins), while within the country it was called alternately, perhaps as early as the end of John Hyrcanus' rule, *Beth Din ha-Gadol* and *Sanhedrin*.

The Sanhedrin (*Beth Din ha-Gadol*) in the Hasmonean period was quite obviously fundamentally different in character from the institution of the same name which existed during the time of Herod and thereafter. The Hasmonean Sanhedrin was a political body, that is, the central governmental tool of the nation, which together with the Hasmonean High Priest-King functioned as a legislative body by virtue of its constitutional prerogatives; the post-Hasmonean Sanhedrin ceased to be a political body, simply becoming a judicial-religious institution. The Hasmonean Sanhedrin, which was composed of all the important classes in the nation, reflected the political reality of Judea, i.e., the relation of the classes to one another and the relation of all of them to the Hasmonean ruler. With the end of the Hasmonean dynasty this character of the Sanhedrin faded away until it finally disappeared in the time of Herod. All that remained was the religious function or, at best, a faint shadow of previous activities.

It is therefore a mistake to try to reconstruct the administrative procedures in force in the Sanhedrin during the Hasmonean period on the basis of the material which has been preserved in the talmudic sources and in the Mishnah. These sources are most familiar with practices current in the Sanhedrin in the post-Hasmonean period. Such practices were for the most part undoubtedly the outgrowth of new development in the life of the country which had begun with the decline of the Hasmonean dynasty. Only a minute part of them may, perhaps, be attributed to the earlier period.[15]

As noted above, so long as Simeon the Hasmonean ruled there were no upheavals in the country and there was no deterioration in the relations between the people and their central government on the one hand, and the ethnarch on the other. Simeon was a ruler who did not deviate from the obligations imposed on him by the constitution of 141, and for this reason he left behind a good name in Jewish literary tradition.

This state of affairs did not end when John Hyrcanus came to power. Simeon's son seems to have continued for many years to govern in the tradition which he had received and made no attempt to introduce changes in the Sanhedrin by curtailing its authority, or by shifting the center of gravity in the Sanhedrin to the side he favored.

However, that which John Hyrcanus deliberately refrained from doing during the early period of his rule came about as a result of the internal development of the Hasmonean state after the death of Simeon. This development bore within it the seed of the upheavals which flared up towards the end of John Hyrcanus' life and to an even greater degree, during the reign of King Jannaeus Alexander. Responsible for it was the Hellenistic influence which had penetrated the various components of the Hasmonean state and substantially changed its character. This change was expressed mainly in two matters: first in the general administration of the country; but even more in the preferential treatment of the military — a direct corollary of the Hasmonean policy of conquest. These facts compelled John Hyrcanus to deviate at the end of his rule from the arrangement in the Sanhedrin which he had taken over from his father and which was based on an equilibrium among the representatives of the classes constituting the supreme ruling body of the nation. To understand this entire process it is necessary to review the development of the foundations of the Hasmonean state from John Hyrcanus onward. Such a survey is designed to elucidate the nature of the new element which struck root in the

Hasmonean state and led to the serious upheavals which undermined the unity that had prevailed under Simeon. Ultimately, these influences brought about the collapse of the entire structure which had been established through the labor of the people and the Hasmonean leadership.

C. The Administrative Division, the Tax System and the Military Organization

The principal elements required for the maintenance of any kind of political order in modern as well as in ancient times are as follows: a) an administration characterized by stability and a degree of order; b) a tax system with definite collection arrangements; and c) a military force to defend the country against foreign and domestic enemies.

The Hasmonean state was no exception to the rule. Like other states, it had to consider these three elements from its very inception. While not all the phases of this development are known, the general lines are entirely clear.

The basis of a well-organized political administration is the division of the state into administrative districts. This is necessary both for the preservation of law and order and for the efficient collection of taxes. The Hasmoneans were also familiar with this rule. They solved the problem that faced them in a rather original manner. The administrative division of the Hasmonean state was based on two elements: a) the Jewish, religious factor, growing out of the ancient division into *mishmarot* (i.e. shifts of priests, Levites, and Israelites assigned to assist in the Temple service) which may already have been in effect during the period of the First Temple, but in any case, obtained after the return from the Babylonian Exile; b) the foreign, Hellenistic practice of dividing a country into toparchies which the Hasmoneans inherited from the Seleucids and partly also from the Ptolemaic tradition in Palestine. The Hasmoneans utilized both systems by superimposing the secular division into toparchies onto the religious division into *mishmarot*. As a result every *mishmar* was tantamount to a toparchy. This was the rule, although in practice there were undoubtedly many exceptions. This process was initiated by Jonathan the Hasmonean, and his successors continued in his path, marking out many *mishmarot* and toparchies. In the time of Jannaeus Alexander there were no fewer than twenty-four toparchies, corresponding to the twenty-four *mishmarot*.[16]

The Hasmoneans, as we have noted, borrowed the division into toparchies from both the Seleucids and the Ptolemies. The reason no doubt was that the toparchy appeared to be an efficient administrative unit, especially for the collection of taxes. For this aspect of the government seemed progressively more vital to the Hasmoneans as they took the path of military conquest and required ever increasing sums of money in order to maintain their numerous forces of mercenaries, which served both for conquest and defense.

The principles on which the tax policy of the Hasmoneans was based and the reaction which it evoked among the people will now be discussed. Although the taxation system of the Hasmoneans is for the most part obscure, the Hasmoneans presumably levied taxes on the people according to a system which was meaningful for them. It may also be assumed that the taxes aroused the hatred of large sections of the population and their religious leaders against the rulers. In this connection it might be mentioned that in his famous order in favor of Hyrcanus II, Julius Caesar found it necessary to stress the obligation of the people to pay to the former the tithes which they had contributed to his predecessors (*Ant.* XIV, 203). This emphasis in the order of Julius Caesar clearly indicates[17] that there was strong opposition to these payments among large sections of the people. Also instructive is the serious complaint presented to Pompey by representatives of "the nation," i.e., the Pharisees (*Ant.* XIV, 41): "...while the nation . . . asked not to be ruled by a king, saying that it was the custom of their country to obey the priests of the God who was venerated by them, but that these two [Aristobulus and Hyrcanus], who were descended from the priests, were seeking to change their form of government in order that they might become a nation of slaves."

"To change their form of government" undoubtedly refers to establishing a monarchy, which the Pharisees regarded as slavery. Their view was primarily based on biblical passages in the Pentateuch (cf. Lev. 25:55 and other texts) and in the Prophets (particularly "the manner of the king" described in I Sam. 8:11–17). But this opinion of the Pharisees also resulted from their experience under the rule of the Seleucids and the Hasmonean kings. A clear idea of the tax burden imposed on the Jews by the Seleucids can be obtained from the alleviations they were granted by Demetrius I and Demetrius II (I Macc. 10:28–30; 11:34–35). True, it seems that upon the liberation of Judea in the days of Simeon most of the Seleucid taxes which had oppressed the people were repealed. But a small state cannot exist either without any taxes, and Simeon and his son John Hyrcanus also obviously taxed the people. Jewish literary tradition may have preserved details of the introduction of the tithe as a national tax by Johanan the High Priest, i.e., John Hyrcanus. The Jerusalem Talmud relates,[18] "At first the tithe was divided into three parts; one-third was given to priests and Levites known [to the donors], one-third went to the treasury, and one-third was given to the poor and to the scholars who were in Jerusalem." The *barayta* is an ancient one, and it apparently alludes to the introduction of the tithe as a tax payable to the ruler by virtue of his priesthood and his political power (this being the significance of "one-third to the treasury").[19]

This tax, it appears, was not the only one levied by John Hyrcanus. The Hasmonean policy of conquest began to assume serious proportions in his day: John Hyrcanus expanded the country's borders into Idumaea, Moab, and Samaria, and apparently got as far as Galilee. These conquests were achieved in part with the help of mercenaries who constituted a heavy drain on the treasury. And the maintenance of the Jewish forces, who were undoubtedly more numerous than the mercenaries, also required considerable funds. All these sums the people had to make available to the High Priest in the form of taxes. Nevertheless, it is safe to assume that the burden which John Hyrcanus imposed on the people was not unbearable. Despite all the conquests, the Hasmonean state was still at the beginning of its expansion and its financial needs did not exceed reasonable proportions.

The situation changed radically when Jannaeus Alexander began his wars of conquest on the eastern and western borders. These wars, which continued intermittently throughout Jannaeus' long reign, required money to an extent to which the people in Judea were not accustomed. They regarded the king as a marauder who was sucking the blood of the citizen in order to satisfy his lust for conquest. The Pharisee poet who made a point of stressing that the King Messiah would not "multiply for himself gold and silver for war"[20] meant to imply that such was not the case in his own day; the Hasmoneans, and King Jannaeus in particular, were squeezing the people dry by heavy taxes and accumulating treasures of gold and silver in order to make war on foreign countries. And evidently the Hasmonean conqueror did not hesitate to outdo his father in the amount of taxes levied on the people. Even if Jannaeus did not wish to do so, he was compelled to follow the path of the Hellenistic kings and adopt their efficient method of taxation. The closest example for Jannaeus to emulate was provided by the Seleucids. In the Seleucid kingdom there were two main types of taxes collected in cash; the φόρος, or the tax levied on subject peoples who enjoyed no special privileges, and the ἐπικεφάλαιον or poll-tax.[21] It is not likely that the φόρος was imposed by Jannaeus on the Jewish people in Judea liberated from the yoke of foreigners. Most probably such a tax was imposed in Jannaeus' kingdom only on those foreigners who refused to embrace Judaism but were nevertheless not expelled; for it is not reasonable to assume that all the foreigners who were conquered by Jannaeus were either converted or forced to leave.

On the other hand, it seems that we cannot avoid the conclusion that Jannaeus did collect an annual poll-tax from all inhabitants of the country, Jews and non-Jews alike.

The Pharisees, the spokesmen of the broad masses of the people, must have regarded the poll-tax as a direct outcome of Jannaeus' policy of conquest. Both activities — the conquests and the levying of tax — were anathema to the Pharisees, since they were not in keeping with the tradition of government by the High Priests. The latter had not aspired to excessive secular power, bent upon the conquest of unclean lands of gentiles, nor had they burdened the people with new taxes; they had observed the precepts of the Torah and judged the people in accordance with them. It was the perverted ways of the Hasmonean High Priests, so like the ways of the gentiles, that had brought on — so the Pharisees felt — all the trouble of heavy taxation which was meant to cover the cost of spilling blood in order to expand the secular power. This explains the remarks of the delegation to Pompey on behalf of "the nation" with respect to the "change" in the form of government which the Hasmoneans had imposed on the people in order to reduce them to "slaves;" the cruel exploitation of the people for the political and military needs of the Hasmonean rulers was very much like their exploitation by the Seleucids, their previous masters; in both cases it was slavery.

The third factor supporting the existence of the Hasmonean state was its military power. This element served as an instrument of defense, but to a much greater extent it was a tool of expansion and conquest.

It is quite certain that, quantitatively speaking, the Jews constituted the bulk of the armies of the Hasmonean rulers, including Jannaeus'. Among the powers which the nation vested in Simeon the Hasmonean was, as noted above, command of the popular army. This authority meant nothing unless it is assumed that the commander had the right to mobilize troops from among the people, when he deemed it necessary.[22] As the Hasmonean wars of conquest became more frequent and greater in scope, the enlistment of the Jewish inhabitants of the country was stepped up. This is particularly true of Jannaeus who waged war for thirty years and required tens of thousands of soldiers.

But the Hasmoneans could not depend solely on the citizens' army. The Jewish farmers were not professional soldiers, whereas the enemy primarily used mercenaries trained in the art of war. There was no choice but to confront these professionals with equally well-trained soldiers, and this of course meant mercenaries. Thus it came about that the Hasmonean High Priests, whose fathers had fought the Syrians and forced them out of the country, found it necessary to bring them back as mercenaries and to rely on their help in their wars of conquest. This was the course adopted by John Hyrcanus and, on a much wider scale, by Jannaeus Alexander.

D. The Rift between John Hyrcanus and the Pharisees

It was only natural that the policy of conquest, which was a central element in the regimes of the Hasmoneans who succeeded Simeon, led to far-reaching changes in the structure of Jewish society. As this policy took root, there was a corresponding rise in the importance of those groups which approved of it and helped carry it out by actively participating in the establishment of the military power and in the campaigns of conquest. These circles belonged mainly to the noble and wealthy families, whose representatives sat in the *Ḥever ha-Yᵉhudim* (the Sanhedrin) as "princes of the nation" (ἄρχοντες τοῦ λαοῦ; cf. above) and who cooperated with the Hasmonean High Priest and King in matters of foreign and domestic policy. As supporters of the policy of conquest, these nobles constituted an elite military caste which belonged to the inner circle of the Hasmonean ruler. These men not only accompanied him in battle but also served him as a privy council in time of peace when important political decisions had to be taken.[23]

The noble families were the principal force within the nation on whom the Hasmonean conquerors could rely. Particularly important was the support given by the representatives of these circles, who sat in the Sanhedrin, to the policy of conquest. It is hardly likely that the early Hasmonean rulers, that is, Simeon and John Hyrcanus, were free to go to war — even if it were only for expansionist purposes — without consulting the Sanhedrin. It was therefore of decisive importance that the central governing body of the nation should contain at least one group backing the policy of the rulers. With the progressive crystallization of the policy of conquest in the time of John Hyrcanus, its endorsement by the nobles in the Sanhedrin became increasingly necessary. For it must be assumed that the relations within the Sanhedrin became more and more strained as the wars against the pagan countries intensified under John Hyrcanus. The scholars who sat in the Sanhedrin began to be apprehensive about the influence of idolatry among the people, and they opposed the policy of the Hasmonean High Priest, designed to enlarge the area of the country

at the expense of the gentiles. We learn (Yer. Shab. 1, 4) that "Jose ben
Jo'ezer of Zereda and Jose ben Johanan of Jerusalem decreed that the
heathen countries and glassware should be subject to uncleanness." This
prohibition, it would seem, reflects the internal struggle within the *Hever
ha-Y*hudim* at the time of John Hyrcanus — when this "pair" of rabbis was
active[24] — between the Sages, i.e., the Pharisees, who opposed the aggressive
policy of the Hasmonean High Priest and ethnarch, and the representatives
of the nobles, i.e., the Sadducees, who supported the growing conquests
of the territories occupied by the gentiles. It was only natural for John
Hyrcanus to regard the Sadducees as his allies, for he realized that without
their help his hands would be tied and he would be unable to carry out
his plans. For this reason he moved closer and closer to the representatives
of the aristocracy within the *Hever ha-Y*hudim* until he finally decided to
take a decisive step: he abandoned the policy inherited from his father
Simeon, of maintaining a balance of power within the central council of the
nation and shifted the center of gravity to the Sadducean "princes of the
nation" by openly going over to their side. This is the historic fact which
underlies the statement in the Babylonian Talmud (B*r. 29a) that "Johanan
the High Priest [John Hyrcanus] officiated as High Priest for eighty years
[forty, according to another version, but actually it was thirty], and in
the end became a Sadducee."

The change which took place in John Hyrcanus' attitude towards the
Pharisees and his joining the representatives of the aristocracy in the *Hever
ha-Y*hudim* are described in two sources in the style of a semi-legendary
tale. These sources are particularly important because they call our
attention to the fact that in addition to the political-social reason described
above, the rift within the *Hever ha-Y*hudim* in the days of John Hyrcanus
also involved an aspect connected with John Hyrcanus personally. One
version of the story has been preserved in Josephus' *Antiquities* (XIII,
288–98). It reads as follows:

> John Hyrcanus once invited the Pharisees to a feast, and when
> he saw that they were having a very good time, he began by
> saying that they knew he wished to be righteous and in every-
> thing he did to please God and them — for the Pharisees profess
> such beliefs; at the same time he begged them, if they observed
> him doing anything wrong or straying from the right path,
> to lead him back to it and correct him. But they testified to
> his being altogether virtuous, and he was delighted with their
> praise. However, one of the guests, named Eleazar, who had an

evil nature and took pleasure in dissension, said: 'Since you have asked to be told the truth, if you wish to be righteous, give up the High Priesthood and be content with governing the people.' And when Hyrcanus asked him for what reason he should give up the High Priesthood, he replied: 'Because we have heard from our elders that your mother was a captive in the reign of Antiochus Epiphanes.' But the story was false, and Hyrcanus was furious with the man, while all the Pharisees were very indignant. Then a certain Jonathan, one of Hyrcanus' close friends, belonging to the school of the Sadducees, who hold opinions opposed to those of the Pharisees, said that it had been with the general approval of all the Pharisees that Eleazar made his slanderous statement; and this, he added, would be clear to Hyrcanus if he inquired of them what punishment Eleazar deserved for what he had said. And so Hyrcanus asked the Pharisees what penalty they thought he deserved — for, he said, he would be convinced that the slanderous statement had not been made with their approval if they fixed a penalty commensurate with the crime — and they replied that Eleazar deserved stripes and chains; for they did not think it right to sentence a man to death for calumny, and anyway the Pharisees are naturally lenient in the matter of punishments. At this Hyrcanus became very angry and began to believe that the fellow had slandered him with their approval. And Jonathan in particular inflamed his anger, and so worked upon him that he brought him to join the Sadducean party and desert the Pharisees, and to abrogate the regulations which they had established for the people, and punish those who observed them. Out of this, of course, grew the hatred of the masses for him and his sons.

In the continuation of the story, Josephus says (*ibid.*, 299–300) that John Hyrcanus managed to appease the people and end his rule in peace, leaving behind a good name.

The second version is found in a *barayta* in the Babylonian Talmud (Qid. 66a), and both in its general content and in many of the details it is very similar to the story in Josephus. The *barayta* reads as follows:

It once happened that King Yannai [Jannaeus] went to Koḥalith in the wilderness and conquered sixty towns there. On his return he rejoiced exceedingly and invited all the Sages of Israel. Said he to them, 'Our forefathers ate mallows when they were engaged in the building of the [second] Temple; let us too eat mallows in memory of our forefathers.' So mallows were served on golden tables, and they ate. Now, there was a man there, frivolous, evil-hearted and worthless, named Eleazar ben Po'yra, who said to King Yannai, 'O King Yannai, the hearts of the Pharisees are against thee.' 'Then what shall I do?' 'Test them by the plate between thine eyes.' So he tested them by the plate between his eyes. Now, an elder, named Judah ben Gᵉdidya, was present there. Said he to King Yannai, 'O King Yannai! let the royal crown suffice thee, and leave the priestly crown to the seed of Aaron.' (For it was rumored that his mother had been taken captive in Modiin.) Accordingly, the charge was investigated, but not sustained, and the Sages of Israel departed in anger. Then said Eleazar ben Po'yra to King Yannai: 'O King Yannai! That is the law even for the most humble man in Israel, and thou, a King and a High Priest, shall that be thy law [too]?' 'Then what shall I do?' 'If thou wilt take my advice, trample them down.' 'But what shall happen with the Torah?' 'Behold, it is written down[25] and lying in the corner: whoever wishes to study, let him go and study!' . . . Straightway, the evil burst forth through Eleazar ben Po'yra, all the Sages of Israel were massacred, and the world was desolate until Simeon ben Sheṭaḥ came and restored the Torah to its pristine [glory].

Even though the *barayta* speaks of "King Yannai," that is Jannaeus, too much importance should not be attributed to the difference in the name of the Hasmonean ruler in the two sources. There is every reason to assume that the Talmud, like Josephus, is referring to John Hyrcanus.[26]

Both versions of the story revolve about the demand of one of the Pharisees (according to Josephus his name was Eleazar, and this must be the Eleazar ben Po'yra of the *barayta*; however, in the *barayta* the demand to relinquish the priesthood is attributed to Judah ben Gᵉdidya) to separate the crown from the priesthood, with the Hasmoneans retaining only the former. But there is a significant difference between the two versions. The *barayta* speaks of the priesthood as such, without qualification. In other words, the Pharisee demanded that the Hasmonean ruler renounce not only the High Priesthood but the priesthood as such, and leave it "to the seed of Aaron." The implication is that the Hasmonean is not of the seed of Aaron the Priest: he had been profaned because of his mother having been taken captive at Modiin!

Josephus, on the other hand, relates that Eleazar demanded that John Hyrcanus relinquish the High Priesthood and be content with the royal crown.

It seems that the correct tradition has been preserved in the *barayta* and that Josephus misinterpreted the excellent source he had before him[27] by rendering it "High Priesthood" instead of "priesthood."

Nevertheless, it would appear that Josephus' version retains indications of the true tradition. According to *Antiquities*, John Hyrcanus received the Pharisees in a friendly manner and emphasized that "they knew he wished to be righteous,"[28] and he begged them that if they observed him "straying from the right path,[29] to lead him back to it and correct him;" and then Eleazar rose and told John Hyrcanus that if he wished "to be righteous"[30] he should give up the "High Priesthood."

This emphasis in the words of the Hasmonean cited in *Antiquities* is lacking in the talmudic tale. But it is precisely this emphasis which is part of the true, early tradition concerning the episode and it fits in with the version of the Pharisees' demand related in the *barayta* in Qiddushin. For we must ask: what reason did John Hyrcanus have for stressing his "righteousness" to the Pharisees? It seems that this aspect of the narrative in *Antiquities* reflects the dispute between John Hyrcanus and the Pharisee extremists who denied his being of the seed of Aaron, and regarded him profaned owing to the rumor that his mother had been taken captive in Modiin. In order to refute that assertion, John Hyrcanus asked the Pharisee Sages to express their opinion on his "righteousness," and by so doing admit that he was a legitimate priest and his priesthood lawful and righteous. Such an expression of opinion about the "righteousness" of his priesthood was very important to John Hyrcanus because of the Scriptural text which explicitly links "righteousness" with the priesthood (cf. Ps. 132:9).[31]

It is most likely that the gathering described in both stories we are considering was convoked by John Hyrcanus in order to put an end to the slanderous campaign being waged against him by an extreme wing of the Pharisees and to obtain the confirmation of his priesthood by the Sages. But what happened was the exact opposite of what he had expected. His adversaries found an opportune moment to hurl all their venom in his face. This personal attack revealed to John Hyrcanus the gulf that separated him from the Pharisees and it hastened the split between the two sides. The Hasmonean realized that not only matters of foreign policy but also domestic affairs connected with him personally urgently required that he sever altogether his connection with the Pharisees and join the Sadducees.

The effects of that decision were felt in the *Ḥever ha-Yᵉhudim* (Sanhedrin) and in the entire country. It appears that John Hyrcanus removed many of the Pharisees from the *Ḥever ha-Yᵉhudim* on suspicion of their being hostile to him personally and to his foreign policy plans, and replaced them with Sadducees. This additional strength in the central council of the nation provided the Hasmonean with a firm guarantee that his will would not be frustrated by dangerous adversaries who relied primarily on their religious influence among the masses. In order to reduce this influence as much as possible, John Hyrcanus issued a decree annulling a number of regulations which had been promulgated by the Pharisees. We learn that "Johanan the High Priest set aside the confession of the tithes. He also abolished the wakers and the strikers. Until his days the hammer used to beat in Jerusalem. And in his days one had no need to enquire concerning *dᵉmai*."[32] The *mishnah* is obscure, and the rabbis have struggled to discover the correct interpretation.[33]

The reference to the tithes was construed to mean that only if the tithe was actually presented was a confession made. The wakers were believed to be the persons whose duty it was to proclaim, "Awake, why sleepest Thou, O Lord? Arouse Thyself, cast not off for ever" (Ps. 44:24). The rabbis explained this to mean either that the Jews happened to be in distress or that the reference was to the Lord's sleeping when the Jews provoked Him (Job 17:2). The rabbis also advanced various explanations concerning the "strikers" who struck the sacrificial calf between the horns, despite the view that this act rendered the animal ritually unfit. Referring to the hammer beating in Jerusalem, the rabbis explained that this meant at the beginning of John Hyrcanus' incumbency. They also held that it was no longer necessary to inquire concerning the *dᵉmai* — the grain of doubtful tithing — since there were now "pairs" of scholars beginning with Jose ben Jo'ezer and Jose ben Johanan.[34]

Even though these interpretations are supported by quite an ancient tradition, they seem artificial and implausible. The rabbis tried to interpret the ancient regulations which were not clear to them, but they apparently had no real knowledge of the subject. Hence, it may be assumed that they are merely passing on conjectures which they received from their predecessors, rather than explanations reflecting a reliable and correct tradition. This is particularly true of the explanations of "the wakers" and "the strikers." These interpretations impress us as being midrashic in nature, without a trace of fact.[35]

However, a closer examination of the *mishnah* in question may show that it actually deals with only one consistent subject: the abolition of a number of matters connected with tithing. The beginning of the *mishnah* states that "Johanan the High Priest" set aside the confession of the tithes, reference being to the second tithe (Deut. 26:12-15). This regulation was instituted, it seems, after John Hyrcanus inaugurated a new arrangement in the payment of tithes in general; as stated in the Jerusalem Talmud in the above-cited reference, the tithe was divided into three parts — one-third was given to priests and Levites who were known to the donors, one-third went to the treasury, and one-third was given to the poor and to the scholars in Jerusalem, who were no doubt also included among the needy. This procedure was carried on in compliance with the wishes of the authorities, most likely on behalf of the *Hever ha-Yehudim* (Sanhedrin), and in particular on behalf of Johanan, the High Priest and head of the *Hever ha-Yehudim*. Thus, there was no longer any need for the confession of each individual, since the authorities saw to it that the tithes were really allocated. The Pharisees were dissatisfied with this regulation, or, more precisely, with the abolition of the confession of tithes. They regarded this act as a serious violation of an explicit precept of the Torah, and they denounced the Hasmonean High Priest who had presumed to do so.[36] The abolition of the confession of tithes apparently also brought in its wake the annulment of a number of customs which depended on the allocation of the tithes.

An important principle, which was observed from the beginning of the Second Temple period, was that every religious practice incumbent on the majority of the population should originate from the central religious body of the nation, that is, from the *Beth Din ha-Gadol*. This seems to have been the custom as early as the time of Ezra and Nehemiah: the Feast of Tabernacles was celebrated in accordance with instructions from "the heads of fathers' houses of all the people, the priests, and the Levites" and from Ezra.[37] Throughout the Second Temple period the fixing of the leap year and the sanctification of the new moon were also accomplished on the instructions of the central authority. Most probably the matter of tithes and the question of *demai* were among the subjects the observance of which at the proper time also engaged the attention of the chief religious authority of the nation. When the time came for allocating the tithe and it was necessary to inquire about *demai*, the *Beth Din ha-Gadol* would send specially appointed persons to inform the people of Jerusalem and of the entire country, in the name of the authorities, that they were required to allocate the tithe.[38] These agents of the Court — so it seems — were dubbed "wakers" and "strikers," apparently because they prompted the people to fulfil their duty, both by reprimanding them and by striking on the doors of their houses with a stick. The Court did not content itself with that and ordered that the time for allocating tithes also be publicly announced in another manner: the streets of Jerusalem would be struck with a hammer as a sign that it was time for tithing.

This interpretation sheds light on the statement in the *mishnah* that Johanan the High Priest abolished the "wakers" and the "strikers", that until his time the hammer used to beat in Jerusalem, and that in his days there was no longer any need to inquire concerning *d·mai*.

The "wakers" and the "strikers" as well as the hammer that used to beat in Jerusalem until the days of Johanan the High Priest thus served the *Beth Din ha-Gadol* as a means of proclaiming the allocation of tithes and of sounding a warning in the period that preceded the time of John Hyrcanus.

However, this warning and announcement by the central authority was entirely devoid of any coercive character. The allocation of tithes was actually left to each individual. As the Jerusalem Talmud says (Ma'as. Sh. 5, 9). "There were those who did allocate [tithes] and there were those who did not."

This was the state of affairs when John Hyrcanus decided to assume the responsibility of seeing to it that the precept was actually observed. As pointed out above, it was Johanan the High Priest who introduced a new arrangement for tithing; the act was implemented on behalf of the authorities, and accordingly, the method of its execution was changed. No longer was there any need for "wakers" and "strikers," nor for the hammer that previously used to beat in Jerusalem. John Hyrcanus, the vigorous Hasmonean High Priest and ethnarch, did not hesitate to abolish these obsolete methods of bringing the matter to the attention of the people, which were not suited to the new state.

The same applies to the necessity of inquiring about *d·mai*. Since the tithe had become the responsibility of the central authority there was no longer any need to inquire about *d·mai*, for everyone concerned with strict observation of the precept could rely on the government to do its duty.[39] This explanation of the obscure *mishnah* may very well supplement the important information supplied by Josephus at the end of his account of the split between John Hyrcanus and the Pharisees, namely, that after he joined the Sadducees, John Hyrcanus abrogated the regulations of the Pharisees and imposed penalties on those who observed them (*Ant.* XIII, 296). Josephus did not explain the nature of the Pharisee regulations which were abolished by John Hyrcanus. It seems that we will not err if we juxtapose the *mishnah* interpreted above with the information preserved in Josephus' *Antiquities*.

John Hyrcanus' reason for abolishing the regulations of the Pharisees is quite clear: the Hasmonean High Priest intended to deprive the Pharisees of the initiative in religious matters, thereby curtailing their great influence with the masses. Since he not only held the highest political office in the nation, i.e., the ethnarchy, but also the supreme religious office, the High Priesthood, he wished to be the real mover and doer also in matters of religious observance. This he wished to achieve not in accordance with the regulations of the Pharisees, but with those of their rivals, and he acted to weaken their influence among the masses after their power had already been reduced in the *Ḥever ha-Yᵉhudim* (Sanhedrin).

The practical significance of this turn of events was a decline in the prestige of the Pharisaic *halaḵa* and the rise of the Sadducean *halaḵa* as a determining factor in the life of the people. Such a development was doubtlessly a bitter blow for the Pharisees and they most likely tried to prevent it at any price. They were apparently willing to compromise, and this would explain the statement of Josephus that precisely after the serious break between John Hyrcanus and the Pharisees there was peace between them which lasted the rest of his lifetime. Moreover, the entire Jewish literary tradition testifies to the fact that the same man who after having served as High Priest for "eighty" or "forty" years and "in the end became a Sadducee," was in the last analysis regarded as "originally righteous."

E. Internal Developments in the Hasmonean State under Jannaeus Alexander

However, the breach was healed only on the surface; deep down the rift gnawed at the nation and the quarrel gathered momentum. For even if the personal differences between the High Priest John Hyrcanus and the Pharisees were smoothed out in the *Ḥever ha-Yᵉhudim*, there were still differences of principle which could not be glossed over. This conflict had no connection whatsoever with the personality of the Hasmonean High Priest, but stemmed from the internal transformations which began to evolve in the Hasmonean state in the first half of John Hyrcanus' rule. It is quite clear that these changes were an expression of the internal logic in the development of the Hasmonean revolution from a fighting religious movement to a national-political movement with an aggressive attitude towards the neighboring countries at whose expense it strove with ever-increasing vigor to expand. This development did not originate in the strong will and arbitrariness of a masterful individual, and it could not be halted by his decree. The course of events in revolutionary Judea was determined in 162 B.C.E. When it became obvious that the Hasmonean party was not satisfied with the religious freedom that it had achieved, but was striving to attain political and national freedom and to establish a state independent of the Seleucid kingdom, the path of future development was absolutely clear. This path led to the establishment of a Judean kingdom on a par with other kingdoms, that is, a kingdom based like them on military and economic power, on conquests and expansion at the expense of its neighbors, on the one hand, and on mounting administrative strength under the leadership of the ruling dynasty and of the rich and powerful families, on the other. These paramount factors — the development of the army and of the economy, the conquest of countries which were large in proportion to the area of the Jews until the Hasmonean revolt, and the establishment of a new administration under the leadership of the rulers and the aristocracy — inevitably led to a deep change in the life of the people. Conspicuous signs of this change appeared during the rule of John Hyrcanus. The most important was the new attitude of this Hasmonean High Priest towards the traditional policy within the *Ḥever ha-Yᵉhudim*. The policy which John Hyrcanus inherited from his father, Simeon, has been defined as the maintenance of a balance of power in the *Ḥever ha-Yᵉhudim*. But owing to the rise in the prestige and importance of the rich and prominent families in the expanding state, John Hyrcanus found it necessary, as we have seen above, to abandon that policy and rely on the upper-class families which supported his conquests. The Talmud sums up the change in Hyrcanus' attitude in a few telling words: "and in the end he became a Sadducee."

However, this development was then only in its incipient stage. The Hasmonean dynasty had just begun to carry out its task of converting the narrow area occupied by the Jews into a state expanding to the east and to the west and having the dimensions of all of Palestine. The goal was reached at the end of Jannaeus Alexander's reign. But at the same time, the changes within the Jewish society which began to appear at the time of John Hyrcanus reached their culmination, and the crisis burst out in the open. As a matter of fact, even Jannaeus' kingdom was originally based on important elements of the conventional internal order of the nation. We have seen that the administrative divisions of the Hasmonean state were based on a synthesis of the religious subdivision into *mishmarot* (shifts of priests) and *maʿamadot* (deputies of the laymen) and the division into toparchies based on Seleucid-Ptolemaic example. The development was a protracted one, and it ended, as noted above, in the days of Jannaeus

Alexander, who set the number of toparchies at twenty-four, as against twenty-four *mishmarot*.[40] This parallelism was by no means fortuitous. A religious nuance in Jannaeus' policy of conquest was also discovered by Klein with respect to the cities of asylum.[41]

It may well be Jannaeus hit upon the idea of setting the number of the country's administrative units at twenty-four, as against the twenty-four units of the religious administration, in order to forge a link between the religious and the political order in the Hasmonean kingdom and to win favor with the Pharisee circles who manifested deep hostility to him. Jannaeus established a kingdom which approximated the dimensions of King David's, and he may have wished to divide it into twenty-four secular administrative units as against the twenty-four units of the traditional religious division in the early Israelite kingdom. It is reasonable to assume that Jannaeus resorted to this way of securing the good-will of the Pharisees only towards the end of his reign,[42] but there is no doubt that his kingdom had originally been built on strong religious foundations. The Pharisees' denunciation of him stemmed to a very large degree from partisan conflict.

This is not to say that all of the Pharisees' charges were false or exaggerated. Consciously or otherwise, Jannaeus deviated from the framework of government which the Pharisees favored, and he drew ever closer to the practices of the Hellenistic monarchs in administering the Hasmonean state; this applied both to foreign and domestic affairs, but above all, to the Hellenistic conception of his kingdom, which pretended to be the Kingdom of Israel.

With respect to domestic policy, it may be said that the administration absorbed further Hellenistic elements in Jannaeus' time, despite the fact that it was precisely this ruler who perfected and expanded the existing administrative division of the country and strengthened its Jewish character by fixing the number of toparchies at twenty-four, as against the twenty-four *mishmarot*. Even though definite information that the government administration in Judea was composed of unmistakably Hellenistic elements dates only from Herod's period,[43] there is no doubt that Jannaeus admitted considerable Hellenistic influences into the administration of his state. This was a necessary consequence of the policy of conquest which Jannaeus pursued throughout his long reign. At the end of Jannaeus' time the Hasmonean state attained proportions never dreamt of by the early Hasmoneans,[44] and it was only natural that the conquered areas should require a ramified and well-ordered bureaucracy. This need was felt primarily in the area of tax collection. Although there is no explicit testimony on this point, it is obvious that the Hasmonean conquerors (and in particular Jannaeus, who more than his predecessors realized that the extent of his conquests made efficient administration a vital need) learned the art of administration from countries in which this talent was most developed, that is, from Ptolemaic Egypt and the Seleucid state (even though the latter was undergoing a steady decline while the Hasmonean dynasty was growing in strength). The Hellenistic elements were felt in tax policy,[45] in municipal administration — particularly in the administration of the conquered gentile cities — and, it would appear, in land policy as well.

With respect to the administration of the conquered gentile cities, it is sheer exaggeration to say that the practical effect of Jannaeus' conquests was nothing but destruction.[46] Only those gentile cities were laid waste which were conquered in the storm of war and whose inhabitants refused to embrace Judaism.[47] Moreover, it is very doubtful whether even in these cases Jannaeus always followed this rule inflexibly. He was probably not unaware of the loss to his treasury caused by the ravage of the gentile towns and villages which he conquered and the annihilation of their population. Most of these places were presumably allowed to stand undamaged, on condition that they pay tribute to the Hasmonean conqueror. It is also likely that the orderly administrative machinery functioning in the gentile cities since the times of Ptolemaic and Seleucid rule was not abolished, but was retained and served the needs of Jannaeus' treasury. To what extent the Hellenistic bureaucracy of the gentile cities which came under Jannaeus' rule exerted an influence on the administration of Jerusalem in particular, and of the ancient Jewish settlements in general, is not known. But there is no reason to suppose that no change at all took place. Hellenistic influence was undoubtedly also felt in the strictly Jewish areas of Jannaeus' kingdom; all that is open to question is the extent of this influence.

We may safely assume that there was also considerable Hellenistic influence in King Jannaeus' land policy. That policy became a matter of cardinal importance in Jannaeus' time because the land holdings of the king were increasing constantly owing to the widespread conquests. The property of the gentiles who were killed, expelled or subdued by the sword was for the most part expropriated, becoming the possession of the conqueror. First of all, Jannaeus came into the real property of the conquered gentile cities. By virtue of the ancient law of war and the Hellenistic view of the rights of the victor, the land conquered from the gentiles in the coastal plain of Western Palestine and in Transjordan became the personal property of the Hasmonean king.[48]

What did King Jannaeus do with the extensive areas which fell into his hands? Part of them, the land of highest quality, no doubt became his private property. This custom had already been followed in the ancient kingdoms of the East, such as the Persia of the Achaemenidae,[49] and the Hellenistic conquerors had taken it over *in toto*.[50] There is no reason to believe that Jannaeus did not follow their example. The best of the conquered lands were transferred to the Hasmonean dynasty in the time of King Jannaeus and thus constituted an important supplement to its great wealth. It may be that the expression "the king's mountain," which is applied in talmudic and midrashic literature to a good part of the hills of Judea and Ephraim, has its origin in the fact that these areas were the private property of the king, Jannaeus it seems.[51]

But it is beyond doubt clear that Jannaeus did not take *all* of these areas for himself. Even after he appropriated the first-rate land, large tracts still remained which he could dispose of as he pleased. It is reasonable to suppose that these surplus lands served Jannaeus as a most important and convenient instrument for the furtherance of an efficient and beneficial domestic policy. Jannaeus made use of these extra lands in his possession to facilitate the implementation of his daring plan of conquest both militarily and financially. He apparently did not pass out the land to all those who wanted some, but distributed it only to persons who accepted certain military obligations, particularly the duty to take part in the king's battles in time of need. Jannaeus was above all a soldier and during his long reign he needed fighting men. The farmers who obtained lands from the king did not thereby become military settlers, in the style of the κληροῦχοι in Ptolemaic Egypt. It appears more likely that Jannaeus followed the system laid down by the Seleucid agricultural settlement policy: the Seleucid kings settled farmers on the surplus land of the ruler[52] and granted them certain privileges in the first few years, for example, he reduced their taxes (sometimes up to ten years), built houses[53] for them and provided them with similar benefits; the only obligation imposed on them in return was to supply the king with soldiers in time of need.[54] It may be assumed than an important goal of Jannaeus was to bolster the security of the conquered land by settling Jewish farmers in its midst: this was the practice of the Seleucids in certain cases when the security of the country required the support of elements loyal to the government.[55] Evidently Jannaeus also followed this method in order to establish security and peace in the areas conquered from the gentiles in the coastal plain to the west, and in Transjordan to the east.[56]

In addition to the military aspect, it appears that there was also a financial factor involved in Jannaeus' utilization of his surplus lands. The protracted military campaigns and the maintenance of mercenaries obviously constituted a heavy expense. Consequently, Jannaeus was constantly, both in war and peace, in need of large sums of money, and there is no doubt that he sought new sources. One of these, as we have seen above, were the taxes he levied on the people. But it is unlikely that these sums were sufficient to cover all his needs, which were increasing in keeping with the expansion of the kingdom from year to year. It thus appears that Jannaeus did not hesitate to convert part of the land he owned into cash by selling plots to anyone who was willing to buy. This use of χώρα βασιλική was practiced in the Seleucid kingdom.[57] The Seleucid kings used to sell part of their domains in periods of financial difficulty, for example in times of war, when the royal treasury was empty and there was urgent need of funds to pay mercenaries.[58] The lands that were sold became the private property of the purchasers.[59] Jannaeus apparently followed the practice of the Seleucid kings.

As the legal owner of large tracts of land, which he could use as he saw fit, Jannaeus no doubt had almost unlimited influence over a large part of the nation. The power to grant land to whoever he wished, and to the extent that he wished, in effect placed the keys to the national economy, which was an agricultural one, in the king's hands. This means that Jannaeus actually ruled entirely free of restraints, even though theoretically he was obliged to govern jointly with the *Ḥever ha-Yᵉhudim*. This fact bred in the resolute Hasmonean king the feeling that he possessed unlimited power and drew him dangerously close to the Hellenistic conception of the nature of the monarchy. In contrast to the early Hasmoneans — Simeon and John Hyrcanus — Jannaeus tended to cut himself off from the central council of the nation as his military aspirations broadened, and with them the extent of his economic activity.

The internal development of Jannaeus' kingdom in the Hellenistic pattern paralleled its external form, as expressed to a pronounced degree in the Hasmonean royal court of the time. This important fact is abidingly clear from the events that occurred in Jerusalem around the time of the death of Queen Salome. Josephus relates (*Ant.* XIII, 408 ff.) how the Pharisees made themselves masters of the entire kingdom during the queen's reign and how they eliminated a number of their Sadducee rivals. Finally, a delegation of Sadducees called on the queen and complained about the high-handed actions of their adversaries: "...and they reminded her of all that they had achieved in the face of danger, whereby they had shown their unwavering loyalty to their master and had therefore been judged worthy by him of the greatest honors . . . They also said that if their adversaries were to be contented with those already slain, they would bear with equanimity what had taken place, out of genuine devotion to their masters; but if, on the other hand, these men were to continue in the same course, let them, they begged, at least be given their freedom; for they would never bring themselves to seek any means of safety but what should come from her, and would welcome death in her palace... It would be disgraceful both for them and for her who ruled as queen, they added, if, being abandoned by her, they should be given shelter by the enemies of her husband; for Aretas the Arab and the other princes would consider it of the utmost value to enlist such men as mercenaries, whose very name, they might say, had caused these princes to shudder before they had heard it [spoken aloud] . . . Speaking in this vein at great length, they called upon the shades of Alexander . . ." This vivid description by Josephus (which he most likely took from the same putative source on the history of the Hasmonean dynasty that also supplied "the document" on Jannaeus' conquests in Moab[60]) provides us with a picture of the relationship between Jannaeus and his comrades-in-arms and of the manner of life at the king's court as it really was, without embellishment. We see before us a group of nobles and warriors proud of the victories which they achieved together with the late king, who have remained loyal to him and his house even after his death and are prepared to die on the threshold of the palace so long as they gain the confidence of the queen, the successor of their late lord. They do not want to exchange their master and his royal house for another, be he Nabatean or anyone else. They are not mercenaries who offer their life and their sword to the highest bidder, but nobles bound to their king and to the legitimate royal family of their people, preserving with pride the memory of the deeds they performed for its glory. During Jannaeus' lifetime these nobles frequented the royal court and watched over the safety of their king and comrade-in-arms in the many wars in which they fought at his side. They also shared thoughts and deeds with him in times of peace as a council of advisers in the political negotiations with the neighboring rulers from without, and with the political rivals from within. This was then the picture of the Hasmonean king — a monarch surrounded by Sadducee nobles from the distinguished families of Judea who together with him formed a closed, aristocratic body administering the affairs of the country on the basis of perspicacious observation of the military and political situation at home and abroad.[61] This picture brings to mind a typical Hellenistic kingdom, Macedonia, for example, in which the warrior nobles around the king were regarded as his "comrades" (ἑταῖροι) in arms and in counsel — and in feasting and carousing as well — and the king himself as *primus inter pares*. More simply, Jannaeus' relationship with the Sadducee nobility of his court did not differ in the slightest from the relationship of any Hellenistic king to his high-born comrades-in-arms who also filled high positions both in the army and the civil administration. This means that during Jannaeus' reign the Hasmonean royal court was modeled on the Hellenistic pattern, i.e., according to a hierarchy of "friends" (φίλοι) and "close friends" (φίλοι ἐν τοῖς μάλιστα), etc., with which we are familiar in the various Hellenistic courts.[62] Indeed, even in John Hyrcanus' entourage we find a "close friend" (φίλος ἐν τοῖς μάλιστα) of the High Priest and ethnarch, certainly not just a friend but the holder of a very high court position, namely the same Jonathan who incited John Hyrcanus against the Pharisees, as related above (*Ant.* XIII, 293). Jannaeus' court doubtlessly included a large number of "friends of the king" of various degrees and much more in keeping with the Hellenistic pattern than in the time of John Hyrcanus, the High Priest.[63]

When Queen Salome was stricken with the illness from which she never recovered, Aristobulus seized the fortresses "where his father's friends had been stationed," that is, the former dignitaries of Jannaeus' court who had appeared before the queen to complain of the high-handedness of the Pharisees, relying on the close friendship that had existed between them and her husband (cf. above).

In the same speech these men had particularly pointed out that Jannaeus had rewarded them for their faithful service. It is quite certain that the reward was in the form of material grants, primarily in landed property and also in high military and administrative posts. And the nobles, for their part, are bound to him by ties of loyalty and serve him throughout his reign heedless of danger to themselves. This, too, is an authentic Hellenistic feature of Jannaeus' kingdom. The king and the band of nobles attached to his court are one inseparable body, united by their social status, and above the people and consequently distinct from it. This close-knit body has but a single ambition: to magnify the glory of the Hasmonean house and kingdom.

This ambition drew Jannaeus and his Sadducean, aristocratic, court party closer to a Hellenistic foreign policy than any other Hasmonean ruler had been. Such a policy contained two basic elements: military conquests on the one hand, and political negotiations with the neighboring gentile states on the other.

There is no doubt that, of the two, war and conquest came first. Jannaeus' political negotiations were simply "a continuation of war by other means." The supreme goal remained the same: expansion, the bursting of existing boundaries, and one conquest succeeding another. The implementation of such a policy would have presented no problem had Jannaeus been the ruler of a truly Hellenistic state. But that was not the case.

The Hasmonean state, as it was established and its original form determined at the National Assembly of Jerusalem in 141 B.C.E., was not based on the omnipotent rule of the High Priest and ethnarch. Under the covenant of 141 B.C.E., the policies of the Hasmonean rulers were first supposed to have been discussed between the Hasmonean ruler and the groups representing the people in the *Ḥever ha-Yᵉhudim*. Without the consent of the *Ḥever ha-Yᵉhudim*, the High Priest was not authorized to conduct negotiations with other states or to declare war, just as his powers were limited in promulgating rules in the sphere of religion or domestic affairs.[64]

Simeon, as we saw above, meticulously observed this basic proviso of the agreement of 141 B.C.E. His son, John Hyrcanus, behaved in a similar fashion for many years, until the outbreak of the quarrel with the Pharisees discussed above. But even after that break, John Hyrcanus did not dare to abrogate the fundamental proviso of the accord of 141 B.C.E. He continued to govern with the concurrence of the *Ḥever ha-Yᵉhudim*, except that the center of gravity within the *Ḥever* was shifted to the side of the Sadducees, who were Hyrcanus' allies and collaborated with him. For this reason his actions should not be characterized as illegal or unconstitutional. At most, the Pharisees could charge that his regulations were not in accord with "the tradition of the fathers," that is, with their own regulations. As we have seen, the Pharisees finally found it necessary to compromise with John Hyrcanus and to accept at least part of his decisions. The constitution of 141 B.C.E., which was based on a partnership between the High Priest and the *Ḥever ha-Yᵉhudim*, was not impaired and was passed on to Jannaeus intact.

The rise to power of this son of John Hyrcanus constituted a turning point in Hasmonean policy. All indications are that Jannaeus was the first of the Hasmoneans to wear a crown,[65] which is enough to tell us about the character of the man. Jannaeus was not content with the rank of ethnarch to parallel that of High Priest. He regarded nothing less than the kingship, symbol of real rule, as befitting him.

This decision of Jannaeus seems to have stemmed from his comparative evaluation of the ruling power vested in the Hasmonean ethnarch under the constitution of 141 B.C.E. and that exercised by a king.

The powers of the Hasmonean ethnarch have been described above. Their scope was limited by the constitutional factor of the *Ḥever ha-Yᵉhudim*. Any attempt to break out of the constitutional framework was necessarily regarded as malfeasance on the part of the ethnarch. The sovereign of the Hasmonean state in practice as well as in theory — so long as the constitution of 141 B.C.E. was observed — was the people in Judea. The Hasmonean ethnarch was the head of the people only on condition that he faithfully carry out the duties imposed on him by the nation. The moment the people believed that the leader it had chosen had abused his office, it had the right to supplant him.

This was a government of the people and for the people. From this aspect — and from this aspect alone — there was a similarity between the constitution which the young Hasmonean state adopted in 141 B.C.E. and the constitutions of republican Rome and of the various *poleis* in classical Greece. In all three the actual rulers were merely officials appointed by the will of the people — in republican Rome and in the Greece of the *polis*, for a specific period, and in Hasmonean Judea, beginning with 141 B.C.E., for an unlimited time.

In the second half of the second century B.C.E. this form of popular government held complete sway in republican Rome, even though signs of degeneration were already increasing. This was not the case in the Hellenistic East. The classical *polis* form of government ceased to exist in Greece with the rise of the Hellenistic period and the concomitant emergence of the period of the Hellenistic monarchy. This was the era when government was synonymous with unrestrained autocracy, absolutism. The Hellenistic ruler, whether he was a powerful king or the master of a small principality (δυνάστης), was all-powerful, and within the territory under his domination his word was law. The people, as we stressed at the beginning of this chapter, declined in that period to the status of the ruler's subjects, and it was consequently unthinkable that they should take a part in the government. Together with the *polis* as the political expression of the classical era, the people as the repository of sovereignty likewise disappeared in the Hellenistic period. They were supplanted by the monarchy as the form of absolute government, with the king as sovereign.

This was the political reality obtaining in all the Hellenistic states, in the entire East. On the whole, it may be said that the political system created in the Hasmonean kingdom in 141 B.C.E. was odd compared with the governments of the surrounding countries. The first Hasmonean rulers, Simeon and John Hyrcanus, adhered to the undertaking they had assumed and honored the constitution of 141 B.C.E. This is true even of

John Hyrcanus, despite the quarrel that broke out between him and his Pharisee partners within the *Ḥever ha-Yᵉhudim*. In spite of the Hellenistic influence which began to penetrate into the administration and the army of the Hasmonean state during the rule of John Hyrcanus, the latter remained immune to the allurements of absolute rule which prevailed in the Hellenistic world about him. There is, of course, no way of knowing whether John Hyrcanus' adherence to his rank of ethnarch stemmed from the fact that he really preferred the office created by the Jewish people, and legally handed to him, to the foreign Hellenistic type of kingship — even though the latter would have bestowed upon him infinitely more power than that which he enjoyed in his capacity as Jewish ethnarch. The desire to replace his "Jewish" office with the "modern" Hellenistic one may not have been unknown to John Hyrcanus — particularly owing to his quarrel with the Pharisees and his difficulties in the *Ḥever ha-Yᵉhudim* in general. Whatever his reasons for remaining faithful to the constitution of 141 B.C.E. — it is a likely conjecture that the perspicacious High Priest was of the opinion that the time was not yet ripe for a change. It is a historical fact that John Hyrcanus and his son Judah Aristobulus I (the latter perhaps because he did not have sufficient opportunity, his rule lasting only one year) retained their office as ethnarchs and did not replace it with a Hellenistic monarchy.

But what seemed right to these two Hasmoneans did not meet with Jannaeus' approval. We have seen above how in his time Hellenistic influence grew progressively in all areas of the Hasmonean state: in the army, in the administration, and in domestic and foreign policy, and how, most importantly, Jannaeus' conception of the nature of government approached the absolutist Hellenistic view as the extent of his conquests increased and his influence on the broad classes of the nation mounted. Moreover, Jannaeus' whole career as statesman, as soldier and conqueror is testimony to the fact that his strongest character trait was an unbridled lust for power. This nature of his did not allow Jannaeus to yield to the will of others and aroused his opposition to any individual or public body that might constitute an obstacle to his ambitions. It is thus clear that Jannaeus rejected altogether his father's position of ethnarch because it was passed on to him with the provision that he work hand-in-hand with the central legislative body of the people, the *Ḥever ha-Yᵉhudim* (Sanhedrin), and be dependent on its approval. It was different with the Hellenistic kinsghip, which was dependent on no external element and was based on the willpower of the strong individual who was his own master and who was not bound to seek the approval of anyone for his actions. It was natural for a man like Jannaeus to find satisfaction in this Hellenistic form of government and to prefer it to the type of government he had inherited from his father.

This means that Jannaeus' ambition, as soon as he replaced the position of ethnarch with the kingship, was to free himself of the bothersome dependence on the *Ḥever ha-Yᵉhudim*. This plan of Jannaeus' apparently found supporters in the military clique at the royal court, whose representatives no doubt sat together with other Sadducees in the *Ḥever ha-Yᵉhudim*. This clique saw in Jannaeus' ambitions a lofty goal, and in his personality an earnest guarantee of its achievement. Before these nobles, who took pride in their wealth and their distinguished birth, there appeared a military leader imbued with the spirit of adventure and striving for conquests and glory, a man not overly concerned with the affairs which constituted the world of the Pharisees, but who was given over completely to one grand purpose: to glorify the Hasmonean kingdom and to turn it into a powerful force, enjoying influence and honor in the Hellenistic world about it. The military caste around Jannaeus bound its fate to his, since only from him could it expect a distinguished economic and social status within the nation or, more correctly, a controlling position in the administration of the country. The whole nationalist, political plan of the conquest of a greater Palestine was entirely Jannaeus', and so it also appeared to the military clique. It was obvious to its members that the *Ḥever ha-Yᵉhudim* had no part in it. Moreover, the members of the military clique knew that the Pharisees in the *Ḥever ha-Yᵉhudim* regarded the entire plan with unconcealed hostility. This fact, which was as clear to Jannaeus as it was to his Sadducee comrades-in-arms, gave them the idea of abolishing the central governing body of the nation, by means of which the Pharisees could frustrate the great political and military plan of the king and his comrades.

F. The Clash between Jannaeus Alexander and the Pharisees. Civil War

This brings us to the dangerous crisis which befell the *Ḥever ha-Yᵉhudim* during Jannaeus' reign. For there can be no doubt that the breach which occurred in the *Ḥever ha-Yᵉhudim* in the days of John Hyrcanus had been healed only on the surface. We have seen above that not only did John Hyrcanus shift dominance of the *Ḥever ha-Yᵉhudim* to its Sadducee members, but that he even gave preference to their interpretation of the Law. And what was even more dangerous in the eyes of the Pharisees, he opened the way for the Sadducean *halaka* to reach the people, so that in the course of time it might displace the Pharisaic *halaka* and substantially reduce its influence among the broad masses. Apprehensive about such a development, the Pharisees tended to compromise with John Hyrcanus, and so peace was restored until his death.[66]

Nevertheless, the breach in the *Hever ha-Yᵉhudim* remained. The Sadducees not only did not really yield the advantage they had gained in the days of John Hyrcanus, but with Jannaeus' rise to power they even extended it to a dangerous degree. As we have already seen, Jannaeus was interested in strengthening the position of the Sadducee faction in the *Hever ha-Yᵉhudim*, because they were in accord with his view that the Hasmonean state ought to expand its boundaries as much as possible, at the expense of the gentile territories. The Sadducees' motive was that their unqualified support of Jannaeus would raise them to the uppermost rung of the state hierarchy and, in addition, would yield them material advantages from the king. With the active backing of these allies, Jannaeus sought to establish in the Hasmonean state a government based on a Hellenistic foundation, i.e., absolute rule not subject to any central body and deriving its legal power from the rights conferred upon it by the people. In brief: Jannaeus and his followers intended to govern the country on the pattern of the neighboring gentile states.

In the eyes of the Pharisees this course of events was extremely dangerous. The danger was a double one. In the first place, it was obvious that the form of government agreed upon in 141 B.C.E. was deliberately being destroyed by Jannaeus and his comrades, with the clear aim of replacing it with a form of government borrowed from the gentiles. The constitution of 141 B.C.E. reserved an important, if not exclusive, role for the scholars in the central council of the nation so that they were not only able to influence the practical day-to-day policy carried out in the council, but also to integrate their principles into the various branches of state administration, for example, in the courts, in worship, in relations between the people and the state and, what was most important to them, in the foreign policy which determined Israel's relations with other nations. The advantage granted to the Sadducees by John Hyrcanus, and to an even greater extent by Jannaeus, deprived the Pharisees of a large part of their lawful share in the government of the state.

But the Pharisees regarded the danger lying in wait for the entire nation as a result of Hasmonean policy in general, and of Jannaeus in particular, as infinitely greater than the threat to their own status in the government. The danger was universal, the Pharisees reasoned, because the Hasmoneans, and particularly Jannaeus, strove to use the entire nation in order to achieve their private political aims. The Pharisees saw in the concentration of the two offices, the kingship and the High Priesthood, in the hands of this dynasty the ominous instrument with which the Hasmoneans were attempting to carry out their designs. Such concentration meant that the Hasmoneans not only conducted the temporal affairs of the nation but — and this the Pharisees considered far more important — they also held the reins of religious affairs, so that they were in a position to mold the nation's religious and moral character in accordance with their secular ambitions.

The Pharisees regarded this state of affairs as intolerable, and they were firm in their resolve to separate the two offices. They insisted that the Hasmoneans content themselves with the monarchy and relinquish the High Priesthood. What was the political significance of this demand? In order to understand this we must recall the Pharisees' view of the role of religion in the life of the Jewish people. The Pharisees regarded religion as the sum and substance of the Jewish people. Religion in their opinion should embrace the nation's life in all its manifestations; in economic affairs and labor, art and thought, law and politics, the life of society and of the individual. In the Pharisaic view, every step of the individual and society, their entire manner of life, were subject to the supreme authority of the Torah and the divine precepts. They regarded the religious leadership as nothing less than the absolute master of all aspects of the nation's daily life. Consequently, the relinquishment of the High Priesthood which the Pharisees demanded of the Hasmoneans actually meant divesting them of internal leadership. They would only retain possession of "the royal crown," that is, those matters which the Pharisees regarded as being outside the bounds of the nation's life. And not only were such matters not essential for the continuation of national life and did not imbue it with any special character, but, on the contrary, they were at variance with the nation's true destiny. For the institution of the state and the foreign conquests, and its position in relation to the neighboring countries and its negotiations with them, drew the nation close to the gentiles and opened the door wide to alien influence. In the eyes of the Pharisees, therefore, the Hasmonean state had become a strictly secular one, filled with the abominations which they ascribed to the heathens.[67] Such a state was not the Pharisaic ideal. The Hasmonean state, which had blurred the boundaries between Israel and the nations and drawn the Chosen People close to the way of life of the gentiles, had caused it to forget the cardinal fact in its life which had determined its character forever: its existence as a holy people. For this reason the state which the Hasmonean dynasty had founded could not satisfy the yearnings and the hope of the Pharisees. These could be satisfied only by the kingdom of Messiah of the House of David. That kingdom alone they regarded as the fitting framework for the life of the Chosen People. But the advent of the Messianic Age called for difficult and careful preparation. For the Pharisees such preparation meant the hegemony of the Torah in the life of the nation as axiomatic and as the foundation stone of its development.

From this point of view, it is understandable why the Pharisees wished to concentrate the religious leadership of the nation in their own hands, after wresting it from the Hasmonean line.

Christian scholars have dealt harshly with the Pharisees because of the one-sided view in the New Testament. According to this conception the Pharisees were seekers of power and honor as well as hypocrites whose religion consisted in the formal observance of the practical precepts. Their primary concern was to dominate the people, whom they subjected to a heavy burden of trivial precepts which petrified the spirit of those who performed them, and deprived the nation of any possibility of free and fruitful religious development.

There is, no doubt, a grain of truth in these charges. Nevertheless, precisely this opinion testifies to a complete lack of understanding of the historical phenomenon known as the Pharisaic sect. With hardly a discordant note,[68] Christian scholars have not perceived the deep moral responsibility which was the foundation underlying all the actions of the Pharisees and the inspiration of their movement. The men who wished to wrest the religious leadership of the nation from the Hasmoneans and concentrate it in their own hands were not moved simply by a lust for power or because they were mendacious religious hypocrites whose aim was to entangle the simple masses in their web of deceit.[69] They were motivated primarily by a conviction that the domination of the Jews by religion was an effective means of educating them in the spirit of the Law and thus preparing them for the Kingdom of the Messiah. The Pharisees did not forget that it had been the Hasmonean house which had entered the stage of history as the defender of the Jewish religion against a Hellenistic king bent on destroying it and replacing it with Hellenistic culture, and they did not lose sight of the fact that this same Hasmonean dynasty had later changed its colors and tried to adapt the achievements of the Hellenistic states to various spheres of activity in the new Judean state. In the eyes of the Pharisees, this Hasmonean house, which had gone from bad to worse, from John Hyrcanus "the Sadducee" to Jannaeus "the wicked," constituted a serious hindrance in the nation's way to the Kingdom of the Messiah.

For this reason the Pharisees were convinced that it was their duty to assume the religious leadership of the nation after removing it from the untrustworthy hands of the Hasmonean dynasty. For the Hasmoneans as the nation's religious leaders were abusing their religious authority; they were betraying their mission and were sinking the holy nation in the mire of the unclean Hellenistic kingdom they had established for themselves. They, the Pharisees, on the other hand, would lead the nation toward its true destiny: they would imbue it with the spirit of holiness so that it would be worthy of welcoming the King Messiah when the time came.[70]

Part of the battle waged over this religious-political goal was the opposition of the Pharisees to the aim of Jannaeus and his Sadducee comrades to abolish the *Ḥever ha-Yᵉhudim* (Sanhedrin) and to institute an absolutist regime on the pattern of the gentile kings. In this struggle over the *Ḥever ha-Yᵉhudim* the Pharisees reasoned that even though they did not entirely control the body, it was a rather effective instrument for influencing the country's foreign and domestic policy. The abolition of the *Ḥever ha-Yᵉhudim* would deprive the Pharisees of any possibility of making their voice heard in public and of preventing actions which did not seem to fit their interpretations of the *halaḵa*.

The religious goal of the Pharisees stood counter to Jannaeus' vision of kingship. Jannaeus wished to be an absolute monarch in the style of the neighboring Hellenistic kings. The practical import of this was that he strove to gain the whip hand, dominating both the secular and the religious spheres, and to suppress every other power in the state.

This ambition of Jannaeus' was completely at odds with the aim of the Pharisees. The Sanhedrin was the most important center of power in the nation, and it was supported by the Pharisees, the religious leaders of the broad masses, who regarded it as an effective instrument for spreading their influence (cf. above). So long as this center of power existed, Jannaeus could not achieve his purpose. He had the choice of renouncing his desire for absolute rule or of dissolving the central council of the people which stood in his way. Jannaeus' personal traits, similar to those of a true Hellenistic ruler, did not allow him to adopt the course of renunciation. Still less would he deign to submit to the wishes of those whom he regarded merely as subjects who were bound to do his bidding.

But this objection was negligible compared with the opposition aroused by the principal demand of the Pharisees — that he relinquish the High Priesthood and with it the religious leadership of the people. It is perfectly obvious that had Jannaeus agreed to this demand, it would have led to the gravest consequences for the Hasmonean dynasty. For of the two positions occupied by the Hasmoneans there is no doubt that the religious office was held in higher regard by the Pharisees and by the nation as a whole, the temporal office being considered only subsidiary. By giving up the High Priesthood, Jannaeus would be surrendering the vital part of his authority as the leader of the nation, and would debase himself in its eyes to the rank of a man in charge of inconsequential matters. The Pharisees were well aware of all this. That is why they were willing to exercise restraint when Jannaeus assumed the kingship; in fact, they were even prepared to acquiesce in that *fait accompli* despite the serious contradiction between acceptance of the Hasmonean monarchy and the hope for the Kingdom of Messiah of the House of David. That was the line of action which the Pharisees followed in the time of Queen Salome, and peace was restored in the land. In that period they acted as if they were the masters of the Hasmonean state. But while they devoted themselves to day-to-day administrative matters — for these men never denied the importance of mundane affairs — they no doubt considered such matters trivial compared with making the Torah dominant in the life of the nation, which they hoped would pave the way for the coming of the Messiah. Compared to that preoccupation, which was paramount in the nation's interest, there was no lasting value to Queen Salome's concern with foreign affairs, and the Pharisees let her have her way, especially since the queen, for her part, did not interfere in their province, after Jannaeus' bitter experience with this militant sect.

With Jannaeus it was different. In contrast to the Pharisees, who demonstrated by their conduct, described above, that they were entirely lacking in awareness of the actual situation of the nation (i.e., of the Hasmonean kingdom), Jannaeus and his Sadducee friends were imbued with the facts of the existence of the Hasmonean state, full of vitality and striving for territorial, military and economic expansion, and giving no thought to the Kingdom of the Messiah, which they considered illusory. It was to this reality that Jannaeus wished to bind the people. Under no circumstances, therefore, even if he had not subscribed to the Hellenistic idea of absolute rule, could Jannaeus have renounced the religious leadership in favor of the Pharisees. For by so doing he would with his own hands be alienating the nation from the Hasmonean kingdom and pushing it into a world of Messianic hopes, which lived only in the spirit of the Pharisees. Jannaeus himself would thus be undermining the foundations of his state and of the Hasmonean dynasty: the state would lose its support in the nation and would remain suspended in mid-air, for the people would see no purpose in it as compared with the blessings it might expect from the future Kingdom of the Messiah, and sooner or later would turn its back on the state. The worth of the Hasmonean dynasty would fall in the eyes of the people, who would think that they need not accept its authority and that they could not look to it for salvation. That would come from the Kingdom of the Messiah and from the men who were guiding them towards it, whereas the Hasmoneans would only be an insignificant factor. Their absence would not be felt and they would be doomed to extinction.

For these reasons Jannaeus rejected both of the Pharisees' demands: to retain the Sanhedrin and to relinquish the High Priesthood. When the Pharisees realized that Jannaeus was adamant, and that there was no hope of compromise, they drew a dangerous arrow from their quiver aimed at no less than the legitimate existence of the kingdom of the Hasmonean House. We have seen above that the Pharisees were willing to acquiesce in the kingship which Jannaeus arrogated to himself, despite its inherent contradiction with the idea of the kingdom of the House of David, provided that Jannaeus would agree to the two demands noted above. But when they saw that Jannaeus stubbornly continued to refuse, and that his hostility to their policies was steadily growing, they proclaimed: not only have the Hasmoneans usurped the High Priesthood, but even the kingship is not legitimately theirs. There is no royal family in Israel but the House of David: "Suffer not a stranger to sit on his throne, nor let others any longer inherit his glory; for by Thy holy name Thou didst swear unto him, that his light should never be quenched."[71] The sons of the Hasmoneans were simply usurpers who had occupied the throne by sheer force. This propaganda against the Hasmonean house was brilliantly expressed in one of the chapters of the Psalms of Solomon, a Pharisaic source which dates in part from the time of Jannaeus:

"O Lord, Thou art our King for ever and ever,
For in Thee, O God, doth our soul glory.
How long are the days of man's life upon the earth?
As are his days, so is the hope [set] upon him.
But we hope in God, our deliverer;
For the might of our God is for ever with mercy,
And the kingdom of our God is for ever the nations in
                                                    judgement.
Thou, O Lord, didst choose David [to be] king over Israel,

> And swardst to him touching his seed that never should his
> kingdom fail before Thee
> But, for our sins, sinners rose up against us;
> They assailed us and thrust us out;
> What Thou hadst not promised to them, they took away [from us]
> with violence.
> They in no wise glorified Thy honorable name;
> They set a [worldly] monarchy in place of [that which was] their
> excellency;
> They laid waste the throne of David in tumultuous arrogance.
> But Thou, O God, didst cast them down, and remove their seed from
> the earth,
> In that there rose up against them a man that was alien to our race.
> According to their sins didst thou recompense them, O God;
> So that it befell them according to their deeds.
> God showed them no pity;
> He sought out their seed and let not one of them go free.
> Faithful is the Lord in all His judgements
> Which He doeth upon the earth (17:1–11).[72]

Jannaeus did not fail to react to this dangerous propaganda. After he abolished the Sanhedrin,[73] the differences between the two factions grew more and more acute, until a critical point was reached. A single spark was enough to ignite a general conflagration.[74]

The spark was touched off on the occasion of the Feast of Tabernacles, but Josephus, who reports the incident, does not say what brought it about. He relates that the people once rebelled against Jannaeus at the Feast of Tabernacles, as the king stood beside the altar about to perform the sacrifice, and pelted him with citrons shouting "son of the captive woman."[75] Jannaeus was not one to take such an insult. He sent his Pisidian and Cilician mercenaries against the people; according to Josephus, six thousand persons were killed that day. In addition, Jannaeus had a wooden barrier built around the altar and the Sanctuary to separate him from the people (*Ant.* XIII, 372–4; *War* I, 88–9). On that occasion Jannaeus succeeded in putting down the revolt, but the ferment which began only awaited a favorable opportunity to burst out with greater intensity.

This occurred when Jannaeus suffered a crushing defeat at the hands of Obedas, King of the Nabataeans, apparently in the area of Gaulanitis.[76] The Judaean army fell into an ambush and was put to rout, and Jannaeus fled to Jerusalem. Upon learning of the king's defeat, his adversaries revolted and took up the sword against him. For six years the country was in the throes of a bloody civil war and, according to Josephus, no less than fifty thousand men of the king's enemies were killed. Perhaps the number is exaggerated, but in any case the country suffered great hardship and its strength was totally sapped. Jannaeus was willing to reach a compromise with his rivals, but they were stubborn and inflexibly rejected his proffered hand; they wanted to be rid of their hated king.[77] They appealed to Demetrius Eukairos, the Seleucid monarch, for aid. Jannaeus encountered Demetrius accompanied by the rebels, near Shechem. Each army tried to entice the enemies' troops over to its own side: Demetrius — Jannaeus' mercenaries, and Jannaeus — the Jews with Demetrius who, according to Josephus, numbered twenty thousand. Jannaeus was defeated in the ensuing encounter and fled to the hills with the remnants of his loyal soldiers. In the end, however, some six thousand of the Jews in Demetrius' camp repented of what they had done and went over to Jannaeus. Demetrius left the country, and the civil war in Judea continued. Finally, Jannaeus succeeded in overcoming the rebels in open battle. The survivors fled to a place whose name is not clear,[78] and were captured by Jannaeus, after a siege. According to Josephus, eight hundred of them were executed with great cruelty. Even though the details are surely exaggerated, there is no doubt about the cruelty, keeping in mind that the protracted war had inflamed passions on both sides, apart from the fact that cruelty is a common characteristic of civil wars. Jannaeus was certainly not one to display magnanimity and in this case, he had every reason to act severely in order to provide an object lesson. Indeed, the Pharisees were so alarmed that eight thousand of them fled the country and did not return until after the death of the hated king.[79]

Jannaeus finally tired of the civil war and of the unending struggle against the Pharisees and, according to the sources, advised his wife Salome before his death to compromise with the Pharisees.[80] This appears very probable, since Jannaeus felt that the civil war was undermining the strength of the kingdom, which was bound to fall into the hands of its neighbors if the internal strife did not cease. However, it was precisely this decision of Jannaeus' that hastened the end of the Hasmonean kingdom. When Salome, in compliance with her husband's request, allowed the Pharisees to run the country as they saw fit, those religious statesmen finally proceeded to put their central idea into practice. Essentially, as we have seen above, their ideology was ridden with contempt for the values of the earthly kingdom and a preference for the "eternal" values, that is, religion. Provided they were allowed to do as they pleased, the Pharisees did not undermine the foundation of the Hasmonean kingdom. But the moment it seemed to them that their aims were in jeopardy, they did not hesitate to sacrifice the national state, so long as they would be in a position to strive for the Kingdom of the Messiah. That is how they acted during the quarrel of Jannaeus' two sons before Pompey. At that time the Pharisees feared that Aristobulus, who resembled his father, would triumph. They therefore suggested to the Roman conqueror that he abolish the Hasmonean kingdom altogether, since it was not consonant with Jewish tradition. From the point of view of these religious statesmen, this was a consistent position. The national kingdom and the messianic one were at odds, and one could not be ushered in unless the other were turned out.

NOTES AND BIBLIOGRAPHY

NOTES

CHAPTER I
THE POLITICAL BACKGROUND

1 Curtius Rufus, VI, 9, 34, relates that Alexander the Great and one of his commanders, Philotas, spoke Greek and not Macedonian to the soldiers and courtiers, so they would be understood by everyone who heard them (i.e., not only by the Macedonians but by the Greeks as well). For the Macedonian language see I. Kallerēs, *Les anciens Macédoniens*, I, Athens, 1954; H. Berve, *Das Alexanderreich auf prosopographischer Grundlage*, I, Munich, 1926, pp. 112 ff.

2 For the phalanx see E. J. Bickermann, *Les Institutions des Séleucides*, Paris, 1938, pp. 55 ff. The creation of the phalanx was the work of King Philip, see Diodorus XVI, 3, 2.

3 For Macedonia and Macedonians see O. Hoffmann, *Die Makedonen, ihre Sprache und ihr Volkstum*, Göttingen, 1906; O. Hoffmann and F. Geyer, "Makedonia," *RE*, Vol. 27, pp. 638 ff.; K. J. Beloch, *Griechische Geschichte* (2nd ed.), IV, 1, Berlin, 1925, pp. 1 ff.; Kallerēs, *op. cit.*, pp. 1 ff.

4 Scholars of our day are divided in their estimation of the historical role of Philip. Some follow Demosthenes in depicting him as the barbarian monarch of a barbarian nation which had set out to subjugate Greece. On the other hand, other historians (the first among them being J. G. Droysen, whose book about Alexander the Great [*Geschichte Alexanders des Grossen*] had appeared in 1833) have noted that the era of the rule of the Greek *polis* was over, and the role Philip played in Greece was not only not negative but, on the contrary, most praiseworthy, since he gave Greece, divided as she was, national unity. The historians' approach to the events of the 4th century also dictates their general evaluation of the Macedonians. Some consider them a semi-barbarian people — the product of a mixture of Greeks and Illyrian and Thracian tribes, while others regard them as a Greek tribe like all the others. For an account of modern opinions cf. Kallerēs, *op. cit.*, pp. 20 ff., 30 ff. For Philip's conquests and the history of his time see A. W. Pickard–Cambridge, "The Rise of Macedonia" and "Macedonian Supremacy in Greece," *CAH*, VI (chaps. VIII–IX), pp. 200 ff. and 244 ff.; G. Glotz – R. Cohen, *Histoire greque*, III, Paris, 1936, pp. 226 ff.; A. Momigliano, *Filippo il Macedone*, Florence, 1934; F. Wüst, *Philipp II von Makedonien und Griechenland in den Jahren von 346 bis 338*, Munich, 1938.

5 The "King's Peace" is also known as the "Peace of Antalcidas" from the name of the Spartan politician who played a major role in the negotiations between the Greeks and the Persian king. The text of the agreement was preserved in Xenophon's *Hellenica*, V, 1, 31. It is not in fact an agreement, and even less a "pact" but an order sent by King Artaxerxes to the Greeks. It reads as follows: "King Artaxerxes thinks it just that the cities in Asia should belong to him, as well as Clazomenae and Cyprus among the islands and that the other Greek cities, both small and great, should be left independent, except Lemnos, Imbros and Scyros; and these should belong, as of old, to the Athenians. But whichever of the two parties does not accept this peace, upon them I will make war, in company with those who desire this arrangement, both by

land and by sea, with ships and with money' (from the Engl. transl. by Carleston L. Brownson in the Loeb Classical Library). This decree provoked great indignation in Greece, especially in Athens; cf. the oration by the illustrious Athenian writer Isocrates, *Panegyricus*, published six years after the agreement was concluded and containing sharp criticism of it and of those Greeks who had willingly accepted it.

6   In 380 Isocrates published his political program based on a national war by a united Greece against Persia (see his famous oration *Panegyricus*, mentioned above). In Philip's time he returned to this plan suggesting to the King of Macedonia that he take the initiative in uniting Greece and proclaiming war against Persia. According to Isocrates it was desirable for the Greeks to abolish Persian power once and for all, but if this plan proved unfeasible, they might content themselves with annexing a large part of Asia Minor (from Cilicia to Sinope) to Macedonia. Here, in Isocrates' opinion, it would be possible to establish Greek colonies capable of absorbing all of Greece's surplus population. In this way the danger of severe social revolutions resulting from large numbers of unemployed people would be obviated (*Philippus* 120). Yet Isocrates' plan remained "a voice that crieth in the wilderness." In 354 Demosthenes had warned the Athenians not to let themselves be dragged into the maelstrom of a war with Persia, since the expense would be prohibitive; in the year of the battle of Chaeronea (338), and later on, the Greek patriots regarded the Persian king as their natural ally in their war against Macedonia.

7   For the exact number of Greek soldiers in Alexander's army (allies and mercenaries) see Berve, *op. cit.*, pp. 141 ff. The number of Greek mercenaries in Darius' force is unknown. The estimate of 20,000 "foreign mercenaries" in the battle of Granicus, of whom 18,000 were killed by Alexander's forces (Arrian, *Anabasis*, I, 14, 4; 16, 2) is certainly a product of the imagination; the estimate of 5,000 men (Diodorus XVII, 7, 3) is more plausible.

8   See above, note 6.

9   The main crisis took place in 330, a short time after Darius' death, when Alexander's revised policy also demanded new men. In that year, Philotas, Parmenion's son, was accused of high treason and put to death. Directly afterwards Parmenion, too, was killed by Alexander's secret order. The removal of Parmenion's influential family cleared the way for the promotion to key positions in the army of young officers who were Alexander's friends. A short time afterwards, Cleitus, one of Philip and Alexander's senior commanders, was killed by the latter's own hand, and though this was done in a drunken fit to Alexander's subsequent profound regret, the real cause of the quarrel between the two men was mainly political. Cleitus had criticized Alexander's new policy and dared to show his preference for Philip over his son. For an analysis of the sources concerning these events see F. Cauer, *Philotas, Kleitos, Kallisthenes*, Leipzig, 1893; and cf. W. W. Tarn, "Alexander: The Conquest of the Far East," *CAH*, VI (chap. XIII).

10   Alexander's campaign was recorded by many writers of his own day and the period shortly after his death. These men, some of whom had actually taken part in the campaign, strove to embellish the heroic deeds of the king by imaginary features. The works of Ptolemy (later to become king of Egypt) and Aristobulus are very important: both were participants in Alexander's campaign and presented a faithful description of events, since they each had a thorough knowledge of all matters concerning the army and the administration in Alexander's time. The whole rich literature of the primary sources has not been preserved, and information must be drawn from later sources. These are: Arrian, Diodorus, Plutarch, Curtius Rufus and Justin, whose works are also important for portraying events in Palestine. Arrian, a high-ranking Roman official in the East in the 2nd century C.E., is considered the best source. He made use of the works of Ptolemy and Aristobulus and, having himself been a military commander and administrator, reported the battles and political events with true understanding of

their significance. Diodorus, a Greek historian of the 1st century B.C.E., wrote a "universal history" (*Bibliotheca historica*) of which the seventeenth volume is devoted to Alexander. He had neither knowledge of military matters nor a critical sense towards his sources; nevertheless, in his book was preserved important information derived not from official Macedonian sources but, apparently, from the stories of Greek mercenaries who had participated in Alexander's campaign. Plutarch wrote *The Life of Alexander* as part of his series of biographies of illustrious men. He had read all the sources, both the good and the bad, but utilized mainly those containing accounts of Alexander's private life. In accordance with his aim he centered his narrative around Alexander's personal activities, being less concerned with the historical background. Curtius Rufus (1st century C.E.) also used diverse sources (some of them reliable), yet he mingles history with empty rhetoric and it is sometimes difficult to pierce the literary shell to reach the grain of historical truth. Nevertheless, many incidents were preserved in Curtius Rufus which have no parallel in other accounts, but evidently derive from reliable sources. The worst of them all is Justin whose information should not be accepted uncritically. There is an abundant modern literature on Alexander. Important works are: Droysen's above mentioned *Geschichte Alexanders des Grossen* (reprinted several times since it first appeared in 1833); J. Kaerst, *Geschichte des Hellenismus* (2nd ed.), I, Leipzig, 1917; U. Wilcken, *Alexander der Grosse*, Leipzig, 1931; G. Radet, *Alexandre le Grand*, Paris, 1931; W. W. Tarn, *Alexander the Great*, 2 vols., Cambridge, 1948; L. Homo, *Alexandre le Grand*, Paris, 1951.

[11] For Alexander's stay in Egypt see V. Ehrenberg, *Alexander und Aegypten*, Leipzig, 1926.

[12] See below, p. 61.

[13] This is an assumption of Kaerst's, which was accepted by several other scholars. It particularly relies upon the fact that Alexander attempted to penetrate into the Ganges Valley, but was forced to withdraw by the Macedonian army's opposition to his project.

[14] Of his plan to make himself master of the West as far as the "Pillars of Hercules" (Gibraltar) we are told by Alexander's notes published after his death (Diodorus XVIII, 4, 4). But there is no assurance of their historical validity.

[15] Alexander's son by his wife Roxane, daughter of a Bactrian prince, was born a few months after his father's death and was at once acknowledged as king by the Macedonian generals. Together with him, Alexander's brother, Philip Arrhidaeus, simple-minded and in everybody's opinion unfit to rule, was also proclaimed king. His election to this high office was due to a quarrel among various elements in the Macedonian army.

[16] For the Diadochi period see Kaerst, *op. cit.*, II, Leipzig, 1926; W. W. Tarn, "The Heritage of Alexander," *CAH*, VI (chap. XV); P. Jouguet, *L'Impérialisme Macédonien et l'hellénisation de l'Orient*, Paris, 1926, pp. 139 ff.; M. I. Rostovtzeff, *The Social and Economic History of the Hellenistic World*, I, Oxford, 1941, pp. 126 ff.

[17] See above, note 15.

[18] The Persian Phrataphernes and the Bactrian Oxyartes, who remained in their satrapies, as well as the Indian kings in the valley of the Indus (Punjab) should be cited as exceptions.

[19] See Diodorus XIX, 55, 3. Seleucus answered "that he was not bound to undergo a public investigation of his administration of this country, which the Macedonians had given him in Alexander's lifetime in exchange for his services."

[20] Philip Arrhidaeus and his wife were assassinated in 317 by Olympias, Alexander's mother, as a consequence of bloody clashes which had broken out in Macedonia. Olympias herself was put to death about a year later by order of the Macedonian regent, Cassander. In 311–310, Alexander's son, a twelve-year old boy, and his mother Roxane were also slain by order of Cassander.

[21] See below, chapter III.

[22] For the Ptolemaic Kingdom and its internal organization see A. Bouché–Leclerq,

Histoire des Lagides, I–IV, Paris, 1903–7; E. R. Bevan, *A History of Egypt under the Ptolemaic Dynasty*, London, 1927; Rostovtzeff, *op. cit.*, I, pp. 255 ff.; II, pp. 870 ff.

23 Cf. J. Herrmann, "Zum Begriff γῆ ἐν ἀφέσει," *Chronique d'Égypte*, 30 (1955), 95 ff.

24 Cf. Rostovtzeff, *op. cit.*, II, pp. 726 ff.

25 For the Ptolemaic army see J. Lesquier, *Les institutions militaires de l'Égypte sous les Lagides*, Paris, 1911; G. T. Griffith, *The Mercenaries of the Hellenistic World*, Cambridge, 1935, pp. 108 ff.

26 Isolated papyri from Egypt were already beginning to appear at the end of the 18th century, but only at the end of the 19th century did papyri found in excavations or offered for sale in Egypt become available in increasing quantities, enabling scholars to appreciate fully the great value of this source for research into the political, economic, juridical, and cultural aspects of life in Egypt in the Ptolemaic-Roman-Byzantine periods. The deciphering of papyri and their historical interpretation have since then become a special branch of science. Now some 30,000 published papyri (including ostraca) are available to scholars. Egypt is quite probably the only land of the Hellenistic-Roman world whose life has been satisfactorily revealed. Among the abundant literature on the papyri see L. Mitteis und U. Wilcken, *Grundzüge und Chrestomathie der Papyruskunde*, I–II, Leipzig, 1912; W. Schubart, *Einführung in die Papyruskunde*, Berlin, 1918; J. G. Winter, *Life and Letters in the Papyri*, Ann Arbor, 1933; K. Preisendanz, *Papyruskunde und Papyrusforschung*, Leipzig, 1933. The papyri are of great value for research into the life of the Jews in Egypt. Cf. V. Tcherikover and A. Fuks, *Corpus Papyrorum Judaicarum*, I–II, Cambridge, Mass., 1957–60. For the Zenon papyri see below, Chapter III.

27 For the Seleucid Kingdom and its organization see E. R. Bevan, *The House of Seleucus*, I–II, London, 1902; A. Bouché-Leclercq, *Histoire des Séleucides*, I–II, Paris 1913–4; Bickermann, *Institutions des Séleucides*. For the Seleucid army cf. Bickermann,

op. cit., pp. 51 ff. For the campaign of Antiochus III in the East see M. Holleaux, "Rome and Macedon: the Romans against Philip," *CAH*, VIII (chap. VI), pp. 138 ff.; Bevan, *op. cit.*

28 See V. Tcherikover, *Die hellenistischen Städtegründungen von Alexander bis auf die Römerzeit*, Leipzig, 1927 (Philol. Suppl. XIX).

29 Modern scholars have frequently tended to exaggerate the importance of the Hellenization of the East in general, and in particular to consider the Seleucid kings as Hellenizers par excellence, carrying the flag of Greek culture among the backward peoples of the East. Cf. for instance, Ed. Meyer, *Blüte und Niedergang des Hellenismus in Asien*, Berlin, 1925, p. 46. Yet as research into the sources advances, the East assumes ever-growing importance and such renowned scholars as Rostovtzeff, Bickermann and others, are currently inclined to deny the Seleucids their role as "Kulturträger" and, on the contrary, stress the power of the East; cf. for this problem Rostovtzeff, *op. cit.* I, p. 502; Bickermann, *op. cit.*, pp. 170 ff.; M. Launey, *Recherches sur les armées hellénistiques*, II, Paris, 1950, pp. 1087 ff.

30 For the "Cities," "the Dynasts," and the "Peoples" as political units enjoying a measure of autonomy within the framework of the Seleucid Empire, cf. Bickermann, *op. cit.*, pp. 164 ff; Rostovtzeff, *op. cit.*, I, p. 502.

31 For the Ptolemaic Empire cf. Beloch, *op. cit.* (2nd ed.), IV, 2, Berlin, 1927, pp. 319 ff.; D. Cohen, *De Magistratibus Aegyptiis externas Lagidarum regni provincias administrantibus*, Hague, 1912.

32 For details of the 4th and 5th Syrian Wars see below, Chapter III.

33 For the political history of the 3rd century B.C.E. and, in particular, for the Syrian Wars, cf. W. W. Tarn, "The Struggle of Egypt against Syria and Macedonia," *CAH*, VII (chap. XXII), pp. 669 ff.; M. Cary, *A History of the Greek World from 323 to 146 B.C.* (2nd ed.), London, 1951, pp. 79 ff.

34 For Antiochus Epiphanes see Chapter V below.

CHAPTER II
THE CULTURAL BACKGROUND

[1] The first scholar to recognize the particular nature of the Hellenistic Age was J. G. Droysen who devoted a detailed study to it. See his *Geschichte des Hellenismus*, I–II, published in 1836–43 (new ed. in 3 vols., Basel, 1952). In later literature the following should be noted: B. Niese, *Geschichte der griechischen und makedonischen Staaten seit der Schlacht bei Chaeronea*, I–III, Gotha, 1893–1903; J. Kaerst, *Geschichte des Hellenismus* (2nd ed.), II, Leipzig, 1926; K. J. Beloch, *Griechische Geschichte*, IV, 1–2, Berlin, 1925–7; *CAH*, VI–VII; W. W. Tarn, *Hellenistic Civilisation* (3rd ed.), London, 1953; M. I. Rostovtzeff, *Social and Economic History of the Hellenistic World*, I–III, Oxford, 1941; M. Cary, *A History of the Greek World from 323 to 146 B.C.* (2nd ed.), London, 1951.

[2] Plutarch, in the biographies of Demetrius, Eumenes and Pyrrhus, skillfully depicted the typical personalities of the era: Demetrius, the adventurer, in pursuit of honor and royal splendor, equally devoted to the pleasures of life in peacetime and to camp life during war. Eumenes — a clever and cunning Greek who invented innumerable stratagems and succeeded in maintaining his position within the hostile Macedonian world for many years thanks to his extraordinary capacity for extricating himself from every complicated situation. Pyrrhus — an outstanding military commander who regarded the subjugation of other countries as his mission, sought to conquer for himself a land whose dimensions and international value would be appropriate to him, but finally fell victim to his own drive for power. Sudden changes in the course of their lives are typical of all these Hellenistic heroes. In the battle against Antigonus, Eumenes headed an army of more than 40,000 men, yet after his defeat he was betrayed by his soldiers, handed over to Antigonus, and put to death. Demetrius was king of a huge kingdom in 301, yet after the battle of Ipsus he lost all he had and became a kind of pirate. Later he obtained the crown of Macedon and gathered a tremendous host in order to reconquer the East, but was defeated by Pyrrhus and ended his life as Seleucus' captive. In Pyrrhus' life, too, there were frequent and violent changes, and if it is kept in mind that each sudden change in the life of one of the mighty would immediately be reflected by similar changes for a large number of small people dependent upon him — tens and hundreds of officers and officials and thousands of soldiers — no wonder that the belief in the power of fate ($(τύχη)$) became a basic feature in the philosophy of Hellenistic man.

[3] For the papyri from Zenon's archives, see below, Note [4] p. 310.

[4] "Turn night into day" — *PSI* 514. For the organization of the work on Apollonius' estates see P. Viereck, *Philadelpheia; die Gründung einer hellenistischen Militärkolonie in Ägypten*, Leipzig, 1928, pp. 30 ff.; C. C. Edgar, *Zenon Papyri in the University of Michigan Collection*, Ann Arbor, 1931, Introduction, pp. 27 ff.; C. Préaux, *Les Grecs en Égypte d'après les archives de Zénon*, Brussels, 1947, pp. 48 ff.

[5] *PCZ* 59532.

[6] *PCZ* 59087.

[7] Apollonius and Zenon were certainly not the only men of this kind, devoted solely to the accumulation of riches yet at the same time displaying extraordinary powers of organization. Cleomenes too, was apparently such a man — a Greek from Naucratis, very capable in financial matters, who was appointed by Alexander to direct Egypt's economic affairs and is to be credited with the building of Alexandria — see H. Berve, *Das Alexanderreich auf prosopographischer Grundlage*, II, Munich, 1926, pp. 210 ff. Harpalus, Alexander's minister of finance, who embezzled state funds and turned into a dangerous adventurer, was also the same kind of man — see Berve, *ibid.*, pp. 75 ff.; W. W. Tarn, "Greece: 335 to 321 B.C.," *CAH*, VI (chap. XIV), pp. 450 ff.

[8] For the Museum and the Library in Alexandria see E. R. Bevan, *A History of*

Egypt under the Ptolemaic Dynasty, London, 1927, pp. 124 ff. A. Bouché-Leclercq, *Histoire des Lagides*, IV, Paris, 1907, Index (p. 359), s.v. Bibliotheques; E. A. Parsons, *The Alexandrian Library, Glory of the Hellenic World*, London, 1952.

9   For the games in classical Greece see: E. N. Gardiner, *Olympia: its History and Remains*, Oxford, 1925; *idem, Athletics of the Ancient World*, Oxford, 1930; C. A. Forbes, *Greek Physical Education*, New York and London, 1929; G. Glotz–R. Cohen, *Histoire Grecque*, I, Paris, 1925, pp. 513 ff.; J. Jüthner, "Herkunft und Grundlagen der griechischer Nationalspiele," *Die Antike*, 15 (1939), 231 ff.

10   The Isthmian games were at first consecrated to the local god, Melicertes (perhaps the Greek derivative of the ancient Phoenician god Melkart) and only later transferred to the name of Poseidon.

11   The first *gymnasia* in Athens were built in the 5th century B.C.E. According to the evidence of the author of *The Constitution of the Athenians* (a work ascribed to Xenophon, but in fact written by an unknown Athenian oligarch at the time of the Peloponnesian War), the wealthy Athenians possessed several *gymnasia* and private rooms for baths. Yet the *demos* (the people) had also built themselves *palaestras* (places for physical education) and bathhouses which were open to the masses (*ibid.*, 2, 10). The education of *ephebes* in Athens is mentioned only from the 4th century onwards, and there is insufficient evidence of their existence before that. Our information about the education of youths in the classical period in cities other than Athens and Sparta is very meager, and does not provide a clear picture.

12   For instance, the philosopher Xenophanes, and the great poets Sophocles and Euripides. Cf. H. Diels, *Die Fragmente der Vorsokratiker* (6th ed.), I, Berlin, 1951, p. 128; J. Burckhardt, *Griechische Kulturgeschichte*, IV (= *Jacob Burckhardt-Gesamtausgabe*, XI), Basel, 1931, pp. 207 ff.; Glotz–Cohen, *op. cit.*, II, Paris, 1931, p. 596.

13   For the *gymnasium* education in the Hellenistic Age cf. A. H. M. Jones, *The Greek City from Alexander to Justinian*, Oxford, 1940, pp. 220 ff.

14   An illuminating example of the national Pan-Hellenic value of the athletic games in the Hellenistic period is to be found in the inscriptions of the city of Magnesia on the river Maeander in Asia Minor, which came to light in excavations at the end of the 19th century. At the end of the 3rd century B.C.E., the citizens of the city decided to honor the city goddess Artemis (who "revealed herself," as it were, to the citizens in a sort of miracle) by organizing athletic games for her every four years, on the pattern of the Pythian games. Having obtained the approval of the priests at Delphi, they sent messengers throughout the Greek world (the kings, the Greek leagues in Greece, and the Hellenistic cities of Greece and Asia Minor — as far as distant Persia) in order to secure the participation of those Greeks in the games. Dozens of positive answers given to the messengers were carved on stone — a memorial for future generations; it was these inscriptions which were found in the excavations and now offer abundant material for the evaluation of the Pan-Hellenic nature of athletic games in the Hellenistic period. Cf. O. Kern, *Die Inschriften von Magnesia am Maeander*, Berlin, 1900, nos. 16–17.

15   For the Greek religion in general, see particularly the following works of M. P. Nilsson: *Geschichte der griechischen Religion*, I–II, Munich, 1941–50; *A History of Greek Religion* (transl. from the Swedish) (2nd ed.), Oxford, 1949; *The Minoan-Mycenaean Religion and its Survival in Greek Religion* (2nd ed.), Lund, 1950; *Greek Popular Religion*, New York, 1940. For the administration of religious affairs by the polis, see G. Busolt, *Griechische Staatskunde* (3rd ed.), I, Munich, 1920, pp. 514 ff. It should be noted that, apart from the city officials appointed by lot or elected to manage religious affairs, there were also special priests and priestesses learned in the cult of a particular deity who served it only. These functions were sometimes hereditary; thus, for instance, the priesthood of the mysteries of Eleusis near Athens was the monopoly of two ancient families only. Yet these priests were experts in certain questions rather than religious teachers, and their influence on spiritual

life in Greece was not marked. Religious movements which arose time and again in Greece (such as the Orphic movement) were not connected with the priests, but developed among communities with similar religious tendencies.

16   In Pericles' time a law was issued in Athens permitting the prosecution of persons not believing in the gods or spreading impious opinions on the heavenly bodies (Plutarch, *Life of Pericles*, 32). The philosopher Anaxagoras, who maintained that the sun was a red-hot stone and the moon a lump of earth drawing its light from the sun, was the first victim of this law; he succeeded in escaping from Athens. Pericles' learned mistress, Aspasia, was also accused of impiety and Pericles had to exert great effort to secure her acquittal. The poet Diagoras of Melos was sentenced to death and had to flee for his life. The Sophist Protagoras may also have had to stand trial for heresy, but escaped from Athens before the court met and his books were burned publicly in the market place; there are, however, scholars who doubt the reliability of this report. Euripides too was accused of the same offense, but he came to no harm; cf. Glotz—Cohen, *op. cit.*, II 428 ff.; J. B. Bury, "The Age of Illumination," *CAH* V (chap. XII), pp. 382 ff.

17   The Panathenaia were held annually, but from the 6th century on the practice was introduced of celebrating them with much greater pomp every fourth year. The festival included games (horse-races, athletic events, competitions in recitation and music) and, in particular, a festive procession with the participation of all the high officials, members of the council, military leaders, etc. The procession passed beyond the limits of the city, ascended the Acropolis, and ended at the entrance to the Pantheon, the great temple of the goddess Athena. The festival, which included the offering of rich sacrifices, was financed by the city treasury.

18   Not without cause did the Old Oligarch (the author of *The Constitution of the Athenians*, 3, 8) unleash his bitter mockery of the Athenians, who could not devote themselves to the affairs of law and justice because they were always too busy celebrating festivals. In other Greek cities, too, festivals in honor of various gods were celebrated with great pomp, cf. P. Stengel, *Die griechischen Kultusaltertümer* (3rd ed.), Munich, 1920, pp. 218 ff.

19   A detailed description of the festivals in Magnesia on the river Maeander is given by Kern, *op. cit.*, nos. 98, 100. For the festivals and games in the Hellenistic cities in general see Jones, *The Greek City*, pp. 227 ff.

20   On the cult of rulers in the Hellenistic Age see E. Kornemann, "Zur Geschichte der antiken Herrscherkulte," *Klio*, 1 (1902), 51 ff; Kaerst, *op. cit.*, II, pp. 376 ff.; W. S. Ferguson, "The Leading Ideas of the New Period," *CAH*, VII (chap. I), pp. 13 ff.; L. R. Taylor, *The Divinity of the Roman Emperor*, Middletown, Conn, 1931, pp. 1–34.

21   Thus, for instance, Alexander the Great, the founder of Alexandria in Egypt, was regarded as the city's official god.

22   Entire books of the works of pre-Socratic Greek philosophers have not survived; fragments were collected by Diels, *op. cit.* For the beginning of philosophy in Greece see J. Burnet, *Early Greek Philosophy* (3rd. ed), New York, 1920 [4th ed., New York, 1958; Ed.]; T. Gomperz, *Griechische Denker; eine Geschichte der antiken Philosophie* (4th ed.), I, Berlin, 1922 (Engl. transl.; *Greek Thinkers; History of Ancient Philosophy*, I, London, 1901); E. Zeller, *Die Philosophie der Griechen in ihrer geschichtlichen Entwicklung dargestellt* (6th ed.), I, 1–2, Leipzig, 1919–20; [W. K. C. Guthrie, *A History of Greek Philosophy*, I, Cambridge, 1962; Ed.]

23   Of the enormous literature on Plato mention should be made of the following: U. Wilamowitz-Moellendorff, *Platon* (2nd ed.), I–II, Berlin, 1920; A. E. Taylor, *Plato* [(7th ed.), London, 1960; Ed.]; E. Barker, *Greek Political Theory; Plato and his Predecessors* (4th ed.), London, 1951, pp. 109 ff.; W. W. Jaeger, *Paideia; die Formung des griechischen Menschen* (2nd ed.), II, Berlin, 1954 (Engl. transl.: *Paideia; the Ideals of Greek Culture*, II, New York, 1943). On the idea of the "Good" see *Republic*, VI, 19, pp. 508 ff. Of the creator who made the gods, man, and the animals, Plato speaks in *Timaeus*, 5, pp. 27 ff.

24 On Aristotle see W. W. Jaeger, *Aristoteles;
Grundlegung einer Geschichte seiner Entwicklung*
(2nd ed.), Berlin, 1955 (Engl. transl.:
*Aristotle; Fundamentals of the History of his
Development* [2nd ed.], Oxford, 1948).

25 Several schools of philosophy were
founded by Socrates' pupils: the Cynic
school — by Antisthenes; the Cyrenaic
school — by Aristippus; the Megarian
school — by Eucleides. Of these three
schools, only the Cynics continued their
activity during the whole Hellenistic-
Roman period. Plato's school, known as
Academy, underwent several stages of
development, and the ideas of the great
teacher changed in the course of time. The
school of Aristotle's disciples was called
Peripatos; in keeping with the spirit of their
teacher, the scholars developed various
branches of science; thus, for instance, Theo-
phrastus laid the foundations of botany.

26 For the philosophy of the Stoics and the
Epicureans, see M. Pohlenz, *Die Stoa;
Geschichte einer geistigen Bewegung*, I–II, Göt-
tingen, 1948–9; A. E. Taylor, *Epicurus*,
London, 1911.

27 On Hellenistic science see W. H. S. Jones
and T. L. Heath, "Hellenistic Science and
Mathematics," *CAH*, VII (chap. IX), pp.
284 ff.; Tarn, *Hellenistic Civilisation*, pp. 261 ff.

28 See above, pp 23 ff.

29 Examples from Egypt (papyri and inscriptions) are cited by R. Taubenschlag,
*The Law of Greco-Roman Egypt in the Light of
the Papyri* (2nd ed.), Warsaw, 1955, pp.
104 ff. For the Hellenistic army in different
lands and for mixed marriages cf. M.
Launey, *Recherches sur les armées hellénistiques*,
II, Paris, 1950, Index (p. 1301), s.v.
marriages mixtes.

30 Cf. V. Tscherikower, *Die hellenistischen
Städtegründungen von Alexander dem Grossen bis
auf die Römerzeit*, Leipzig, 1927, pp. 190 ff.

31 *Ibid.*, pp. 68, 203.

32 Thus, particularly in the Phoenician
cities which were already familiar with
Greeks before the Hellenistic Age, and
even more so after the Macedonian conquest, when the Greek population increased.
On the other hand, those cities would not
give up their bonds with the local culture;
the inscriptions on their coins were not

only in Greek (as Hellenistic custom re-
quired) but also Phoenician; cf. E. C. F.
Babelon, *Les Rois de Syrie, d'Arménie, et de
Commagène*, Paris, 1890, pp. CIV–CVIII; B.
V. Head, *Historia Numorum; a Manual of Greek
Numismatics* (2nd ed.), Oxford, 1911, p. 790.

33 The papyri provide numerous examples
of Egyptians using Greek names and of
Greeks who took Egyptian names; Egyptian
deities were given Greek names, and many
Greeks participated in Egyptian cults. The
language was also sometimes spoken by
Greeks. For the fusion of both parts of the
population cf. W. Schubart, *Einführung in
die Papyruskunde*, Berlin, 1918, p. 317; L.
Mitteis — U. Wilcken, *Grundzüge und Chrestomathie der Papyruskunde*, I, 2: U. Wilcken,
"Chrestomathie der Papyruskunde," Leipzig, 1912, nos. 50–2; M. I. Rostovtzeff,
"Ptolemaic Egypt," *CAH*, VII (chap. IV),
pp. 144 ff.; H. I. Bell, *Egypt from Alexander
the Great to the Arab Conquest*, Oxford, 1948,
pp. 38 ff.

34 In many papyri, especially from southern Egypt (Thebes) the following formula
is often encountered: "So-and-so wrote for
so-and-so since the latter cannot read or
write." For this question cf. R. Calderini,
"Gli ἀγράμματοι nell'Egitto greco-romano,"
Aegyptus, 30 (1950), 14 ff.

35 Posidonius of Apamea in Syria is perhaps
the only Easterner who played an important
part in the development of Greek culture in
the Hellenistic Age; Nicolaus of Damascus,
the famous Greek historian and a follower of
Herod, and the poet Meleager of Gadara,
also deserve mention.

36 Cf. Schubart, *op. cit.*, pp. 64 ff.; J. G.
Winter, *Life and Letters in the Papyri*, Ann
Arbor, 1933, pp. 192 ff., 238 ff.

37 For the *gymnasia* in Egyptian villages
see Launey, *op. cit.*, II, pp. 836 ff.; A. H. M.
Jones, *The Cities of the Eastern Roman
Provinces*, Oxford, 1937, p. 309; Rostovtzeff,
*Social and Economic History of the Hellenistic
World*, III, p. 1395, note 121.

38 Change of name (not only a man's own
name, but at times also that of his parents)
was an official matter in Egypt and required
the government's permission. Examples in
the papyri are quite numerous: see, for
instance, the cases mentioned in Schubart,

op. cit., p. 333. For Asian lands see for instance, F. Cumont, *Fouilles de Doura-Europos* [*1922–1923*], Paris, 1926, pp. 356, 443.

39   This opinion is already known from the works of Herodotus who identifies the Greek gods with the deities of Eastern lands and Egypt, *e.g.*, Zeus with Amon, Dionysus with Heracles, Aphrodite with Astarte, etc. Cf. I. M. Linforth, *Greek Gods and Foreign Gods in Herodotus*, Berkeley, 1926 (University of California Publications in Classical Philology, vol. 9 no. 1).

40   The papyri from the temple of Sarapis in the vicinity of Memphis offer the most convincing example of the existence of various kinds of ancient Egyptian cults under the rule of the Ptolemies. All the ancient rituals, such as funeral ceremonies on the occasion of the death of the sacred bull Apis, were preserved in this temple unchanged. Not only did the religious service in all its minutest details remain in the hands of the local priests, but the attitude of the Egyptian priests of the temple towards strangers (in one particular case towards a Macedonian soldier residing in the temple) demonstrates open hostility. See U.Wilcken, *Urkunden der Ptolemäerzeit* [*ältere Funde*], I, Berlin, 1922–27. The same picture we see in the temple of Horus in Edfu; cf. M. Alliot, *Le culte d'Horus à Edfu au temps des Ptolémées*, Cairo, 1949 (Institut français d'archéologie orientale, Bibliothèque d'étude, T. 20 Fasc. 1). Three cities in Asia Minor and Syria were called by the Greeks "Hierapolis," i.e., "the holy city" since they had been known as the centers of important cults before the Hellenistic age; from this it may be concluded that the Greeks did not flout the sanctity of the holy sites of ancient cults but accorded them official recognition.

41   In Egypt, for instance, the Greeks lived according to the principles of Hellenistic law (which was a synthesis of the laws of different Greek cities, cf. R. Taubenschlag, "The ancient-Greek-city laws in Ptolemaic Egypt," *Actes du Ve Congrès international de papyrologie*, Brussels, 1938, pp. 471 ff.), while the Egyptian population continued to live according to the ancient Egyptian law called the "land law." The "land law" was officially recognized by the king as a law binding upon the Egyptians. Legal disputes between Egyptians were also brought before Egyptian judges (*laokritai*, i.e., "the people's judges"); cf. for the Egyptian law under the Ptolemies Mitteis—Wilcken, *op. cit.*, II, 1: L. Mitteis, "Grundzüge der Papyruskunde," Leipzig, 1912, *passim;* E. Seidl, *Ptolemäische Rechtsgeschichte*, Erlangen, 1947 [2nd., enlarged, ed. Glückstadt, 1962; Ed.]; Taubenschlag, *op. cit.*, pp. 7 ff. and *passim*. The existence of documents from Babylon, written in cuneiform script, attests to the continuation of the ancient legal tradition even under the rule of the Seleucids. Cf. O. Krückmann, *Babylonische Rechts- und Verwaltungsurkunden aus der Zeit Alexanders und der Diadochen*, Weimar, 1931.

42   See above, note 33.

43   On mixed marriages between Macedonian soldiers and Eastern women, and on the mixed population in the cities (such as Antioch) see above, p. 14.

44   The prohibition of marriages (*epigamia*) between citizens of Naucratis and Egyptians is known to us from one papyrus of the Roman period. Cf. Mitteis — Wilcken, *op. cit.*, I, 2, no. 27.

45   This is the origin of the double name of almost every Hellenistic city in the East— its ancient Eastern name and the new Greek one; for instance, Berythus — Laodicea, Damascus — Demetrias, Hamath — Epiphaneia, Nisibis — Antioch, etc., etc. Big cities were also built near ancient villages such as Alexandria in Egypt, near the Egyptian village of Rhacotis (it is worth noting that in documents written in Demotic, Alexandria is always called by its Egyptian name, Rhacotis). Sometimes a new city was founded through the *synoikismos* (fusion of several villages) on orders from above (for example, the capital of Armenia, Tigranocerta, was founded through the fusion of twelve neighboring villages); sometimes, by the transfer of the population from one city to another (thus the Greeks were transferred from Canopus to Alexandria, and the local population of Babylon to Seleuceia). Cf. Tscherikower, *op. cit.*, pp. 190 ff.

CHAPTER III

THE POLITICAL SITUATION FROM 332 TO 175 B.C.E.

1 Hecataeus wrote a book on the history of Egypt (Αἰγύπτιακά or Αἰγυπτια καὶ ἱστορίαι); according to Josephus (*Against Apion* I, 183, 214), he also wrote a separate work on the Jews (περὶ αὐτῶν Ἰουδαίων συνέγραψε βιβλίον). Fragments from Hecataeus were preserved in Diodorus (XL, 3) and in Josephus (*Against Apion* I, 183 ff.). Yet only the fragments in Diodorus were considered by scholars as authentic, while those in Josephus were regarded as a Jewish forgery and called "Pseudo-Hecataeus;" see Schürer, *Geschichte*, III, pp. 603 ff. Research in the 20th century however has provided several proofs of the authenticity of the fragments in Josephus; cf. H. Lewy, "Hekataios von Abdera περὶ Ἰουδαίων," *ZNW*, 31 (1932), 117 ff. Hereafter the evidence from Hecataeus preserved in Josephus will be accepted as accurate historical information.

2 There has been no special research on Josephus' methods of describing early Hellenism from Alexander the Great down to Antiochus Epiphanes, but the notes of R. Marcus to his translation of Josephus in the Loeb Classical Library are particularly important, as are his appendices to the translation: Vol. VI, pp. 498 ff., vol. VII, pp. 732 ff.

3 For the dating of the *Letter of Aristeas*, see E. Bickermann, "Zur Datierung des Pseudo-Aristeas," *ZNW*, 29 (1930), 280 ff.; A. Momigliano, "Per la data e la caratteristica della lettera di Aristea," *Aegyptus*, 12 (1932), 161 ff.

4 The Zenon papyri were published mainly in the following editions:

a) *Pubblicazioni della Società Italiana per la Ricerca dei Papiri Greci e Latini in Egitto*: *Papiri Greci e Latini*, IV–VII, Florence, 1917–1925.

b) C. C. Edgar, *Zenon Papyri in the University of Michigan Collection*, Ann Arbor, 1931.

c) *Zenon Papyri* (ed. by C. C. Edgar), I–IV, Cairo, 1925–31 (Cairo Musée des antiquités égyptiennes: Catalogue général des antiquités égyptiennes, nos. 59001–59800).

d) *Zenon Papyri* (ed. by C. C. Edgar), V, Cairo, 1940 (Publications de la Société Fouad I de papyrologie, textes et documents).

e) *Zenon Papyri* (ed. by W. L. Westermann et. al.), I–II, New York, 1934–1940.

f) *Catalogue of the Greek Papyri in the John Rylands Library, Manchester*, IV (ed. by C. R. Roberts and E. G. Turner [nos. 554–717]), Manchester, 1952.

The literature on Hellenistic Egypt based on the Zenon papyri (especially on agricultural questions) is very rich. See the most important studies: M. I. Rostovtzeff, *A large Estate in Egypt in the Third Century B. C.*, Madison, 1922; Edgar, *Zenon Papyri in the University of Michigan Collection*, Introduction; C. Préaux, *Les Grecs en Egypte d'après les archives de Zenon*, Brussels, 1947. For Palestine according to the Zenon papyri see V. Tcherikover, "Palestine in the Light of the Zenon Papyri" (Hebrew), *Tarbiz*, 4 (1933), 226 ff., 354 ff.; 5 (1934), 37 ff.

5 The papyrus was published for the first time by H. Liebesny in the papyrological journal *Aegyptus*, 16 (1936), 257 ff.; it was republished in *Sammelbuch griechischer Urkunden aus Ägypten*, Wiesbaden, 1955, no. 8008. The papyrus was written circa 261 B.C.E. (the year 24 or 25 of Ptolemy II Philadelphus' reign). Cf. M. I. Rostovtzeff, *The Social and Economic History of the Hellenistic world*, I, Oxford, 1941, pp. 340 ff.

6 For these historians see above, note 10 to Chapter I.

7 The literature on Alexander's visit to Jerusalem is profuse. Cf. J. Klausner, *History of the Second Temple* (Hebrew) (2nd ed.), II, Jerusalem, 1951, pp. 95 ff.; J. Gutmann, "Alexander of Macedon in Palestine" (Hebrew), *Tarbiz*, 11 (1940), 271 ff.; V. Tcherikover, *Hellenistic Civilization and the Jews* (transl. from the Hebrew), Philadelphia, 1959, pp. 42 ff.

8 It is worth noting that the legend about Alexander's meeting with the Jews reap-

pears in a slightly different form in a Jewish story introduced into a Greek book on Alexander. The book, known as *Pseudo-Callisthenes*, contains a collection of different legends which the Greeks told about their great king. In this Jewish addition Alexander asks the Jewish priests what god they worship, and the priests answer: "We serve one God who created heaven and earth and all things in them. But no man is able to tell His name." And to this Alexander replies: "As servants of the true God go in peace, go. For your God shall be my God." See R. Marcus' Josephus in the Loeb Classical Library, VI, Appendix C, pp. 513 ff.

9 Cf. A. Schalit, "A Chapter in the History of the Party Conflict in Jerusalem at the End of the Fifth Century and at the Beginning of the Fourth Century B.C.E." (Hebrew), *Commentationes Judaico-Hellenisticae in Memoriam Johannis Lewy*, Jerusalem, 1949, pp. 252 ff.; Marcus, *ibid*, pp. 498 ff; For a different view cf. now J. D. Purvis, *The Samaritan Pentateuch and the Origin of the Samaritan Sect*, Cambridge, Mass., 1968, pp. 88 ff. New evidence which has come to light since this chapter was written, changes the view expressed by the author on the historicity of Sanballat in Alexander's time. See F. M. Cross, "The Discovery of the Samaria Papyri," *BAr*, 26 (1963), 110 ff., (Ed.).

10 Cf. Tcherikover, *Hellenistic Civilization and the Jews*, pp. 45 ff. These imaginary accounts are only a fraction of similar tales about Alexander told at different periods both in Eastern and Western countries. Cf. also R. Merkelbach, *Die Quellen des Griechischen Alexander-Romans*, Munich, 1954.

11 In the Talmud, Samaritans are called *Cutim*.

12 βουλευταί, members of the council, from βουλή (Boule) – council. This refers to members of the Council of Elders (γερουσία) in Jerusalem. The figure 1,000 is a common exaggeration in the spirit of midrashic legends.

13 $M^e g$. *Ta'an.*, pp. 339-40. Cf. also Deut. R., 13,5.

14 See below, pp. 215.

15 See below, pp. 192.

16 Curtius, IV, 8, 9–10: "This sorrow [on the death of Hector, son of Parmenion] was made greater by news of the death of Andromachus, to whom he had given the charge of Syria; the Samaritans had burned him alive. To avenge his murder he hastened to the spot with all possible speed and on his arrival [in Samaria?] those who had been guilty of so great a crime were delivered to him."

17 Eusebius, *Chronicon*, ed. by A. Schöne, II, Berlin, 1866, p. 114; and cf. Schürer, *Geschichte*, II, p. 195.

18 *Ant.* XVI, 142; cf. M. Avi-Yonah, *Historical Geography of Palestine* (Hebrew) (2nd ed.), Jerusalem, 1951 [3rd ed., Jerusalem, 1962; Ed.], pp. 128–129.

19 The *Scholion* on $M^e gillat$ *Ta'anit*, while relating that an envoy of the Emperor Gaius Caligula visited the cities of Palestine, says; "before he arrived in Antipatris he got the letter that Caligula was murdered" ($M^e g$. *Ta'an.*, p. 344); see also the passage in M. Git. 7,7: "and he was on the point of going from Judea to Galilee, if he got as far as Antipatris and then turned back." Cf. also *Midrasch Mischle* (ed. by S. Buber, Vilna, 1893) and *Yalkut Shimoni* to Prov. 9:2; The Acts of the Apostles, 23:31 ff.

20 "The people of Sardes and the rest of the Lydians were granted the right to practice the ancient Lydian law and proclaimed free" (Arrian, *Anabasis*, I, 17, 4); in the Ionian cities he abolished the oligarchies, re-established the democracies, and "restored the laws of each of them," (*ibid.*, I, 18, 2). He granted the Arabs and Indians the right "to rule according to their laws" (*ibid.*, VII, 20, 1. εἴπερ οὖν καὶ Ἀράβων, κρατήσας ἐπιτρέψειεν αὐτοῖς, καάπερ Ἰνδοῖς, πολιτεύειν κατὰ τὰ σφῶν νόμιμα). According to Strabo (XVI, 1, 11 [741]) he granted the Arabs "the ancestral independence which they had before" (ἐπιτρέψαντα τὴν πάτριον αὐτονομίαν ἔχειν ἥν εἶχον πρότερον). In Egypt Alexander organized a government modeled on ancient Egyptian tradition (Curtius IV, 7, 5: *conpositisque rebus ita, ut nihil ex patrio Aegyptiorum more mutaret*).

21 The satraps Arimmas and Asclepiodorus are designated as governors in charge of the whole of Syria (Arrian, *op. cit.*, III, 6, 8).

Others were appointed to rule over Coele-Syria – such as Parmenion (Curtius IV, 1, 4) Andromachus (*ibid.*, IV, 5, 9), and Menon (*ibid.*, IV, 8, 11; cf. Arrian, *op, cit..* II, 13, 7). For this question cf. Gutmann, "Alexander of Macedon in Palestine," *loc. cit.*, pp. 275 ff.; H. Berve, *Das Alexanderreich auf prosopographischer Grundlage*, II, Munich, 1926, pp. 38, 60, 88, 259, 302. The question is not at all clear in our sources, and sometimes contradictory information appears; for instance, Andromachus is noted in one place as the governor of Syria, and elsewhere as the governor of Coele-Syria. Parmenion certainly held his office only temporarily, during the time of the conquest.

22 Diodorus XVIII, 3, 1; 39, 6; Curtius X, 10, 2; Justin XIII, 4.

23 Diodorus XVIII, 43: Appian, *The Syrian Wars*, 52.

24 The coin was found in the excavations of Beth-zur (see O. R. Sellers, *The Citadel of Beth-zur*, Philadelphia, 1933, pp. 73 ff.) and belongs to the series of coins bearing the inscription יהד. E. L. Sukenik ("Paralipomena Palaestinensia," *JPOS*, 14 [1934], 181), was doubtful as to the reading of יחזקיהו (Hezekiah), however the majority of scholars regard the reading as correct (cf. N. Avigad, "A New Class of *Yehud* Stamps," *IEJ*, 7 [1957], 149 note 10). As to the time it was minted, the coin could also belong to the Persian period, and this is supported by the fact that the Jewish names Uriah and Ba'ana appear on seals together with the inscription יהד (*Yehud*) in the Persian period (cf. Avigad, *ibid.*, pp. 146 ff.). If indeed the coin belongs to the Persian period, then there is no connection whatsoever between the Hezekiah whose name appears on the coin and the Hezekiah in Hecataeus, unless it is assumed that the latter began to serve as High Priest when still under the Persians, for in 312, according to Hecataeus, he was 66 years old (Avigad, *ibid.*, p. 149; M. Narkis, *Coins of Palestine* [Hebrew], II, Jerusalem, 1938, pp. 37 f., 86).

25 The name Antigonus is one of the first Greek names which appeared among the Jews (Antigonus of Soko) and it may perhaps be supposed that this was connected with the popularity the Diadoch Antigonus Monophthalmus enjoyed among the Jews.

26 Cf. *Against Apion* I, 186 and *Ant.* XII, 9, with *Ant.* XII, 6, and *Against Apion* I, 210.

27 See *Letter of Aristeas*, 12 ff.

28 Concerning the situation in the Persian period, see Ed. Meyer, *Die Entstehung des Judentums*, Halle, 1896, p. 130.

29 τὴν δὲ τοῦ πλήθους προστασίαν δίδοσθαι... τῷ δοκοῦντι τῶν ἱερέων φρονήσει καὶ ἀρετῇ προέχειν.

30 See V. Tcherikover, "Palestine under the Ptolemies," *Mizraim*, 4–5 (1937), pp. 32 ff.

31 For the importance of timber in the Hellenistic economy see Rostovtzeff, *op. cit.* II, Oxford, 1941, pp. 1168, 1254 ff.

32 See Polybius V, 67; and cf. the opinion of F. W. Walbank, *A Historical Commentary on Polybius*, I, Oxford, 1957, pp. 592 f.

33 The official name "Syria and Phoenicia" is mentioned not only in the Vienna papyrus but also in the decree in the *Letter of Aristeas*, 22. On the other hand, the historians did not commonly use the correct name for this administrative district in the Ptolemaic period, although it does occasionally appear. In non-official documents the name "Syria" is encountered. See, for instance, *PSI* 324; *PCZ* 59012, line 125.

34 See Tcherikover, "Palestine under the Ptolemies," *loc. cit.*

35 On the Nabataeans and Hauran in the Zenon Papyri, see below, note 3 to chapter IV.

36 On the relations between the Nabataeans and Ptolemy Philadelphus see *e.g.* W. W. Tarn, "Ptolemy II and Arabia," *JEA*, 15 (1929), 22.

37 Τῶν δὲ στρατευομένων καὶ τῶν ἄλλων τῶν κατοικούντων ἐν Συρίαι καὶ Φοινίκηι.

38 See above, p. 23.

39 See *PCZ* 59006; *PCZ* 59004. And cf. the inscription in *Supplementum Epigraphicum Graecum*, 8 (1937), no. 269, and also P. Roussel, "Epitaphe de Gaza commémorant deux officiers de la garnison ptolémaique," *Aegyptus*, 13 (1933), 145 ff; M. N. Tod, "A Greek Epigram from Gaza," *loc. cit.*, 152 ff.

40 See for instance, D. Cohen, *De Magistratibus Aegyptiis externas Lagidarum regni*

provincias administrantibus, Hague, 1912, pp.
1 ff.

41 See for instance, Polybius V, 87, 6, and
cf. H. Bengtson, *Die Strategie in der hellenistischen Zeit*, III, Munich, 1952, pp. 168 ff.
The latter claims the existence of a special
commissioner in Syria and Phoenicia with
the title of *strategos*.

42 For different forms of the royal Ptolemaic legislation see M.–T. Lenger, "Les lois
et ordonnances des Lagides," *Chronique
d'Égypte*, 19 (1944), 108 ff.

43 This division into *hyparchies* did not leave
its mark upon the terminology of the period
which succeeded Ptolemaic times. The
literary sources dealing with Palestine make
no mention of *hyparchies*. [For the origin of
the administrative unit *hyparchy* cf. now A.
Schalit, *König Herodes*, Berlin, 1969, pp.
187 ff. Ed.]

44 For this office see the Vienna papyrus,
right-hand column, lines 18 ff. Among
other prerogatives he had the right to sell
people into slavery in accordance with the
law pertaining to the leasing of property.

45 For the tax-farmers, see Rostovtzeff,
op. cit., I, p. 345.

46 For this papyrus see Tcherikover,
"Palestine under the Ptolemies," *loc. cit.*,
pp. 40 ff.

47 Maresha (Marissa) was an important
center in the Idumaean region. Its economic
importance is attested by the existence of a
colony of Hellenized Sidonians organized
in an association of their own; their tombs
have been discovered by archaeologists.
See J. P. Peters and H. Thiersch, *The
Painted Tombs in the Necropolis of Marissa
[Mareshaḥ]*, London, 1905. Moreover, it can
be seen from the map that Maresha was
situated at the crossroads of the Gaza–Jerusalem and Ashkelon–Hebron commercial
routes. Nevertheless, Maresha could certainly not compete with the large coastal
cities. For Maresha see also *PCZ* 59006,
line 65.

48 See Nicanor's letter in *PSI* 594, dealing
with the gifts he sent to Apollonius.

49 See the list of 66 names in Tcherikover,
"Palestine under the Ptolemies," *loc. cit.*,
pp. 61 ff. If we add to this list another 11
names from among the native population,

we shall arrive at a total of 78 men,
including Zenon. Yet we must consider the
fact that the lists which have reached us
were preserved by chance. Other lists, had
they been found, would have supplied
additional names.

50 Cf. for instance, *PCZ* 59012.

51 For this see H. A. Thompson, "Syrian
wheat in Hellenistic Egypt," *Archiv für
Papyrusforschung*, 9 (1930), 207 ff.

52 Cf. the distribution of wines among
Apollonius' agents in *PCZ* 59007. Concerning the Roman period, we have the
evidence of Strabo XVI, 2, 9 [751–752],
saying that Laodicea on the sea-shore was
rich in wines and exported most of them
to Alexandria.

53 See *PCZ* 59009 and *PSI* 628, in which
Diodorus appears as the man in charge of
frankincense; ἐπὶ τῆς λιβανωτικῆς.

54 The slave girl bought by Zenon in Birta
in the land of the Ammonites was 7 years
of age. See *C. P. Jud.* no. 1. Of the four
slaves sent by Tobiah two were 10 years
of age and the others were 7 and 8. See
ibid., no. 4. The slaves bought by Zenon
in Idumaea, *PCZ* 59015 *verso*, were also, it
seems, very young (παῖδες). See also below,
pp. 90 ff.

55 Cf. *P. Lille* 29 = L. Mitteis – U.
Wilcken, *Grundzüge und Chrestomathie der
Papyruskunde*, II, 2 (L. Mitteis, "Chrestomathie"), Leipzig, 1912, no. 369: Μηθενὶ
ἐξέστω σώματα πωλεῖν [ἐπ'] ἐξαγωγῆι

56 See *PCZ* 59093, and below, pp. 91 ff.

57 So, for instance, S. Zeitlin, "The Tobias
Family and the Hasmoneans," *PAAJR*, 4
(1932), 180.

58 This is the sole occasion on which the
sources speak of such payment. The sums
offered by the contenders for the High
Priesthood at the time of Antiochus Epiphanes which are mentioned in II Maccabees, 4, have a different connotation.

59 For the chronological problems connected with the rise of Joseph son of
Tobiah and his son Hyrcanus cf. Tcherikover, *Hellenistic Civilization and the Jews*, pp.
128 ff.

60 See Polybius V, 66 f.

61 For the events of 217 and the battle of
Raphia cf. Polybius V, 79 ff. Among the

abundant modern literature on the Fourth Syrian War, see B. Niese, *Geschichte der griechischen und makedonischen Staaten seit der Schlacht bei Chaeronea*, II, Gotha, 1899, pp. 364 ff; E. R. Bevan, *The House of Seleucus*, I, London, 1902, pp. 300 ff. A. Bouché-Leclercq, *Histoire des Séleucides*, I, Paris, 1913, pp. 127 ff.; K. J. Beloch, *Griechische Geschichte* (2nd ed.), IV, I, Berlin, 1925, pp. 687 ff.; W. W. Tarn, "The Struggle of Egypt against Syria and Macedonia," *CAH*, VII (chap. XXII), pp. 723 ff.

62 For Dositheus, son of Drimylus, see *C. P. Jud.* no. 127. The papyrological material makes it possible to trace the rise of Dositheus in the administration and society of Ptolemaic Egypt. See A. Fuks, "Dositheos son of Drimylos: A Prosopographical Note," *Journal of Juristic Papyrology*, 7–8 (1953–1954), 205 ff.

63 This assumption would also fit in with the putative date at which both books were written. II Maccabees was written in the Hellenistic Age, while III Maccabees was apparently written in the Roman period.

64 For this inscription see H. Gauthier and H. Sottas, "*Un décret trilingue en l'honneur de Ptolémée IV*, Cairo, 1925. Sottas thought the inscription included the word Eleazar, which could lead to far-reaching conclusions concerning the situation in Judea. However, this reading has been proved unfounded by W. Spiegelberg ("Beiträge zur Erklärung des neuen dreisprachigen Priesterdekretes zu Ehren des Ptolemaios Philopator," *Sitzungsberichte der philosophisch-philologischen und der historischen Klasse der Bayerischen Akademie der Wissenschaften zu München*, Munich, 1925 [4. Abh.]), and scholars who came after him, though F. M. Abel, *Histoire de la Palestine*, I, Paris, 1952, p. 83, repeats Sottas' erroneous reading.

65 On the Fifth Syrian War, see Bevan, *op. cit.*, II, pp. 29 ff.; Bouché-Leclercq, *op. cit.*, I, pp. 167 ff., and especially the brilliant exposition of M. Holleaux, *Etudes d'épigraphie et d'histoire grecques*, III, Paris, 1942, pp. 317 ff.

66 *PL*, vol. 35, col. 562: *Pugnantibus contra se Magno Antiocho et ducibus Ptolemaei, in medio Judaea posita in contraria studia scindebatur, aliis Antiocho, aliis Ptolemaeo faventibus.*

67 *Ibid.*, col. 563; *Cumque Antiochus teneret Judaeam, missus Scopas, Aetholus, dux Ptolemaei partium, adversus Antiochum fortiter dimicavit cepitque Judaeam, et optimates Ptolemaei partium secum abducens, in Aegyptum reversus est.*

68 On Daniel as a historical source, see below, Chapter V.

69 For the interpretation of this verse see also D. R. Schlatter, "Die B ᵉne pariṣim bei Daniel," *ZAW*, 14 (1894), 145 ff; E. Taeubler, "Jerusalem 201 to 199 B.C.E.; on the history of Messianic movements," *JQR* (n.s.), 37 (1946–7), 1 ff., 125 ff., 249 ff.

70 Cf. E. Bickermann "La Charte séleucide de Jérusalem," *REJ*, 100 (1935), 4 ff.

71 For the list of the High Priests in Josephus, see below, p. 110.

72 From the translation by G. H. Box and W. O. E. Oesterley in *The Apocrypha and Pseudoepigrapha of the Old Testament*, ed. by R. H. Charles, I, Oxford, 1913.

73 See *Ant.* XII, 142.

74 See *Ant.* XII, 142: κατὰ τοὺς πατρίους νόμους.

75 Cf. Holleaux, *op. cit.*, II, Paris, 1938, p. 92.

76 See E. Bickermann, *Der Gott der Makkabäer*, Berlin, 1937, p. 53.

77 See II Macc. 4:11. This Johanan was a priest of the Hakkoz family and his son was one of the two envoys Judah Maccabee sent to Rome. See I Macc. 8:17.

78 See J. F. Moore, "Simeon the Righteous," *Jewish Studies in Memory of Israel Abrahams*, New York, 1927, pp. 348 ff.

79 See II Macc. 3.

80 Cf. E. J. Bickermann, *Les Institutions des Séleucides*, Paris, 1938, pp. 164 ff.

CHAPTER IV
SOCIAL CONDITIONS

1 See *C. P. Jud.* 2a = *PCZ* 59004. For the Zenon papyri dealing with Palestine, see V. Tcherikover, "Palestine in the Light of the Zenon Papyri" (Hebrew), *Tarbiz*, 4 (1933), 226 ff., 354 ff.; 5 (1934), 37 ff., and *idem*, "Palestine under the Ptolemies," *Mizraim*, 4–5 (1937), 9 ff.; cf. also J. M. Harper, Jr., "A Study in the Commercial Relations Between Egypt and Syria in the Third Century Before Christ," *American Journal of Philology*, 49 (1928), 1 ff.; L. H. Vincent, "La Palestine dans les papyrus ptolémaïques de Gerza," *RB*, 29 (1920), 161–202; F. M. Abel, "Marisa dans le papyrus 76 de Zénon," *ibid.*, 33 (1924), 566–574; *idem*, "La liste géographique du papyrus 71 de Zénon," *ibid.*, 32 (1923), 406 ff.

2 See *PCZ* 59006. There appear, one after another, Gaza, Maresha and Adoraim (in its Greek transcription 'Αδώρεον).

3 On Hauran in the Zenon papyri, see *PCZ* 59008, line 35, and *PSI* 406. Nabataeans are mentioned in *PSI* 406, when two of Zenon's men (Drimylus and Dionysios) came into contact with them.

4 This list is in *P. Iand.* inv. 413 *verso*, which was published as document no. 3 in *C. P. Jud.* The Idumaean name Kousnatanos is one of the many names derived from that of the Idumaean god Kos. See, for instance, J. P. Peters and H. Thiersch, *The Painted Tombs in the Necropolis of Marissa* [*Marêshah*], London, 1905, pp. 44 ff., 54.

5 Cf. the text of the order in H. Liebesny, "Ein Erlass des Königs Ptolemaios II Philadelphos über die Deklaration von Vieh und Sklaven in Syrien und Phönikien (PER Inv. N². 24.552 gr.)," *Aegyptus*, 16 (1936), 257 ff. See especially the right-hand column lines 12 ff., which deal with the local women whom the soldiers took for themselves.

6 This papyrus gained much attention in research literature because of its mention of Tobiah's men who established military settlements. See the bibliography attached to *C.P. Jud.* no 1.

7 On slavery in the Ptolemaic kingdom, see W. L. Westermann, *Upon Slavery in Ptolemaic Egypt*, New York, 1929; *idem*, *The Slave Systems of Greek and Roman Antiquity*, Philadelphia, 1955.

8 A detailed discussion on this papyrus is to be found in Tcherikover, "Palestine under the Ptolemies," *loc. cit.*, pp. 68 ff. For another point of view, cf. M. I. Rostovtzeff, *A large Estate in Egypt in the Third Century B.C.*, Madison, 1922, p. 33, and *idem*, *The Social and Economic History of the Hellenistic World*, III, Oxford, 1941, p. 1394.

9 For Heracletus, see Tcherikover, *ibid.*, p. 63.

10 Pegai (Πηγαί, Pegae – "the springs") may be identified with the modern Rosh ha-'Ayin, near Petaḥ Tiqva of today. See also *Ant.* XII, 261, and cf. D. A. Alt, "Pegai," *ZDPV*, 45 (1922), 221 ff. The city Antipatris was founded on the same site in Herod's times.

11 This interpretation, however, involves a certain change in the text of the papyrus as published in *PSI* 406 (ἱέρεαν instead of ιερεα). See Tcherikover, "Palestine in the Light of the Zenon Papyri," *loc. cit.*, p. 232.

12 For the explanation of this decree see W. L. Westermann, "Enslaved Persons who are Free," *American Journal of Philology*, 59 (1938), 1 ff. Cf. also Rostovtzeff, *Social and Economic History*, I, pp. 340 ff., III, pp. 1400 ff. Rostovtzeff (*ibid.*, I, p. 342) raises the question whether the Greek ruling class had not turned the traditional Eastern forms of slavery, which were less rigid, into the strict Greek ones.

13 See Tcherikover, "Palestine under the Ptolemies," *loc. cit.*, p. 86 note 87.

14 Beth-anath, which appears in *PCZ* 59011, *PSI* 594, column III, and *PCZ* 59004, is apparently to be sought in Lower Western Galilee, to the east of Acco (Ptolemais), despite difficulties stemming from locating the site there. Cf. F. M. Abel, *Géographie de la Palestine*, II, Paris, 1938, pp. 265 ff.; M. Avi-Yonah, *Historical Geography of Palestine* (Hebrew), (2nd ed.), Jerusalem,

1951 [3rd ed., Jerusalem, 1962, Ed.], p. 136. Cf. also W. F. Albright, "Contributions to the Historical Geography of Palestine," *AASOR*, 2–3 (1921–2), 20.

15   In *PSI* 554, the name Beth-anath is not mentioned, just as there is no mention of any other geographical place-name in Palestine; yet it may be assumed almost with certitude that this papyrus refers to Apollonius' estate in Galilee. Although the papyrus has lacunae, it is possible to discern that this is a letter dealing with agricultural questions. The names of its sender and addressee have not survived, although the latter may have been Apollonius himself. The sole first name appearing in various fragments of the papyrus is that of Melas, who is also mentioned in *PCZ* 59004, line 30; 59019, line 9; 59131; *PSI* 594.

16   See the Vienna Papyrus (above, note 5 to Chapter III), left column, line 18.

17   In the document the name Ἰεδδοῦς appears, yet there is no doubt that this is a variant of the Hebrew name Jaddua, just as Ἰησοῦς is of Joshua. In *Ant.* XI, 302, 306, 322, 347, Jaddua is transcribed as Ἰαδδοῦς.

18   See *PCZ* 59015 verso — five letters which Zenon wrote to various officials of the Ptolemaic administration in Palestine after leaving the country. They deal with slaves Zenon had bought in Maresha in Idumaea and who had run away from him. See above, p. 74.

19   B. Mazar [Maisler], in "The House of Tobiah" (Hebrew), *Tarbiz*, 12 (1941), 122, had already suggested that there is a connection between the Tobiads in the Hellenistic Age and the son of Tabeel [*ben Tov'al*] in Isaiah 7:6. See the grounds for this assumption in his article "Ben Tabal and Beth Tuviya" (Hebrew), *Eretz Israel*, 4 (1956), 249 ff.

20   The remains in 'Irāq al-Amīr have been described by numerous scholars. A detailed description is given by H. C. Butler, "Ancient Architecture in Syria" *Princeton University Archaeological Expeditions to Syria in* 1904–1905, Div. 2, Section A, Pt. 1, Leyden, 1907, pp. 1–25. For the problem of the character of the remains cf. O. Plöger, "Hyrkan im Ostjordanland," *ZDPV*, 71

(1955), 70 ff. and especially 73–8. See also C. C. McCown, "The 'Araq el-Émir and the Tobiads," *BAr*, 20 (1957), 63 ff. As to the name Tobiah carved upon a rock in 'Irāq al-Amīr, opinions concerning the date of the inscription are divided. Thus, for instance, L. H. Vincent, "La date des épigraphes d'"Arâq el-Emîr," *JPOS*, 3 (1923), 67, is of the opinion that paleographically, the inscription belongs to the time of Ptolemy Philadelphus, and that the Tobiah of the inscription is identical with the Tobiah in the Zenon papyri; Mazar, however ("Ben Tabal and Beth Tuviya," *loc. cit.*, p. 250), holds that paleographical considerations make it possible to attribute the date to an earlier period, i.e., the end of the 6th or the beginning of the 5th centuries, and that this inscription may refer to the Tobiah in Zech. 6:9.

21   The following are the papyrological documents from Zenon's archives connected with the Tobiads: a) *PCZ* 59003 = *C.P. Jud.* no. 1; b) *PCZ* 59004 = *C.P. Jud.* no. 2a; c) *PCZ* 59005 = *C.P. Jud.* no 2b; d) *PCZ* 59802 = *C.P. Jud.* no. 2c; e) *P. Lond.* inv. 2358 (A), first published in *C.P. Jud.* no. 2d; f) *PCZ* 59076 = *C.P. Jud.* no. 4; g) *PCZ* 59075 = *C.P. Jud.* no. 5.

22   See *C.P. Jud.* no. 2a line 6: Σουραβιτ... οις and *ibid.* no. 2d, line 15.

23   Josephus mainly emphasizes the activity of Hyrcanus, the son of Joseph son of Tobiah, and is completely silent on the ancient bonds between the Tobiads and Transjordan. For the dating of the architectural remains, in view of the fact that Josephus ascribes vast construction works to Hyrcanus, cf. Vincent, "La date des épigraphes d' 'Arâq el-Emïr," *loc. cit.*, pp. 55 ff.; W. F. Albright, *The Archaeology of Palestine* (rev. ed.), New York, 1956, pp. 149 ff.

24   On the whole, the narrative does not show a favorable attitude toward the other sons of Joseph son of Tobiah, and provides no details on their lives. They are by far less wise than Hyrcanus, and envy him.

25   In a number of mss. of *Ant.* (XII, 158) the king is called Ptolemy Euergetes, while the VF and Epitome (E) mss., as well as the Latin translation, omit the words "Euer-

getes father of Philopator." It seems, however, that this was a deliberate omission in order to avoid contradictions in the chronology of Josephus. It also stands to reason that the source from which Josephus drew his information wished to distinguish between Ptolemy III Euergetes I and Ptolemy VII Euergetes II, and therefore emphasized in his account the fact that Euergetes was the father of Philopator.

26 Of the abundant literature on the rise of Joseph son of Tobiah and his son Hyrcanus, see H. Willrich, *Juden und Griechen vor der Makkabäischen Erhebung*, Göttingen, 1895, pp. 91 ff.; A. Büchler, *Die Tobiaden und die Oniaden im II Makkabäerbuche und in der verwandten jüdisch-hellenistischen Literatur*, Vienna, 1899, pp. 43 ff.; Ed. Meyer, *Ursprung und Anfänge des Christentums*, II, Stuttgart and Berlin, 1921, pp. 128 ff.; J. Wellhausen, *Israelitische und jüdische Geschichte* (8th ed.), Berlin, 1921, pp. 229 ff.; W. Otto, "Hyrkanos," *RE*, vol. 17, pp. 527 ff.; A. Momigliano, "I Tobiadi nella preistoria del moto maccabaico," *Atti della Reale Accademia delle Scienze di Torino*, 67 (1931–2), 165 ff.; S. Zeitlin, "The Tobias Family and the Hasmoneans," *PAAJR*, 4 (1932–3), 169 ff.; M. Holleaux, *Études d'épigraphie et d'histoire grecques*, III, Paris, 1942, pp. 337 ff.; Plöger, "Hyrkan im Ostjordanland," *loc. cit.*, pp. 70 ff. A number of scholars (for instance, Otto) stress the fact that the passages in *Ant.* XII, 221 ff., dealing with Hyrcanus and his attitude toward his brothers are couched in a less legendary style than previous ones; accordingly they point out that Josephus may have used an additional source for them. But this hypothesis is not mandatory.

27 On the system of tax-collection in Ptolemaic Egypt, cf. U. Wilcken, *Griechische Ostraka aus Ägypten und Nubien*, Leipzig, 1899, in particular pp. 513 ff., and C. Préaux, *L'économie royale des Lagides*, Brussels, 1939, pp. 450 ff.

28 According to *Ant.* XII, 175 f., the Ptolemaic revenue from the districts of Syria and Palestine amounted to 8,000 talents, and Joseph son of Tobiah promised to double this sum, i.e., to collect 16,000 talents. This amount seems exaggerated when compared with other extant information concerning the revenues of Egypt at the time of Ptolemy Philadelphus. Thus, for instance, in his commentary to Daniel 11:5, Hieronymus says that Ptolemy Philadelphus had a total annual income of 14,800 talents from Egypt proper; and according to Diodorus XIX, 56, 5, the income of Antigonus' kingdom amounted to 11,000 talents. For the total income of the Ptolemies cf. also Préaux, *op. cit.*, pp. 424 ff.

29 See *Ant.* XII, 175 ff. Josephus does not use the correct administrative designation for the area under Ptolemaic rule in southern Syria and Palestine at that period, viz., "Syria and Phoenicia," but speaks of Coele-Syria, Phoenicia, Judea, and Samaria, thus confusing, as is his wont in such matters, conditions obtaining in an earlier period with those of his own time.

30 The source which Josephus uses does not express either any feeling of revulsion with regard to the immoral methods of its heroes, Joseph and Hyrcanus.

31 Compare the liberal attitude of Joseph son of Tobiah towards the dietary laws with that of the heroes of the Book of Daniel or of the martyrs at the time of Antiochus' persecution (II Macc. 6–7; see also IV Maccabees). This approach may also be compared with that of the author of the *Letter of Aristeas*, 128 ff.

32 This is, of course, a distinctly legendary feature since there is no reason to think that the sons of Joseph son of Tobiah and the grandsons of Tobiah, who had maintained close connections with Ptolemy Philadelphus and Apollonius, did not receive, as Hyrcanus, a proper education.

33 See V. Tcherikover, *Hellenistic Civilization and the Jews* (transl. from the Hebrew), Philadelphia, 1959, pp. 129 f.

34 It may be assumed that the sons of Joseph son of Tobiah must have been among the heads of the pro-Ptolemaic aristocracy whom Hieronymus mentions in his commentary on Daniel. Cf. Hieronymus' commentary on Daniel 11:13–4 in F. Jacoby, *Die Fragmente der Griechischen Historiker*, II, D (Text), Berlin, 1929, 260 F 45, p. 1224.

35 Josephus, in *Ant.* XII, 229, conforming to his practice, does not add "the Just" to

the name of Simeon the High Priest, since in accordance with his account, Simeon I is the one called "the Just" (*Ant.* XII, 43). For this question see also G. F. Moore, "Simeon the Righteous," *Jewish Studies in Memory of Israel Abrahams*, New York, 1927, pp. 348 ff., who doubts, though without sufficient basis, the very existence of Simeon I. This assumption is accepted by J. Jeremias, *Jerusalem zur Zeit Jesu*, II B, Leipzig, 1937, p. 5 note 1. Cf. also J. H. Weiss, *Dor Dor we-Dorshaw* (*Zur Geschichte der jüdischen Tradition*) (Hebrew; 4th ed.), I, Vilna, 1904, pp. 78 ff., Graetz,*Geschichte*, II, 2, p. 235; S. Krauss, "The Great Synod," *JQR*, 10 (1898), 347 ff.

36   While the document *C.P. Jud.* no. 1 speaks of "Birta" ('εν Βίρται τῆς 'Αμμανίτιδος), Josephus in *Ant.* XII, 230 tells about the building of βᾶρις meaning fortress, a word which also appears in other places in Josephus' works. [For the word and its meaning see C. B. Welles, *Royal Correspondence in the Hellenistic Period*, New Haven, 1934, pp. 320 f. s.v. βᾶρις; the material in Josephus appears in A. Schalit, *Namenwörterbuch zu Flavius Josephus*, Leyden, 1968 (*A Complete Concordance to Flavius Josephus*, ed, by K. H. Rengstorf, Suppl. I), and in the forthcoming vol. I of the Complete Concordance to Josephus. [Ed.]

37   It must be emphasized that Josephus tells that it was Hyrcanus who had built Birta; he completely ignores the fact that Hyrcanus actually returned to his ancestors' homeland and to a region which had long been the stronghold of their power.

38   See above, p. 82.

39   See *Ant.* XII, 236.

40   This was already the time of Seleucus IV's rule. The question is whether ties between Hyrcanus and Onias III on the one hand, and Heliodorus on the other, were developing at that time. See also Plöger, "Hyrkan im Ostjordanland," *loc. cit.*, pp. 78 ff.

41   On Hyrcanus as the possible author of the Book of Ecclesiastes see E. Renan, *Histoire du peuple d'Israël*, IV, Paris, 1893, p. 275.; H. Gressman, "Die ammonitischen Tobiaden," *Sitzungsberichte der Preussischen Akademie der Wissenschaften*, Berlin, 1921,

pp. 670 f.; and L. Herzfeld, *Geschichte des Volkes Jisrael* (2nd. ed.), I, Leipzig, 1863, pp. 194 ff. According to the opinion of Herzfeld and his followers, such as Gressmann, there is a connection between Hyrcanus' rise and the Messianic hopes of the people.

42   According to Neh. 11:10–4, 1,192 priests were living in Jerusalem; 1 Chron. 9:13 puts the figure at 1,760. These figures correspond to the view that the 1,500 priests mentioned in Hecataeus were those living within the boundaries of the city of Jerusalem. Cf. also A. Büchler, *Die Priester und der Cultus im letzten Jahrzent des Jerusalemischen Tempels*, Vienna, 1895, p. 49. Yet it is certain that the total number of priests was far greater. The Hasmoneans of Modiin may serve as an example of priests whose permanent residence was outside the city. For priests in provincial cities cf. again Büchler, *op. cit.*, pp. 159 ff. A different opinion about the 1,500 priests mentioned in Hecataeus is expressed by S. Klein, *Erez Yehuda* (Hebrew), Tel Aviv, 1939, pp. 37 ff., but his arguments are hardly convincing.

43   On Hecataeus and Jews see also H. Lewy, "Hekataios von Abdera περὶ 'Ιουδαίων," *ZNW*, 31 (1932), 117 ff.

44   See above, p. 54.

45   This passage, as well as the following ones from the *Letter of Aristeas*, are taken from the English translation by M. Hadas, *Aristeas to Philocrates*, New York, 1951.

46   See II Macc. 3:10 ff.

47   See *Ant.* XII, 145. The main discussion is in E. Bickermann, "Une proclamation Séleucide rélative au temple de Jérusalem," *Syria*, 25 (1946–8), 67 ff.

48   See, for example, Wellhausen, *op. cit.*, p. 229 note 1; Willrich, *op. cit.*, pp. 107 ff.; Moore, "Simeon the Righteous," *loc. cit.*, pp. 361 ff.; Ed. Meyer, *op. cit.*, p. 130 note 1.

49   Is this an instance of duplication with Manasseh of the story about Sanballat and the foundation of the Samaritan temple? Cf. *Ant.* XI, 302 f.

50   The family of Hezir (see Neh. 10:21; I Chron. 24:15) became quite famous, because of the inscription discovered by De Saulcy in 1854 and published ten years

later by C. J. M. de Vogüé. See the latter's work *Le Temple de Jérusalem*, Paris, 1864. S. Klein, *Judisch-Palästinisches Corpus Inscriptionum*, Vienna, 1920, pp. 14 ff., attempted to bolster the assumption that the priests whose names are engraved in the inscription belonged to the Boethusians, a family the foundations of whose greatness were laid in Herod's time. Accordingly, Klein quite arbitrarily reads *Beney Baytos* instead of *Beney Yosef* which appears in the inscription. N. Avigad, who made a careful study of the inscription, came to the conclusion that for paleographical reasons it must be attributed to approximately the first half of the 1st century B.C.E. See his *Ancient Monuments in the Kidron Valley* (Hebrew), Jerusalem, 1954, pp. 59 ff.

51   For this matter cf. the famous words of Josephus in *Against Apion* I, 60; "Ours is not a maritime country; neither commerce nor the intercourse which it promotes with the outside world has any attraction for us."

52   See Neh. 3; Ben Sira, 38.

CHAPTER V

THE HELLENISTIC MOVEMENT IN JERUSALEM
AND THE PERSECUTIONS OF ANTIOCHUS

1 Of the abundant literature on the Book of Daniel see especially the commentaries of A. A. Bevan, *A Short Commentary on the Book of Daniel*, Cambridge, 1892; J. A. Montgomery, *A Critical and Exegetical Commentary on the Book of Daniel*, Edinburgh, 1927 (in *The International Critical Commentary*), and in particular of R. H. Charles, *A Critical and Exegetical Commentary on the Book of Daniel*, Oxford, 1929. Cf. also H. H. Rowley, "The Unity of the Book of Daniel," *HUCA*, 23, I (1950–1), 233 ff., and *idem*, "The Composition of the Book of Daniel," *Vetus Testamentum*, 5 (1955), 272 ff. See also M. A. Beek, *Das Danielbuch; sein historischer Hintergrund und seine literarische Entwicklung*, Leyden, 1935; H. L. Ginsberg, *Studies in Daniel*, New York, 1948.

2 The article by E. Täubler, "Jerusalem 201 to 199 B.C.E. On the History of the Messianic Movement," *JQR* (n.s.), 37 (1946–7), 1 ff., may serve as an example of an exaggerated use of the Book of Daniel.

3 The best text of I Maccabees is that of W. Kappler in *Septuaginta*, *Vetus Testamentum Graecum*, Auctoritate Societatis Litterarum Gottingensis editum, Vol. IX, fasc. 1: Maccabaeorum liber I, Göttingen, 1936, and of II Maccabees of W. Kappler and R. Hanhart in *ibid.*, vol. IX, fasc. 2: Maccabaeorum liber II, Göttingen, 1959. The ancient Latin translations are also important for determining the right version. See D. de Bruyne – D. B. Sodar, *Les anciennes traductions latines des Machabées*, Abbaye de Maredsous, 1932. Among the numerous commentaries on the Books of the Maccabees particular note should be taken of those by C. L. W. Grimm to I Maccabees, Leipzig, 1853, and to II Maccabees, Leipzig, 1857 (in O. D. Fritzsche and C. L. W. Grimm, *Kurzgefasstes exegetisches Handbuch zu den Apokryphen des Alten Testaments*, Lfg. 3 and 4) which laid the foundations of the scholarly interpretation of these books; of K. F. Keil, *Commentar über die Bücher der Makkabäer*, Leipzig, 1875; and of H. Bévenot, *Die beiden Makkabäerbücher, übersetzt und erklärt*, Bonn, 1931, all in German. See also the commentary in French by F. M. Abel, *Les Livres des Maccabées*, Paris, 1949, and in English by J. C. Dancy, *A Commentary on I Maccabees*, Oxford, 1954. Cf. the following studies dealing in general with the Book of the Maccabees: B. Niese, *Kritik der beiden Makkabäerbücher; nebst Beiträgen zur Geschichte der Makkabäischen Erhebung*, Berlin, 1900; R. Laqueur, *Kritische Untersuchungen zum zweiten Makkabäerbuch*, Strassburg, 1904; J. Wellhausen, "Über den geschichtlichen Wert des zweiten Makkabäerbuchs im Verhältnis zum ersten," *Nachrichten von der Königl. Gesellschaft der Wissenschaften zu Göttingen*. Philologisch-historische Klasse, 1905, pp. 117 ff.; H. W. Ettelson, "The Integrity of I Maccabees," *Transactions of the Connecticut Academy of Arts and Sciences*, 27 (1925), 249 ff,; E. Bickermann, "Makkabäerbücher," *RE*, Vol. 27, pp. 779 ff.; A. Momigliano, *Prime linee di storia della tradizione maccabaica*, Torino, 1931; K. D. Schunck, *Die Quellen des I, und II. Makkabäerbuches*, Halle, 1954.

4 Not only Judah Maccabee, but the whole of the Hasmonean family are the heroes of the book. For the time the book was written cf. Momigliano, *op. cit.*, p. 34; E. J. Bickermann, *Der Gott der Makkabäer*, Berlin, 1937, p. 145. In the eyes of the book's author the Hasmoneans alone were those into whose hands the salvation of Israel was committed.

5 Here is the list of the documents included in I Maccabees:

a) A letter from the Jews of Gilead to Judah and his brothers asking for assistance against the pagans, 2:10–3.

b) The covenant between Judah and Rome, 8:22–32.

c) A letter from Alexander Balas to Jonathan, 10:18–20.

d) A letter from Demetrius I to the Jews, 10:26–45.

e) A letter from Demetrius II to Jonathan, 11:30–7.

f) A letter from Antiochus VI to Jonathan, 11:57 (actually a brief extract from a document rather than the document itself).

g) A letter from Jonathan to Sparta, 12:6–18.

h) A letter from the King of Sparta to Onias, the High Priest, 12:20–3.

i) A letter from Demetrius II to Simeon, 13:36–40.

j) A letter from the Spartans to Simeon, 14:20–3.

k) The decision of the people to put Simeon at the head of the nation, 14:27–45.

l) A letter from Antiochus VII to Simeon, 15:2–9.

m) A letter from the Consul Lucius, 15:16–21.

6 The author of I Maccabees does not invent non-existent victories, but sometimes he avoids matters which are not to the credit of the Hasmonean family, and particularly of Simeon. Thus, for instance, II Macc. 14:17 tells of the defeat Simeon suffered in a battle against Nicanor, while I Maccabees is silent about this in a parallel passage.

In the course of the 19th century I Maccabees was definitely preferred by leading scholars. Niese, in his book mentioned above (note 3), tried to reverse this judgment and gave preference to II Maccabees. The value of his study lies in the fact that he revealed the worth of II Maccabees as a historical source, and pointed out its literary and historiographic qualities against the background of the "pathetic" Hellenistic historiography of the era. Yet, in his desire to prove the indisputable importance of II Maccabees, and to emphasize its value as a source, Niese neglected I Maccabees to such a degree that he doubted the very existence of Mattathias the Hasmonean because he is not mentioned in II Maccabees. A more balanced approach is displayed by Wellhausen in the study mentioned above (note 3). While

emphasizing the dominant value of I Maccabees, he does not deny the importance of II Maccabees. Recent examination of II Maccabees in the light of new documentary material, proves that it should be dealt with more attentively than even Wellhausen did; however, Niese's one-sided view should be avoided.

7 See II Macc. 2:19 ff.

8 Cf. the legendary description of Heliodorus in II Macc. 3; the account of Antiochus Epiphanes' death, his repentance, and the letter he was supposed to have written to the Jews before his death (*ibid.* 9); Judah Maccabee's dream before the last battle with Nicanor (*ibid.* 15:11 ff.); etc.

9 The fact that Jason does not mention the Hasmonean family at all may be additional proof of the fact that he wrote at an earlier period. Jason's cognomen "of Cyrene" proves that he was not born in Judea, and it is difficult to tell how well he knew Palestine. In contrast to I Maccabees, II Maccabees does not indicate a thorough knowledge of the geography of the land.

10 On the nature of Hellenistic historiography see in particular P. Scheller, *De hellenistica historiae conscribendae arte*, Diss., Leipzig, 1911.

11 The reconstruction of the history of the great families which determined the character of Jewish society in those fateful generations involves the analysis of information provided in the Books of Ezra and Nehemiah, II Maccabees, Josephus, and the talmudic sources. I Maccabees, which is wholly devoted to the history of the Hasmoneans, hardly adds anything to the elucidation of this problem.

12 See above, p. 110.

13 See above, p. 103.

14 See below, p. 125.

15 There are scholars, such as L. Herzfeld, *Geschichte des Volkes Jisrael* (2nd ed.), I, Leipzig, 1863, p. 218, who thought that here the reading should be *Minyamin* instead of *Binyamin*, relying upon the assumption that the priestly family of that name, one of the *mishmarot* of the Temple (Neh. 12:5, 17; I Chron. 24:9), was meant. But it now seems that one should follow the

ancient Latin translator, who here reads *Bilgga* instead of *Binyamin* (*de tribu Balgea*) – cf. I. Chron. 24:14. Since it cannot be assumed that the Latin translator attributed Simeon's origin to the Bilgah family on his own responsibility, it must be assumed that he found this information in an early Greek text which he used for his translation. See also Abel, *Les Livres des Maccabées*, p. 316.

16 The term in Greek is προστάτης. This may be assumed to have been a traditional Jewish office in the Temple. See, for instance, Jer. 20:1: "chief governor in the House of the Lord," or II Chron. 24:11: "the chief priest's officer," which is rendered in the Septuagint as προστάτης.

17 For the office of *agoranomos* in the Palestinian cities see also *Ant*. XVIII, 149, which says that Agrippa served as *agoranomos* in the city of Tiberias.

18 For a detailed analysis of the episode concerning Heliodorus see E. Bickermann, "Héliodore au temple de Jérusalem," *Annuaire de l'Institut de Philologie et d'Histoire Orientales et Slaves*, 7 (1939–44), 5 ff.

19 See II Macc. 3:10–1; IV Macc. 4:3.

20 Cf. Polybius XXVI; Livy XLI, 20; Diodorus XXIX, 32: XXXI, 16.

21 On Antiochus Epiphanes' methods as the founder of Hellenistic cities in his kingdom, see V. Tscherikower, *Die hellenistischen Städtegründungen von Alexander dem Grossen bis auf die Römerzeit*, Leipzig, 1927, pp. 176 ff.; cf. also A. H. M. Jones, *The Cities of the Eastern Roman Provinces*, Oxford, 1937, pp. 250 ff.

22 See V. Tcherikover, "Antiochus' Persecutions and their Problems" (Hebrew), *Eshkolot* (Σχολια – *Commentationes de Antiquitate Classica*), 1 (1954), 91.

23 The Apamea peace treaty, following Antiochus III's defeat in the battle of Magnesia, imposed hard conditions upon the Seleucid kingdom (Polybius XXI, 42; Diodorus XXIX, 10; Livy XXXVIII, 38; Appian, *The Syrian Wars*, 38 ff.) which lost areas to the north of Taurus in Asia Minor, and was forced to pay heavy tribute. In addition, it had to provide hostages and accept restrictions of its military power (*e.g.*, a prohibition of keeping elephants and warships).

24 A negative evaluation of Antiochus as a realistic politician may be found in W. G. A. Otto, "Zur Geschichte der Zeit des 6. Ptolemäers," *Abhandlungen der Bayerischen Akademie der Wissenschaften*, phil.-hist. Klasse, Munich, 1934. A much more positive opinion is expressed by W. W. Tarn, *The Greeks in Bactria and India* (2nd ed.), Cambridge, 1951, pp. 183 ff. For an evaluation of Antiochus' policy cf. also E. Reuter, *Beiträge zur Beurteilung des Königs Antiochos Epiphanes*, Diss., Münster, 1938.

25 The sale of priestly offices was a normal practice in the Hellenistic Age, in Asia Minor as well as in Egypt. On buying the office of High Priest in the traditions dating from the end of the Second Temple Period see G. Alon, *Studies in Jewish History in the time of the Second Temple, the Mishnah and the Talmud* (Hebrew), I, Jerusalem, 1957, pp. 60 ff. Cf. also II Macc. 11:3.

26 The first opinion is expressed by Ed. Meyer, *Ursprung und Anfänge des Christentums*, II, Stuttgart and Berlin, 1921, p. 145; the second by Bickermann, *Der Gott der Makkabäer*, pp. 59ff.; see also the next note.

27 This is also the opinion of B. Niese, *Geschichte der griechischen und makedonischen Staaten seit der Schlacht bei Chaeronea*, III, Gotha, 1903, p. 96, and of E. R. Bevan, *The House of Seleucus*, II, London, 1902, p. 169. This interpretation fits in with Antiochus' general policy, and the parallel between the Antiochenes of Jerusalem and the Seleucians of Gaza and the Antiochenes of Acco-Ptolemais, who appear on the coins of Gaza and Acco, confirms the assumption that Jerusalem was transformed into a Greek *polis* with the name Antioch, in the same way as Acco-Ptolemais changed its name to Antioch, and Gaza to Seleuceia. Regarding Bickermann's theory as expressed in his above-mentioned book, cf. V. Tcherikover, "*Antiochia in Jerusalem*" (Hebrew), *J. N. Epstein Jubilee Volume*, Jerusalem, 1950, pp. 61 ff.

28 See above.

29 Cf. I Macc. 1:14–5: "And they built a *gymnasium* in Jerusalem according to the manner of the Gentiles. They also submitted themselves to uncircumcision, and repudiated the holy covenant; yea, they

joined themselves to the Gentiles, and sold themselves to do evil." See also II Macc. 4:14–5: "that the priests were no longer interested in the services of an altar, but despising the sanctuary and neglecting the sacrifices, they hurried to take part in the unlawful displays held in the palaestra after the quoit-throwing had been announced – thus setting at nought what their fathers honored and esteeming the glories of the Greeks above all else."

30 For the phenomenon of the *gymnasium* becoming the province of the well-to-do, see A. H. M. Jones, *The Greek City from Alexander to Justinian*, Oxford, 1940, p. 224.

31 For the number 3,000, see II Macc. 4:40. This is the number of men Lysimachus, Menelaus' brother, armed against the rebels in Jerusalem.

32 This is Bickermann's opinion; see *Der Gott der Makkabäer*, pp. 63 ff.

33 See above, note 21.

34 Until Antiochus' persecutions however, there was no direct activity on the part of the Jewish Hellenizers against the Jewish religion.

35 It is worth noting that Josephus, who had read neither Jason of Cyrene's works nor II Maccabees, says nothing about Jason's reform. Instead, he associates the changes introduced by the Hellenizers with Menelaus and the Tobiads. It follows that subsequent generations regarded Jason as only an insignificant and fleeting personality, while the Tobiads, and Menelaus, who was connected with them, remained in the memory of the people as the true implementors of the revolution.

36 See *War* I, 31; if Jason's name is substituted for Onias' in this passage, it could be supposed that Jason had two clashes with the Tobiads: first in 171 and again in 168. But to which of these two clashes is Josephus referring when speaking about a clash between the High Priest and the Tobiads? It seems that he confused both of them. The end of the passage corresponds better to the events of 168, but the beginning, describing the banishment of the Tobiads from the city, induces another impression. In 168 Menelaus did not leave the city but shut himself up in the

akra, and the Tobiads presumably did likewise. We may conjecture, therefore, that the passage was based upon the events of 171, but in his hurry to pass on to the history of Antiochus' persecutions, Josephus combined them with those of the year 168. Cf. V. Tcherikover, "War I, 1, 1 as a Historical Source" (Hebrew), *Madda'ey ha-Yyahadut*, I, Jerusalem, 1926, p. 197; idem, *Hellenistic Civilization and the Jews* (transl. from the Hebrew), Philadelphia, 1959, pp. 392–5.

37 See above, note 25.

38 Only II Maccabees gives an account of the circumstances of Onias' death, and his murder by Andronicus. In *War* I, 33, Josephus states explicitly that Onias son of Simeon, i.e., Onias III, founded the Temple of Onias in Egypt, in which case he could not have been murdered by Andronicus in Antioch during the period to which II Maccabees refers. Cf. also *War* VII, 23. Even from *Antiquities* XII, 237, it appears that Onias died a natural death, yet the founder of the Temple of Onias, according to this work, was Onias IV and not Onias III. Some difficulty arises from Diodorus XXX, 7, 2 (cf. also John of Antioch, frag. 58, *apud* C. W. L. Müller, *Fragmenta Historicorum Graecorum*, IV, Paris, 1851, p. 558), who relates that Antiochus ordered Andronicus to be put to death not because the latter had murdered Onias, but because he had killed Seleucus IV's son. It seems however that neither Josephus' narrative, nor the traditions about Onias preserved in the Talmud or in the commentary on the Psalms of Theodore of Mopsuestia (see Schürer, *Geschichte*, III, pp. 144 ff. and F. Bäthgen, "Siebenzehn makkabäische Psalmen nach Theodor von Mopsuestia," *ZAW*, 6 [1886], 276 ff.) can altogether discredit the detailed and consistent record of II Maccabees. Even the contradiction between II Maccabees and Diodorus can be reconciled; see also Tcherikover, *Hellenistic Civilization and the Jews*, p. 469 note 40.

39 See II Macc. 4:44 ff. Ptolemy, son of Dorymenes, who later played an important part in the military actions against the rebellious Hasmoneans, appears here for the first time as one of the representatives

of the anti-Jewish policy at the court of Antiochus.

40　The studies of Otto and Bickermann have lent weight to the theory that two campaigns by Antiochus IV in Egypt should be taken into account, the first in 169 and the second in 168. As for the second, nobody doubts its chronology, since it is known that Antiochus retreated from Egypt for the last time after the ultimatum of Popillius Laenas, the Roman representative. The date of this ultimatum is to be placed very shortly after the Roman victory over Macedon at Pydna (22 June, 168 – a date which is absolutely certain). Yet there are problems concerning the date of Antiochus' first campaign. Papyrus no. 583 in the *Catalogue of the Greek Papyri in the John Rylands Library*, *Manchester*, IV, Manchester, 1952, provides the information that in November 170 time reckoning in Egypt was already fixed according to the joint reign of both kings, Ptolemy Philometor and Ptolemy Euergetes, and it is generally accepted that the joint rule of the two brothers started only after the end of Antiochus' first Egyptian campaign. Accordingly this campaign should be ascribed to the year 170 and not 169. See C. Préaux, "Eric G. Turner, *A Ptolemaic Vineyard Lease*, Bulletin of the John Rylands Library 31 (1948), pp. 3–16 et 1 pl.," *Chronique d'Egypte*, 24 (1949), 134; A. Aymard, "Tutelle et usurpation dans les monarchies hellénistiques," *Aegyptus*, 32 (1952), 85 note 2. Bickermann, in an excellent analysis in *Chronique d'Egypte*, 27 (1952), 396 ff. ("Sur la chronologie de la sixième Guerre de Syrie") defends his previous opinion in a comprehensive discussion of all the problems, and as long as no additional evidence to the contrary has appeared, we may abide by his chronological theory.

41　*P. Tebtunis*, III, 698. We cannot fix the date with certainty, but it may be assumed that the ceremony took place in Memphis at the time of Antiochus' second campaign. Antiochus no longer felt under any obligation to Ptolemy Philometor after the latter had openly conspired with the enemies of the Seleucid kingdom.

42　See in particular Otto, "Zur Geschichte der Zeit des 6. Ptolemäers," *loc. cit.*, pp. 80 ff. Sources concerning the context of the ultimatum offered by Popillius Laenas are very numerous. See Polybius XXIX, 27; Diodorus XXXI, 2; Livy XLV, 12; Appian, *The Syrian Wars*, 66; Justin XXXIV, 3, and others. The day on which the ultimatum was delivered to Antiochus by Popillius Laenas may truly be considered as the turning point in the history of Antiochus' kingdom.

43　*Against Apion* II, 83: *..cum non esset hostis, et super nos auxiliatores suos et amicos adgressus est,......*

44　It seems that the news of the rebellion of the city of Aradus in Phoenicia (of which Hieronymus speaks in his commentary on Daniel 11:44), belongs here, too.

45　Antiochus' second visit to Jerusalem is also mentioned in the sources. Of his first visit in 169, Daniel (11:28) writes: "And he shall return to his own land with great substance; and his heart shall be against the holy covenant; and he shall do his pleasure, and return to his own land"; and of the second visit in 168: "..and he shall return, and have indignation against the holy covenant, and shall do his pleasure; and he shall return, and have regard unto them that forsake the holy covenant" (*ibid.* 11:30). Read side by side dispassionately the two passages can only be interpreted as referring to two similar actions. Attempts to prove that the first passage relates to a personal visit of Antiochus, while the second deals with the sending of his messenger, Apollonius, are pointless.

46　The settlement of Roman legionaries in Italian cities by the second Triumvirate led to a social revolution, and later even to an attempt at a defensive war by the Italians against the legionaries. See R. Syme, *The Roman Revolution*, Oxford, 1939, pp. 207 ff. Daniel's phrase "and shall divide the land for a price" (11:39) indicates that the soil of Jerusalem, which until then had been in the hands of the Jews, was divided wholly or partly among the new settlers.

47　The reading "people of a foreign god" instead of "with a foreign god" has been accepted by the majority of scholars.

Charles, *op. cit.*, p. 316, leaves the customary vocalization in "fortresses" and translates the sentence as follows: "He shall use for the strongest fortresses the people of a strange god." Montgomery, *op. cit.*, p. 463 reads: "And he shall make for defenders of fortresses a people of a foreign god."

48 For the Macedonians as a pseudo-ethnic group in the Hellenistic Age see M. Launey, *Recherches sur les armées hellénistiques*, I, Paris, 1949, pp. 321, 330, 360 ff. And see above, pp. 7–8.

49 See, for example, Dancy, in his commentary on I Maccabees (above, note 3), p. 73.

50 Cf. also the threat of Ptolemy Euergetes in the story of the rise of Joseph son of Tobiah (*Ant.* XII, 1959). See also I Macc. 3:36; II Macc. 11:2.

51 Baal-Shamin was the chief Syrian god, whose cult spread all over the area. See H. Seyrig, "Antiquités Syriennes," *Syria*, 14 (1933), 238 ff.; 26 (1949), 29 ff. Cf. also M. Avi-Yonah, "Mount Carmel and the God of Baalbek," *IEJ*, 2 (1952), 122.

52 Dushara was at first the desert god of the Arabs. Later he became the god of wine and was identified with Dionysus. For him see also J. Gutmann, "The Canaanite God Shadrapa and His Nature" (Hebrew), *J. N. Epstein Jubilee Volume*, Jerusalem, 1950, p. 74.

53 Cf. *M^eg. Ta'an.* 337: "On the twenty-third of Marḥeshwan the *Soreg* in the court was razed. For the Gentiles built there a sacred place and brought prostitutes there, and when the Hasmoneans were victorious, they took it from them and demolished it."

54 See Bickermann, *Der Gott der Makkabäer*, p. 114.

55 The fact that the *Ḥasidim*, decided to join Mattathias the Hasmonean, in spite of his intention to fight on the Sabbath, testifies that they were not simply imbued with a blind, fanatical faith, but knew how to relax the strict observance of the laws where this could have endangered the rebel movement.

56 Cf. Bickermann, *op. cit.*, pp. 117 ff.

57 See Tcherikover, "Antiochus' Persecutions and their Problems," *loc. cit.*, pp. 86 ff.

58 See Otto, "Zur Geschichte der Zeit des 6. Ptolemäers," *loc. cit.*, p. 85, and I. Heinemann, "Wer veranlasste den Glaubenszwang der Makkabäerzeit?," *MGWJ*, 82 (1938), 161 ff. in contrast with Bickermann, *op. cit.*, 127 ff., and Dancy, *op. cit.*, p. 75, who deny the existence of the general decree.

59 See II Macc. 6:1, for the identification of the man ("Geron, the Athenian" being a personal name and not "an old man of Athens"); cf. I. and L. Robert, "Bulletin Epigraphique, " *REG*, 64 (1951), 130.

60 See II Macc. 6–7, and cf. IV Maccabees.

61 This is Bickermann's theory, *op. cit.*

62 See above, note 59.

63 See I Macc. 1:60; II Macc. 6:10.

CHAPTER VI

THE HASMONEAN REVOLT AND JUDAH MACCABEE'S WAR AGAINST THE SYRIANS

1   See B. Niese's edition, *Flavii Iosephi Opera*, 7 vols., Berlin, 1885–1894; it is also worthwhile comparing the English translation by H. St. Thakeray and R. Marcus (last three books of *Antiquities* by L. H. Feldman), published in the Loeb Classical Library (Vols. II-VIII), London, 1927-1965.

2   Our sources do not specify the lapse of time between the beginning of the religious persecution until the outbreak of the revolt at Modiin. It may, however, reasonably be assumed that even before the open rebellion there were many acts of opposition to the orders of King Antiochus IV, who in effect abrogated the Jewish religion; otherwise, the religious persecution in itself cannot be understood. The king and his officials apparently gave credence to the assurance of the Hellenizers and hoped that the people would accept the royal command without opposition. When the first instances of disobedience occurred, they regarded them as isolated acts and severely punished the people involved, in the belief that such measures would intimidate others into compliance with the royal injunctions. In any event, the account in the First Book of Maccabees makes it clear that opposition was essentially passive — even though it is difficult to believe that there were no cases of active resistance as well, unorganized though they may have been. The story of the death of many Jews who refused to fight on the Sabbath (I Macc. 2:29–38; II Macc. 6:11) proves that passive opposition continued even after the first military actions took place. For a different view see Chapter V, above.

3   Eusebius (*Onomastikon*, ed. by E. Klostermann, Leipzig, 1904, p. 132, lines 16–7) defines its position reckoning the distance from Diospolis (Lod); according to his usual practice, this indicates administrative affiliation.

4   However the phrase ἄρχων καὶ ἔνδοξος καὶ μέγας might indicate that what is meant is not necessarily an official position.

5   See also II Macc. 5:27.

6   As we shall see (p. 172 below), the same mountains served as a refuge for Judah and his men after the defeat at Beth-zacharia, and until the battle of Elasa.

7   On the *akra* see p. 134 above.

8   M. Avi-Yonah, *Historical Geography of Palestine* (Hebrew), (3rd ed.), Jerusalem, 1962, pp. 32 f.

9   Avi-Yonah, *loc. cit.*

10   See also Josephus, *Ant.* XII, 261.

11   This situation did not change even after the district of Akrabattine was joined to Judea at a later period, for then, too, the road to Anuath Borcaeus remained in Samaria.

12   Cf. *Ant.* XIV, 458; and cf. W. F. Albright, "New Identifications of Ancient Towns," *BASOR*, 9 (1923), 7 f.

13   *Josippon*, ed. by S. Huminer, Jerusalem, 1956, p. 82.

14   Appian, *Syriaca*, 62.

15   Strabo, XVI, 2, 25; Diodorus, XVI, 41, 3.

16   *E.g.*, Jaffa and Jabneh (Jamnia) whose attitude to the Jews living there is described in II Macc. 12:3–8.

17   F. M. Abel, in his commentary to the Book of Maccabees (*Les Livres des Maccabées*, Paris, 1949), p. 60, is of the opinion that the best point of attack is the stretch of road between the hill and Upper Beth-horon.

18   The author of the Book of Maccabees, who is mainly interested in what took place in Judea, naturally ignores the real reasons for this royal journey.

19   On this title and the responsibilities it carried, see M. Avi-Yonah, *op. cit.*, p. 32.

20   Polybius, 5:65 and 79.

21   See also *Josippon*, p. 83. The figures given in the course of the story likewise contradict the previous ones; according to I Macc. 4:1, Gorgias took six thousand men with him; according to verse 15 in the same chapter, three thousand of the enemy army were killed.

22 Including Abel, *Les Livres des Maccabées*, p. 68.

23 See N. Avigad, "New Light on the MSH Seal Impressions," *IEJ*, 8 (1958), 117 ff.

24 See Abel, *loc. cit.*

25 From his position at Mizpeh Judah Maccabee had the choice of either first marching on Jerusalem, in the event of an attack by the garrison stationed there, or towards Emmaus, if that direction appeared more dangerous; the second alternative is what actually happened.

26 Cf. Deut. 20:5–9.

27 M. Avi-Yonah, "The 'War of the Sons of Light and the Sons of Darkness' and Maccabeean Warfare," *IEJ*, 2 (1952), 2 f.

28 It is typical of our two sources that whereas the author of the First Book of Maccabees explains the interruption of the pursuit of Nicanor on sound strategic grounds, the author of the Second Book of Maccabees (8:26) attributes the move to the advent of the Sabbath — a religious viewpoint versus a political one.

29 Lysias' campaign is attributed to "the next year," i.e., 148 according to the Seleucid reckoning, or 164/3 B.C.E.

30 In the brief language of the source; "And they came to Idumaea and encamped at Beth-zur," a version infinitely better than the reading, "And they came into Judea," to which a number of commentators still subscribe.

31 According to II Macc. 11:6, Lysias laid siege to Beth-zur, although from I Macc. 4:61 it appears that the place was fortified only afterwards, so that it was not yet in a position to withstand a siege during Lysias' first campaign.

32 Later on, as ruler of the state, Jonathan could employ coercive measures; he mobilized forty thousand men (I Macc. 12:41), which is an indication of the size of the total population.

33 The letter in II Macc. 11:27 ff., fits in here very nicely.

34 See pp. 81–83 above.

35 Diodorus, XIX, 98–9, testifies to these efforts.

36 Cf. the account of Jonathan's times, I Macc. 9:35; see p. 184 below.

37 Ἐν τῇ Ἰδουμαίᾳ τὴν Ἀκραβαττήνην; the Latin translation separates the two: *in Idumaea et eos qui erant in acrabassene.*

38 It is mentioned as a toparchy of Judea by Josephus, *War* III, 53–4. The only time the Jews both controlled Samaria and were in a position to implement this annexation was from the period of Hyrcanus I to that of Hyrcanus II.

39 On the problems connected with this area, see B. Mazar, "The Tobiads," *IEJ*, 7 (1957), 137–45, 229–38.

40 As opposed to the opinion of Abel, *Les Livres des Maccabées*, pp. 89–90.

41 N. Glueck, "Exploration in Eastern Palestine, III," *AASOR*, 18–19 (1937–39), *passim.*

42 Cf. N. Glueck, *ibid.*, pp. 153–5.

43 M. Avi-Yonah, *Historical Geography*, p. 34.

44 This was also the view of the present writer; see *ibid.*, pp. 160 f.

45 See Abel, *Les Livres des Maccabées*, p. 98.

46 See Abel, *op. cit.*, p. 93. It is doubtful, however, whether the name Tob may be sought in Khirbat at-Tayyiba between Zorah and Bozrah (Bezer), for most of the places with this name were once called Ophrah, Ephraim, etc. The fact that Charax is mentioned in connection with the people of Tob points to a location in southern Bashan.

47 In the manuscripts the versions Αρβανοις, Αρβαττοις, Ακραβαττοις, Αρβακτοις are to be found. It is, of course, also possible to think of 'Arzaba in Galilee, as well as Arubboth-Narbata; this last identification seems more likely. See Abel, *op. cit.*, pp. 95 f.

48 The usual identifications are: Bosora — Buṣrā Askī Shām; Bosor — Buṣr al-Ḥarīrī; Alema — 'Almā; Casphon — Khasfīn; Maker (in some MSS; Maked) — Tell al-Jāmid near al-Maqārīn (this identification, proposed by Abel in "Topographie des campagnes Maccabéennes," *RB*, 32 (1923), 517 ff., seems more plausible than that with Tell Miqdād, subsequently suggested by Abel himself in his *Géographie de la Palestine*, II, Paris, 1938, p. 378); Carnaim — ash-Shaykh Saʻad; see Avi-Yonah, *Historical Geography*, pp. 154, 157 f.

49 It should of course be kept in mind that

Bosora was then not yet the metropolis and capital of the province of Arabia.

50   This name is omitted in I Maccabees; it is added in *Ant.* XII, 340.

51   In Josephus (*Ant.* XII, 340) Casphon and Maker are combined into one name; Χασφομάκη.

52   Abel, "Topographie des Campagnes Maccabéennes," *loc. cit.*, p. 519.

53   We cannot, of course, accept the common version, which has it that Timotheus appeared in Judea. What is meant is that he planned to reconquer Judea after defeating its army.

54   According to Josephus (*Ant.* XII, 348) the Jews crossed "the Great Plain," the Valley of Jezreel, but from I Macc. 5:52, it follows that the reference is to "the great plain over against Beth-shean" (τὸ πεδίον τὸ μέγα κατὰ πρόσωπον Βαΐθσαν) i.e., the plain of Beth-shean itself.

55   According to Josephus, *Ant.* XII, 349, this was a triumphal march beginning with their departure from Beth-shean; however, I Macc. 5:54 maintains, more realistically, that the celebration began only when the caravan reached Jerusalem.

55   The version in some MSS is Σαμαρειαν Samaria, but there is no doubt that the version Μαρισαν in other MSS is the correct one.

57   The information in I Macc. 6:20 and 52, to the effect that even in the early stages of the war the Hasmoneans already knew how to build siege engines is refuted by the fact that, despite years of effort, they did not capture any fortress, until the time of Simeon, who built the first siege engine (καὶ ἐποίησεν ἑλεόπολιν) during the investment of Gezer (I Macc. 13:43).

58   Josephus (*War* I, 41) speaks of 50,000 foot soldiers, 5,000 cavalry, and 80 elephants.

59   There is nothing surprising about their appearance at Modiin; on their way to Beth-zur the Syrians in any case had to advance along the coast, and they may have taken the opportunity to revenge themselves on the town from which their main enemies came.

60   See O. R. Sellers, *The Citadel of Beth-zur,* Philadelphia, 1933 and now also *idem et al.,*

"The 1957 Excavation at Beth-zur," *AASOR*, 38 (1968).

61   See J. W. Crowfoot, *The Buildings at Samaria*, London, 1942, pp. 24 ff.

62   The place suggested by Abel (Topographie des Campagnes Maccabéennes, *RB*, 33 [1924], 214 ff.), Ballūtat al-Yerza, does not fit for two reasons: it is a hill, and not a plain, and the site lies too far to the north.

63   "And when they saw the strength of the royal army... they turned away from them."

64   The author attributes the surrender of Beth-zur to the fact that it was a sabbatical year, and perhaps hints that it would be a good idea to abrogate it during wartime, just as the prohibition against fighting on the Sabbath had been repealed earlier (I Macc. 2:41).

65   The topographical situation necessitates acceptance of the version of Berzetho in *Ant.* XII 397, and not Bethzetho, as Abel suggests (*Les Livres des Maccabées*, p. 135) on the basis of some variants of I Macc. 7:19.

66   There are, however, MSS which raise the number of dead to 50,000.

67   This maneuver demanded considerable daring. Judah placed himself between Nicanor and the base of the king's army in Jerusalem, which meant that in the event of defeat he would be trapped between his enemies. On the other hand, the element of surprise was in his favor. Having learned the lesson of the battle near Kapharsalama, and knowing that Judah held the mountains of Gophna *north* of the road, Nicanor did not expect an attack from the *south.*

68   According to *Ant.* XII, 411.

69   According to I Maccabees, Nicanor fell at the beginning of the battle, while according to Josephus (*Ant.* XII, 406), it was at the end. Josephus praises Nicanor's courage, a rare occurrence in Jewish historiography with respect to the nation's enemies.

70   Some MSS designate the place where Bacchides encamped as Βερεαν, Βερεθ.

71   Abel, "Topographie des campagnes Maccabéennes," *loc. cit.*, pp. 383 ff. Abel's later suggestion (*Géographie de la Palestine*, II, p. 312) that we should read ΑΔΑΣΑ here

instead of the supposedly erroneous rendi-
tion ΑΛΑΣΑ is unacceptable on topographical grounds. Adasa, which lies between
Berea and Jerusalem, was exposed to attack
on both sides, and it is inconceivable that
with only three thousand men Judah would
dare to seize this dangerous position in face
of an enemy force several times his own
strength (in the battle against Nicanor the
numerical ratio was entirely different).

[72] Abel, "Topographie des Campagnes
Maccabéennes," *loc. cit.*, pp. 385 ff.; later
on Abel accepted the Michaelis-Yeivin
theory — see below and the next note.

[73] S. Yeivin, "Topographic Notes"
(Hebrew), *BIES*, 8 (1941), 83 f. This view
was already expressed by J. D. Michaelis
in his annotated German translation of the
First Book of Maccabees, Götingen, 1778,
pp. 193–94.

CHAPTER VII

THE FIRST HASMONEAN RULERS: JONATHAN AND SIMEON

1   υἱοὶ 'Ιαμβρι in Greek (I Macc. 9:36); in *Ant.* XIII, 11, they are erroneously called the sons of Amaraios (οἱ 'Αμαραίου παῖδες). The name יעמרו appears in an Aramaic inscription found at Medeba (Clermont-Ganneau cited by Schürer, *Geschichte*, I, p. 224 note 3).

2   [A. Schalit, *König Herodes*, Berlin, 1969, pp. 168 f. Ed.]

3   According to Graetz's conjecture (*Geschichte*, III, pp. 10 f., cf. also p. 565 notes 1, 5), this was the barrier called *soreg* and this action of Alcimus' is hinted at in M. Mid. 2, 3: "Within it was the *soreg* ten hand-breadths high. There were thirteen breaches in it; these had been originally made by the king of Greece [through their loyal servant, Alcimus], and when they repaired them they enacted that thirteen prostrations should be made facing them." Schürer, *Geschichte*, I, p. 225 note 6, disputes Graetz's view, since we have no evidence that the *soreg* existed prior to the Temple of Herod. In either case, there is reason to believe that Alcimus' intention was to do away with the partition between that part of the Temple which only Jews were permitted to enter and the area which could also be entered by non-Jews.

4   So called in I Macc. 9:54.

5   Gen. R. 65 (pp. 742 ff.).

6   However, the amazing similarity of the account of the state of affairs at the beginning of Alcimus' priesthood in the days of Judah Maccabee and of conditions when Jonathan assumed the leadership, is noteworthy. In both periods Alcimus and Bacchides are allies, in both periods the situation quiets down after the victory of the Greeks, and in both periods Bacchides leaves the country before complete calm is restored. Is this perhaps the case of a single set of facts being applied to two different events?

7   Josephus (*Ant.* XIII, 25) misunderstood I Macc. 9:61, to mean that Bacchides killed these 50 men because they did not carry out their promise to deliver Jonathan to him.

8   [See M. Avi-Yonah, *Historical Geography of Palestine* (Hebrew), (3rd ed.), Jerusalem, 1962, pp. 103 f. Ed.]

9   Here the author of I Maccabees employs an archaistic note, when he compares this beginning of the Hasmonean monarchy to the period of the Judges.

10   A point of interest is that Jonathan did not officiate as High Priest on the Day of Atonement which falls only four days before the Feast of Tabernacles: the festival (*ha-ḥag* — and *ḥag* used without qualification always refers to the Feast of Tabernacles) on which "the daughters of Jerusalem came out and danced," was still considered more important than the Day of Atonement, (Mᵉ. Ta'an, 4, 8 and as it also appears from Neh. 8:13–18).

11   I Macc. 10:25–45, and from that source in *Ant.* XIII, 48 ff.

12   Ed. Meyer, *Ursprung und Anfänge des Christentums*, II, Stuttgart and Berlin, 1921, pp. 254 f.

13   Meyer, *op. cit.*, p. 255 note 1, also is of the opinion that the authenticity of this document should not be doubted. But he points out that since the letter was translated from Greek into Hebrew, and then back into Greek, it is likely that some unintentional alterations of the original crept in. [See also the interpretation of the document given in M. Stern, *The Documents on the History of the Hasmonaean Revolt* (Hebrew), Tel-Aviv, 1965, pp. 97 ff. Ed.]

14   So his full name is given in *Ant.* XIII, 88.

15   So Josephus states explicitly (see *Ant.* XIII, 114).

16   The city is mentioned in II Sam. 13:23; apparently it is identical with the Ephrain of II Chron. 13:19.

17   "Ramathaim-zophim, of the hill-country of Ephraim" (I Sam. 1:1).

18   See E. Renan, *Histoire du peuple d'Israel*, IV, Paris, 1893, p. 401 note 3.

19   In addition to Josephus' account on this point, we have that of Diodorus Siculus, who states (XXXIII, 4) that in his war against the rebels, Demetrius was aided by

"an important foreign force" (ξενικὴ δύναμις ἀξιόλογος).

20 Χαλφὶ in I Macc. 11:70; Χαψαῖος in *Ant.* XIII, 161.

21 Wellhausen doubts whether Jonathan renewed the alliance with Rome after the battle of Hazor. In the first place, he maintains, there simply was not enough time to send emissaries from Jerusalem after the battle at Hazor, which is far away from Jerusalem, and before the new battle against Syria, which is recounted below. Secondly, Jonathan and Simeon were fighting on behalf of Antiochus and Tryphon, as vassals of the Syrian kingdom as it were, and the dispatch of ambassadors to Rome, Syria's enemy, might have aroused the suspicion that they were conspiring to transfer their allegiance to Rome (J. Wellhausen, *Israelitische und jüdische Geschichte* [8th ed.], Berlin, 1921, p. 255 note 1); Schürer, (*Geschichte*, I, p. 237 note 33) for his part, doubts the authenticity of the documents, at least insofar as they refer to Sparta. But these doubts are not well-founded. The ambassadors might have been dispatched from somewhere other than Hazor, and even at a time when Jonathan was away from Jerusalem. As for arousing suspicion about throwing off the Syrian yoke with Roman help, Jonathan's letter to Sparta was likely to have precisely the opposite effect. For the letter recalls that even in the days of Onias — who was not an independent ruler but a vassal of the Ptolemies or the Seleucids — an alliance was concluded between Judea and Sparta, hence it was also permissible for him, Jonathan, to make treaties despite his being a vassal of the king of Syria. Furthermore, since the beginning of the period of frequent changes on the Syrian throne, Jonathan stopped fearing the Syrian kings; on the contrary, those usurpers were afraid of him. And he certainly had no compunction about drawing suspicion on himself by sending emissaries to Rome and Sparta. It is self-evident that Jonathan attached importance to an alliance with Rome. At that period, the kings of both Syria and Egypt stood in dread of Rome, and because of that fear Ptolemy Philometor

did not dare place the crown of Asia on his head.

22 J. Derenbourg, *Essai sur histoire et la géographie de la Palestine*, I, Paris, 1867, p. 99 note 1.

23 *Meg. Ta'an.*, p. 322.

24 See Schürer, *Geschichte*, I, p. 238 note 34.

25 Cf. Ezra 2:33 and M. 'Arak. 9, 6. The phrase in M. 'Eduy. 7, 5, *Yaqim ish Hadar* should read *Yaqim ish Ḥadid*.

26 See Graetz, *Geschichte*, III, pp. 19 f.

27 See Ezra 3:7 and Jonah 1:3. Tarshish is apparently the Spanish city of Tartessus.

28 Thus in *Ant.* XIII, 210. This may be Beth-shiqma, a place unknown today. [Perhaps it is to be identified as al-Jumayza, northeast of Lake Kinnereth. Ed.].

29 On its artistic aspect, see J. Klausner, *In the Days of the Second Temple* (Hebrew) (3rd ed.), Jerusalem, 1954, pp. 210 ff.

30 *Meg. Ta'an.*, p. 319.

31 This is the content and purpose of the first letter which appears at the beginning of II. Macc. (1:1-9).

32 Archeological excavations at Gezer have brought to light the remains of a palace built for the governor appointed by the Hasmonean rulers. Under the remains was found a Greek inscription cursing Simeon for what he did to the pagan residents of Gezer (See J. B. Frey, *Corpus Inscriptionum Iudaicarum*, II, Rome, 1952, no. 1184). In excavations near Gezer a number of Hebrew-Greek inscriptions have been found consisting of the Hebrew words תחם גזר and the Greek name Αλκιου, or simply the two Hebrew words. The Greek name, in the opinion of scholars, is that of the person who carved the inscriptions, while תחם גזר indicates the "Sabbath bounds," i.e., the limit up to which it was permissible to go from the city of Gezer on the Sabbath. But it is unlikely that in the days of the early Hasmoneans it was already customary to mark the Sabbath bounds by special inscriptions. And even if they did, what is a Greek name doing on such purely religious inscriptions? It appears that the words תחם גזר mean: up to here are the plots and fields which belong to the city of Gezer

('*burah shel 'ir* — the outskirts of a city — in the language of the Mishnah [M. 'Eruv. 5:7]), and from here onward is the territory of another city; and the Greek name is that of the official in charge of fixing the boundaries. These inscriptions undoubtedly date from the times of the last of the Hasmoneans who used both Hebrew and Greek even on their coins.

33   G. Hölscher, *Palästina in persischer und hellenistischer Zeit*, Berlin, 1903, pp. 87 f., is of a different opinion.

34   See *M*ᵉ*g. Ta'an.*, *loc. cit.*

35   In *War* V, 139, the deed is attributed vaguely to the Hasmonean kings.

36   This is the view of Wellhausen, *op. cit.*, p. 260 note 2; Meyer, *op. cit.*, II, p. 264 note 1, finds no contradiction between *Antiquities* and I Maccabees and thinks it more natural to attribute the leveling of the hill of the *akra* to the time of its conquest by Simeon.

37   See Strabo, XVI, 2, 28 [759].

38   Derenbourg, *op. cit.*, pp. 450 ff.

39   See p. 257 below. [And cf. also A. Schalit, *op. cit.*, pp. 781 ff. Ed.].

40   [The period covered by the document was also limited by verse 14:41: "until a faithful prophet should arise." Ed.].

41   [The orders date from 142 B.C.E. Concerning the document see M. Stern, *op. cit.*, pp. 128 ff. On the date, see F. Münzer, "Das Konsulpaar von 139 v. Chr." *KLIO*, 24 (1931), 333 f. Ed.].

42   See I Macc. 15:32.

43   And not by Arsaces himself, as stated in I Macc. 14:2–3. [The name Arsaces has in effect been used there as a generic term, applying to all the Parthian kings. Ed.].

44   Κέδρων in the Septuagint (I Macc. 15:39) and Gedor in the Vulgate. In Schürer's opinion (*Geschichte*, I, p. 255), this is the Arab village Qatra, the present-day Gederah. The Syrian translation erroneously renders it Hebron instead of Kedron, while in Graetz' opinion (*op. cit.*, III, p. 16), it should be Ekron instead of Kedron. [Cf. also M. Avi-Yonah, *op. cit.*, p. 110. Ed.].

45   See above, pp. 200–201.

46   Erroneously given as Dagon in *Ant.* XIII, 230.

47   Or, according to *Ant.* XIII, 230 f., he killed the sons later on.

CHAPTER VIII

JOHN HYRCANUS I

1　See p. 206 above.

2　And not in 130–129 B.C.E., as Wellhausen and Niese affirm, in line with Porphyrius. See Ed. Meyer, *Ursprung und Anfänge des Christentums*, II Stuttgart and Berlin, 1921, p. 268 note 1.

3　Plutarch, *Regum et imperatorum apophtegmata*, 184 E–F.

4　See *Ant.* XIII, 245 ff. This fact is particularly stressed by the Greek writers who deal with the wars of Antiochus VII. See Diodorus, XXXIV, 1.

5　See Porphyrius, in Eusebius' *Chronicon* ed., by A. Schöne, I, Berlin, 1866, p. 255; Diodorus, *loc. cit.*

6　As in Josephus' account, *Ant.* XIII, 247.

7　Herod, too, sought for money in David's tomb. See *Ant.* XVI, 179 ff.

8　On Alexander Balas, see above, pp. 187 ff.

9　So says Josephus, who thus understood the biblical report; see *Ant.* IX, 277–9; X, 184; XI, 19, 85.

10　Ḥag. 25a.

11　Lam. R. 3, 7

12　Cf. G. Hölscher, *Palästina in persischer und hellenistischer Zeit*, Berlin, 1903, pp. 75, 81 ff.; J. Klausner, *Jesus of Nazareth* (trans. from the Hebrew), New York, 1929, p. 135 and note 2.

13　See J. Klausner, *History of the Second Temple* (Hebrew) (2nd ed.), II, Jerusalem, 1950, pp. 194 f.

14　See *Ant.* XI, 341.

15　M*e*g. *Ta'an.*, p. 339.

16　Cf. "the Elders of the South," "Our Masters of the South" (Z*e*v. 22b; Y*e*v. 45a and elsewhere); Δαρῶμα in Eusebius; *Doroma* in Hieronymus. Also see *Aruch Completum*, ed. by A. Kohut (2nd ed.), Vienna, 1926, III, s.v. *Darom*, and S. J. Rapoport, *Erech Millin*, Prague, 1854, s.v. *Darom*.

17　According to *Ant.* XIII, 276.

18　*Ant.* XIII, 280. This view Josephus derived from Nicolaus of Damascus, who regarded it as an explanation for the "defeat" of the Greeks, which he considered a greater shame than accepting a bribe.

19　M*e*g. *Ta'an.*, pp. 319, 320.

20　*Op. cit.*, p. 338.

21　[For a different interpretation of this passage in the commentary, see now A. Schalit's remarks in his *Namenwörterbuch zu Flavius Josephus*, Leiden, 1968 (*A Complete Concordance to Flavius Josephus*, ed. by K. H. Rengstorf, Suppl. I. Ed.)].

22　Sota 33a; parallel passages also in Yer. Sota 9, 13; Cant. R. 8, 11; Tosef. Sota 13, 5 (p. 319). It is worth noting that the Voice (*Bat-qol*) spoke in Aramaic, the language of the common people in Judea at the time, of which Josephus uses a number of words in his writings.

23　Ben-Sira, 50:25–6; see M. H. Segal, *The Complete Book of Ben Sira* (Hebrew), Jerusalem, 1953, pp. 348 f.

24　See below.

25　The fact that John Hyrcanus rebuilt the walls of Jerusalem is specifically mentioned at the end of I Maccabees.

26　A. Alt identifies the place with the modern Rosh ha-'Ayin, near Petaḥ-Tiqwa: see his "Pegai," *ZDPV*, 45 (1922), 221 ff.

27　In Mendelssohn's view (L. Mendelssohn, "Senati Consulta Romanorum quae sunt in Iosephi Antiquitatibus," *Acta Societatis Philologae Lipsiensis*, V, Leipzig, 1875, pp. 135 ff.), both these documents pertain to the war of Hyrcanus I against Antiochus VII Sidetes. Despite the fact that the second document speaks of "Antiochus, the son of Antiochus," which could only apply to Antiochus IX Cyzicenus, since Antiochus VII Sidetes and Antiochus VIII Grypus, were sons of Demetrius and not of Antiochus, Mendelssohn asserts that the two references must be to Antiochus Sidetes and that the name of his father was incorrectly given in the second document. According to Josephus (*Ant.* XIII, 278) Antiochus Cyzicenus was only able to devastate the country, but made no conquests, whereas Antiochus Sidetes actually conquered cities and harbors in Judea and forced John Hyrcanus to accept harsh peace terms. However, it is hard to believe that two documents so different from one another in content and style refer to the same matter; and it is even more difficult to accept the assumption that a gross error in the name of the king's father could have crept into an official paper. It therefore seems more reasonable to suppose that while the first document refers to Antiochus Sidetes because it mentions Fannius, the son of Marcus, who was praetor in 132 B.C.E., the second refers to Antiochus Cyzicenus, who also devastated Judea, as Josephus testifies, and may also have con-

quered Jaffa, Gezer and other places, and by this very decree of the Roman Senate he was forced to forgo his war against Hyrcanus and retire to Tripolis. Cf. Schürer, *Geschichte*, I, pp. 261 f., and particularly p. 262 note 7; J. Juster, *Les Juifs dans l'Empire Romain*, I, Paris, 1914, pp. 133 ff. [Cf. also M. Stern, "The Relations between Judaea and Rome during the Rule of John Hyrcanus" (Hebrew), *Zion*, 26 (1961) 1 ff. Ed.]

28 See below, pp. 269 ff.

CHAPTER IX

JUDAH ARISTOBULUS AND JANNAEUS ALEXANDER

1 Quoted by Josephus, *Ant.* XIII, 319.

2 Josephus possessed genuine Hebrew historical sources only up to the end of the princedom of John Hyrcanus; I Maccabees and "The Chronicles of Johanan, the High Priest," mentioned at the end of I Maccabees, which may be the source of the *barayta* in Qid. 66a.

3 Josephus does not attempt to reconcile the contradictions in his sources. [For a different evaluation of the personalities of the Hasmonean rulers, see now A. Schalit, *König Herodes*, Berlin, 1969, p. 762 and note. Ed.].

4 M. Narkiss, *Coins of Palestine* (Hebrew), I, Jerusalem, 1936, p. 97.

5 See Strabo, XVI, 2, 40 [762]. [For another view on the question see below, note 65 to chap. XI. Ed.].

6 Cf. E. Renan, *Histoire du peuple d'Israel*, V, Paris, 1893, p. 110 note 1.

7 For some inexplicable reason, Ed. Meyer *Ursprung und Anfänge des Christentums*, II, Stuttgart and Berlin, 1921, p. 274 note 4, considers it impossible that this territory in Upper Galilee, which was not large, should have been conquered in the course of one year.

8 On Jannaeus Alexander see J. Klausner, *When a Nation Fights for its Freedom* (Hebrew) (9th ed.), Tel Aviv, 1955, pp. 116–91.

9 See also E. Renan, *op. cit.*, V, p. 111 note 2.

10 This point has been emphasized by V. Tcherikover, *Hellenistic Civilization and the Jews* (transl. from the Hebrew), Philadelphia, 1959, pp. 251 ff. Cf. also E. J. Bickermann, *The Maccabees*, New York, 1947, pp. 75 ff.

11 Yer. Sheᵛv. 9, 2; *Midrasch Tehillim* (*Schocher Tob*), ed. by S. Buber, Vilna, 1891, 92:11, p. 410. [Cf. now M. Stern, "The Political Background of the Wars of Alexander Jannai" (Hebrew), *Tarbiz*, 33 (1964), 331 note 37. Ed.].

12 These stories about Ptolemy's atrocities should also be treated with caution, even though they are not implausible. With

regard to what Greek authors say about a Greek king we may ask, in the language of the Talmud: "Why should they lie?"

13 [See Tcherikover, *op. cit.*, p. 98. Ed.].

14 [Cf. also Eusebius, *Onomastikon*, ed. by E. Klostermann, Leipzig, 1904, p. 22. Ed.].

15 [See M. Avi-Yonah, *Historical Geography of Palestine* (Hebrew) (3rd ed.), Jerusalem, 1962, p. 117. Ed.].

16 M. Suk. 4, 9.

17 Tosef. Suk. 3, 16 (p. 197).

18 Suk. 48b.

19 See J. Klausner, *History of the Second Temple* (Hebrew) (2nd ed.), III, Jerusalem, 1951, pp. 120 f.

20 Sota 22b.

21 Thus in *Ant.* XIII, 377; according to *War* I, 93, the number was 8,000.

22 According to *War, ibid.*, only 10,000.

23 The first form is in *Ant.* XIII, 380, and the second in *War* I, 96. According to S. Klein, *Erez Yᵉhuda* (Hebrew), Tel Aviv, 1939, pp. 41 f., 80, 239 ff., this was Beit ha-Meleḳ, identical with Har ha-Meleḳ. See also his article, "Βεμσελις–Βαιθομμις, Βαιθομμη" in *Tarbiz*, 1, 1 (1930), 136–44. And cf. below, note 78 to chap. XI.

24 "When King Jannaeus put the Rabbis to death" (Sota 47a); "When King Jannaeus slew our Rabbis" (Sanh. 107b in the uncensored editions).

25 M. Avot, 1, 8. [For the "Pairs" (*Zugot*) cf. C. Tchernowitz, *Tolᵉdoth Ha-Halakah — History of Hebrew Law* (Hebrew), IV, New-York, 1950, pp. 141 ff.; S. B. Hoenig, *The Great Sanhedrin*, Philadelphia, 1953, pp. 36 ff., 44 ff. and *passim*. Ed.].

26 Yer. Ḥag. 2, 2.

27 Yer. Naz. 5, 5; Gen. R. 91 (pp. 1115 ff.). Cf. also a shorter version in the Babylonian Talmud, Bᵉr. 48a. Schürer's statement about "the strange taste and the strange morality" (*Geschichte*, I, pp. 279 f.) with reference to this legend is difficult to understand. It is after all only a witty popular legend, which does not profess to be esthetic or moral.

28 Cf. J. Klausner, *Jesus of Nazareth. His*

Life, Times and Teaching (transl. from the Hebrew), New York, 1929, pp. 349 ff.

29   Graetz, *Geschichte*, III, 1, p. 129 note 5.

30   [For a different evaluation cf. above, note 3. Ed.].

31   For a detailed discussion of this matter, cf. the reference cited in note 8 above. [On the significance of the dispute between the Hasmoneans and the Pharisees, which continued until the time of Herod, cf. A. Schalit, "Die frühchristliche Überlieferung über die Herkunft der Familie des Herodes", *ASTI*, 1 (1962), 109 ff. Ed.].

32   [Identified by some scholars with the modern Rosh ha-'Ayin, near Petaḥ Tiqwa. Ed.].

33   The city is mentioned in Ezra 2:33, and in M. 'Arak. 9, 6; it is near Modiin.

34   [For the developments in Syria during this period see A. R. Bellinger, "The End of the Seleucids," *Transactions of the Connecticut Academy of Arts and Sciences*, 38 (1949), 78 ff. Ed.].

35   On the Decapolis, see G. Hölscher, *Palästina in persischer und hellenistischer Zeit*, Berlin, 1903, pp. 58 ff.

36   [See M. Avi-Yona, *op. cit.*, p. 162. Ed.].

37   *Maseket Soferim*, ed. by M. Higger, New-York, 1937, 1, 8. In my opinion תורתן של אלכסנדרוס is the correct version, and not תורתן של אלכסנדריים.

38   For a detailed discussion, cf. Hölscher, *op. cit.*, pp. 90 ff.; M. Avi-Yona, *op. cit.*, pp. 45 ff.

39   Undoubtedly Abel-shittim (Num. 33: 49), and not Abel-beth-maacah in the far north.

40   See the detailed list of Syncellus, ed. by W. Dindorf, I, Bonn, 1829, pp. 558 f. On the list of conquests in Moab cf. A. Schalit, "Alexander Jannai's Conquests in Moab" (Hebrew), *Eretz-Israel*, 1 (1951), 104 ff.

41   On the territorial expansion and military importance of Jannaeus' kingdom, cf. M. I. Rostovtzeff, *The Social and Economic History of the Hellenistic World*, II, Oxford, 1941, p. 841; A. H. M. Jones, *The Herods of Judaea*, Oxford, 1938, p. 11.

42   [On Machaerus, see M. Avi-Yona, *op. cit.*, p. 167. Ed.].

43   Hölscher, *op. cit.*, pp. 92 f.

44   [See S. Klein, *Eretz Yehuda*, pp. 81 f.; *idem*, '*Ever Ha-Yarden Ha-Yehudi* (Hebrew), Vienna, 1925, p. 15. And see below, chap. X. Ed.].

45   See J. Klausner, *History of the Second Temple*, III, p. 95, contradicting his statement previously expressed in *In the Days of the Second Temple* (Hebrew), Jerusalem, 1954, p. 211, that it was built by John Hyrcanus.

46   See F. M. Abel, "La Maison d'Abraham à Hebron," *JPOS*, 1 (1920–1), 138 ff.

47   And cf. Klausner, *In the Days of the Second Temple*, pp. 223 f. On this golden vine, cf. H. Willrich, *Das Haus des Herodes zwischen Jerusalem und Rom*, Heidelberg, 1929, pp. 174 f. [See now A. Schalit's remarks on this question in *König Herodes*, p. 8 note 28. Ed.].

48   J. Klausner, *Israelite History* (Hebrew) (which preceded *History of the Second Temple*), I, Odessa, 1909, pp. 260–4. Cf. also *idem*, *In the Days of the Second Temple*, pp. 151–5.

49   On the *Letter of Aristeas* and its tendency, cf. V. Tcherikover, "The Ideology of the Letter of Aristeas," *Harvard Theological Review*, 51 (1958), 59 ff. See also above, pp 54, 106, 110.

50   From the English translation by M. Hadas, *Aristeas to Philocrates* (*Letter of Aristeas*), New York, 1951, pp. 107, 112–5.

51   On Jannaeus' coins, see M. Narkiss, *op. cit.*, pp. 32 ff., 97 ff.; cf. also L. Herzfeld, *Handelsgeschichte der Juden des Alterthums* (2nd ed.), Braunschweig, 1894, pp. 76 f.

CHAPTER X
QUEEN SALOME ALEXANDRA

1 Without a *waw*, in accordance with the system of *defective* spelling (i.e. devoid of *matres lectionis*) and perhaps on the basis of the Aramaic form שְׁלָמָה, as conjectured by G. Dalman in *Jesus-Jeschua*, Leipzig, 1922, p. 13. שלמ צי‎ן without either the first or second *waw* is already extant in an Aramaic inscription. See A. Cowley, *Aramaic Papyri of the Fifth Century B.C.*, Oxford, 1923, pap. 81, line 2, pp. 192 and 198.

2 Eccl. R. 7, 11, on the verse "Wisdom is good."

3 Sifra (Commentar zu Leviticus), ed. by J. H. Weiss, Vienna, 1862, p. 110b.

4 Lev. R. 35, 8.

5 *Meg. Ta'an.* p. 342.

6 Shab. 16b, and Ta'an. 23a, according to Tosaf. to Shab. 16b, s.v. *de'amar*. The word is missing in the published editions of the tractate Ta'anit.

7 Tosef. Bek. 7, 3 (p. 541).

8 See also J. Klausner, *History of the Second Temple* (Hebrew) (2nd ed.), III, Jerusalem, 1950, p. 161.

9 See M. Narkis, *Coins of Palestine* (Hebrew), I, Jerusalem, 1936, p. 33; A. Reifenberg, *Ancient Jewish Coins* (2nd ed.) Jerusalem, 1947, p. 15.

10 *Meg. Ta'an.* p. 319.

11 *Loc. cit.*

12 *Ibid.*, p. 321.

13 See *ibid.*, p. 342 f.

14 *Ibid.*, p. 318.

15 See his *Essai sur l'histoire et la géographie de la Palestine*, Paris, 1867, p. 444 note 6.

16 See above, p. 269 ff; and Klausner, *op. cit.*, III, p. 84.

17 Qid. 66a. See also Klausner, *ibid.*, pp. 137 f.

18 Sota 47a.

19 Yer. Ḥag. 2, 2.

20 M. Avot, 1, 8.

21 See Klausner, *op. cit.*, III, p. 154.

22 Cf. I. Halevy, *Dorot Harischonim* (Hebrew), I. c, Berlin and Vienna, 1923, pp. 506–46.

23 [Cf. H. Buchheim, "Die Orientpolitik des Triumwirn M. Antonius," *Abhandlungen der Heidelberger Akademie der Wissenschaften*, Philos-hist. Klasse, 1960, Abh. 3, p. 16, Ed.]

24 Lev. R. 35, 10 (from the English transl. ed. by H. Freedman and M. Simon, London, 1939, p. 452); and cf. parallel passages in the Babylonian Talmud, Ta'an. 23a, and in Sifra, ed. by Weiss, p. 110b.

25 See, *e.g.*, the legends about the Nazirite sacrifice and the grace after meals, involving Jannaeus and Simeon ben Sheṭaḥ, recounted in detail in Klausner, *op. cit.*, III, p. 154; and cf. above, p. 233.

26 Ber. 48a, and elsewhere.

27 See *Meg. Ta'an.* pp. 342 f.

28 Mekhilta de-Rabbi Ishmael, ed. with an Engl. transl. by J. Z. Lauterbach, III, Philadelphia, 1949, p. 170.

29 It is worth noting this special expression, which was used by two Sages who lived during the height of the Hasmonean dynasty's power. See also Pes., 54b and Luke 2:25. For this expression cf. J. Klausner, *The Messianic Idea in Israel* (Hebrew) (3rd ed.), Tel-Aviv 1950, p. 250 note 16.

30 *Zomem*-witness: collusive witness; plural: *zomemim*.

31 Mak. 5b; Tosef. Sanh. 6, 6 (p. 424).

32 M. Sanh. 6, 4; Yer. Ḥag. 2, 2; Sifri, Deut. 221.

33 See Klausner, *History of the Second Temple*, III, p. 159, and above, p. 191.

34 Derenbourg, *op. cit.*, p. 69 note 1.

35 I Macc. 12:33, and above, p. 000.

36 Yer. Sanh. 6, 5.

37 Deut. R. 3, 5.

38 Sanh. 19a–b.

39 Derenbourg, *op. cit.*, pp. 146 ff. attributes his story in its entirety to Hyrcanus II, who was afraid to try Herod for having killed Hezekiah the Galilean in the presence of Shema'ya the head of the Sanhedrin. Shema'ya, Avṭalyon's "colleague," rebuked the members of the Sanhedrin for fearing to issue a just verdict against Herod. I do not know why Derenbourg saw fit to distort all the historical names, without exception: not Jannaeus but Hyrcanus, not Simeon

ben Sheṭaḥ but Shᵉmaʿya, while the slave becomes Herod and the person killed, Hezekiah.

40   Shab. 14b and 16b; Yer. Kᵉt. 8, 11.

41   See S. Daiches, "Aramaic Inscriptions from the Days of Ezra" (Hebrew), *Ha-schiloah*, 17 (1907), 511–5.

42   J. Klausner, *Jesus of Nazareth, His Life, Times and Teaching* (transl. from the Hebrew) New York, 1929, p. 195.

43   M. ʿEduy. 1, 12; Tosef. ʿEduy., 1, 6 (p. 455).

44   M. ʿEduy. 8, 4. Cf. E. Ben-Yehuda, *Until When was Hebrew Spoken* (Hebrew), New York, 1919, pp. 72–100.

45   Ben-Yehuda, *op. cit.*, pp. 121–4.

46   In the Jerusalem Talmud, this is followed by the statement, "and it was a minor matter in his eyes to divorce her" (Yer. Kᵉt. 8, 11).

47   In the Jerusalem Talmud, this is followed by the statement, "and it was still a minor matter in his eyes to divorce her" (*loc. cit.*).

48   The Jerusalem Talmud has the following version: "a man may buy glasses and bowls, and plates with his wife's *kᵉtubba*."

49   Kᵉt. 82b.

50   *Loc. cit.*

51   Cf. J. Klausner, *The Second Temple in its Greatness* (Hebrew), Tel-Aviv, 1930, pp. 113–4.

52   Yer. Kᵉt. 8, 11.

53   Literally "the House of the Book," meaning the Bible.

54   Qid. 30a; Ḥag. 15b.

55   B. Batra 21a.

56   See Schürer, *Geschichte*, II, p. 494.

57   This conjecture is supported by several considerations. First, Derenbourg, *op. cit.*, p. 249 end of note 2, has already pointed out that "it is difficult to believe that the Jews could have devoted their attention to an institution of this kind during the incumbency of this High Priest [Joshua ben Gamala]." Secondly, Schürer himself (*Geschichte, loc. cit.*) admits that "the ruling [of Joshua ben Gamala] stipulates the extended existence of schools for youth." Finally, what Philo, who lived before the time of the High Priest Joshua ben Gamala, and Josephus, who was the contemporary of this High Priest, say about the education of children in Palestine (see Philo's *The Embassy to Gaius*, 115, and Josephus' *Against Apion*, II, 204) clearly proves that long before the time of Joshua ben Gamala the Torah was taught to the youth and that Jewish children were well-versed in its laws and precepts. Indeed, the Babylonian Talmud itself says (B. Batra 21a) that even before Joshua ben Gamala's ruling "they... made an ordinance that teachers of children should be appointed in Jerusalem," and later on, but still before the time of that High Priest, "they... ordained that teachers should be appointed in each prefecture." And cf. W. Bacher, "Das altjüdische Schulwesen," *JjGL*, 6 (1903), 58, who conjectures that instead of Joshua ben Gamala it should be Joshua ben Pᵉraḥya, who lived one generation before Simeon ben Sheṭaḥ. Cf. also Klausner, *Jesus of Nazareth*, p. 193 note 1. Dalman, *op. cit.*, pp. 30 f. rejects everything written on this subject in the Babylonian and Jerusalem Talmuds, but without a detailed analysis nor adequate scientific foundation.

58   Qid. 66a.

59   *The Embassy to Gaius, loc. cit.*

60   Yer. Kᵉt. 8, 11.

61   Shab. 14b, 16b. Cf. Klausner, *History of the Second Temple*, III, p. 79.

62   Yer. Shab. 1, 1.

63   Shab. 16b.

64   M. Avot, 1, 8–9.

CHAPTER XI

DOMESTIC POLITICS AND POLITICAL INSTITUTIONS

1   See chapter I above.

2   On this subject, cf. E. J. Bickermann, *Les Institutions des Séleucides*, Paris, 1938, p. 164.

3   Evidence of this may perhaps be found in the role played by the High Priest in the legend about Alexander the Great in Palestine; see *Ant.* XI, 317 ff.

4   On these matters, cf. V. Tcherikover, *Hellenistic Civilization and the Jews* (transl. from the Hebrew), Philadelphia, 1959, pp. 119 ff.; cf. also A. Schalit, *Encyclopaedia Biblica* (Hebrew), II, Jerusalem, 1954, cols. 816–25, s.v. Hellenism; and see also pp. 99 ff above.

5   Cf. the summarizing comments of F. M. Abel, *Les Livres des Maccabées*, Paris, 1949, *ad* 15, 1; cf. also Schürer, *Geschichte*, I, p. 249 note 17; Y. Yadin, *The Scroll of the War of the Sons of Light Against the Sons of Darkness*, Oxford, 1962, p. 44 note 6. According to D. Flusser, "The Apocryphal Book of *Ascensio Isaiae* and the Dead Sea Sect," *IEJ*, 3 (1953), 34 ff., ἐθνάρχης is a translation of the Hebrew title *Sar 'am El* (שר עם אל), but this is disputed by Yadin, *loc. cit.* These views reflect a basic error. The interpretation given to the word ασαραμελ, σαραμελ is not correct; for detailed evidence of this see A. Schalit, *König Herodes*, Berlin, 1969, Appendix XIV, pp. 781 ff. The title ἐθνάρχης τῶν Ἰουδαίων, that is "the ruler of the Jews," is the less common term used to indicate the lay authority of the High Priest.

6   Cf. the remarks of Schürer, *op. cit.*, I, p. 269 note 25, who shares the view of the *Hever* as an all-embracing body.

7   Sanh. 82a; 'Av. Zara 36b.

8   A partial exception to this are the coins of King Jannaeus, which omit mention of *Hever ha-Yehudim*. This omission, however, stems from the revolution in Jannaeus' conception of his kingship, which is discussed below.

9   S. B. Hoenig, *The Great Sanhedrin*, Philadelphia, 1953, pp. 32 ff. identifies Simeon the Just with Simeon the Hasmonean, but this is without foundation.

10   Cf. M. Sanh. 1, 5–6.

11   Cf. M. Ḥag. 2, 2; Ḥag, 16b; Yer. Ḥag. 2, 2.

12   On this entire matter, cf. J. Derenbourg, *Essai sur l'histoire et la géographie de la Palestine*, Paris, 1867, p. 91.

13   Cf. I. Macc. 16:14.

14   Cf. note 7, above.

15   According to M. Sanh. 11, 2 (see also Tosef. Ḥag. 2, 9 [p. 235] and Sanh. 88b) in addition to the Great Sanhedrin (*Beth Din ha-Gadol*), there were also three 23-member courts in Jerusalem: one of them met at the entrance to the Temple Mount, one at the door of the Temple Court, and one in the Hall of Hewn Stones. J. Klausner (*History of the Second Temple* [Hebrew], Jerusalem, 1950 (2nd ed.), III, p. 97) assumes that the *Hever* or the Sanhedrin "was composed of these three courts together with the president (*Nasi*) and his deputy (*Av Beth Din*)." The matter cannot be settled on the basis of the available evidence. Nor is it possible to determine whether these three small courts functioned alongside the Great Sanhedrin even in Hasmonean times, or whether the information in the Mishnah, the Tosefta and the Talmud should be attributed to later periods.

16   The following toparchies existed in the days of Jannaeus Alexander: Jerusalem, Jericho, Mizpeh, Beth-zur, Keilah, Beth-ha-Kerem, Ephraim, Lod, Ramathaim, Gedor, Jaffa, Gezer, Akrabatta, Narbata, Eastern Idumaea, Western Idumaea, Jabneh, Arbel, Migdal, Zippori, Arab, Upper Galilee, Betharamatha, and Abel. On this whole question, see A. Schalit, *König Herodes*, pp. 205 f.; *idem*, *Roman Administration in Palestine* (Hebrew), Jerusalem, 1937, pp. 23 ff., and the studies of S. Klein cited there.

17   As E. E. Urbach rightly pointed out. See his "Political and Social Tendencies in Talmudic Concepts of Charity" (Hebrew), *Zion*, 16 (1951), 11.

18   Ma'as. Sh. 5, 9; and cf. Yer. Sota 9, 11.

19   Cf. Urbach, *loc. cit.*

20   The Psalms of Solomon, 17:33.

21   Cf. Bickermann, *op. cit.*, pp. 106 ff.

22   Our sources are entirely silent concerning the method for carrying out the mobilization and the principles by which it operated. Apparently there was a more or less fixed arrangement concerning the obligation of military service in the Hasmonean period. There is reason to believe that the distinction between voluntary wars (wars not commanded by the Torah) and obligatory wars (wars commanded by the Torah) dates to the early days of the Maccabean revolt. According to the Mishnah, in an obligatory war "all go forth, even a bridegroom from his chamber and a bride from her canopy" (M. Sota 8, 7; cf. Tosef. Sota, 7 [p. 309, line 25]). The war of religion in the time of Mattathias the Hasmonean and Judah Maccabee was an obligatory war, whereas the wars which followed were at best, in the eyes of the Pharisees, optional wars. The relations between Jannaeus and his Jewish troops are discussed in detail in Schalit, *König Herodes*, pp. 170–2.

23   See below.

24   According to A. Geiger, *Urschrift und Übersetzungen der Bibel*, Breslau, 1857, p. 64 (cf. also G. Foot Moore, *Judaism*, I, Cambridge, 1946, p. 45) Jose ben Jo'ezer was one of the sixty *Ḥasidim* murdered by Bacchides the Syrian, on the advice of Alcimus, the High Priest. But this is not plausible, as proved by Hoenig, *op. cit.*, pp. 29 f.

25   This is the original reading. See E. E. Urbach, *Gershom G. Sholem Jubilee Volume* (Hebrew), Jerusalem, 1958, p. 55 note 52; A. Schalit, "Kritische Randbemerkungen zu Paul Winters 'On the Trial of Jesus'," *ASTI*, 2 (1963), 86–102.

26   It has been seen above that the Talmud, too, is cognizant of the fact that Johanan the High Priest (i.e., John Hyrcanus) became a Sadducee "in the end." The passage in B^er. 29a goes on to say: "Abaye said: 'Johanan is the same as Jannai,' Raba said: 'Johanan and Jannai are different: Jannai was originally wicked and Johanan was originally righteous'." This indicates that Abaye interpreted the name Jannai as another form, no doubt a

diminutive, of the name Johanan. Even though, from the aspect of historical truth, Raba is right, Abaye's opinion, at any rate, indicates that the name "Jannai," being an accepted form of the name Johanan, cannot constitute a serious obstacle to the view expressed above that the *barayta* in question refers to John Hyrcanus — provided that this opinion is supported by other facts. The argument in favor of this opinion is that the Talmud is also aware of the change which occurred in John Hyrcanus' attitude towards the Pharisees, whereas Jannaeus was basically wicked, that is, he did not have to change his mind at all and become a Sadducee. Cf. also the comments of Klausner, *op. cit.*, III, pp. 138–9.

27   Josephus evidently based his description on a comprehensive account of the Hasmonean dynasty, detailing its history from beginning to end. Josephus made use of a Greek translation of that account, which had originally been written in Hebrew. Cf. the remarks on this subject in my "Alexander Jannai's Conquests in Moab" (Hebrew), *Eretz Israel*, I (1951), 119 ff.

28.   In Greek: . . . καὶ ὡς ἴσασιν μὲν αὐτὸν βουλόμενον εἶναι δίκαιον.

29   In Greek: . . . καὶ τῆς ὁδοῦ τῆς δικαίας ἐκτρεπόμενον.

30   In Greek: . . . εἰ δέλεις εἶναι δίκαιος.

31   Does this view have its origin in, or is it at least influenced by, the fact that the High Priests were the sons of Zadok (*ẓedeq* — righteousness)?

32   M. Ma'as. Sh. 5, 15; M. Sota 9, 10; cf. also Tosef. Sota 13, 9–10 (pp. 319–20); Yer. Sota 9, 11.

33   In addition to the reference in the Tosefta cited in the previous note, cf. Yer. Ma'as. Sh. 5, 9; Sota 48a.

34   Yer. Ma'as. Sh. 5, 9; cf. also parallel passages cited above.

35   Klausner, *op. cit.*, p. 101, who bases himself on Graetz, actually only repeats what is said in the Jerusalem Talmud and in the Tosefta.

36   Cf. Yer. Ma'as. Sh. 5, 9: "and he abolished the confessions of tithes — which was a shameful thing."

37 Neh. 8:13. That instructions were really given then by the central religious body in Jerusalem to all the people to observe the Feast of Tabernacles is implied in verse 15: "And that they should publish and proclaim in all their cities, and in Jerusalem, saying: 'Go forth unto the mount . . .'."

38 Cf. Midrasch Tannaim zum Deuteronomium (ed. by D. Hoffmann), Berlin, 1909, *ad* 26:13, pp. 175 f.; Yer. Sanh. 1, 2.

39 The Jerusalem Talmud, *loc. cit.* relates that Johanan the High Priest appointed "pairs" and consequently there was no need to inquire about *demai*. These "pairs" were obviously official agents empowered by the High Priest to forcibly execute the allocation of tithes.

40 Despite the reservations of M. Avi-Yonah, *Historical Geography of Palestine* (Hebrew) (3rd ed.), Jerusalem, 1962, p. 63, there is no reason for doubting the correctness of S. Klein's assumption in *Sefer ha-Shana shel Erez Yisra'el* (Hebrew), I, Tel-Aviv, 1923, pp. 24–41; II, 1926, pp. 17–24 (cf. also S. Klein, *Galiläa von der Makkabäerzeit bis 67*, Vienna, 1928, pp. 44 ff. and my remarks in *Roman Administration in Palestine*, pp. 23 ff.) on the connection between the 24 shifts of Temple attendants and the toparchial system. The view that the process of fixing toparchies ended at the time of Jannaeus, should be accepted. This subject is discussed at greater length in Schalit, *König Herodes*, pp. 205 ff.

41 Cf. S. Klein, "A Chapter in Palestine Research Towards the End of the Second Temple" (Hebrew, English summary), *Magnes Anniversary Book*, Jerusalem, 1938, pp. 216–23.

42 There appears to be a kernel of truth in Josephus' statement in *Ant.* XIII, 401–4, that Jannaeus advised his wife Salome before his death to make peace with the Pharisees and seek their favor.

43 According to *War*, I, 479, and *Ant.* XVI, 203, Mariamne's sons threatened that after their accession to power they would make "village clerks" (κωμογραμματεῖς) out of the sons born to Herod by his other wives, that being a fitting position for persons with their level of education. It is reasonable to suppose that there were also "local clerks" (τοπογραμμτεῖς). Likewise, we know of "elders" (γέροντες), "a council" (βουλή), and *synedria* (συνέδρια), during the period of Herod's successors. There is no doubt that all these Hellenistic administrative elements familiar to us mainly from Ptolemaic Egypt were also present in Herod's kingdom (on all these matters, see my *Roman Administration in Palestine*, pp. 22 f., and the references cited there).

44 A summary of the conquests is given in *Ant.* XIII, 395–7; cf. A. Schalit, "Alexander Yannai's Conquests in Moab," *op. cit.*, 104–21.

45 See pp. 265 ff. above.

46 This is the opinion, first and foremost, of Ed. Meyer, *Ursprung und Anfänge des Christentums*, II, Stuttgart and Berlin, 1921, pp. 279 ff.

47 An example is the city of Pella as related in *Ant.* XIII, 397. An even more striking instance is the destruction of Gaza — *Ant.* XIII, 362–4.

48 Cf. the remarks at the beginning of this chapter.

49 Details of the private property of the king of Persia and members of his family have been preserved for us by Xenophon, in *Anabasis*, I, chap. 4 § 9; chap. 2 § 7; one should also compare the information in Neh. 2:8 about the park, undoubtedly the king's forest, from which Asaph the keeper had to supply Nehemiah with the timber needed "to make beams for the gates of the castle which appertaineth to the house, and for the walls of the city, and for the house that I shall enter into." In general, cf. M. I. Rostovtzeff, *The Social and Economic History of the Hellenistic World*, I, Oxford, 1941, pp. 332, 336, 385; II, Oxford, 1941, pp. 1168 ff.

50 The private property of the kings of Persia changed hands upon the conquest of the Persian kingdom by Alexander the Great and the establishment of the kingdoms of his successors after his death. One can trace, for example, the ownership of the forests of Lebanon from the kings of Persia to Antiochus III (information about the holdings of the Roman emperors is another question and does not fall within the scope

of our present subject). There is no doubt that the park referred to by Nehemiah was the king's forest in Lebanon, which not only supplied lumber for building the royal fleet but which provided all the lumber required by the royal economy in the whole of Syria. Of course, the ownership of the forests of Lebanon, together with that of all the private property of the kings of Persia, passed to the Hellenistic conquerors, i.e., to Alexander the Great, to Antigonus Monophthalmus, and then to the Seleucids (and perhaps also to the Ptolemies, to the extent that they ruled over that part of Syria). Indeed, we learn in *Ant.* XII, 141, about a gift of lumber from Lebanon made by Antiochus III to the Temple in Jerusalem. There is no doubt that Antiochus III was repeating a deed of Artaxerxes; he made a contribution to the Jewish Temple from his private forests in Lebanon.

51   On the concept, "the king's mountain," cf. the detailed study of S. Klein, *Erez Yᵉhuda* (Hebrew), Tel-Aviv, 1939, pp. 41 ff., 239 ff., who was the first to suggest the connection between "the king's mountain" and the landed property of the rulers in Palestine. Klein is of the opinion that the expression is older and that it was current among the people during the period of Ptolemaic rule in Palestine. Even if we accept this assumption, it does not change in the least the fact that the Hasmonean rulers gained possession of large tracts of superior quality land which they extended with the conquest of the neighboring countries.

52   These lands were called χώρα βασιλική ("the king's land"); on this institution in the Seleucid kingdom, cf. Bickermann, *op. cit.*, pp. 180 ff.; Rostovtzeff. *op. cit.*, I, pp. 465, 468, 493 f., 503, 589; *idem, Studien zur Geschichte des römischen Kolonates*, Leipzig, 1910, pp. 246 ff.

53   An instructive example of this method of agricultural settlement was the transporting of two thousand Jewish families from Mesopotamia and Babylonia to Phrygia and Lydia at the command of Antiochus III, *Ant.* XII, 147–53; see A. Schalit, "The Letter of Antiochus III to

Zeuxis regarding the Establishment of Jewish Military Colonies in Phrygia and Lydia," *JQR.* (n.s.), 50 (1959–60), 289 ff.

54   This does not mean that the king required all the farmers who received land to serve in his army. It appears that every settlement or every clan was required to furnish only a certain number of soldiers, as determined by the king, cf. Bickermann, *op. cit.*, pp. 83 f.

55   The settlement of the Jews in Phrygia and Lydia (cf. note 53 above) served this purpose, as we learn from the wording of the letter of Antiochus III (*Ant.* XII, 149): "Learning that the people in Lydia and Phrygia are revolting . . . I determined to transport two thousand Jewish families with their effects from Mesopotamia and Babylonia to the fortresses and most important places."

56   Herod repeated Jannaeus' presumed act of settling Babylonian Jews in Trachonitis (*Ant.* XVII, 23–31).

57   Cf. Rostovtzeff, *Studien zur Geschichte des römischen Kolonates*, pp. 248 ff.

58   The dependable choice of action in such instances, however, was the expropriation of the treasures of the wealthy temples in the country; cf., for example, I Macc. 6:1–4; *Ant.* XII, 354–5; Polybius, XXXI, 9(11); Porphyr. ap. Hieronym. (on Daniel 11:44–5): Antiochus Epiphanes. Antiochus III, finding himself in financial straits, also made an effort to plunder the treasury of a rich temple, and died in the attempt (cf. Diodorus XXIX, 15 Dindorf [*Exc. de virt. et vitiis*, p. 298, Val.; pars I, p. 273, § 247 Büttner-Wobst]; XXVIII, 3 [*Exc.* p. 293, Val.; pars I, p. 270, § 236 B–W]; Polybius, XXXI 9 [11], [Exc. p. 145, Val.]; pars II, p. 186, § 103 A. G. Roos; all passages are quoted by M. Holleaux, *Études d'épigraphie et d'histoire grecques*, III, Paris, 1942, pp. 258 ff.). Seleucus IV tried to plunder the Temple in Jerusalem (II Macc. 3:6 ff.); the plunder of the Temple by Antiochus Epiphanes (I Macc. 1:21; II Macc. 5:21); and, in general cf. Bickermann, *op. cit.*, pp. 121 ff.

59   This was the rule in the Seleucid kingdom, in contradistinction to Ptolemaic Egypt, where the "sale" of the γῆ βασιλική

land was only in the nature of a lease, since the king had never relinquished ownership. In both theory and practice, he was entitled at any time to expropriate the land that had been "sold." Cf. C. Préaux, *L'économie royale des Lagides*, Bruxelles, 1939, pp. 459 ff.; Rostovtzeff, *Studien zur Geschichte des römischen Kolonates*, p. 249.

60   Cf. note 44 above.

61   For the interpretation of *Ant.* XIII, 408 ff., cf. J. Wellhausen, *Die Pharisäer und die Sadducäer*, Hannover, 1924 (2nd ed.), pp. 98 f.; and cf. also Schalit, *König Herodes*, p. 17 notes 62–3.

62   On the various ranks at the Seleucid royal court cf. Bickermann, *op. cit.*, pp. 40 ff.; on the ranks at the Hellenistic courts in general, cf. G. Corradi, *Studi ellenistici*, Torino, 1929, pp. 256–343.

63   This heightened addiction to Hellenistic practices was also expressed, *inter alia*, by "the king's friends" dressing according to the latest Hellenistic fashion of the royal court. Josephus relates a typical example concerning the "friends" of Aristobulus II. When the king appeared before Pompey in order to dispute with his brother Hyrcanus he was surrounded by "some young swaggerers" (τοὺς νέους καὶ σοβαρωτέρους), no doubt a group of noble "friends," who wore purple robes; their hair was made up, and they all wore metal (i.e., gold) ornaments (*Ant.* XIV, 45). The king wished to impress the Roman commander and so he and his entourage appeared in the festive robes of the court. Naturally, all that splendor was not the innovation of Aristobulus. He no doubt became acquainted with the custom at his father's court. (In another place [*Ant.* XIII, 427] mention is made of the κόσμος βασίλειος that is, the royal magnificence displayed by Aristobulus even while Salome was alive; it is safe to assume that during the queen's reign the ruling Pharisee statesmen managed to remove the foreign influence from the daily life of the Hasmonean royal court.)

64   Simeon the Hasmonean's commission (I Macc. 14:14) stated that no person had the right to contradict anything spoken by him or to call a meeting without his permission, or even to wear purple or a gold clasp. In other words, the people undertook to obey the constitution which conferred on Simeon the highest rank in the state and put in his hands the supervision of law and order. However, the covenant of 141 B.C.E. was undoubtedly bilateral: it obligated both parties. Just as it forbade any individual to behave as he liked, so it imposed the same prohibition on Simeon and his successors.

65   According to Josephus (*Ant.* XIII, 301; *War* I, 70) Aristobulus was the first Hasmonean High Priest to assume the title of king. Contradicting Josephus is the testimony of Strabo, XVI, 2, 40, (p. 762), that the first Hasmonean king was Alexandros, i.e., Jannaeus Alexander. The Greek geographer was probably right, because his view is supported by the evidence of the coins of Aristobulus, which describe him only as "High Priest" (the inscription of Aristobulus' coins is: "Judah the High Priest and *Ḥever ha-Yᵉhudim*") and of Jannaeus' coins which also bear the title of king. (Two varieties of Jannaeus' coins are extant: one has the double inscription, יהונתן המלך on one side and Αλέξανδρος βασιλεύς on the other, and the second has only a Hebrew inscription [or יהונתן [ינתן] הכהן הגדול וחבר היהודים [the significance of the omission of the reference to the *Ḥever ha-Yᵉhudim* on one type of coins will be discussed below]). Schürer, *op. cit.*, I, p. 274 note 5, who prefers Josephus' information, explains away Strabo's conflicting statement by saying that the latter ignored Aristobulus' kingship because it lasted only a year. This argument is unconvincing, because Strabo does relate interesting details about Aristobulus' rule which prove that he was fully informed about his life. It is inconceivable that the most important detail of Aristobulus' reign — if it were really true — would elude him (the passage about Aristobulus, the "Philhellene" [Φιλέλλην] which appears in *Ant.* XIII, 319, is taken from Strabo, who cited Timagenes as his authority). The information in Josephus about Aristobulus I's accession to the throne is also suspect for chronological reasons. On this, cf.

Schalit, *König Herodes*, pp. 743–4. For another opinion, see chap. IX above.

66   It may well be that John Hyrcanus, on his part, also paved the way for a compromise by refraining from adopting really harsh measures against the Pharisees, even though we know that he put down by force the riots that broke out against him (cf. *Ant.* XIII, 296).

67   A hint of the opinion of the Hasmonean state commonly held in Pharisaic circles is revealed by the Pharisee author of the Psalms of Solomon, 8:5–14, 17:5–12.

68   Such an exception is the English scholar R. T. Herford who has laid down his views in his well-known book *The Pharisees*, London, 1924.

69   To the discerning eye, the description of the Pharisees in the New Testament appears one-sided if only because the Talmud itself mentions with disapproval certain types of Pharisees who acted out of ulterior motives (various terms of opprobium applied to the Pharisees, some of them whose meaning is not clear, are found in: M. Sota 3, 4; Yer. Pe'a 8, 8; Sota 22b; Yer. Sota 5, 7; Yer. B^er. 9, 7).

70   These matters are discussed in A. Schalit, "Die frühchristliche Überlieferung über die Herkunft der Familie des Herodes," *ASTI*, 1 (1962), 109–60.

71   From the *Haftara* Benedictions.

72   17:1–11. This chapter of the Psalms of Solomon was no doubt written shortly after Pompey's conquest of Jerusalem and the fall of the Hasmonean House in 63 B.C.E., as is proved by the clear allusions to events which occurred during and after the siege. Nevertheless, it may be cited as evidence of the propaganda employed by the Pharisees against Jannaeus. What the Pharisee poet, the contemporary of Jannaeus' sons, says about the Hasmonean House, is completely in accord with the opinion of the Pharisees about the same royal family at the time of Jannaeus himself.

73   The abolition of the Sanhedrin is reflected in the coins of Jannaeus (see note 65 above) on which the inscription "*Hever ha-Y^ehudim*," was dropped. This was done, no doubt, because the institution no longer

existed at the time: it had been abolished at the order of Jannaeus the absolute monarch.

74   The story in Gen. R. 91 (pp. 1115–7) (and cf. Eccl. R. 7, 11; Yer. Naz. 5, 5; Yer. B^er. 7, 2) about the strained relations between Jannaeus and Simeon ben Sheṭaḥ is devoid of historical value. (Thus, rightly, Schürer, *op. cit.*, I, pp. 279 f.; apparently Derenbourg, *op. cit.*, pp. 96 ff., is of the opinion that it should be regarded as a factual account. This is disputable.) Nevertheless, it reflects the lack of confidence that prevailed on both sides.

75   In M. Suk. 4, 9, we find the account of an incident which is similar to the story in *Antiquities*, but the Mishnah does not give the name of the person involved: "To [the priest] who performed the libation they used to say, 'Raise thy hand,' for on a certain occasion, a certain man poured out the water over his feet, and all the people pelted him with their etrogs." The parallel story in Tosef. Suk. 3, 16 (p. 197), is more detailed: "Once there was an incident with a Beothusian, who poured the libation water over his feet, and all the people pelted him with their etrogs, and the horn of the altar became damaged and the Temple service was cancelled that day, until they brought a lump of salt and placed it upon it so that it should not be seen to be damaged..." The same episode is recounted in the Babylonian Talmud (Suk. 48b): "Our Rabbis taught, It once happened that a certain Sadducee... etc." There is no way of knowing whether these sources are referring to the episode with Jannaeus related in *Antiquities*.

76   The name of the place is not clear; cf. Schürer's remark, *op. cit.*, I, p. 281 note 17; and cf. also Marcus' note to *Ant.* (Engl. transl. in Loeb Classical Series) XIII, 375.

77   Josephus relates (*Ant.* XIII, 376) that when Jannaeus asked his rivals what they wanted of him and he would do it, they replied that all they wished was for him to die.

78   The version in *Ant.* XIII, 380, is Βαιθόμη while *War* I, 96, employs the term Βεμεσελίς. According to Klausner,

op. cit., p. 153, the first version indicates the name Beth Ḥoma. The second version has been interpreted by Klein, (*Tarbiz* [Hebrew], I [1930], 137), as Beth ha-Meleḳ. For an identification of the place, see F. M. Abel, *Géographie de la Palestine*, Paris, 1933, II, p. 278, s.v. Bethommé. For a different explanation of the name Βαιθόμη. see A. Schalit, *Namenwörterbuch zu Flavius Josephus* (*A Complete Concordance to Flavius Josephus*, ed. by K. H. Rengstorf, suppl. I), Leiden, 1968, p. 39, *ad* Δοσίθεος.

[79] All these events are related in *Ant.* XIII, 376–83 and *War*, I, 90–8. An echo of the events has also been preserved in the talmudic sources (Sota 47b; Sanh. 107b in the uncensored editions; cf. Derenbourg, *op. cit.*, pp. 93 f.). According to the Talmudic legend, the Pharisees who fled or hid included Joshua ben Peraḥya and Simeon ben Sheṭaḥ (*loc. cit.*), as well as Judah ben Ṭabbay, who fled to Alexandria (Yer. Ḥag. 2, 2).

[80] *Ant.* XIII, 400–2. A similar story appears in the Talmud (Sota 22b).

BIBLIOGRAPHY

CHAPTER I

THE POLITICAL BACKGROUND

K. J. Beloch, *Griechische Geschichte* (2nd ed.), IV, 1, Berlin, 1925

H. Berve, *Des Alexanderreich Prosopographischer Grundlage*, I, Munich, 1926

E. R. Bevan, *The House of Seleucus*, I–II, London, 1902
A History of Egypt under the Ptolemaic Dynasty, London, 1927

E. J. Bickermann, *Les institutions des Séleucides*, Paris, 1938

A. Bouché-Leclercq, *Histoire des Lagides*, I–IV, Paris, 1903–7
Histoire des Séleucides, I–II, Paris, 1913–4

J. G. Droysen, *Geschichte Alexanders des Grossen*, 1833 (new ed., vol. I in *Geschichte des Hellenismus*, Basel, 1952)

V. Ehrenberg, *Alexander und Aegypten*, Leipzig, 1926

G. Glotz — R. Cohen, *Histoire grecque*, III, Paris, 1936

G. F. Griffith, *The Mercenaries of the Hellenistic World*, Cambridge, 1935

P. Jouguet, *L'impérialisme macédonien et l'Hellénisation de l'Orient*, Paris, 1926

J. Kaerst, *Geschichte des Hellenismus* (2nd ed.), I, Leipzig, 1917

M. Launey, *Recherches sur les armées hellenistiques*, I–II, Paris, 1949–50

J. Lesquier, *Les institutions militaires de l'Égypte sous les Lagides*, Paris, 1911.

L. Mitteis — U. Wilcken, *Grundzüge und Chrestomathie der Papyruskunde*, I–II, Leipzig, 1912

M. I. Rostovtzeff, *The Social and Economic History of the Hellenistic World*, I–III, Oxford, 1941

W. W. Tarn, *Alexander the Great*, 2 vols, Cambridge, 1948
"Alexander: The Conquest of the Far East," *CAH*, VI (chap. XIII)
"The Heritage of Alexander," *CAH*, VI (chap. XV)
"The Struggle of Egypt against Syria and Macedonia," *CAH*, VII (chap. XXII)

V. Tscherikower, *Die hellenistischen städtegründungen von Alexander dem Grossen bis auf die Römerzeit*, Leipzig, 1927

V. Wilcken, *Alexander der Grosse*, Leipzig, 1931

CHAPTER II

THE CULTURAL BACKGROUND

H. I. Bell, *Egypt from Alexander the Great to the Arab Conquest*, Oxford, 1948

K. J. Beloch, *Griechische Geschichte*, IV, 1–2, Berlin, 1925–7

E. R. Bevan, *A History of Egypt under the Ptolemaic Dynasty*, London, 1927

A. Bouché-Leclercq, *Histoire des Lagides*, I–IV, Paris, 1902–7

J. G. Droysen, *Geschichte des Hellenismus*, I–III 1833–43 (new ed. in 3 vols. Basel, 1952)

W. S. Ferguson, "The Leading Ideas of

the New Period," *CAH*, VII (chap. I)

G. Glotz — R. Cohen, *Histoire grecque*, I, Paris, 1925

F. Gomperz, *Griechische Denker: eine Geschichte der antiken Philosophie* (4th ed.), I, Berlin 1922 (Engl. transl: *Greek Thinkers: History of Ancient Philosophy*, I, London, 1901)

A. H. M. Jones, *The Cities of the Eastern Roman Provinces*, Oxford, 1937
The Greek City from Alexander to Justinian, Oxford, 1940

A. H. M. Jones — T. L. Heath, "Hellenistic Science and Mathematics," *CAH*, VII (chap. IX)

J. Kaerst, *Geschichte des Hellenismus* (2nd ed.), II, Leipzig, 1926

E. Kornemann, "Zur Geschichte der antiken Herscherkulte," *Klio*, 1 (1902)

M. Launey, *Recherches sur les armées hellénistiques*, I–II, Paris, 1949–50

L. Mitteis — U. Wilcken, *Grundzüge und Chrestomathie der Papyruskunde*, I–II, Leipzig, 1912

B. Niese, *Geschichte der griechischen und makedonischen Staaten seit der Schlacht bei Chaeronea*, I–II, Gotha, 1893–1903

M. P. Nilsson, *Greek Popular Religion*, New-York, 1940
Geschichte der griechischen Religion, Munich, 1941–50

M. Pohlenz, *Die Stoa; Geschichte einer geistigen Bewegung*, I–II, Göttingen, 1948–9

M. I. Rostovtzeff, *Social and Economic History of the Hellenistic World*, I–III, Oxford, 1941
"Ptolemaic Egypt," *CAH*, VII (chap. IV)

W. Schubart, *Einführung in die Papyruskunde*, Berlin, 1918

W. W. Tarn, *Hellenistic Civilisation* (3rd ed.), London, 1953

R. Taubenschlag, *The Law of Greco-Roman Egypt in the Light of the Papyri* (2nd ed.), Warsaw, 1955

A. E. Taylor, *Epicurus*, London, 1911

V. Tscherikower, *Die hellenistischen Städtegründungen von Alexander dem Grossen bis auf die Römerzeit*, Leipzig, 1927

J. O. Winter, *Life and Letters in the Papyri*, Ann Arbor, 1933

CHAPTER III

THE POLITICAL SITUATION FROM 332 TO 175 B.C.E.

M. Avi-Yonah, *Historical Geography of Palestine* (Hebrew) (3rd ed.), Jerusalem, 1962; English revised and enlarged edition: *The Holy Land from the Persian to the Arab Conquests* (536 B.C. to A.D. 640), Grand Rapids, Michigan, 1966

K. J. Beloch, *Griechische Geschichte* (2nd ed.), IV, 1, Berlin, 1925

H. Bengtson, *Die Strategie in der Hellenistischen Zeit*, III, Munich, 1952

E. R. Bevan, *The House of Seleucus*, I, London, 1902

E. Bickermann, "Zur Datierung des Pseudo-Aristeas," *ZNW*, 29 (1930), 280 ff. 98
"La Charte séleucide de Jérusalem," *REJ*, 100 (1935), 4–35
Les institutions des Séleucides, Paris, 1938

A. Bouché-Leclercq, *Histoire des Séleucides*, I, Paris, 1913

D. Cohen, *De Magistratibus Aegyptus externas Lagidarum regni provincias administrantibus*, Hague, 1912

F. M. Cross, "The Discovery of the Samaria Papyri, "*BAr*, 26 (1963), 110–21

A. Fuks, "Dositheos son of Drimylos: A Prosopographical Note," *Journal of Juristic Papyrology*, 7–8 (1953–4), 205–9

J. Gutmann, "Alexander of Macedon in Palestine" (Hebrew), *Tarbiz*, 11 (1940), 271–94

M. Holleaux, *Etudes d'épigraphie et d'histoire grecques*, II–III, Paris, 1938–42

J. Klausner, *History of the Second Temple* (Hebrew), II (5th ed.), Jerusalem, 1958

H. Lewy, "Hekataios von Abdera περὶ Ἰουδαίων," *ZNW*, 31 (1932), 117–32

H. Liebesny, "Ein Erlass des Königs Ptolemaios II Philadelphos über die Deklaration von Vieh und Sklaven in Syrien und Phönikien (PER Inv. Nr. 24.552 gr.)," *Aegyptus*, 16 (1936), 257–91

R. Merkelbach, *Die Quellen des Griechischen Alexander-Romans*, Munich, 1954

A. Momigliano, "Per la data e la caratteristica della lettera di Aristea," *Aegyptus*, 12 (1932), 161–72

J. F. Moore, "Simeon the Righteous," *Jewish Studies in Memory of Israel Abrahams*, New York, 1927, 348–64

B. Niese, *Geschichte der griechischen und makedonischen Staaten seit der Schlacht bei Chaeronea*, II, Gotha, 1899

J. P. Peters — H. Thiersch, *The Painted Tombs in the Necropolis of Marissa* [Marîshah], London, 1905

J. D. Purvis, *The Samaritan Pentateuch and the Origin of the Samaritan Sect*, Cambridge, Mass., 1968

M. I. Rostovtzeff, *The Social and Economic History of the Hellenistic World*, I–III, Oxford, 1941

A. Schalit, "A Chapter in the History of the Party Conflict in Jerusalem at the End of the Fifth Century and at the Beginning of the Fourth Century B.C.E." (Hebrew), *Commentationes Judaico-Hellenisticae in Memoriam Johannis Lewy*, Jerusalem, 1949

D. R. Schlatter, "Die Bᵉne pariṣim bei Daniel," *ZAW*, 14 (1894), 145–51

E. Schürer, *Geschichte des Jüdischen Volkes im Zeitalter Jesu Christi*, I–III, (3rd–4th ed.) Leipzig, 1901–1909

E. L. Sukenik, "Paralipomena Palaestinensia," *JPOS*, 14 (1934), 178–84

W. Tarn, "The Struggle of Egypt against Syria and Macedonia" *CAH*, VII (chap. XXII)

V. Tcherikover, "Palestine in the Light of the Zenon Papyri" (Hebrew), *Tarbiz*, 4 (1933) 226–47, 354–65; 5 (1934), 37–44

"Palestine under the Ptolemies," *Mizraim*, 4–5 (1937), 9–90

Hellenistic Civilization and the Jews (transl. from the Hebrew), Philadelphia, 1959

CHAPTER IV

SOCIAL CONDITIONS

F. M. Abel, "La liste géographique du papyrus 71 de Zénon," *RB*, 32 (1923), 406–15

"Marisa dans le papyrus 76 de Zénon," *RB*, 33 (1924), 566–74

E. Bickermann, "Une proclamation séleucide relative au temple de Jérusalem," *Syria*, 25 (1946–8), 67–85

A. Büchler, *Die Priester und der Cultus im letzten Jahrzent des Jerusalemischen Tempels*, Vienna, 1895

Die Tobiaden und die Oniaden im II Makkabäerbuche und in der verwandten jüdisch-hellenistischen Literatur, Vienna, 1899

H. C. Butler, "Ancient Architecture in Syria": The Ledja, *Princeton University Archaeological Expeditions to Syria in 1904–*1905, Div. 2, Section A, Pt. 1, Leyden, 1919

H. Graetz, *Geschichte der Juden von den ältesten Zeiten bis auf die Gegenwart*, III, 1–2, (5th ed.), Leipzig, 1905–6

H. Gressmann, "*Die ammonitischen Tobiaden*," *Sitzungsberichte der Preussischen Akademie der Wissenschaften*, Berlin, 1921, 663–71

J. M. Harper Jr., "A Study in the Commercial Relations Between Egypt and Syria in the Third Century Before Christ," *American Journal of Philology*, 49 (1928), 1–35

M. Hengel, *Judentum und Hellenismus; Studien zu ihrer Begegnung unter besonderer Berücksichtigung Palästinas bis zur Mitte des 2. Jh. v. Chr.*, Tübingen, 1969

L. Herzfeld, *Geschichte des Volkes Jisrael* (2nd ed.), I, Leipzig, 1863

M. Holleaux, *Études d'épigraphie et d'histoire grecques*, III, Paris, 1942

S. Klein, *Erez Yehuda* (Hebrew), Tel Aviv, 1939

S. Kraus, "The Great Synod," *JQR*, 10 (1898), 347-77

H. Liebesny, "Ein Erlass des Königs Ptolemaios II Philadelphos über die Deklaration von Vieh und Sklaven in Syrien und Phönikien (PER Inv. no. 24.552 gr.)," *Aegyptus*, 16 (1936), 257-91

B. Maisler (Mazar), "The House of Tobiah" (Hebrew), *Tarbiz*, 12 (1941), 109-23
"Ben Tabal and Beth Tuvia" (Hebrew), *Eretz Israel*, 4 (1956), 249-52

C. C. McCown, "The 'Araq el-Emir and the Tobiads," *BAr*, 20 (1957), 63-76

Ed. Meyer, *Ursprung und Anfänge des Christentums*, II, Stuttgart and Berlin, 1921

A. Momigliano, "I Tobiadi nella preistoria del moto maccabaico," *Atti della Reale Accademia delle Scienze di Torino*, 67 (1931-2), 165-210

G. F. Moore, "Simeon the Righteous," *Jewish studies in Memory of Israel Abrahams*, New York, 1927

W. G. A. Otto, "Hyrkanos," *RE*, vol. 17, 527-34

O. Plöger, "Hyrkan im Ostjordanland," *ZDPV*, 71 (1955), 70-81.

C. Préaux, *L'économie royale des Lagides*, Brussels, 1939

E. Renan, *Histoire du peuple d'Israel*, IV, Paris, 1893

M. I. Rostovtzeff, *The Social and Economic History of the Hellenistic World*, I-III, Oxford, 1941

V. Tcherikover, "Palestine in the Light of the Zenon Papyri" (Hebrew), *Tarbiz*, 4 (1933), 226-47, 354-65; 5 (1934), 37-44
"Palestine under the Ptolemies," *Mizraim*, 4-5 (1937), 9-90
Hellenistic Civilization and the Jews (transl. from the Hebrew), Philadelphia, 1959

L. H. Vincent, "La Palestine dans les Papyrus Ptolemaïques de Gerza," *RB*, 29 (1920), 161-202
"La Date des épigraphes d' 'Arâq el-Emîr," *JPOS*, 3 (1923), 55-68

J. Wellhausen, *Israelitische und jüdische Geschichte*, (8th ed.), Berlin, 1921

W. L. Westermann, "Enslaved Persons who are Free," *American Journal of Philology*, 59 (1938), 1-30

U. Wilcken, *Griechische Ostraka aus Ägypten und Nubien*, Leipzig, 1899

H. Willich, *Juden und Griechen vor der Makkabäischen Erhebung*, Göttingen, 1895

S. Zeitlin, "The Tobias Family and the Hasmoneans," *PAAJR*, 4 (1932), 169-223

CHAPTER V

THE HELLENISTIC MOVEMENT IN JERUSALEM AND ANTIOCHUS' PERSECUTIONS

F. M. Abel, *Les Livres des Maccabées*, Paris, 1949

M. A. Beek, *Das Danielbuch; sein historischer Hintergrund und seine literarische Entwicklung*, Leyden, 1935

A. A. Bevan, *A Short Commentary on the Book of Daniel*, 1892

E. R. Bevan, *The House of Seleucus*, II, London, 1902

E. Bickermann, "Makkabäerbücher," *RE*, vol. 27, 779-800
Der Gott der Makkabäer, Berlin, 1937

"Heliodore au temple de Jérusalem," *Annuaire de l'Institut de Philologie et d'Histoire Orientales et Slaves*, 7 (1939-44), 5-40

J. C. Dancy, *A Commentary on I Maccabees*, Oxford, 1954

H. W. Ettelson, "The Integrity of I Maccabees," *Transactions of the Connecticut Academy of Arts and Sciences*, 27 (1925), 249-384

I. Heinemann, "Wer veranlasste den Glaubenszwange der Makkabäerzeit" *MGWJ*, 82 (1938), 145-72

A. H. M. Jones, *The Cities of the Eastern Roman Provinces*, Oxford, 1937

R. Laquer, *Kritische Untersuchungen zum zweiten Makkabäerbuch*, Strassburg, 1904

Ed. Meyer, *Ursprung und Anfänge des Christentums*, II, Stuttgart and Berlin, 1921

A. Momigliano, *Prime Linee di Storia della Tradizione Maccabaica*, Torino, 1931

J. A. Montgomery, *A critical and Exegetical Commentary on the Book of Daniel*, Edinburgh, 1927

B. Niese, *Kritik der beiden Makkabäerbücher; nebst Beiträgen zur Geschichte der Makkabäischen Erhebung*, Berlin, 1900
Geschichte der griechischen und makedonischen Staaten seit der Schlacht bei Chaeronea, III, Gotha, 1903

W. G. A. Otto, "Zur Geschichte der Zeit des 6. Ptolemäers," *Abhandlungen der Bayerischen Akademie der Wissenschaften*, phil.-hist. Klasse, Munich, 1934

K. D. Schunck, *Die Quellen des I. und II. Makkabäerbuches*, Halle, 1954

V. Tcherikover (Tscherikower), "War I, I, I as a Historical Source" (Hebrew), *Madda'ey ha-yahadut*, I, Jerusalem, 1926
Die hellenistischen städtegründugen von Alexander dem Grossen bis auf die Römerzeit, Leipzig, 1927
"Antiochia in Jerusalem" (Hebrew), *J. N. Epstein Jubilee Volume*, Jerusalem, 1950, 61–7
"Antiochus' Persecutions and their Problems" (Hebrew), *Eshkolot* (Εχολια — *Commentationes de Antiquitate Classica*), 1 (1954), 86–109
Hellenistic Civilization and the Jews (transl. from the Hebrew), Philadelphia, 1959

J. Wellhausen, "Über den geschichtlichen Wert des zweiten Makkabäerbuches in Verhältnis zum ersten," *Nachrichten von der Königl. Gesellschaft der Wissenschaften zu Göttingen*, philologisch-historische Klasse, 1905

CHAPTER VI

THE HASMONEAN REVOLT AND JUDAH MACCABEE'S WAR AGAINST THE SYRIANS

F. M. Abel, "Topographie des Campagnes Maccabéennes," *RB*, 32 (1923), 495–552; 33 (1924), 201–17, 371–87; 34 (1925), 194–216; 35 (1926), 206–22, 510–33

E. Avissar, *The Wars of Judas Maccabaeus* (Hebrew), Tel Aviv, 1968

M. Avi-Yonah, "The Battles in the Book of the Maccabees" (Hebrew), *Y. Levi Memorial Volume*, Jerusalem, 1939, 13–24 (reprinted in: M. Avi-Yonah, *Essays and Studies in the Lore of the Holy Land* [Hebrew], Tel Aviv, 1954)
Carta's Atlas of the Period of the Second Temple: The Mishnah and the Talmud (Hebrew), Jerusalem, 1966

M. Avi-Yonah — Y. Aharoni, *Macmillan Bible Atlas*, New York, 1968

G. Hölscher, "Die Feldzüge des Makkabäer Judas," *ZDPV*, 29 (1906), 133–51

O. Plöger, "Die Feldzüge der Seleukiden gegen den Makkabäer Judas," *ZDPV*, 74 (1958), 158–88

E. Schürer, *Geschichte des jüdischen Volkes im Zeitalter Jesu Christi*, I (3rd–4th ed.), Leipzig, 1901

M. Stern, *Documents for the History of the Hasmonean Revolt* (Hebrew), Tel Aviv, 1965

S. Wibbing, "Zur Topographie einzelner Schlachten des Judas Makkabäus," *ZDPV*, 78 (1962), 159–70

CHAPTERS VII–X

JONATHAN AND SIMEON; JOHN HYRCANUS I; JUDAH ARISTOBULUS AND JANNAEUS ALEXANDER; QUEEN SALOME ALEXANDRA

F. M. Abel, *Les Livres des Maccabées*, Paris, 1949

M. Avi-Yonah, *Historical Geography of Palestine* (Hebrew) (3rd ed.), Jerusalem, 1962; English revised and enlarged edition: *The Holy Land from the Persian to the Arab Conquests* (536 B.C. to A.D. 640), Grand Rapids, Michigan, 1966

W. Bacher, "Das altjüdische Schulwesen," *JjGL*, 6 (1903), 48–81

A. R. Bellinger, "The End of the Seleucids," *Transactions of the Connecticut Academy of Arts and Sciences* 38 (1949), 51–102

E. Bickermann, *Der Gott der Makkabäer*, Berlin, 1937
The Maccabees, New York, 1947

H. Buchheim, "Die Orientpolitik des Triumwirn M. Antonius," *Abhandlungen der Heidelberger Akademie der Wissenschaften, philosophisch-historische Klasse*, 1960

J. C. Dancy, *A Commentary on I Maccabees*, Oxford, 1954

J. Derenbourg, *Essai sur l'histoire et la géographie de la Palestine*, I, Paris, 1867

H. Graetz, *Geschichte der Juden von den ältesten Zeiten bis auf die Gegenwart*, III, 1 (5th ed.) Leipzig, 1905

L. Herzfeld, *Handelsgeschichte der Juden des Altertums* (2nd ed.), Braunschweig, 1894

G. Hölscher, *Palästina in der persischer und hellenistischer Zeit*, Berlin, 1903

J. Klausner, *History of the Second Temple* (Hebrew), II, (2nd ed.), Jerusalem, 1951
In the Days of the Second Temple (Hebrew), Jerusalem, 1954

When a Nation Fights for its Freedom (Hebrew) (9th ed.), Tel Aviv, 1955

Ed. Meyer, *Ursprung und Anfänge des Christentums*, II, Stuttgart and Berlin, 1921

B. Niese, *Kritik der beiden Makkabäerbücher; nebst Beiträgen zur Geschichte der Makkabäischen Erhebung*, Berlin, 1900

A. Reifenberg, *Ancient Jewish Coins*, Jerusalem, 1947

A. Schalit, "Alexander Jannai's Conquests in Moab" (Hebrew), *Eretz-Israel*, 1 (1951), 104–21
"Die frühchristliche Überlieferung über die Herkunft der Familie des Herodes" *ASTI*, 1 (1962), 109–60
König Herodes, Berlin, 1969

E. Schürer, *Geschichte des jüdischen Volkes im Zeitalter Jesu Christi*, I (3rd–4th ed.), Leipzig, 1901

M. Stern, "The Relations between Judea and Rome during the Rule of John Hyrcanus" (Hebrew), *Zion*, 26 (1961), 1–22
"The Political Background of the Wars of Alexander Jannai" (Hebrew), *Tarbiz*, 33 (1964), 325–36
The Documents on the History of the Hasmonean Revolt (Hebrew), Tel Aviv, 1965

V. Tcherikover, *Hellenistic Civilization and the Jews* (transl. from the Hebrew), Philadelphia, 1959

J. Wellhausen, *Israelitische und jüdische Geschichte*, Berlin, 1914

S. Zeitlin, *The Rise and Fall of the Judaean State*, I, Philadelphia, 1962.

CHAPTER XI

DOMESTIC POLITICS AND POLITICAL INSTITUTIONS

F. M. Abel, *Géographie de la Palestine*, I–II, Paris, 1933–8

Les Livres des Maccabées, Paris, 1949

M. Avi-Yonah, *Historical Geography of Palestine* (Hebrew) (3rd ed.), Jerusalem, 1962; English revised and enlarged edition: *The Holy Land from the Persian to the Arab Conquests* (536 B.C. to A.D. 640), Grand Rapids, Michigan, 1966

E. Bickermann, *Les Institutions des Séleucides*, Paris, 1938

G. Corradi, *Studi ellenistici*, Torino, 1929

J. Derenbourg, *Essai sur l'histoire et la géographie de la Palestine*, I, Paris, 1867

D. Flusser, "The Apocryphal Book of Ascensio Isaiae and the Dead Sea Sect," *IEJ*, 3 (1953), 30–47

A. Geiger, *Urschrift und Übersetzungen der Bibel*, Breslau, 1857

R. T. Herford, *The Pharisees*, London, 1924

S. B. Hoenig, *The Great Sanhedrin*, Philadelphia, 1953

M. Holleaux, *Études d'epigraphie et d'histoire grecques*, III, Paris, 1942

J. Klausner, *History of the Second Temple* (Hebrew), I–III (2nd ed.), Jerusalem, 1951

S. Klein, *Sefer ha-Shana shel Erez Israel* (Hebrew), I, Tel Aviv, 1923, 24–41; II, 1926, 17–24

Galiläa von der Makkabäerzeit bis 67, Vienna, 1928

"A Chapter in Palestine Research Toward the End of the Second Temple" (Hebrew), *Magnes Anniversary Book*, Jerusalem, 1938, 216–23

Erez Yehuda (Hebrew), Tel Aviv, 1939

Ed. Meyer, *Ursprung und Anfänge des Christentums*, I–III, Stuttgart and Berlin, 1921

G. F. Moore, *Judaism*, Cambridge, 1946

M. I. Rostovtzeff, *Studien zur Geschichte des römischen Kolonates*, Leipzig, 1910

The Social and Economic History of the Hellenistic World, I–III, Oxford, 1941

E. Schürer, *Geschichte des jüdischen Volkes im Zeitalter Jesu Christi*, I–III (3rd–4th ed.), Leipzig, 1901–1909

A. Schalit, *Roman Administration in Palestine* (Hebrew), Jerusalem, 1937

"Alexander Yannai's Conquests in Moab" (Hebrew), *Eretz-Israel*, 1 (1951), 104–21

"The letter of Antiochus III to Zeuxis Regarding the Establishment of Jewish Military Colonies in Phrygia and Lydia," *JQR* (n.s.), 50 (1959–60), 289–318

"Die frühchristliche überlieferung über die Herkunft der Familie des Herodes," *ASTI*, 1 (1962), 109–60

"Kritische Randbemerkungen zu Paul Winters' 'On the Trial of Jesus'", *ASTI*, 2 (1963), 86–102

Namenwörterbuch zu Flavius Josephus (A Complete Concordance to Flavius Josephus, ed. by K. H. Rengstorf, Supplement I), Leiden, 1968

V. Tcherikover, *Hellenistic Civilization and the Jews* (transl. from the Hebrew), Philadelphia, 1959

E. E. Urbach, "Political and Social Tendencies in Talmudic Concepts of Charity" (Hebrew), *Zion*, 16 (1951), 1–27

Y. Yadin, *The Scroll of the War of the Sons of Light Against the Sons of Darkness* (transl. from the Hebrew), Oxford, 1962

INDEX OF NAMES AND PLACES

THE HELLENISTIC WORLD ON THE EVE OF THE MACCABEAN REVOLT

MACEDONIA
PELLA

EPIRUS

ATHENS

SPARTA

Black Sea

SINOPE

BITHYNIA
PERGAMUM
PAPHLA-GONIA
PONTUS

PERGAMUM
SARDES
GALATIA

KINGDOM

MILETUS
APAMEA
CAPPADOCIA

A R

PHRYGIA

Mediterranean Sea

CRETE

CILICIA

EDESSA

S E L

CYPRUS

ANTIOCH

ARADUS

DAMASCUS

TYRE
COELE
SYRIA
SYRIA

PALESTINE

ALEXANDRIA

JERUSALEM
GAZA
SAMARIA

P
T
O
L
E
M
A
I
C

A R A B I

K
I
N
G
D
O
M

MEMPHIS

E G Y P T

Nile R.

Red Sea

0 50 100
miles
CARTA, Jerusalem